Reparations for Slavery and the Slave Trade

Reparations for Slavery and the Slave Trade

A Transnational and Comparative History

Ana Lucia Araujo

BLOOMSBURY ACADEMIC
LONDON · NEW YORK · OXFORD · NEW DELHI · SYDNEY

BLOOMSBURY ACADEMIC
Bloomsbury Publishing Plc
50 Bedford Square, London, WC1B 3DP, UK
1385 Broadway, New York, NY 10018, USA

BLOOMSBURY, BLOOMSBURY ACADEMIC and the Diana logo are trademarks
of Bloomsbury Publishing Plc

First published in 2017
Reprinted in 2020

Copyright © Ana Lucia Araujo, 2017

Cover image: Slaves reunion. Washington, DC, c. 1916 (© Shorpy) √

Ana Lucia Araujo has asserted their right under the Copyright, Designs and Patents Act,
1988, to be identified as Author of this work.

A catalogue record for this book is available from the British Library.

A catalog record for this book is available from the Library of Congress.

ISBN: HB: 978-1-3500-1059-8
PB: 978-1-3500-1060-4
ePDF: 978-1-3500-1061-1
eBook: 978-1-3500-1058-1

Typeset by RefineCatch Limited, Bungay, Suffolk
Printed and bound in Great Britain

To find out more about our authors and books visit www.bloomsbury.com
and sign up for our newsletters.

CONTENTS

ILLUSTRATIONS

ACKNOWLEDGMENTS

The idea of writing this book can be traced back to 2005, when I was conducting research in the National Archives of Republic of Benin in West Africa. I found many newspaper articles from the 1990s in which the problem of reparations for slavery, the Atlantic slave trade, and colonization was discussed on an almost daily basis. Whereas my work focused on the memorialization of slavery in the South Atlantic world, in 2008, I had the great luck of becoming a professor in the historically black Howard University, in Washington, DC, an institution created just after the abolition of slavery, during the Reconstruction period, and whose initial mission was to remedy the exclusion of African Americans from higher education. Howard University is itself a site of memory of slavery and emancipation and its very existence is closely related to the need to redress the horrible legacies of slavery and racial segregation in the United States.

More than a decade later, the issue of symbolic reparations for slavery has gained great importance in Europe, Africa, and the Americas, either through public apologies and commemoration activities or through the construction of monuments and memorials for the victims of the Atlantic slave trade. Gradually, governments as well as prominent authorities and groups embraced the memorialization of slavery, to the point it became a central trend in many former slave societies. Despite these changes, the debates on material reparations remain very contentious. It was time to gather the materials I had accumulated over the years, conduct new research, and dedicate time to write a book on the history of reparations for slavery and the Atlantic slave trade.

I presented parts of this book in seminars and conferences held in the United States, the Netherlands, France, and Germany. In February 2015 and October 2016, I presented in the Howard University Seminar "Slavery, Memory, and African Diasporas." I thank the seminars' participants for their comments. I also discussed one chapter of this book in the DC Area African American Studies Seminar in September 2016. I thank Jay Driskell for the opportunity to share my work with this amazing group of scholars, and for his enlightening and detailed written comments. I also discussed sections and chapters of this book in the International Workshop "Global Slavery and Exhibitionary Impulse," at Leiden University, Leiden, Netherlands, in June 2015; the Annual Convention of the Association for the Study of African American Life and History, held in September 2015; the international conference The States of Memory of Slavery: International Comparative Perspectives. La mémoire de l'esclavage dans tous ses états. Perspectives internationales comparées (École des Hautes Études en Sciences Sociales), in October 2015; the 17th Annual International Conference of the Gilder Lehrman Center for the Study of Slavery, Resistance, and Abolition (Yale University) in October 2015; the Princeton African Humanities Colloquium "African Memory and the Crisis of the Present" (Princeton University) in November 2015; the lecture series The Framing of Race (Oberlin College) in April 2016; the international conferences La traite des noirs, l'esclavage et les mémoires des ports (Université du Havre), in May 2016, Lieux de mémoire européens held in Hanover, Germany, in November 2016, and Traces and Memories of Slavery in the Atlantic World (Université de Montpellier) in December, 2016. I thank Wayne Modest, Damian Pargas, Abdoulaye Gueye, Johann Michel, Marcela Echeverri, David Blight, Simon Gikandi, Matthew Rarey, Eric Saunier, Etienne François, Thomas Serrier, Bernard Michon, and Lawrence Aje for inviting me to give keynote addresses and to present my work in these meetings.

Several scholars helped through this process, by providing me with references and comments. Alice L. Baumgartner graciously sent me a copy of the excellent paper on abolition of slavery in Mexico she presented in the annual conference of the Gilder Lehrman Center in 2015. Andrew Maginn provided me with valuable references regarding Haiti's debt and the discussion on the US recognition of Haitian independence. I am also thankful to Adam Rothman, Beatriz Mamigonian, Claudia Andrade Santos, Eduardo Silva, Fernando Costa da Conceição, Humberto Adami Santos Junior, Ivana Stolze Lima, Júnia Furtado, Maria Helena Machado, Manisha Sinha, and Deadria Farmer-Paellmann, who patiently answered my questions and provided me with references. Joanne Pope-Melish generously gave me a copy of Levi Hart, "Thoughts on the Subject of Freeing the Negro Slaves" whose original had disappeared from the collections of the Connecticut Historical Society. Olivette Otele encouraged me and provided me with useful references. I am grateful to Roy Finkenbine for sharing with me references on his important work on reparations for slavery in the United States. I thank Rebecca J. Scott and Michael Zeuske for providing me with valuable information regarding the case of Andrea Quesada in Cuba. I am indebted to Gracelaw Simmons of the Board of Directors of the Royall House Slave Quarters in Medford, Massachusetts, for directing me to primary sources on Isaac Royall and Belinda Sutton.

The staff of the archives and libraries in three continents helped me finding documents and gave me precious advice. In the United States, members of the staff of Howard University Library were extremely helpful in assisting me to locate and order documents and books. My thanks go especially to Marcus E. Haynes from the Interlibrary Loan Service, and Ruth Rasby, Head of Access Services and Digitization. At the Moorland-

Spingarn Center, I thank archivists Joellen ElBashir and Kenvi Philips for their help. Moorland-Spingarn Research Center is Howard University's precious jewel. Also, I am grateful to Museu Berardo (Lisbon, Portugal) for allowing me to use the image of a painting from its collections.

I am also indebted to the staff of the National Archives in Washington, DC, including Thomas Eisinger, but especially Miranda Booker-Perry who helped me explore the records of the ex-slaves pensions' movement. At the Connecticut Historical Society, I thank Barbara Austen. The staff of the Beinecke Library at Yale University, the Library of Congress and its Manuscript Division, and the New York Public Library were extremely helpful in finding valuable documents for my research. In France, I am grateful to the staff of Bibliothèque Nationale de France, Paris; and in the Republic of Benin, I thank the archivists of the Archives Nationales, in Porto Novo. In Brazil, I thank the librarians and archivists of Biblioteca Nacional of Rio de Janeiro, Arquivo Público do Rio Grande do Sul, and Instituto Histórico Geográfico Brasileiro for orienting me and helping me finding existing primary and secondary sources.

Edna G. Medford, chair of the Department of History and Bernard A. Mair, Dean of the College of Arts and Sciences supported my work by making my sabbatical research leave possible, without which it would be impossible to complete this book. Kristy Johnson edited early drafts of chapters of this book. During the years I conducted research for this book I was assisted by Howard University's doctoral candidates Kate McMahon, Erica Metcalfe, Arlisha Norwood, and Marcus Weise. I also thank many dear colleagues and friends, who supported me in various ways during this process. Dale T. Graden and Alex Borucki read the second chapter and gave me many valuable recommendations and corrections. Leslie Schwalm read and commented the third chapter, and I did my best to incorporate all her suggestions. I am particularly grateful to Daniel Domingues da Silva, who read two chapters and provided me with important comments and detailed corrections. Lisa Earl Castillo has been a supportive friend and colleague with whom I exchanged thoughts during all the long process that ended with the publication of this book.

At Bloomsbury, Claire Lipscomb enthusiastically supported this project in its initial stages. Emma Goode did a wonderful job from the beginning to the end. I thank her for all the assistance she provided me starting with the manuscript submission, the conception of the cover, until its publication. I also express my gratitude to the generous scholars who reviewed the book proposal and the book manuscript. Their comments and suggestions helped me to improve the final version of the book.

My parents Gilberto Araujo and Syrlei Araujo provided me with comfort, love, and care during my trips to Brazil. When I was finishing writing this book, my dear uncle and brother, Paulo Roberto Oliveira de Araujo (1951–2016) left us to join the ancestors, but his memory and legacy will always be with me. Most importantly, this book would not exist without my husband's support. Alain Bélanger encouraged me during this long journey, with positive words, and wise advice. His love and support is what keep me alive and moving. As always, this book is dedicated to him. Aby, our furry feline friend, not only inspired me with his beauty, but also helped me to wake up early in the morning to write this book.

Introduction

Reparations in the
Past and Present

From 1517 until 1867, slave ships carried approximately 12.5 million
enslaved Africans to the Americas. In West Africa and West Central Africa,
African men, women, and children were killed in the wars that produced
captives for the slave trade. Others perished during the lingering journeys
walking from the hinterland to the coast and though the long waiting period
of confinement in slave depots. Whereas nearly 2 million Africans were
killed before being forced into the vessels that carried them through the
Atlantic Ocean, another 1.8 million did not survive the horrors of the
Middle Passage. Approximately 10.7 million enslaved men, women, and
children disembarked alive in the Americas.[1] Revisiting this human tragedy
and its enduring reverberations, this book chronicles the history of the
demands of reparations for slavery and the Atlantic slave trade.

The past three decades witnessed an increasing number of ventures
memorializing slavery in the Americas, Europe, and Africa.[2] Many of these
initiatives were eventually transformed into official projects. Yet, the
construction of monuments and memorials neither healed the wounds of the
slave past, nor mitigated the legacies of slavery. Instead it made more visible
the scars of racial violence and racial inequalities of which black populations,
most of whom are descendants of slaves, are still the main victims in former
slave societies. In this new context, in which public memory of slavery is
increasingly institutionalized, demands of financial and material reparations
for slavery and the Atlantic slave trade are again resurfacing, against the
odds of many scholars and activists who by the end of the twentieth century
declared the case for financial and material reparations dead.

In this book, I argue that not only are these demands not dead, but they
have a long and persevering history. During slavery times, written records
show that enslaved and freedpeople rarely employed the term reparation in
association with bondage. Instead they evoked it by using synonyms such as

redress, compensation, indemnification, atonement, repayment, and restitution. Yet, since the eighteenth century, enslaved and freed individuals started conceptualizing the idea of reparations in correspondence, pamphlets, public speeches, slave narratives, and judicial claims, written in English, French, Spanish, and Portuguese. In different periods, despite the legality of slavery, slaves and former slaves showed how conscious they were of having been victims of an injustice. They were aware they provided unpaid labor to their owners contributing to their wealth. They also fought back and demanded compensations when they were unlawfully held in captivity. Drawing from this consciousness, the trailblazers who addressed the first demands to governments and former masters for reparations clearly stated that not only must they be freed, but that they were owed financial and material restitutions.

Historically, the term reparation has been employed to convey the idea of making amendments for past wrongs.[3] During the twentieth century, the idea of reparation appeared in international law and in the human rights field to describe the redress of physical, material, or moral damage inflicted on an individual, a group of individuals, and even a nation. In customary international law, reparation was associated with measures to indemnify nations for wartime damages. But such amendments contain two dimensions. The first is moral or symbolic, and usually consists of apologies and actions to help those who were victims of wrongdoing. The second one carries a financial and material scope. In other words, the victim of past wrongs also obtains money or other possessions, such as land, as payment for the misconduct inflicted. Ultimately, reparation can carry only a symbolic aspect, or also a material and a financial dimension.

Starting at the end of the eighteenth century, during the American Revolutionary War (1775–1783), and especially after 1804, with the victory of the Saint-Domingue Revolution, slavery was gradually abolished in the western hemisphere. In Cuba and the United States, a number of slaves and former slaves individually attempted without success to obtain financial and material reparations for the time they lived in bondage. In contrast, in several former slave societies, including the French and British Caribbean colonies, former masters and planters obtained compensation from their respective governments for the loss of slave property.

In the United States, the period that followed emancipation brought hopes of land redistribution to freedpeople. But these projects failed as well. When Reconstruction ended, and the prospects of obtaining land and full citizenship were replaced with disenfranchisement and increasing racial hatred, former slaves collectively requested financial reparations. During the 1890s, thousands of former slaves petitioned the government of the United States to pass Bills providing them with pensions for the time they were enslaved. The leaders of this movement, which historian Mary Frances Berry examined in detail, conceived the payment of pensions as financial redress for the many years of uncompensated labor that slaves provided to their masters.[4]

The Bills demanding pensions to ex-slaves generated great mobilization and debates, but never passed. Moreover, federal authorities persecuted the leaders of the movement, who were sent to prison, and ultimately never achieved their goal. Meanwhile, during the nineteenth and early twentieth centuries, other former slave societies such as Brazil, Cuba, and Colombia did not witness collective movements demanding reparations for slavery. Although deprived of material resources, freedpeople privileged the struggle for citizenship in these societies where the ideologies of racial democracy and *mestizaje* predominated. But in the period that followed the end of the Second World War, this context started changing especially after the Jewish victims of the Holocaust obtained restitution. In this new landscape in which governments paid compensation to victimized groups, the renewed call for financial, material, and symbolic reparations for more than three centuries of slavery eventually started gaining more public attention.

In 1959, Cuba staged a revolution, which was followed by an extensive agrarian reform and ultimately redistributed land to black Cubans. Meanwhile, in the United States, the Civil Rights Movement hardly ever defended reparations for slavery that were not a central element in its overall agenda. Yet, during the Cold War in the United States, even though reparations activism was constantly associated with Communism, several groups advocating reparations surfaced. During the 1960s, the movement gained new blood with the rise of the Reparations Committee for the Descendants of American Slaves, the Republic of New Africa, and the Black Manifesto. As the end of the Cold War approached, the government of the United States paid financial restitutions to the Japanese Americans who were unlawfully interned in camps during the Second World War. With this precedent, the end of the 1980s and the 1990s provided a new ground for a renewed wave of demands of reparations for slavery. Brazil, Colombia, and Ecuador enacted new constitutions recognizing the right of land ownership for their black communities. In the United States, new organizations combining activism and litigation requesting reparations emerged as well. The echoes of this movement were also heard in Africa, where a group of intellectuals, artists, politicians, and activists issued a document calling for reparations for the Atlantic slave trade and colonialism. With the beginning of the twenty-first century, the United Nations World Conference Against Racism, Racial Discrimination, Xenophobia, and Related Intolerance held in Durban in 2001 recognized slavery and the Atlantic slave trade as crimes against humanity. More than ever, demands of redress acquired a new strength.

As recently as March 2014, the Caribbean Community (CARICOM) accepted a plan focusing on reparations for slavery and native genocide. The program consists of ten points comprising material, financial, and symbolic demands addressed to various European governments including the United Kingdom, Spain, France, Netherlands, Denmark, Sweden, and Portugal. The call for reparations received great attention from the media in European and Caribbean countries, as well as from newspapers in the United States and

Brazil. As a result, few weeks later, the debate on reparations for African Americans reemerged in an article by the acclaimed journalist and writer Ta-Nehisi Coates, as well as in a series of essays published in the *New York Times*.[5] Its echoes persisted during the US presidential campaign of 2016 and still reverberate today.

But despite these continuous movements and the recurring debates on whether governments and other organizations should award reparations for slavery to the populations of African descent, and which forms these reparations should take, to this day no former slave society in the Americas has paid restitutions to the descendants of slaves. Likewise, European countries have not paid financial reparations to their former colonies in the Americas, all of which, at least to some extent, relied on slave labor. Moreover, no African nation obtained any form of reparations for the Atlantic slave trade as well. Although this context suggests a pessimistic perspective, the debates on reparations for slavery remain very alive. Every year demands of redress continue to be the object of lawsuits and Bills and remain present in the public sphere through popular demonstrations, especially when approaching commemorative dates associated with the abolition of slavery.

Drawing from my work on public memory of slavery, this book presents a narrative history of the demands of financial, material, and, to a lesser extent, symbolical reparations for slavery and the Atlantic slave trade. To tell this story, I combined the approaches of social and cultural history, by relying on fieldwork material and a myriad of written primary sources in English, French, Spanish, and Portuguese, including abolitionist pamphlets, correspondence, parliamentary debates, petitions by former slaves, newspaper articles, and congressional Bills as well as public discourses by black activists and politicians in western European countries such as France and the United Kingdom, West Africa, the United States, the Caribbean, and Latin America.

My central argument is that the ways the demands of reparations for slavery and the slave trade have been historically addressed are deeply connected to the peculiarities of the slave systems that prevailed in the societies where they emerged. I argue that these requests are linked to the particular processes that culminated with the abolition of slavery in several countries in the Americas, and also associated with the paths of development taken by these societies during the post-abolition period. I underscore that requests for redress are related to how former slaves and their descendants achieved or at least attempted to achieve citizenship in former slave societies. I show that calls for reparations are also associated with the ways black activists responded to the legal systems that imposed racial segregation and to the ruling ideologies that promoted racism and reinforced white supremacy. I interrogate these debates and demands to understand what they tell us about the societies and the social actors who have addressed them in the past and the present. To this end, I revisit the history of slavery and its aftermath in the Americas to explain the emergence and the persistence of requests of reparations. Exploring the voices of black militants who identified themselves as victims of the Atlantic slave trade and slavery, I show why from the nineteenth century to today the calls for reparations have been emphasized or dismissed in public debates held in African societies that provided slaves to the Americas and in European and American nations that benefited from the slave workforce.

Throughout this book, I explain that reparations go much beyond granting freedom and civil rights, and can take various forms that stand independently. A first step in the reparatory process requires that those who benefit from the wrongdoing offer an apology to those they victimized. Other measures include redressing the original situation as it was before the offense, and offering payment for possible damages. An apology can be understood as symbolic reparation, and does not necessarily need to be followed by the other steps. Ultimately, by examining the multiple dimensions of the discourses requesting reparations, from the abolition era and the post-abolition period until the present, I highlight how and why the requests for reparations have been emphasized or dismissed in public debates by various social actors such as politicians, activists, and government authorities.

Countless works have examined the issue of reparations from various angles, but this is the first book to draw a transnational and comparative narrative history of demands for reparations for slavery. Because the various former slave societies have several elements in common, this history cannot be restrained to national borders. Yet, I call the reader's attention to the fact that even though during slavery, and after its abolition, different societies of the Americas presented many similar elements, they were also marked by numerous differences, but these discrepancies never prevented historians from developing comparisons and providing analyses that transcend local and national contexts.

Likewise, in my role of historian I do not make any recommendations on who should receive reparations, who should pay them, and what amounts are allegedly owed to which specific individuals and groups. This determination should be made by the organizations and the groups that request reparations. Instead, what this book studies is how the idea of reparations emerged, how it was developed over time, who were the social actors who requested it, in which period, and why. Yet, it is worth remembering that the study of slavery and its legacies in former slave societies remains a rough terrain full of quicksand spots and imbricated in power structures. Historians and readers should question who collects historical data, who controls historical records, who regulates the publication of conclusions resulting from academic research on slavery, and how this research has been made available or kept inaccessible to larger audiences.

Despite these limitations of the historian's craft, the analysis of primary sources can reveal how some states, companies, and universities, as well as other individuals and their descendants largely benefited from the slave trade and slave labor. Especially in the first chapter of this book, I show that works written by historians have played and still play an important role either to highlight or to minimize the importance of the wealth generated by the Atlantic slave trade and slavery, by necessarily impacting the discourses of activists who contributed to formulate demands of reparations. Still, historical research can also bring to light how the descendants of slaves remained socially, economically, and politically excluded. Evidently, such body of evidence can eventually support the work of organizations to establish their demands for reparations.

Over the pages that follow, when referring to slaves and former slaves, as well as their descendants and other black and white abolitionists and activists who invoked or formulated demands for reparations for slavery and the Atlantic slave trade, I interchangeably use synonyms such as redress, indemnification, atonement, and restitution. Still, because after emancipation former slave owners and planters also requested payments to cover the loss of slave property, in this book these demands are referred to as financial compensation. These two kinds of payments greatly differ in nature. Whereas financial or material reparations are amendments for slavery and the slave trade as past wrongdoings, financial compensation to slave owners are indemnities paid by governments to former slave owners in order to assure that their losses provoked by emancipation were minimal. But although different, these two forms of payments are interrelated. When governments compromised in indemnifying former masters and planters, they took the clear decision to engage existing resources to subsidize those who over more than three centuries already benefited from slavery, rather than supporting decent work and living conditions to freedpeople.

Although this is a transnational and comparative book, this work is not an exhaustive compilation of demands for reparations for slavery in every single country, a task that would require a multivolume publication. Organized in chronological order, this book is divided into five chapters. Chapter 1, "Greatest Riches From Our Blood and Tears," contextualizes the history of the Atlantic slave trade and slavery in the Americas. I stress that the Atlantic slave trade resulted from the collaboration between African elites, middlemen, and other commoners, with Europeans and their descendants. I also stress that slavery existed both in urban areas and plantation settings. In addition, I underscore that both in the North and in the South Atlantic systems the Atlantic slave trade engendered great economic profits for European and American slaveholding elites as well as for African rulers and middlemen. I show that only a transnational approach, combining history and memory, can consider the complexities of an inhuman system that interconnected three continents for more than three hundred years. Overall, the chapter provides the reader with a general view of the ways the first demands of reparations for slavery surfaced between the late eighteenth and the late nineteenth century.

Chapter 2, "'And What Should We Wait of These Brutish Spirits?'" explores the fallacies of the debates regarding emancipation and abolition of slavery in Europe and the Americas during the eighteenth and nineteenth centuries. By comparing the processes that led to the end of slavery in the American continent, this chapter shows how elite groups emphasized the legality of owning human property, the need of a very gradual emancipation process that would not hurt the slave owners, and the necessity of providing the masters with financial compensation for property loss. Despite this hegemonic view, the chapter brings to light the contrasting views of a small number of abolitionists, who even before the emancipation, defended the need for financial and material reparations to the future freed population. I show that during the period of gradual abolition individuals unlawfully enslaved as well as former slaves requested either the government or their old masters to supply them with pensions or some kind of monetary or material reparations for the time they performed unpaid labor. The study of these few individual calls for redress illuminates the discourses of these first historical actors. I argue that the fight for reparations, although initially in a small scale, has a long history in the Americas.

Chapter 3, "'We Helped to Pay this Cost'," explores the period that followed the abolition of slavery, when new individual and collective demands of reparations for slavery surfaced. The chapter highlights that these emerging demands were closely associated with wider debates about the future of former slave societies. In the United States, Cuba, and Brazil former slaves struggled to get access to civil rights and material resources. While reparations for slavery was not a central claim for the great majority of freedmen and freedwomen, both individually or gathered in organizations, freedpeople addressed demands for reparations to the governments and to their former masters. This chapter illuminates the main arguments advanced by these social actors to defend their calls for reparations for the time they lived in bondage. Combining macro-history, through the study of larger trends in post-slave societies, and micro-history, through the examination of individual cases and smaller groups, I explain what factors favored or prevented the emergence of demands for reparations between the end of the nineteenth century and the two first decades of the twentieth century.

In Chapter 4, "'What Else Will the Negro Expect?'," I discuss how Brazil, Cuba, and the United States addressed symbolic, material, and financial reparations for slavery, starting from the Great Depression and continuing through the Cold War era. During the 1960s, financial and material reparations for slavery were absent from the agenda of the Civil Rights Movement. Yet, after the passing of the Civil Rights Act of 1964, reparations resurfaced in the program of several African American organizations of the Black Power era. During this period, whereas post-revolutionary Cuba led a large agrarian reform that resulted in the redistribution of land to black Cubans, Brazil took an opposite direction through the instauration of a military regime. Despite these contrasting paths, I argue that the era of the

Civil Rights Movement opened an enormous space to reintroduce reparations for slavery in the public debate.

Chapter 5, "'It's Time for Us to Get Paid'," surveys the rise of new demands of reparations for slavery and the Atlantic slave trade in the United States, West Africa, the Caribbean, and South America on the eve of the end of the Cold War. Although initially this wave was rather characterized by demands of symbolic reparations whose focus was the creation of monuments and memorials acknowledging the central role of enslaved men and women in the construction of slave societies, a growing number of organizations and groups started drawing attention to the need for financial and material reparations, by introducing Bills, starting litigation, and organizing demonstrations. For the first time in history, groups identifying themselves as descendants of slaves not only started calls for financial and material restitutions for slavery but also established international connections. I show that despite the specific contexts that oriented power relations and the rise of black organized groups in different parts of the Americas, activism advocating reparations also acquired a transnational scope.

The epilogue, "Unfinished Struggle," draws the main lines that contributed to the construction of particular discourses conveyed by different historical and social actors in the last two centuries in order to situate the current state of the problem of financial, material, and symbolic reparations for slavery. Even though the Atlantic slave trade and slavery were atrocities committed in the past, because their legacies remain alive today, debates, conferences, manifestos, litigation, and demonstrations requesting redress remain on the rise. Therefore, revisiting these past and current debates contributes not only to contextualizing the past, but also to understanding the present in which racial inequalities and white supremacy persist and demands of reparations remain alive.

This book tells the story of demands of reparations for slavery; starting with a history rooted in ideas that came to light during the abolitionist movement and were propagated from the end of the nineteenth century. This historical perspective is crucial because all over the Americas, and especially in Europe and Latin America, many social actors and even academics adhere to the idea that the first demands of reparations for slavery were only initiated as a result of United Nations World Conference Against Racism, Racial Discrimination, Xenophobia, and Related Intolerance held in Durban in 2001. Indeed, the first individual and collective demands of reparations surfaced more than two centuries earlier in the United States and in other former slave societies of the Americas.

This book shows how, to a greater or to a lesser extent, the arguments in favor of or opposed to reparations carried similar elements in societies where slavery existed. I emphasize not only how over time social actors and groups of activists defended or opposed various forms of reparations, but also underscore that from their emergence the movements for reparations were criminalized, dismissed, and rejected, if not ridiculed. Ultimately I explain why the current debates on demands for reparations remain so relevant today in the Americas, Europe, and Africa. To this end, before moving to the first chapter revisiting the history of slavery, I should state that all passages translated to English from French, Portuguese, and Spanish are my own, except otherwise indicated. ✓

1

"Greatest Riches in All America Have Arisen From Our Blood and Tears"

Studying the impacts of the Atlantic slave trade and slavery in Africa and former slave societies is comparable to walk in a minefield. For many decades, either in Europe or in the Americas, the study of slavery was an arena controlled by scholars who often dissociated the economic and human dimensions of the Atlantic slave trade. In this highly politicized terrain, the interplay of history and memory contributed to concealing the role of slavery in the construction of the Americas. It also helped to minimize the importance of the Atlantic slave trade in transforming Europe into a powerful and rich continent. In this scholarly battlefield, dissenting voices were likely to be condemned to the silence of the academic dungeons.

In a similar fashion, in many former slave societies slavery has been concealed from the public space. Whether intentional or not, in many ways this erasure contributed to the silencing of possible demands for redress for past wrongdoings from black social actors, who since the end of slavery had remained not only socially and economically marginalized but had also been prevented from having access to full citizenship. At the same time, it also gave origin to several misconceptions regarding the Atlantic slave trade and slavery. But as over the last three decades the discussion about slavery and its legacies reemerged in the public sphere, old and new ideas gained currency in popular debates. Even though not corroborated by historical research, social actors involved in debating slavery and its current legacies contributed to either reinforce or contest these misleading views, which have been disseminated to larger audiences in history books, school textbooks, visual images, motion pictures, documentary films, plays, novels, museum exhibitions, tourism initiatives, and television series.

The first misleading idea explaining the engines of the Atlantic slave trade is two-pronged. On the one hand, it states that Europeans kidnapped Africans and sold them into slavery. On the other hand, it asserts that Africans enslaved and sold their own brothers. The second misconception is the idea that slavery did not generate profit and was incompatible with capitalism, whereas the third associates the existence of slavery with large plantations and slaveholdings, neglecting its importance in urban areas all over the Americas. The fourth falsehood, still present in popular representations of slavery, emphasizes the cruel and inhumane dimension of slavery in the United States and the British Caribbean as opposed to the milder slave systems of Latin America. By deconstructing these myths and through an overview of the history of slavery and the Atlantic slave trade both in the North and the South Atlantic worlds, this chapter provides the context that helps us to understand the main arguments made by social actors who over the last two centuries defended or opposed the demands of financial, material, and symbolic reparations for slavery. Moreover, by exploring the patterns of the Atlantic slave trade from Africa to the various areas of the Americas and the experiences lived by the enslaved populations and their descendants, it illuminates how economic and human dimensions oriented the further emergence or demise of demands of reparations for slavery in these two continents.

The roots of the Atlantic slave trade

The Atlantic slave trade resulted from the collaboration between different African agents including rulers and middlemen, as well as of slaveholding elites and slave merchants in Europe and the Americas. To a greater or lesser extent, these agents benefited from the wealth engendered by the slave trade and slavery. African elites obtained political and economic power detrimental to the large majority of the victims of wars that led to the enslavement of millions of African men, women, and children. Yet, various groups who spoke different languages such as Yoruba, Fon, and Kimbundu, and practiced different religions such as Islam, Catholicism, Vodun, and Orisha composed the states involved in these wars. In the context of warfare especially, enslavers and captives were not brothers and sisters, but rather enemies and competitors, therefore eligible to be captured, sold to slave merchants, and brought by force to the Americas. Although a small group of Africans benefited from the immediate profits generated by the Atlantic slave trade, the wars and the overall insecurity that nourished its engines had significant and enduring negative impacts on African societies and the great majority of its populations. Still today these effects remain difficult to measure.

In both the North Atlantic and South Atlantic systems the slave trade and slavery propelled the accumulation of wealth and economic development. Whether in Brazil and Cuba, or in the United States, slavery was not in contradiction to the emergence of industrial capitalism. Moreover, albeit with various nuances, slavery existed both in plantation and urban areas all over the Americas. In these two different environments, slave merchants and slave owners submitted enslaved men, women, and children to horrible living and working conditions. Notwithstanding the different legal and religious systems and contrary to many present popular representations, slavery was a cruel and inhumane institution that left permanent scars on the enslaved populations and their descendants in the United States, Latin America, and the Caribbean.

Slavery existed in most world societies since antiquity. It took different forms in various times and places. Based on violence and coercion, slavery was an economic system and institution, regulated by laws and customs that allowed the ownership of men, women, and children. Conceived as commodities, slaves could be bought, sold, beaten, raped, killed, and discarded. But more than only providing forced labor to the master, slaves were submitted to relations of power.[1] The masters were entitled to control the bodies of slaves through the use of physical punishment as well as psychological and sexual abuse. Yet, several societies where slavery existed, at least to some extent, recognized slaves as human beings. On their end, slaves resisted and fought back to escape masters' control.

Whether in Greece, Rome, Egypt, Portugal, Peru, and Mauritania (the latest country to legally abolish slavery, in 1981) slavery existed in both urban and rural areas. Slaves worked in all places where their labor was required. In most societies, men and women inherited slave status from the mother (*partus sequitur ventrem*). But depending on the context, an enslaved man could pass his slave status to his offspring. Many freeborn individuals became slaves through raids and kidnappings, others were made slaves as judicial punishment for crimes like homicide, robbery, adultery, and witchcraft. Once in captivity, they were sold into slavery to other regions. Away from their homelands and families, physical appearance, customs, language, and religion ethnically marked these foreigners as different from the indigenous populations of the new societies to which they were bonded.

Portugal pioneered the European exploration of the coasts of Africa and India. After conquering Ceuta in North Africa, the Portuguese created numerous trading posts along African coastal areas, opening the way to a sustained trade. Portugal was the first European power to establish contact with Africa and to start acquiring West Central African captives. In 1481, after settling along the Gold Coast, the Portuguese initiated the construction of an impressive castle in Elmina, a coastal town located in present-day Ghana. Controlled by the Portuguese, and later under the Dutch and the British jurisdiction, Elmina Castle became an important slave depot, which today attracts thousands of tourists seeking to understand the history of the Atlantic slave trade and the origins of their ancestors deported to the Americas. But once established in West Africa, the Portuguese continued moving eastward.

In 1483, Diogo Cão (1440–1486) arrived on the coast of West Central Africa, where the Portuguese started developing relations with the Kingdom of Kongo, an area encompassing today's northern Angola, Cabinda, the Republic of the Congo, western Democratic Republic of the Congo, and southern Gabon. As part of a project of imperial expansion, which relied on the idea that Africans were pagans and needed to be evangelized, the Portuguese made an alliance with the King of Kongo, Nzinga Nkuwu (?–1506), who accepted baptism and converted to Catholicism. In exchange, the Portuguese provided Nzinga with military assistance to wage war against neighboring states. More importantly, the king supplied the Portuguese with captives for the emerging Atlantic slave trade.[2]

When the Portuguese engaged in exploring the coastal regions of West Africa and West Central Africa, captives from sub-Saharan Africa predominated in the slave trade. During the fifteenth century, purchasing and transporting enslaved Africans through the Atlantic Ocean was much more affordable in comparison with purchasing the increasingly expensive slaves from the Ottoman Empire and the Moroccan state, regions that traditionally provided captives to the European markets through the Saharan routes. Enslaved Africans worked in Portuguese sugarcane plantations of the Atlantic islands along the West African coast, including Madeira, Azores, Cape Verde, Canaries, and São Tomé.[3]

When the Atlantic slave trade emerged, slavery already existed in Africa. In the Kingdom of Kongo slavery was present at least since the fourteenth century, prior to the arrival of the Portuguese.[4] As early as in the fifteenth century, in West Central Africa, men, women, children, and any resource that produced wealth were regarded as capital.[5] But as the contact with the Portuguese expanded, local rulers gathered an increasing number of dependents by relying on acquiring foreign goods like weapons, alcohol, and textiles. Although luxury goods were crucial in expanding influence, as African rulers became deeply involved in Atlantic networks they had to sell into slavery the newly acquired dependents to these same foreigners from whom they obtained imported goods from European traders.[6]

The rise of the Atlantic slave trade impacted African societies in different ways. It also transformed the institution of slavery on the continent. During the era of the slave trade, the current map and frontiers of African states did not exist yet. The populations of a particular village or kingdom neither associated themselves with the entire continent nor carried some kind of pan-African identity. In other words, men and women of sub-Saharan Africa did not see themselves as, nor call themselves "Africans." This common identity emerged much later in the Americas, as the result of the tragedy of slavery, and in Africa, as a response to European colonial rule. In fact, until at least the middle of the nineteenth century, men and women living in the African continent tended to relate themselves to the various villages, states, kingdoms, and empires of different sizes, where they were born. Identifying themselves along ethnic lines, they spoke different languages and carried varied cultural and religious traditions associated with their lineages and clans. In this context, most individuals made captives and sold into slavery were either aliens or undesirable subjects in their home societies, condition that made them salable.[7]

In most African societies, enslaved men and women were outsiders. During the sixteenth century, foreign prisoners captured during wars with the Kingdom of Ndongo or in the regions of Pamzelungu and Anzicon largely fulfilled the demand for slaves in the Kingdom of Kongo.[8] The existence of this external source of supply of slaves usually protected freeborn subjects from being captured and sold into slavery. But the development of the Atlantic slave trade changed this situation. Insecurity increased in West African and West Central African societies, where populations born locally feared to be enslaved.[9]

From the sixteenth century until the middle of the seventeenth century Kongo rulers occasionally denounced Portuguese citizens who enslaved free people and even nobles and sent them to Portugal, São Tomé, and Brazil. Yet, enslaving free indigenous subjects was rather uncommon.[10] In West Africa, for example, the tradition established during the reign of King Wegbaja, who ruled Dahomey approximately from 1645 to 1685, strongly prevented the sale of individuals born within the kingdom. Contravening this custom was considered a major transgression. Rulers enforced this norm so severely that they even prohibited selling female captives who became pregnant during their transit through Dahomey.[11]

The establishment of commercial, cultural, and religious exchanges between the Portuguese and Africans coincided with European expansion in the Americas. West Central African and West African rulers purchased firearms from the Portuguese. The access to these weapons allowed them to continue waging war against neighboring states, which over time impacted the cycle of acquisition of war captives to be sold into slavery. With growing contact with African markets, the Portuguese became central actors in the development of the slave trade to Europe. As early as in the fifteenth century in Senegambia, Portuguese subjects participated in raids and kidnappings. Starting in the seventeenth century, the presence of Portuguese and Brazilians in West Central African ports contributed to the acceleration of existing divisions among states and chiefdoms, which fought each other to gain expansion and control larger numbers of subjects. These various polities competed to expand their territories and dominate larger populations on whom they imposed tributes.[12] In West Africa and West Central Africa, the impacts generated by the European presence and trade differed from one port to another, making it difficult to draw any generalizations. During the summit of the Atlantic slave trade in the eighteenth century, the largest West African ports such as Ouidah and Annamaboe were controlled by local rulers and not by Europeans.[13] But in other West African areas such as the hinterland of Benguela in West Central Africa, the Portuguese organized wars, conducted raids, and kidnapped people to feed slave exports.[14] Ultimately, the interactions between Europeans and Africans oriented the dynamics that made possible the largest transoceanic forced migration of all times. But why enslaved Africans?

Slavery and enslaved Africans in the Americas

When Christopher Columbus (1451–1506) arrived in the Caribbean in 1492, the indigenous groups who had inhabited the Americas for thousands of years organized their societies in different ways. In South America's Andean region, as well as in Mexico and Central America, these populations constructed empires and civilizations of various sizes that reached various levels of development. In Brazil, semisedentary Tupi-speaking peoples lived along the coastal region. Very soon, Columbus and the explorers who followed him identified the presence of gold in the new discovered land—first in the Caribbean islands, and then in Mexico and Central America, regions occupied by the Aztec empire and the Mayan civilization. The conquistadores also found gold deposits along the Inca empire in northwestern South America. The search for gold and silver pushed the Spaniards to conquer the Inca and the Aztec empires. They subjugated and killed the indigenous populations, and eventually colonized the new territory.

Pedro Álvares Cabral (1467–1502) and his fleet landed in Brazil in 1500, marking the beginning of the Portuguese colonial presence in the Americas. But Portugal was not in a position to propel the migration of its own population to settle and colonize the new territory. Unlike the Spanish, during this early period of conquest and colonization of Brazil the Portuguese did not find valuable goods such as gold. Instead they established trading posts along the coast, as they did in Africa, which allowed them to exchange goods with the indigenous groups who lived along the coast. In contrast to colonial North America, where white indentured servants constituted the majority workforce employed in the early seventeenth-century boom of Virginia's tobacco industry, Portugal's population was too small to sustain a significant migratory wave of workers to the Americas.[15] Consequently, both Spanish and Portuguese enslaved indigenous men and women. In the Spanish Americas, the natives performed forced labor in gold and silver mines, whereas in Brazil they extracted *pau-brasil* (brazilwood), a kind of wood that produced a red dye, highly valued in textile production in Europe.

Although it was the cheapest and fastest alternative at hand to the Spanish and Portuguese colonizers, the use of a native workforce faced great obstacles. Estimated at approximately twenty million individuals at the time of the conquest, in the few years that followed the conquest, the native population dramatically declined, killed not only in the wars of conquest, but also by epidemics and extreme working conditions. Between 1540 and 1570, the Portuguese used enslaved indigenous workers in the sugarcane plantations established in northeast region of Brazil. But in several areas natives resisted enslavement by attacking Portuguese settlements and escaping to the interior.

Soon, the existing pool of indigenous workers became insufficient to respond to the high demand for workers in the emerging Brazilian sugar industry.[16] By that time, promoting the immigration of the scarce Portuguese peasant populations to perform agriculture labor in Brazil would require great investment for transportation, relocation, and wages. As the Portuguese already employed enslaved Africans in the sugarcane plantations established in the Atlantic islands of the western African coast during the previous century, turning to sub-Saharan Africa once again was the most logical solution. More importantly, the slave trade generated profits for the Portuguese. Purchasing slaves in West Central Africa and West Africa and transporting them to the Americas to work in sugarcane plantations was more affordable in the long run. It was also less risky than insisting on the enslavement of rebellious natives who were not only unfamiliar with intensive agricultural work but who also resisted enslavement in their own homeland.

Over time, the sustained trade relations between Portugal, West Africa, and West Central Africa contributed to the extensive use of African slave labor in Brazil. In the 1550s, about 10,000 slaves of African descent lived in Lisbon, Portugal's capital. This old presence appears in written documents, heritage sites, and visual images like the Dutch painting representing the King's Fountain Square (Figure 1.1). The image shows male citizens interacting with enslaved black female and male subjects. The slave status of one character is visible through a large chain attached to his neck. The barefoot black men and women perform various activities. Several of them

FIGURE 1.1 Anonymous, *Chafariz d'el Rey in the Alfama District*, c. 1570–1580. Oil on panel. Associação de Coleções, The Berardo Collection, Lisbon, Portugal.

carry water jars on their heads, suggesting their lower status. In the foreground, an elegantly dressed black male rides a horse. Wearing shoes, he is dressed in a black tunic that displays the cross of the Order of Santiago's knights, which implies his upper status.[17] The painting confirms that black individuals were well established in the Iberian Peninsula. But despite this black presence in the Iberian Peninsula during the time of the Atlantic slave trade, most Africans forcibly migrated to the region as slaves. As a consequence, their descendants continued occupying subaltern positions and facing discriminatory policies based on their origin, status, and color.

Over the fifteenth century, the slave trade to the Americas gradually flourished. In 1517 the first enslaved Africans disembarked in Hispaniola, then in the viceroyalties of New Spain (or Mexico) and Peru. In the middle of the sixteenth century slavery became a racialized institution, as Iberians conceived black and slave as synonyms. By 1553, for instance, the population of African descent in New Spain grew so fast that it raised fear among local authorities. The Viceroy Luis Velasco (1511–1564) wrote a letter asking the Spanish Crown to restrict the imports of enslaved Africans, in order to prevent the colony from becoming predominantly black.[18] The decreasing indigenous population and the Iberian demographic context, associated with the previous use of slaves from sub-Saharan Africa in the Atlantic islands were factors that contributed to the intensification of the development of the slave trade to the Americas. In several regions, enslaved Africans progressively replaced indigenous slaves.

Enslaved Africans and their descendants played a crucial role in the economies of Spanish and Portuguese colonies. Still, their importance in different areas varied over time and also depended on the size of existing native populations. At least initially, the colonization of Brazil and the thirteen colonies of North America had similar elements. Both areas were characterized by isolated settlements along the coast, and lacked large and organized Amerindian civilizations, such as the Inca and Aztec empires of the Spanish Americas. However, contrasting Brazil and the Spanish Americas, the colonization of North America relied on the presence of family farms. European settlers had access to land ownership and political power through the participation in elections and local institutions.[19] All over the Americas, African presence had more importance in areas with reduced or scattered indigenous populations than in the regions where the use of enslaved African and native workforces were combined.

Slavery existed in all regions of the Americas, but in societies with slaves, slavery had a marginal role, and the number of slaves was usually small. In contrast, in slave societies the institution of slavery was a central element of social, political, and economic life. Yet, with the development of the plantation system, several societies with slaves became slave societies.[20] Small-scale slavery predominated in mainland Spanish Americas, whereas large-scale plantation slavery prevailed in the Caribbean and Brazil. In these two areas, the production for a market economy reigned, and the number of slaves was significantly larger than in the areas where small-scale slavery existed.

During the sixteenth century, in the Viceroyalty of Peru, encompassing most present-day South American countries of the Andean region, such as Peru, Colombia, Bolivia, and Ecuador, most enslaved Africans performed strenuous work in silver mines. In the Viceroyalty of New Spain, the territories ruled by Spain in North America and Central America, black slaves were employed in textile workshops. By 1570, approximately 20,000 slaves of African descent lived in the region, but by the early seventeenth century their presence increased to nearly 45,000 individuals. In 1640, slaves made up 2 percent of the total population of New Spain, but their number declined significantly in the second half of the seventeenth century. In this same period, the number of slaves in the Viceroyalty of Peru was estimated at approximately 100,000, representing between 10 percent and 15 percent of the total population. Together these two viceroyalties imported between 250,000 and 300,000 enslaved Africans.[21]

The expansion of slave economies in the Americas was highly dependent on the dynamics of the slave trade. Access to ships, credit, and African markets, which relied on political and economic local contexts, determined how successful European empires and kingdoms would be in supplying their colonies with slaves. For example, the slave trade to the Spanish Americas intensified during the Iberian Union (1580–1640), when the Spanish and Portuguese crowns were unified. At the time, the Portuguese obtained the *asiento*, the license provided by the Spanish Crown giving the monopoly of the slave trade to a particular nation. Therefore, the Spanish Americas imported approximately 289,000 enslaved Africans, whereas roughly 188,000 Spaniards arrived in the region.[22] With the end of the Iberian Union in 1640, the slave trade to New Spain started declining and continued decreasing throughout the eighteenth century, when a growing workforce of indigenous populations became available.

The organization of the slave trade presented distinct elements in the various regions of the Atlantic world. In the North Atlantic system, the slave trade tended to follow the so-called triangular model. Slave ships would leave Europe with goods to be sold in African ports in exchange for slaves, who would be transported to the Caribbean and North America. These same ships would bring raw materials from the Americas to Europe, even if in some cases certain goods were shipped to Europe in larger vessels specifically designed for the purpose.[23] In the South Atlantic, the Luso-Brazilian slave trade rather adhered to a bilateral model. In this zone, exchanges often occurred independently from Lisbon. Slave ships traveled directly between Brazilian slave ports and those in West Africa and West Central Africa.[24] From Rio de Janeiro and Salvador, the largest slave ports in the Americas, Portuguese and Brazilian slave merchants transported gold, sugarcane brandies (*gerebitas*, *aguardente* or *cachaça*), tobacco, and gunpowder, as well as manufactured goods such as textiles. Arrived in Luanda, Ouidah, and

Benguela, the major African slave ports, they exchanged these goods for slaves. Yet, this bilateral trade did not exclude the triangular model. Ships transporting goods from Europe, Asia, and the Americas left Portugal and sailed to Africa, to exchange these commodities for slaves, and then crossed again the Atlantic Ocean to eventually arrive in Brazil.[25]

The development of the Atlantic slave trade was deeply entangled with imperial expansion. European rivalries transformed the balance of power in the Americas. They also altered the dynamics of the Atlantic slave trade in Africa. In the course of the seventeenth century, the North Atlantic and South Atlantic systems became the battlefield of disputes among European empires that sought to control the slave trade from Africa to the Americas and to monopolize the emerging and lucrative sugar industry. The Iberian Union affected negatively the relations between Portugal and the Netherlands. The Dutch were the Portuguese's major commercial partner in Brazil but were enemies of Spain against whom they rebelled by declaring independence in 1588 during the Eighty Years' War (1568–1648).

In retaliation, in 1624 the Dutch occupied Salvador, then the Brazilian capital, situated in the colony's second largest sugar-producing captaincy. Although expelled by the Portuguese in the following year, in 1630 the Dutch successfully took control of Recife, the capital of the captaincy of Pernambuco and Brazil's first sugar producer. These conflicts reverberated in Africa as well. In 1637 the Dutch seized Elmina Castle on the Gold Coast. In 1641, they occupied Luanda and eventually controlled the coast of Angola.[26] In 1654, after their expulsion from Brazil, the Dutch massively migrated to the Caribbean, where their colonies expanded.

European rivalries provoked other changes in the Atlantic landscape. The growing colonial competition coincided with the opening of the tobacco industry in Virginia. Moreover, during this period, other European powers secured their position in the Caribbean region. In 1655, Britain took control of Jamaica, and by 1659, France occupied the western part of Hispaniola, which in turn became the colony of Saint-Domingue. Spain kept Cuba, Puerto Rico, and the eastern part of the island (Santo Domingo), present-day Dominican Republic. In Africa, the French and the British seized most of the West African slave trade, even though the Luso-Brazilian slave traders continued controlling the slave trade along the coast of West Central Africa. As the major European empires fought to take over the new colonies in the Americas as well as the slave markets in Africa, the Atlantic slave trade intensified. In the seventeenth century, about 964,700 enslaved Africans were transported to Brazil; 327,000 to the British Caribbean; 104,000 to the Spanish Americas, and 32,800 to the French and British colonies in North America.[27]

In the European colonies in the Caribbean and in Brazil, slavery followed the preexisting plantation model implemented by the Portuguese in the Atlantic islands of West Africa. The traders, who initially acquired wealth in South and Southeast Asia, also provided capital, credit, and technology to the development of this emergent sugar industry. Barbados and Martinique developed as the two first slave societies based on plantation regimes.[28] Until the seventeenth century, the size of slaveholdings in these plantations was approximately fifty slaves. By 1600, when sugar prices dramatically increased, Brazil had 200 sugar mills in operation, and produced more than 10,000 tons of sugar annually.[29] Between 1630 and 1640, as Brazil dominated the international sugar production, slave imports intensified.

Dutch colonization transformed the sugar industry in the Americas. During their occupation of Pernambuco, the captaincy became Brazil's main sugar producer. Once in the Caribbean, they provided credit and introduced modern techniques that contributed to the development of sugar plantations and mills in the British and French colonies, which broke Brazil's domination of the world's sugar production.[30] Dutch presence fueled the development of North American colonies. In the 1620s, through the Dutch East India Company, they established the colony of New Amsterdam in present-day New York. In this same period, a group of British Puritans created a settlement in Massachusetts. Then a decade later, other British immigrants established a colony in Maryland.

During the seventeenth century, a plantation system emerged in North America's Chesapeake region, including the colonies of Maryland and Virginia. By that time, enslaved Africans and white indentured servants worked together in agricultural activities.[31] But at the end of the seventeenth century, as the tobacco plantations expanded and the number of indentured white servants decreased, planters started importing a growing number of enslaved Africans. This new context reinforced racial slavery and increased measures segregating blacks and whites. Meanwhile, Brazil positioned itself as the third largest producer of sugar, behind Saint-Domingue and Jamaica. Following various expeditions to the interior of the colony, Portuguese and Brazilian explorers found gold deposits in the region of present-day Minas Gerais.

The discovery of gold propelled the growth of the slave trade to Brazil in the eighteenth century. Whereas in the seventeenth century Brazil imported about one million enslaved Africans, in the eighteenth century this number almost doubled. In the first two decades of the eighteenth century, a gold rush transformed Rio de Janeiro into the most important Brazilian slave port, overtaking Salvador and Recife. During this same period, although the number of slave imports declined in Mexico and Peru, other regions witnessed the opposite movement. By that time, slavery also expanded with the sugar and coffee production in Cuba, with the gold industry in Viceroyalty of New Granada, and with cacao production in Venezuela and Costa Rica. In the Spanish Americas and Brazil, a slave workforce predominated in silver, gold, and diamond mines.

Africans and the Atlantic slave trade

The Atlantic slave trade expanded during the eighteenth century, with full British, French, and Dutch involvement. Britain became the world's premier

European slaving nation, followed by Portugal and Spain. In other areas of the Americas, the slave trade also intensified. In the eighteenth century, slave imports in the British Caribbean are estimated at 1,813,323 slaves. From 1645 to 1776, when the thirteen colonies declared independence from Britain, approximately 281,328 enslaved Africans disembarked in mainland North America, whereas from 1700 to 1800, more than two million Africans were imported to Brazil.[32]

This demand for captives in the Americas contributed to the development of the existing interstate wars in West Africa and West Central Africa, intensifying instability in the region. In the Kingdom of Kongo, this dynamic led to growing rivalries among the candidates to the royal throne and their supporters. These disputes, associated with civil wars, accentuated internal divisions that over time engendered new circumstances in which people who were born free within the Kingdom of Kongo's frontiers were no longer protected as they used to be in the past from being sold into slavery.[33]

Likewise, the Kingdom of Dahomey waged wars against several of its neighbors, including the kingdoms of Onim and Badagry, as well as the Kingdom of Oyo.[34] Still today, the stories of these campaigns appear in applique hangings dispersed in museum collections around the world and in a series of bas-reliefs, representing male and female warriors fighting and killing enemies, which decorate the façades of the royal palaces of Dahomey's capital, Abomey, in present-day Republic of Benin. Dahomean kings also narrated these wars in an extensive correspondence exchanged with the Portuguese rulers during diplomatic missions sent to Brazil between the middle of the eighteenth century and the early nineteenth century to negotiate the terms of the Atlantic slave trade. The letters exchanged between these monarchs illuminate the engines of the Atlantic slave trade in the region of Bight of Benin.

By the end of 1750, Dahomey's King Tegbesu (c. 1728–1774) sent to Brazil a delegation composed of one ambassador, two other individuals, and one interpreter.[35] On September 29, 1750, the diplomatic mission arrived at the then Brazilian capital, Salvador of Bahia. A gun salute solemnly welcomed the group. The ambassador, wearing a gown with a nacreous velvet coat and a headscarf with plumes, was transported to the city in a luxurious palanquin padded with silk. The two other emissaries, dressed in traditional clothes, left the wharf in a sedan chair, followed by four young naked girls who came with them from Dahomey. The lavish procession of West African delegates attracted the population's curiosity. Although the presence of newly arrived and nearly naked enslaved Africans was common in the streets of Salvador, the view of an African emissary sophisticatedly dressed was an exceptional event. The group stayed in a room richly decorated in the College of the Jesuits, located just next to the Cathedral of Salvador, in the Terreiro de Jesus public square.[36]

Dahomean emissaries had to wait almost three weeks before the official meeting with the Portuguese authorities. Meanwhile, the Portuguese and

Brazilian officials invited the guests to visit Salvador's churches, convents, and fortresses, but they preferred to wait for the official meeting, before touring the area. Brazil's viceroy, Luiz Peregrino de Carvalho Meneses de Ataíde (1700–1758), the Count of Atouguia, also offered the Dahomean officials Portuguese costumes in velvet and damask, especially tailored for the official diplomatic audience. But the ambassador also refused this offer by stating that he and his delegates had to dress according to their home country fashion. During their stay in Bahia, even though they lodged in a Jesuit institution, the group freely practiced their religious rites, apparently with no opposition from the Portuguese officials. On the day of an important religious holiday in their calendar, they even performed a Vodun ceremony, during which they "killed many birds, anointing themselves with their blood, and made a banquet with delicacies prepared at their manner."[37]

The Dahomean ambassador offered as gifts to the viceroy and the King of Portugal two large boxes covered in iron with ornate locks, as well as the four girls who accompanied the embassy.[38] Except for one girl, who became blind after arriving in Bahia, the boxes and the three other girls were sent to Lisbon.[39] Eventually the emissaries departed from Bahia on April 12, 1751, in a vessel carrying 8,101 rolls of tobacco. On June 27, 1752, the same ship returned from West Africa carrying 834 slaves, showing the success of the diplomatic mission in developing the trade relations between Brazil and Dahomey.[40]

During the reign of King Agonglo (r. 1789–1797) wars and revolutions raged in Europe and in its colonies in the Americas.[41] The Atlantic conflicts that followed the French Revolution and led to the Napoleonic Wars (1803–1815) deeply affected France, Portugal, Spain, and Britain. The Saint-Domingue slave revolts provoked the first abolition of slavery by the French Convention in 1794, resulting into the drastic decline of the French slave trade in Ouidah.[42] The problems generated by this decline are visible in the further correspondence between the Portuguese and Dahomean authorities as part of the two kingdoms' reciprocal diplomatic missions.

In May 1795, King Agonglo sent a new embassy to Bahia, with the goal of convincing the Portuguese authorities to transform the port of Ouidah into the exclusive source of slave exports from the Bight of Benin to Brazil. The mission included two representatives of the Dahomean king who were accompanied by an interpreter, Luiz Caetano de Assumpção, an enslaved man identified in the contemporary documents as a "mulatto" who after escaping his master, the administrator of the Portuguese fort, put himself under Agonglo's protection.[43]

In one of the letters, dated March 20, 1795, along with the embassy, the king complained to Bahia's governor about the weight of tobacco rolls imported from Bahia. Confirming the demand for luxury goods in Dahomey, he also requested Bahia's governor to send him other goods such as silks, carved gold, and silver. In addition, he insisted on the old demand to give Ouidah the monopoly of slaves' supply from the Bight of Benin to Brazil, by also asking the governor to forbid Portuguese vessels to trade at the neighboring ports.[44] But the governor rejected the proposal, explaining that the monopoly would not only increase the price of slaves, but also prevent the captains of ships from choosing the slaves.[45]

The content of this letter reveals that products such as firearms, gunpowder, alcohol and tobacco were Dahomey's main imports during the eighteenth and the nineteenth centuries. The introduction of these goods transformed local customs and daily life.[46] Dahomeans employed various kinds of firearms in military campaigns, hunting activities, and defense. European travelers also reported that at their arrival in Abomey, the kingdom's capital, they were saluted by gunfire. Different ceremonies also included firing guns.[47] Although it is hard to determine the extent of consumption of luxury goods in Dahomey, alcohol and tobacco imports were destined for both the ruling class and mass consumption. Whereas tobacco was a native plant from the Americas, the introduction of alcohol was adapted to preexisting consumption habits. European accounts of the late eighteenth century, for example, show that in addition to the consumption of palm wine and a local beer called *pitto*, Europeans introduced several kinds of brandy, wine, and beer.[48] During audiences, ceremonies, and welcome receptions, travelers drank the king's health in small glasses of brandy. Additionally, even though Dahomey had a long-standing local weaving tradition, with the Atlantic slave trade imported cloths such as silk were increasingly consumed by ruling elites. During a visit to the Dahomean court in 1772, the British slave trader Robert Norris (c. 1724–1791) brought "a few pieces of silk for presents," and later the king received him "dressed in a silk night-gown."[49] Norris also attended a procession in which women wore "rich silks, silver bracelets, and other ornaments, coral and a profusion of other valuable beads."[50] In publicly displaying their luxury garments, the members of the royal court sought to affirm their political power.[51]

From Bahia, Agonglo's ambassadors embarked for Lisbon where they received the same refusal to the proposal regarding giving Ouidah the monopoly of the slave trade from the Bight of Benin to Brazil. Once in Lisbon, both Dahomean emissaries were baptized in the Catholic Church. This was an important change in comparison with the behavior of the members of the previous mission sent to Bahia, who insisted in wearing their native costumes in official ceremonies and even performed a Vodun ritual. For the Dahomean ambassadors, accepting the Catholic faith through baptism, as happened centuries before in the Kingdom of Kongo, was probably a necessary step in obtaining a positive answer to their request. Catholicism continued to be an important instrument to reinforce diplomatic and commercial relations with African states.

On their return to Dahomey, the Dahomean embassy was followed by a Catholic mission set up by the Portuguese and composed of two Brazilian-born priests of color Cipriano Pires Sardinha (c. 1749–1797) and Vicente Ferreira Pires (c. 1765–1805?), who intended to convert and evangelize the king of Dahomey.[52] On their arrival in Abomey, King Agonglo received them in an audience. On this occasion, he may have told them that he "was ready to be instructed and baptized in the Catholic faith."[53] The rumors about the king's conversion spread and generated conflicts, which led to his assassination by one of his opponents.[54]

After Agonglo's assassination a series of disputes started. Because there was no consensus on who had the power to choose the new king, periods of succession were characterized by great chaos and instability. These transition phases gave rise to plots involving the mothers and brothers of the aspirant successors. When the new king was eventually chosen, he punished all losing competitors for the throne, and their supporters, selling into slavery and sending the members of the opposed factions to other neighboring regions or to the Americas.[55] Thus, when in 1797, one of the Agonglo's sons was enthroned and became King Adandozan (r. 1797–1818), he penalized all antagonists who to some extent participated in the events related to his father's assassination.[56] The new king quickly gained the reputation of the cruelest ruler in Dahomey's history. Despite earlier evidence of Dahomeans who sold members of the kingdom into slavery, Adandozan became the only monarch to be remembered for selling members of the royal family into slavery.

Rivalries among African states are described in slave narratives as well. Olaudah Equiano or Gustavus Vassa (c. 1745–1797) narrated his youth in Igboland (present-day Nigeria). He explained that his father owned many slaves and that he was trained since his early years in the arts of war. According to him, when the adults were absent, the children were trained to watch if any strangers approached. Equiano's fears of raids and kidnappings were justified. In 1753, two men and a woman abducted him and his sister. Subsequently, as it happened to many other men, women, and children in West Africa, they were brought to the coast, sold to slave merchants, and sent to the Barbados, a colony of the British Caribbean.[57] Likewise, by 1770, Quobna Ottobah Cugoano (c. 1757–1791?), who later became a famous abolitionist, had the same fate. Born in the Fante village of Agimaque or Ajumako in the region of modern-day Ghana, a group of men captured Cugoano when he was playing in the woods with other children. Brought to the coast like Equiano, he was sold into slavery and transported to Grenada, along with other enslaved men, women, and children.[58]

These cases may suggest that kidnapping and selling opponents into slavery were not exceptional events. Yet most individuals were enslaved as a result of warfare. Starting in the eighteenth century, wars and raids were part of the daily life in the hinterlands of Bight of Benin and the Bight of Biafra.[59] Some Africans made prisoners during interstate wars in West Africa left written records narrating their enslavement. For example, at some point between 1728 and 1732, the Dahomean army captured a young male West African healer from the Mahi country (north of the modern Republic of Benin). After being brought to the coast, he was sold to the slave merchants and sent into slavery to Rio de Janeiro, where he was later baptized as Domingos Álvares.[60] In 1739, raiders captured a boy named Broteer Furro (c. 1729–1805) somewhere in the hinterland of the Gold Coast (contemporary Ghana). After the abductors sold him in the coastal town of Anomabu, slave merchants transported him to Barbados, then to Rhode Island, and eventually sold him as a slave in New York, where he was named Venture Smith.[61]

Other West African men lived similar experiences of enslavement. Mahommah Gardo Baquaqua, who was born in Djougou (north of the contemporary Republic of Benin), was sold into slavery in the then province of Pernambuco (Brazil).[62] In his biography, published in the middle of the nineteenth century, he underscored the internal conflicts that led to war in his kingdom:

> The kings are continually quarreling, which quarrels lead to war. [. . .] When a king dies, there is no regular successor, but a great many rivals for the kingdom spring up, and he who can achieve his object by power and strength, becomes the succeeding king, thus war settles the question. [. . .] Slavery is also another fruitful source of war, the prisoners being sold for slaves.[63]

Baquaqua's account confirms that during the period of succession among royal families of Bight of Benin's states, the sale of members from opposing factions into slavery could occur, even though he was not himself enslaved through warfare.

In the early nineteenth century, the Atlantic slave trade continued fueling interstate wars in West Africa, which in turn maintained the production of slaves at a rapid speed. The engines of this cycle are also visible in the correspondence between King Adandozan and the Portuguese officials. As during his father's reign, his rule was a period of political and economic crisis as the slave trade continued to decline in the Kingdom of Dahomey.[64] Not only did Adandozan lose military campaigns led against the Mahi country and the Kingdom of Oyo, but as a consequence of the Napoleonic Wars, in the same year he was enthroned the French abandoned their fortress in Ouidah.[65] In addition, the growing importance of the port of Onim (in today's Nigeria) increasingly threatened the dominance of Ouidah.

In November 1804, Adandozan sent a new delegation to Brazil. In one letter brought by the ambassadors, the Dahomean king complained that the storekeeper of the Portuguese fort added water to the barrels of *aguardente* (a strong alcoholic beverage) with which he bought Dahomey's captives. He also complained that the storekeeper and the new director of the fortress stole and lowered the price of captives: "what is worth one ounce, he buys for one head, whereas the captives that cost thirteen ounces he pays five, and men, and women who cost eight, he pays three."[66] The king showed discontentment because the captains of the Portuguese fort were providing

the traders with misleading information about him. He stressed that
although Africans were illiterate, they fulfilled their word, whereas
Europeans were dishonest: "God granted memory and talent to the White to
know how to read and write, and he gave memory to us only to remember
what is done in the present; we have the elders to remind us what we
forget."[67] He also made a series of complaints about the Portuguese
merchants who used counterfeit gold and silver in buying captives. According
to him, these traders falsified the weight of the goods and also bought
captives with fake pieces of silk and velvet.

Like his father, Adandozan demanded the Portuguese to exclusively trade
in slaves at Ouidah. To justify his request, he warned and scared the Prince
Regent Dom João Carlos de Bragança (1767–1826) by narrating how other
kings in neighboring ports alienated Portuguese traders. According to him,
the King of Badagry allowed the murder of whites and even used the head
of a white as "a calabash for drinking water." Then after enumerating
atrocities committed by his neighbors against European traders, Adandozan
drew up a list soliciting several goods including powder, rifles, *aguardente*,
silks, pipes, and glass.[68] In another letter sent with the embassy of 1805, the
king mentioned he sacrificed eleven men to report on Santa Anna's good
services to his deceased father. After this exercise in intimidation, the king
expressed his wish to discuss with the Prince Regent the opening of
Dahomean gold mines that were "still kept secret." This misleading
information was certainly designed to attract Portuguese interest in valuable
natural resources and perhaps convince the Portuguese to exclusively trade
in Ouidah. At the end of his letter, Adandozan asked the Portuguese Regent
to send him someone "who knows how to manufacture pieces [of cannon],
guns, powder and other things necessary to make war," thirty big hats in
different colors with great plumes, as well as twenty pieces of silk.[69] These
demands confirm the illustrations of European travelogues depicting
Dahomean kings wearing big colorful hats decorated with huge plumes.
Moreover, they suggest that Adandozan, like his predecessors, was also
concerned with the imports of luxury goods.[70] From Bahia, the ambassadors
went to Lisbon and from there back again to Bahia from where they returned
to Dahomey in October 1805.

In 1810, King Adandozan sent his last delegation to Brazil. As, since
1808, the Portuguese court had relocated to Rio de Janeiro to escape the
invasion of Napoléon Bonaparte's army, the ambassadors no longer needed
to travel to Lisbon. Yet, since the transfer of the royal court to Rio de Janeiro,
Portugal and Britain had signed several bilateral treaties to stop the slave
trade. In this context, welcoming the Dahomean representatives in Rio de
Janeiro would certainly be perceived by the British as a gesture of defiance.
As a result, the Prince Regent Dom João Carlos de Bragança prevented the
visitors from traveling to Rio de Janeiro.

In a letter sent with the embassy, the Dahomean king expressed surprise
at the events that forced the transfer of the Portuguese royal court to Brazil.

Showing how aware he was about the Napoleonic Wars, he regretted not being able to assist the Portuguese royal family in the fight against the French: "what I feel the most is to no longer be the neighbor of Our Majesty, and not being able to walk on firm land to give you a help with my arm, so my wish is big, as here I have also fought many wars in the backlands."[71] The king described his military campaigns against the kingdoms of Porto-Novo and Oyo, and the violent incursion by the Dahomean army in the Mahi country. He narrated how his army destroyed the land, killed, and burned the king, and how after the attack, they captured the king's sons, grandsons, and brothers, and killed all his people. He added that a number of enemies were decapitated, their heads nailed to wooden stakes and displayed at the entrance of his palace. After this detailed account of violence, he concluded by stating that he gave all this news "because we are far away, give me also news about the Wars, and also give me news about the wars with the French nation and the others, it will make me happy to know about it."[72]

Adandozan's letter reveals how West Africans were following the Napoleonic Wars, because these events impacted the slave markets in the Americas and the Atlantic slave trade in West African ports. After this account, which demonstrated how powerful the Dahomean army was in comparison with the cowardice of the Portuguese ruler and army, who escaped from Napoléon Bonaparte, Adandozan presented his complaints and requests. First, he asked the Portuguese Regent to send a governor, a priest, and a surgeon to the Portuguese fort. Then he mentioned that the last Dahomean delegation sent to Bahia in 1805 brought twenty-four captives to be sold in exchange for various orders "from the land of the white." Yet, although all these captives arrived alive in Bahia, he had not yet been paid.[73] In addition he also demanded four water pumps and relics to protect his body from the enemy when he went to wars. Curiously, he also expressed his intent to convert to Catholicism and to construct a church in Abomey. To this end, he asked the Prince Regent to send to Abomey two bricklayers to build the temple, and two priests. He also asked for wood, and two bells for the towers, in addition to various images, paintings, and ornaments to decorate the building. He justified this demand by stating that he wanted to please the Prince Regent by founding a church in order to show the whites who visited the Kingdom of Dahomey how loyal and faithful he was to the Portuguese.[74] Like his father, who accepted conversion to Catholicism just to obtain better trade conditions with the Portuguese, Adandozan's wish to construct a chapel in Abomey was certainly an attempt to gain attention from the Prince Regent and have his ambassadors received at Rio de Janeiro, in a period of decline of the Atlantic slave trade. The king's numerous requests highlight the growing dependency on European goods, which increased the need to wage wars to produce more captives.

The diplomatic missions between Portugal, Brazil, and Dahomey shed light on the multiple dimensions of West Africans' participation in the

Atlantic slave trade enterprise. Although showing that Europeans and Africans rulers and middlemen interacted as equals, the letters bring evidence that Dahomeans controlled the port of Ouidah and were often able to use force to intimidate European traders. Moreover, these kings utilized their possible conversion to Catholicism to bargain for better trade conditions with the Portuguese. In their missions to Brazil, Dahomean ambassadors were welcomed with pomp, suggesting that they were treated fairly in Lisbon and Bahia. Yet the letters exchanged between the monarchs feature the kings of Dahomey's numerous complaints, suggesting that in several cases they sold slaves in exchange for counterfeit alcohol and Portuguese goods of cheap quality. More importantly, this extensive correspondence show how West African states increasingly relied on European goods. This dependency intensified warfare, and wars were fought with the only goal of capturing men, women, and children to be sold to the Atlantic market. Even though the great majority of Africans were victims of the inhuman commerce, the lucrative association of slave merchants and slave owners in Europe and the Americas with African rulers and middlemen was used as an argument against future demands of reparations for slavery and the Atlantic slave trade.

Slavery as a profitable institution

As slavery became a very lucrative business in the Americas, in the early eighteenth century, huge estates started emerging in Jamaica and Saint-Domingue, replacing in importance Barbados and Martinique. The rise of the French and the British slave economies in the Caribbean ended the Dutch's prevalence in the region. Gradually, large plantations of over 200 acres and comprising 100 slaves became typical.[75] The enslaved population in the British Caribbean also multiplied exponentially. By 1740, Jamaica became the richest British colony in the region, with a population of 100,000 enslaved individuals.[76] By 1788 this number expanded to approximately 255,000 slaves, who made up 90 percent of its total population.[77] As land ownership concentration amplified, the average number of workers per estate expanded to roughly 200 slaves.[78] This dynamic accentuated the imbalance between blacks and whites; for each white person, there were ten enslaved black individuals and many were born in Africa. In Jamaica, unlike Saint-Domingue, white planters totally controlled plantation and slave ownership, and consequently the free population of color was very small.

Saint-Domingue's enslaved population grew as the production of sugar augmented. In 1700, the number of slaves in the western third of the island was approximately 9,082 individuals.[79] Toward the middle of the eighteenth century, the slave population of Saint-Domingue jumped to 150,000 slaves. This number greatly contrasted with the estimated white population of approximately 14,000 individuals. Although, it is hard to precisely establish population figures for the colony on the eve of the French Revolution, most historians agree that in 1789, there were approximately 465,000 slaves in Saint-Domingue, who counted for almost half of the overall slave population of the Caribbean islands. The disparity between this huge enslaved population and the small number of whites, then estimated at 31,000 individuals, was striking. In addition, the colony maintained a significant free colored population, estimated at 28,000 individuals.[80] Saint-Domingue was also the largest world producer of coffee, and maintained an important production of tobacco and indigo.[81]

Slavery became a dominant component of social, political, and economic life in four distinct areas encompassing the present-day United States: the North, the Chesapeake region, the coastal Low Country of South Carolina, Georgia, and Florida, and the lower Mississippi Valley.[82] In these four areas, slavery developed at a different pace and had particular characteristics. By 1700 Chesapeake's black population was estimated at 16 percent. But the imports of enslaved Africans increased when this region became the leading territory of tobacco industry.[83] During the 1720s, Virginia's slave population also witnessed a substantial natural growth, a tendency that continued over the next decades in other southern colonies. Therefore heavily relying on a plantation economy, Virginia became a slave society. On the eve of the American Revolutionary War, Virginia and Maryland had approximately one-third of the total population of the thirteen colonies and the half of its enslaved population. Slavery generated profits. Even when the gains of the tobacco industry started declining, the use of slave labor continued to be lucrative, expanding into other farming activities, including the cultivation of corn and grains.

Slavery also expanded in the Deep South. South Carolina, unlike Virginia, was a slave society from its foundation. As early as in the 1730s, its rice plantations largely utilized slaves, and blacks clearly outnumbered the white population.[84] But in the middle of the eighteenth century, with the emergence of the rice industry, the plantation system also developed in the Low Country, the region along the coast of South Carolina. Like Virginia and Maryland, this area became a slave society as well. Enslaved women prevailed in these rice plantations, where slave owners relied on their reproductive capacity to maintain the growth of the slave population.[85] The success of the plantation economy was undeniable at the end of the eighteenth century. This period marked not only the persistence but also the great expansion of slavery toward the south of the United States. After the invention of the cotton gin and screw press, cotton production witnessed an extraordinary growth, expanding to the interior of Georgia, South Carolina, Alabama, Mississippi, Louisiana, Arkansas, and even Texas.[86] New crops and new machinery contributed to the wealth of white planters and their associates, confirming the status of slavery as a profitable institution in the United States.[87]

During the eighteenth century, slavery also expanded in the Caribbean. When the British occupied Cuba during the Seven Years' War (1756–1763), the island witnessed a major development in agricultural slavery. At the same time, although slavery remained important in the Spanish Americas and continuously proliferated in the newly independent United States, Brazil became the largest slave society of Latin America. Cotton production developed in Brazilian captaincies of Maranhão and Pernambuco. Cattle ranching also emerged in the center-south region of the colony along with new crops such as rice and coffee.[88] Moreover, after 1791 as the slave revolts disrupted Saint-Domingue's sugar and coffee production, Brazil's sugar industry reemerged in Bahia and Pernambuco.[89] Likewise, Cuban sugar industry also flourished in this period and continued growing during the first half of the nineteenth century, when the island became the world's largest sugar producer, a period known as "second slavery."[90]

Despite a number of similarities, there were important distinctions between the slave systems of Brazil and the Caribbean. Brazilian planters resided in the colony, whereas most planters of the British and French Caribbean were based in England and France. From Europe, they operated their estates with the support of attorneys and managers, who were often slave owners themselves and administered various estates.[91] Both in Brazil and Jamaica, approximately 60 percent of the slaves worked in the fields; about 35 percent performed skilled activities and usually 4 percent were domestic servants. In Brazil enslaved men largely outnumbered enslaved women. Slaves performed the work in the cane fields either in a task system, in which they had to cut a certain amount of cane per day, or in a gang system, in which organized groups worked together cutting cane the entire day, under the supervision of an overseer.[92] In Jamaica, enslaved women predominantly composed the gangs who conducted work in the fields. Enslaved men performed land clearance tasks, which involved removing trees and stones, but all other activities were performed by enslaved men and women of all ages.

At the peak of the Brazilian sugar industry, its plantations had an average of no more than 100 slaves. When the Saint-Domingue slave rebellion started in the late eighteenth century, the average size of slaveholdings in sugar plantations was 185 slaves. A sugar plantation in Jamaica had an average of 154 slaves in 1770, but in 1832, this number increased to 223 slaves.[93] Although behind Cuba, Brazilian production of sugar continued growing during the nineteenth century. From the late eighteenth century, in the absence of competition following the Saint-Domingue Revolution which brought coffee production in that area to a halt, coffee plantations began to emerge in the Paraíba River Valley, in southeastern Brazil. Like sugar, Brazilian coffee benefited from the increasing demand for this product from North American and European markets. It quickly became the country's most important export crop. Slavery was also central to Brazil's gold, indigo, cattle, cotton, and jerked beef industries.

At the end of the eighteenth century, although the population of the United States was twice the size of the Brazilian population, the number of slaves was larger in Brazil. In 1790, the first census of the entire newly independent United States recorded a total of 3,893,635 individuals, including 694,280 slaves and 59,150 free individuals of color.[94] Ten years later, in 1800, the estimated Brazilian population was 1,942,000, including 718,000 slaves, whereas the number of slaves in Cuba and Venezuela were respectively estimated at 212,000 and 112,000. Brazil had also a huge free population of color, especially in the urban areas. Estimated at 587,000 individuals, the number of free coloreds in Brazil was almost ten times the size of the free population of color in the United States.[95]

The workforce of enslaved black men, women, and children was the engine that allowed the development of American societies. Although slavery was highly concentrated in the plantation areas in the Americas, neither in the United States nor in the Caribbean and Latin America can slavery be equated with the plantation system.[96] Enslaved men and women worked everywhere in urban areas. They had different professions and worked as porters, barbers, shoemakers, carpenters, tailors, craftsmen, blacksmiths, hatters, and silversmiths. Enslaved women worked in convents and shops. They were also street vendors, prostitutes, nannies, wet nurses, cooks, washerwomen, and domestic servants.

Whereas towns in the British Caribbean had populations of approximately 15,000 persons, in the Spanish Americas and Brazil cities could have populations averaging between 50,000 to 100,000 individuals. Since the sixteenth century, Mexico City and Lima had huge urban enslaved populations. In Brazil, between the seventeenth and the nineteenth centuries, enslaved men, women, and children could constitute almost half of the population of bigger cities like Salvador and Rio de Janeiro. The eighteenth-century Brazilian mining boom in the area of present-day Minas Gerais, Goiás, and Mato Grosso led to the growth of slave imports. In mining towns like Sabará, Ouro Preto, and Mariana, slaves composed a significant part of the population. A number of enslaved men were itinerant slave miners, known as *faisqueiros*, who worked and lived away from their masters and brought them a fixed amount of gold.[97] Enslaved women were not miners, but worked as wage earners, street vendors or prostitutes, activities that could allow them to purchase their freedom. This mobility created a particular social dynamic in the region.[98]

The use of slave labor was widespread in all spheres of Brazilian society. In urban settings, enslaved men and women also worked autonomously as wage-earning slaves, keeping part of their income and giving the rest to their masters.[99] Compared to Brazil, slavery was present in smaller numbers in various cities of the thirteen colonies and later in the independent United States. Yet, in New York City, Philadelphia, Baltimore, Richmond, Charleston, and New Orleans, slaves performed various kinds of activities.[100] After independence, slavery grew in urban centers of the United States. In cities such as Baltimore and Richmond slaves worked in various industries, including iron manufacture, shipbuilding, and mining.[101]

Urban slavery was prevalent in many areas of the French Caribbean and the Spanish Americas as well. In these urban settings where there were not enough whites, black enslaved men, women, and children acquired better statuses as artisans, vendors, and apprentices.[102] Still, despite the possibilities of social mobility, in a *casta* system which clearly delimitated racial hierarchies, populations of African descent were discriminated against, considered inferior, and confined to the lower social strata.[103] In the Central Valley area in the Central American province of Costa Rica, slaves and free blacks along with natives and mestizos performed not only a variety of domestic tasks but also "raised corn and wheat, cared for livestock, fished, hauled produce, and carried out dozens of other tasks."[104] In South American cities such as Lima, Mexico City, Santiago de Chile, Salvador, and Rio de Janeiro, rich slave owners provided enslaved women, who performed domestic service, with fine clothes and even jewelry. Because owning slaves in these societies was an indicator of wealth, masters dressed their slaves in ways that mirrored privileged economic and social positions.[105] In urban areas, as portrayed in illustrations of European travel accounts (Figure 1.2), it was a typical scene to see a master and a mistress as well as their children

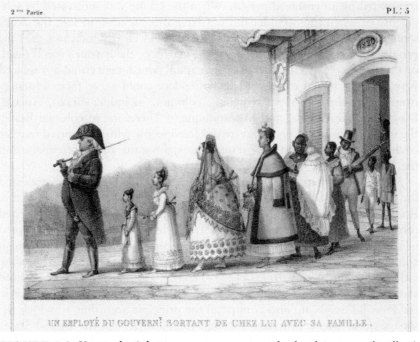

UN EMPLOYÉ DU GOUVERN! SORTANT DE CHEZ LUI AVEC SA FAMILLE.

FIGURE 1.2 *Un employé du gouvernement sortant de chez lui avec sa famille* (A Government Employee Leaving His Home With His Family), in Jean-Baptiste Debret, *Voyage pittoresque et historique au Brésil* (Paris: Firmin Didot Frères, 1834–1839), vol. 2, plate 5.

walking in the streets followed by a line of enslaved men, women, and children as a way to assert prestige and high social status.[106]

Negotiating and resisting

Relations between masters and slaves differed across the Americas. These nuances are not only related to the predominance of Catholicism in Latin America in contrast with the prevalence of Protestantism in North America, but also with the existence of legal systems that shaped these slave societies in different ways.[107] Both in Brazil and the United States, slaves sued their masters to obtain their freedom.[108] But despite the similarities and differences among slavery legal codes, the application of the law in the different localities of the Americas varied.[109] Brazil, for example, had no codes regulating the work and the activities of the enslaved population. Since 1603, the legislation in force in Portugal and its colonies was the collection of ordinances, the *Ordenações Filipinas*, which along the previous *Ordenações Manoelinas* (1513), was highly influenced by the Roman civil law.[110] Still, several articles of the ordinances mentioned slaves. For example, in Brazil, capital punishment was not always applied in cases of murder, even if the crime was committed by an enslaved person. When the killing was motivated by self-defense or when the offender did not have the intention to kill, the death sentence could be excluded. However, Article 41 clearly indicates that the penalty for a slave who kills or hurts the master or the master's son is death on the gallows.[111] In a number of cases, capital punishment could be replaced with *degredo* (penal exile) and the offenders could serve their sentences overseas in the various Portuguese colonies, including Brazil, Angola, Benguela, Macau, Goa, and Mozambique.[112] Therefore, in colonial Brazil, the sentences imposed on enslaved and freedpeople who committed murder could vary depending on the circumstances, the status of the offenders, and that of the victims.

Since early colonization, Brazil and the Spanish Americas incorporated the doctrine of *partus sequitur ventrem* into their legal codes. Derived from Roman law, this doctrine determined that the slave's status was inherited through the enslaved mother. Later in 1662, the same doctrine was adopted in the British colonies, starting in Virginia; up until that time the British common law established that the slave's status was transmitted through the father. Both the *Siete partidas* (1251–1265), a Castilian code that inspired slavery laws in the Spanish Americas, and the *Code noir* (1685), in force in the French Caribbean, also confirmed the principle according to which the slave's status was transmitted through the mother.[113] In the United States slaves were not allowed to legally marry. In Brazil and in the Spanish Americas the Catholic Church performed these marriages with the permission of the masters, even though gender imbalance created obstacles to find suitable spouses.[114]

Manumission contributed to the rapid growth of a black free population in Latin America.[115] In contrast, although self-purchase existed in early colonial North America, starting at the end of the seventeenth century, in the south, various laws imposed restrictions on masters' abilities to manumit their slaves.[116] In 1691, Virginia prohibited manumission within its territory. Thus, any master who freed a slave had to transport the newly freed individual outside the colony. In 1735, South Carolina legislature established a similar restriction.[117] Yet, after the independence, in 1782, the "Act to Authorize the Manumission of Slaves" passed in the Virginia General Assembly. This Act permitted slave owners to emancipate their slaves in their wills, testaments or other written documents presented in front of a court, by excluding the previous restriction of sending newly freed individuals out of the colony.[118] Over the next years, similar laws allowing manumissions passed in Maryland and Delaware.

In the Spanish Americas and Brazil, manumission subsisted until the abolition of slavery.[119] Yet, masters rarely granted unconditional emancipation. Most freed slaves were individuals who over the years were able to gather the necessary amounts to purchase their own freedom, usually in several installments (*coartación* or *coartação*). In other words, manumission was not an indication of the alleged benign nature of Latin American slavery in opposition to the cruel nature of slavery in British colonies. Slaves paid the market price for their own freedom. Moreover, for the masters, granting manumission to certain slaves, especially enslaved women and children, and making it more difficult for African-born men, was a very lucrative strategy that allowed them to reinvest profits in the slave market.[120]

All over the Americas, enslaved men and women daily resisted the hardships of slavery in a variety of ways. In plantation areas, slaves organized strikes, decreased the rhythm of production, and destroyed machinery and tools. Slaves also negotiated with their masters to obtain better work and living conditions. Yet, a number of enslaved men and women could only attempt to escape slavery through more extreme forms of resistance by either running away, organizing rebellions, or forming runaway slave communities. Slaves committed suicide, and also killed their masters and mistresses along with their children. Enslaved women who lived in proximity with their masters in domestic spaces poisoned their owners' food and also committed infanticide as a form of resistance to physical and sexual abuse.[121]

In Brazil, slavery was so pervasive that even the most modest individuals and families would seek to own at least one slave. Moreover, archival records show that in urban areas several former slaves became slave owners.[122] Some slaves possessed slaves as well.[123] In cities like Salvador in Bahia, about 67 percent of the slaveholders owned between one and ten slaves, whereas among the individuals for whom postmortem inventories were registered, only approximately 13 percent did not own any slaves.[124] In the cities, despite having higher mobility, slaves were conceived as commodities exactly

FIGURE 1.3 *Une dame brésilienne dans son intérieur* (A Brazilian Lady in Her Home) in Jean-Baptiste Debret, *Voyage pittoresque et historique au Brésil* (Paris: Firmin Didot Frères, 1834–1839), vol. 2, plate 6.

as they were in the plantation zones. Yet, in the domestic space of urban areas slave owners lived in an environment of proximity with enslaved men, women, and children (Figure 1.3). Because manumission was widely practiced and there was no rigid racial legislation, many foreign observers concluded that social relations between masters and slaves were cordial. These views originated the idea that slavery was milder in Brazil and the Spanish Americas than in the United States.

Prior to 1850, slavery in Brazil and the United States had analogous features, including a similar ratio of slave owners among the free population and of slaves in relation to the total population. Despite these similarities, during the first half of the nineteenth century Brazilian slaveholdings were smaller than in the United States, with fewer estates with very large numbers of slaves. Yet, this situation changed in the middle of the nineteenth century, when the size of slaveholdings in the United States increased. At that point 11 percent of all owners had 20 or more slaves, a ratio found in Jamaica since 1833.[125] When Brazil became the world's largest coffee producer in the 1830s, slaveholdings became more concentrated, comparable to that of the largest sugar estates of the country's northeast region and the Caribbean.

The mortality rate is also a crucial element to determine the work and living conditions of slave populations in the Americas. In sugar plantation areas of Saint-Domingue, Jamaica, and Brazil, the slave mortality rate was much higher than natural growth.[126] To remedy the problem, slave owners relied on massive slave imports from Africa, which were considered cheaper than to "rear Negro children."[127] Contradicting the idea that Brazilian slavery was benign, the life expectancy of young male slaves who worked the cane fields between twelve and sixteen hours daily, in the hot and humid tropical Brazilian northeast region or in the French and British Caribbean, was equally very low. In Saint-Domingue, for example, a contemporary observer emphasized huge death rates among slaves, who were "always dying."[128] Still, in labor regimes such as coffee, tobacco, and cotton plantations, life expectancy was higher, and therefore natural growth existed without the need of slave imports from Africa.[129]

In addition to mortality rates in Brazil, Jamaica, and Saint-Domingue, work accidents were common in sugar mills. After cutting the cane, trimming it, and binding into bundles, slaves transported the sugarcane to the mills. Then they manually inserted the canes through the mill rollers to obtain the cane juice that would be boiled and transformed into crystallized sugar. It happened from time to time that the slaves that worked feeding cane into the mills, in many cases enslaved women, had one or both of their arms or hands crushed in the mill's rollers.[130] In 1730s, an enslaved woman named Marcelina lost one arm at Engenho Santana, in Bahia. According to a traveler's description, a very beautiful enslaved woman named Teresa, also suffered a similar fate. Prior to being enslaved, Teresa was a queen in Cabinda, in West Central Africa. Sold into slavery and sent to Brazil, she worked at Sibiró Mill. Although inexperienced, she was placed to work in the mill. Her two hands were caught in the mill's roller and she had both arms amputated.[131] Likewise, in Mesopotamia plantation in Jamaica, two enslaved women lost an arm and a hand in sugar mill accidents. Bella, a forty-two-year old grass cutter, lost her hand in a mill accident in 1793, but continued cutting grass and cooking over the next twenty years. Rose was a fifty-year old nurse who lost her arm in a mill accident in 1765, but who also continued working carrying water on her head over the subsequent thirty years.[132]

Slaves, but especially enslaved women, were constant victims of physical and sexual violence, even when they worked in domestic environments. In all the Americas, and particularly in the United States, starting in the nineteenth century slave owners largely relied on enslaved women's reproduction capacity to increase the enslaved population. Several slave narratives and other primary sources show the horrors suffered by enslaved women at the hands of abusive masters, mistresses, and overseers. Enslaved in Bermuda, in the British Caribbean, Mary Prince (c. 1788–1833) changed owners four times when she was still a young woman. Separated from her relatives and submitted to strenuous working hours, Prince was physically and psychologically abused by her various masters and mistress. According to her, "there was scarcely any punishment more dreadful than the blows I received on my face and head from her hard heavy fist. She was a fearful woman, and a savage mistress to her slaves."[133] Likewise, Sojourner Truth (c. 1797–1883) faced great hardships as an enslaved woman. Born in the state of New York to enslaved parents, she had twelve siblings, who were gradually separated. Between 1806 and 1810, she experienced being sold three times. Moreover, her master illegally sold out of the state her five-year-old son.[134] Such cases just illustrate how in the nineteenth-century slavery remained a horrible reality not only in the south but also in the north of the United States.

In various parts of the Americas, masters, their male children, overseers, and other male members of the household sexually exploited, tortured, and abused enslaved women and girls. In the United States, one of the most notorious cases of sexual violence inflicted on an enslaved woman was that of Harriet Jacobs (c. 1813–1897). Born in slavery in the state of North Carolina, after the death of her mother she moved to the house of her mother's mistress, with whom she learned how to read and white. After the passing of her mistress in 1825, Jacobs was bequeathed by a man named James Norcom. In her narrative Jacobs reveals that her new master started sexually abusing her when she reached fifteen years old: "I saw a man forty years my senior daily violating the most sacred commandments of nature. He told me I was his property; that I must be subject to his will in all things."[135] As in other regions of the Americas, sexual abuse of enslaved women by white men was tolerated in the United States. Jacobs reports her mistress being jealous and violent as a result of her husband's sexual behavior. Still, she also states that he fathered eleven slaves in his property, an indication that raping enslaved women was not only an acceptable behavior in masters, but also an efficient way to produce new slaves.[136]

With some exceptions, rape and abuse against enslaved women passed in silence. But enslaved women resisted through various means. In 1820, Monica killed her abusive master with an axe blow in a distant farm in Rio Grande do Sul, Brazil. Although she justified her action because she was drunk, she also emphasized in her testimony that she was beaten by her master on a constant basis. Monica was sentenced to 500 lashes and penal exile in Benguela.[137] Like Monica, in 1855, a nineteen-year-old enslaved woman from Missouri, United States, named Celia, killed her master who had been raping her for nearly five years. However, Celia was sentenced to death.[138]

The young Brazilian-born enslaved woman Liberata also experienced sexual violence and psychological abuse. In 1790, when she was ten years old she was sold to José Vieira Rebello, a man who resided near the city of Desterro (present-day Florianópolis).[139] Rebello sexually abused Liberata and manipulated her with the promise of manumission. Within a few years she gave birth to two children. Rebello recognized the paternity of the first female child, who he baptized as Anna Vieira. Yet, as his wife and children condemned the extramarital relations, he refused to baptize the second baby. As late as in 1812, Liberata remained enslaved. She began a relationship with Francisco José, a mixed-race free man, who attempted to purchase her freedom to marry her. But as Rebello rejected the offer, José petitioned the municipal judge in order to obtain Liberata's freedom. Although this case made it to the court, there were certainly many other enslaved women in Latin America whose masters promised freedom in exchange for sex whose stories were forgotten. The horrors of sexual exploitation left deep scars on enslaved women, which were certainly transmitted to their descendants.

White numbers, black bodies

The use of statistical data and demographics to explain the engines of slavery and the Atlantic slave trade has also been an arena of dissent in academic debates, which ultimately influence the discussion about the impacts of the inhumane institution in the Americas. Some scholars have acknowledged the challenges of accurately describing the extreme suffering provoked by these atrocities, but have argued that the use of quantitative data provides clues to understanding the dynamics of the slave trade and its consequences in Africa and the Americas.[140] Yet, statistics do not consider the human dimension of slavery and the Atlantic slave trade. In other words, the debates on the volume of the slave trade to the Americas and its impacts on the African continent have always been politicized because the social actors participating in these debates identify themselves along racial lines, which although constructed in the past still have an impact in the present.

Guyanese historian and activist Walter Rodney was the first scholar to develop the thesis of the impact of the Atlantic slave trade on Africa. His work was largely criticized in a debate dominated by white male English-speaking historians from Britain, Canada, and the United States and from which African and African American scholars were nearly absent.[141] Some of these historians have minimized the impact of massive deportation of enslaved Africans on the continent's depopulation and downplayed the role of the Atlantic slave trade in the development of slavery on African soil.[142] Other scholars, although recognizing that the Atlantic slave trade contributed to the expansion of slavery on African soil, depopulation of the continent, and negative impact on its development, continued placing demographics as a central element of their works, by rarely paying more attention to the human dimension of the slave trade and the individual life paths of enslaved Africans.[143]

After the end of the Second World War, when the Civil Rights Movement and the decolonization struggle emerged, the quantification of population loss, as a result of the Atlantic slave trade, conveyed a neat image of its nefarious effects in Africa. Therefore, numbers offered support and substance emancipation discourses as well as in the formulation of demands of reparations for slavery, the Atlantic slave trade, and colonization. Underestimated or overestimated by governments and activists depending on the political context, these numbers were constantly associated with the existing power structures of racism and white supremacy which prevailed in former slave societies, where black populations remained excluded and marginalized. Ultimately, despite seeming obvious, it was necessary to authenticate that the greater the number of slaves deported to the Americas, the more significant were the human losses imposed on Africa. Moreover, the larger the number of Africans brought to the various parts of the Americas, the more important was their contribution to the development of European and American societies.[144]

Within this context, although usually distant from black social actors, slavery scholars working on demographic data attempted to determine how many captives embarked in African slave ports, how many were killed during the Middle Passage, and how many effectively disembarked in the Americas. Academics, militants, and other members of black communities in Europe and the Americas discussed the volume of the slave trade and its negative effects in Africa, by centering on four kinds of quantitative and qualitative arguments. First, the underdevelopment of African countries has been partially caused by population drain that resulted from the Atlantic slave trade. Second, the Atlantic slave trade engendered the scramble for Africa at the end of the nineteenth century. Third, European colonial rule introduced forced labor on African soil, making the working conditions of millions of individuals very similar to chattel slavery. Finally, colonization extorted Africa's natural resources, and stole its cultural and artistic heritages. Over the second half of the twentieth century, this line of reasoning contributed to the construction of anticolonial discourses that later also supported the discourses developed by social actors advocating reparations to Africa.[145]

The argument underscoring population drain was central to illustrate the damages provoked by the Atlantic slave trade in the African continent.[146] Yet, more accurate estimates on the number of enslaved Africans transported to the Americas were made public only in 1969, when US historian Philip D. Curtin (1922–2009) published a detailed census.[147] Despite being a major scholarly work, Curtin's census came out during the difficult period that followed the Civil Rights Movement, after the assassinations of Malcolm X (1925–1965) and Martin Luther King Jr. (1929–1968). In this context, it was clear for many organizations that emerged as part of the Black Power movement in the United States that the achievement of civil rights through legal means would not end racial hatred and racial inequalities. In this adverse context, Curtin's census established that between 1471 and 1870, 9,566,100 enslaved Africans disembarked in various ports in the Americas. The release of estimates lower than the previous ones generated controversy.[148] Although these debates were restricted to academic circles they were not dissociated from the violent racial and class tensions that marked the end of that decade in the United States. Moreover, even though African Americans were largely absent from academic circles that monopolized the debates on the estimates of the Atlantic slave trade, black activists and social actors identifying as descendants of slaves attended some conferences which discussed the issue.[149] Even though knowing that numbers would never measure the suffering inflicted on enslaved men, women, and children, they understood these estimates as a way to assess the impacts of slavery in Africa and as a symbolic indicator of the atrocities committed against their ancestors.

The efforts to establish an accurate volume for the Atlantic slave trade were systematized and made available online through the *Trans-Atlantic Slave Trade Database: Voyages*. Gathering more than 35,000 slave voyages, this initiative was largely controlled by white male scholars mostly from private US universities.[150] Yet, this important accomplishment did not challenge the tradition established by the scholarship in which human beings who were bought and sold were portrayed as anonymous commodities. In response to this view, over the last decade, academics started considering the human dimension of the Atlantic slave trade, by giving a central attention to the origins and life stories of those who for very long time were faceless and nameless victims.[151] Still, when younger historians published new books centering on the African experience on board of slave ships by relying on available sources, the same scholars who during decades privileged the debate on the numbers game, fiercely criticized these efforts.[152]

The academic debates on how deeply the traffic impacted African societies have also been contentious. Similar to the discussions on the volume of the Atlantic slave trade, these exchanges emerged mostly in white academic circles of Europe and the United States, and not in African institutions. Whereas the figure of 12.5 million enslaved Africans exported to the Americas has supported the thesis that the Atlantic slave trade had negatively affected Africa, slavery scholars also used existing statistic data to minimize this impact. Based in European and US universities, until recently most historians relied mainly on secondary sources and European primary sources. Without conducting fieldwork or archival research in Africa, they often overlooked how the Atlantic slave trade was articulated with the Muslim and internal slave trades.[153]

Over the last twenty years, many historians continued studying slavery confined to national boundaries. They were criticized for missing the connections between the study of slavery in the Americas and the dynamic of the slave trade in Africa. Other works were also contested for failing to place the slave trade as part of a larger oceanic system in which each society involved had its own influential position. Likewise, several scholars overlooked the effects of the Atlantic slave trade in the original regions where Africans were enslaved, in the embarkation and disembarkation ports, and in the European metropoles and colonies that controlled the trade. Despite these shortcomings and occasional disagreements, all these scholars continued to ignore how the dynamic of racial relations affected their scholarship and favored their access to research funds. Most importantly, they failed to connect the history of this human tragedy with its persisting legacies. They refused to question how white supremacy shaped not only their own works but also national historiographies of former slave societies.

Several older and more recent studies show that the ways the slave trade was organized in the South and the North Atlantic systems impacted the volume of gains made by the slave traders and planters. These works emphasized how the slave trade shaped the development of capitalism in the British, French, Dutch, Spanish, and Portuguese empires.[154] But similarities and differences aside, in all slave societies, slavery was an institution that generated profits that ultimately contributed to the growing wealth of European and American nations and to the development of capitalism. These two aspects, frequently mentioned in the discourses of black abolitionists, such as David Walker (1796–1830), who underscored how the "greatest riches in all America have arisen from our blood and tears," have also been explored by historians and by the various social actors who since the era of emancipation formulated demands of reparations for the Atlantic slave trade and slavery.[155]

Slavery as a profitable human atrocity

Examining the mechanisms of the Atlantic slave trade and slavery in Europe, Africa, and the Americas is a necessary step to understanding the various dimensions of the abolitionist debates that considered the need of reparations during the era of emancipation. Both in the North Atlantic or in the South Atlantic systems, slavery and the slave trade generated significant financial profits that greatly benefited merchants, planters, and other elite groups in Europe and the Americas. The Atlantic slave trade also brought economic gains and political power to West Central African and West African rulers who by waging wars obtained captives to be sold in the Atlantic slave trade in exchange for luxury goods and weapons. This cycle of violence and war eventually opened the path for a sustained European presence in these regions that toward the end of the nineteenth century facilitated the establishment of colonial rule in the continent, reason why public demands of reparations for slavery have been always to some extent associated with the discussion of the struggle for decolonization of Africa.

The Atlantic slave trade had enduring nefarious impacts on the great majority of the populations of these African regions, which can hardly be measured through statistical data. In both Africa and the Americas, the Atlantic slave trade and slavery left behind a trail of blood, death, disease, sexual violence, and trauma, experiences that although hard to measure were unquestionably transmitted to later generations. Still today the legacies of these atrocities remain alive in the collective memory of the various populations who were victims of these extreme and complex forms of violence.

Whether in plantations, mills, mines, cattle ranches, jerked meat factories, or in the domestic spaces of household kitchens and gardens in urban areas, the great majority of slaves were submitted to dreadful living and working conditions that included daily physical violence and sexual abuse. Because slavery and the Atlantic slave trade were the engines of an economic system of production, for many decades, historians preferred to focus on its demographic and legal dimensions. These scholars largely failed in providing responses that adequately address the point of view of the victims of this great human tragedy. As the history of slavery is still being written and as the groups who identify themselves as descendants of slaves remain excluded from historical narratives, only an approach combining history and memory can take into account the complexities of an inhuman system that interconnected three continents for more than three hundred years, and that still today fuels debates on the need of measures of symbolic, financial, and material reparation. ʋ ʋ ʋ

2

"And What Should We Wait of These Brutish Spirits?"

In 1804, Saint-Domingue dismantled slavery and its colonial ties with France. Haiti became the first and only independent black republic of the Americas. The years that followed the birth of the black nation were marked by the legal prohibition of the slave trade to the British colonies and by the growing British pressure to stop the slave trade from Africa to the American continent. Yet, the end of slavery in the Americas took almost one century to be accomplished. During the era of emancipation, freed individuals were discriminated against because their skin color and physical features associated them with a whole group of people who just some years before were enslaved. Wageless and very often without access to basic education, freedmen and freedwomen could hardly improve their social and economic position. Despite the variety of paths taken after slavery, these inequalities were perpetuated over the end of the nineteenth century and during the twentieth and twenty-first centuries.

Between 1804 and 1888, all societies in the Americas abolished slavery. But its demise was a lengthy and gradual process. Even in regions traditionally referred by historians as freedom havens, such as the north of the United States and Mexico (where slavery was abolished earlier than in many regions of the Americas) the end of slavery can hardly be defined as a straightforward process. From Cuba to Brazil, public debates among abolitionists and proslavery groups reveal many common features. Slaveholding elites underscored that slavery and the slave trade were legal and that property rights should be respected above all rights. Abolitionists also utilized legal arguments to denounce that thousands of Africans were imported to the Americas illegally, and that it was unlawful to keep in bondage these Africans and their descendants. Moreover, as the internal slave trade continued active in countries like the United States, Brazil, and Cuba, a number of free individuals were also unlawfully enslaved even beyond national borders. These debates shed light on how a variety of social actors conceived property rights and how they envisioned the future of the freed populations in the public sphere. Although some antislavery activists occasionally invoked the need for reparations to former slaves and their descendants, through land redistribution, wages, and education, demands for financial compensation for slave owners always prevailed in these public debates. ✓✓

The gradual end of slavery in the western hemisphere during the long nineteenth century was planned to protect the interests of slaveholders and planters, who to different degrees succeeded in receiving at least some kind of monetary compensation. Likewise, either in the British Caribbean or in Cuba, the creation of apprenticeship systems indirectly rewarded many former masters who were allowed to keep freedpeople under their control by paying them symbolic wages. Yet, though it was a rare occurrence, during the era of gradual abolition a small number of former slaves demanded that either the government or their old masters provide them with pensions or some kind of financial reparations. Although numerically insignificant, these first demands by individuals, that emerged even when slavery was far from being abolished, provide a broader perspective to understanding the discourses of the first social actors who engaged in formulating demands of reparations for slavery and the Atlantic slave trade. These first calls show that demands for reparations have a long history in the Americas.

Reparations in times of revolution

The abolition of the slave trade from Africa was the first of the many steps that eventually led to the prolonged process of emancipation in the Americas. The first measures to prohibit the imports of enslaved Africans to the thirteen British colonies in North America started in the first half of the eighteenth century. Yet, none of these early initiatives were motivated by humanitarian reasons, but rather by fear of slave insurrections led by newly arrived enslaved Africans. Following the Stono Rebellion of 1739, the largest slave revolt of colonial North America, South Carolina banned the importation of enslaved Africans twice. In the periods when international slave trade was resumed, special taxes were created to discourage slave imports.

Winds of change were blowing through Western Europe and in the Atlantic world. Between 1703 and 1714, the War of Spanish Succession opposing France and Spain against Britain, the Dutch Republic, and other European powers such as Prussia and Portugal, took on continental dimensions and eventually consolidated Britain as an imperial power. Some decades later, the Seven Years' War once again opposed all major European powers against one another and marked the disputes between Britain and France over North America. The movements for independence in the Americas were not far behind.

During the American Revolutionary War, the imports of enslaved Africans, who arrived in the colonies on board of British slave ships or via the Royal African Company, were interrupted. The war greatly affected the slave system and the lives of enslaved men and women, giving them the hope of obtaining freedom. Slaves in the northern colonies who joined the

Continental Army were freed and their masters were evidently offered financial compensation.[1] Whereas at least 5,000 black soldiers fought on the patriots' side, approximately 20,000 black Loyalists escaped slavery to join the British lines with the promise of freedom in exchange for their service. After the end of the war, these freedmen continued building their freedom project scattered across the British empire, including the Caribbean, Canada, and Australia, and also in the future British colony of Sierra Leone in West Africa.[2]

As in most movements for independence in the Americas, white colonial elites ultimately controlled the American Revolution. In the areas where the institution of slavery was central to the economy especially, these insurgences were certainly not designed to emancipate the enslaved population. Instead, they were intended to provide selected groups with political and economic autonomy that was denied to them by the European metropoles. Only in Saint-Domingue were slaves and freed populations able to gain control of the anti-colonial struggle. In most cases, even in the areas where slavery was not a central institution, slave owners resisted freeing their slaves and imposed on the enslaved populations the long path of gradual abolition.

In colonies and later independent states like Virginia, the most famous revolutionary leaders such as George Washington (1732–1799), Thomas Jefferson (1743–1826), and James Madison (1751–1836), who later became known as the founding fathers of the United States, continued to be large slave owners until the end of their lives. After the thirteen colonies broke from Britain, neither the Declaration of Independence of 1776, nor the first US Constitution, adopted in 1787, addressed the problem of human bondage, and, indeed, did not even employ the words *slave* or *slavery*.[3] The new Constitution defended the slaveholders, who henceforth were overwhelmingly present in the House of Representatives and the Electoral College. The Constitution also protected slave property, through the Fugitive Slave Clause that established that slaves, apprentices, and indentured servants who escaped from their original states were to be returned to their owners. Moreover, the imports of slaves to the United States extended for more than two decades. Therefore, although acknowledging slavery as evil, all further proposals to abolish slavery in the new independent country included some kind of financial compensation to the slave owners, but no reparations to the former slaves.[4]

After the end of the American Revolutionary War and as the French Revolution emerged in 1789, antislavery activity continued to spread in Europe and the United States. In Britain, former enslaved Africans such as Olaudah Equiano and Ottobah Cugoano joined the abolitionist movement, which by then was becoming popular and gaining great public visibility.[5] Their writings, denouncing the horrors of the slave trade and slavery, reached audiences of thousands of people. Following the end of the war, although slave imports resumed in a number of newly independent states, between 1780 and 1788 the international slave trade was banned in several states in the north and the south, including Pennsylvania, South Carolina, New Jersey, and Massachusetts. This new context opened doors for the passing of gradual emancipation legislation.

Although the first debates to abolish slavery in the thirteen colonies started before the rise of the American Revolutionary War, most laws to abolish slavery were gradually enacted only after the end of the conflict. During the 1770s, several northern states ratified legislation freeing newborns to enslaved mothers. However, many scholars have overestimated the scope of these laws by equating them with the abolition (or gradual abolition) of slavery.[6] In recent days, despite the growing number of new studies on slavery in the north of the United States, this tendency seems to remain alive, in some ways contributing to preserve the myth that depicts the north of the country as the land of the free. One historian, for example, explained that "Vermont, with its tiny population of slaves, provided for immediate emancipation in its 1777 constitution. In 1780, the Pennsylvania state legislature enacted gradual emancipation."[7] Although sometimes referring to gradual emancipation as free womb laws, one scholar stated that "Vermont's Constitution barred both slavery and indentured servitude," when indeed only the children born after the passing of the law were freed.[8] More recently, another historian also affirmed that by "1784 all New England states and Pennsylvania had abolished slavery."[9] In fact, the eighteenth-century emancipation legislation did not liberate any living slaves, but only the future children of enslaved women. In the north of the United States, the slow process of abolition was focused on procedures cautiously designed not to hurt the interests of the slave owners. These measures relied on the idea that perhaps with much time and patience the evil institution would naturally disappear.

In 1777, the Constitution of the new state of Vermont did not free any of its small population of slaves. In fact, the first article of its first chapter, titled "A Declaration of the Rights of the Inhabitants of the State of Vermont," established that "no male person, born in this country, or brought from over sea, ought to be holden by law to serve any person as a servant, slave, or apprentice after he arrives the age of twenty-one years, nor female, in like manner, after she arrives to the age of eighteen years."[10] Despite the new legislation, slavery did not end, but rather continued to exist in Vermont until the early nineteenth century.[11] Yet, a few number of slaves challenged their enslavement in court and were able to obtain financial reparations. In 1778, an enslaved man named Pompey Brakkee, unlawfully maintained in slavery, sued his owner, a Loyalist named Elijah Lovell (1749–1816) of Rockingham, for unpaid labor. Eventually, Brakkee obtained an amount of £400 as reparation.[12]

Following Vermont, Pennsylvania passed its "Act for the Gradual Abolition of Slavery" in 1780. But in reality the new law did not emancipate any existing slaves. Its fourth section mandated that children born to enslaved mothers after the Act's passing were to be freed, but only after reaching twenty-eight years of age.[13] The Act also banned the importation of new slaves and created a mandatory slave register. If the masters failed to comply with the law, unregistered slaves were to be manumitted. Despite these measures, slaveholders continued circumventing the legislation in a variety of ways, among others by importing slaves and transporting pregnant enslaved women to give birth to their children in states where slavery remained legal.[14]

In the colonies of the north, the American Revolutionary War fueled antislavery discourses and an early abolitionist movement, in which enslaved men and women actively participated by petitioning their masters to obtain freedom and in some cases rewards for past services, which can be understood as pioneer demands of reparations for slavery.[15] Inspired by the Enlightenment promoting ideals of liberty and equality, the revolutionary movement contributed to questioning the existence and the morality of slavery, which at least in theory was opposed to republican values.[16] In this context, one of the first demand of reparations for slavery was formulated by an elderly former slave who petitioned the legislature of Massachusetts.

Belinda (c. 1713–179?) was born in a village in West Africa. According to her own story found in the petition, she was captured before the age of twelve years and sold into slavery. Yet, it is hard to know her actual place of birth. The account refers to River Volta, which could suggest a location in the interior of the Gold Coast, but she also mentions the Orisha. This reference suggests that her ethnicity may have been Yoruba and that she was born either in the Bight of Benin or perhaps in the Bight of Biafra.[17] Arrived in the Caribbean, Belinda became the slave of the wealthy Isaac Royall (1672–1739), who was born in Maine and by the age of twenty-eight years old settled in Antigua, where he established a sugarcane plantation.

In 1737, Royall and his family moved to North America, bringing with him twenty-seven slaves. He settled in Massachusetts, and acquired a farm in Medford. After Royall's death two years later, his son Isaac Royall Junior (1719–1781) inherited his assets, including a large property with a mansion and twenty slaves, becoming one of the richest men in the colony.[18] Among these slaves was Belinda. Baptism records of August 14, 1768, reveal that she had two children, a son named Joseph, and a daughter, named Prine.[19] In 1775, during the American Revolutionary War, because of his strong connections with the Loyalists, Royall Junior was forced to escape to Nova Scotia and then to England. He left behind his business, real estate, and slaves, including Belinda. In his will of May 26, 1778, Royall Junior instructed his grandson and executor William Pepperel (1775–1816) to pay Belinda "for three years, £30."[20] Moreover, he also bequeathed Harvard University with land to endow a professorship of law, physics, or anatomy. Eventually the university utilized the funds to create a professorship of law that marked the foundation of Harvard Law School.[21]

In 1778, the state of Massachusetts confiscated Royall Junior's properties. Several of his slaves were manumitted, including Belinda. Soon after she was freed, at approximately sixty-five years of age, she moved to Boston where she lived in poverty. After Royall Junior's death in 1781, it is assumed that Belinda received the amount determined in his will. But three years later, as expected, the payments stopped. Thus, on February 14, 1783, Belinda petitioned the Massachusetts legislature for the first time. She requested a pension as reparations for the unpaid work she provided to the Royalls:

> Fifty years her faithful hands have been compelled to ignoble servitude for the benefit of an Isaac Royall, untill, as if Nations must be agitated, and the world convulsed for the preservation of that freedom which the Almightly Father intended for all the human Race, the present war was Commenced—The terror of men armed in the Cause of freedom, compeeled her master to fly—and to breathe away his Life in a Land, where, Lawless domination sits enthroned—pouring bloody outrage and cruelty on all who dare to be free.[22]

The legislature responded positively to her request, and Belinda obtained an annual pension of £15 12s. taken from the revenues generated by Royall's estate.[23] Two elements can explain this positive outcome. First, her deceased master had already determined in his will to pay her an amount for three years. Second, her case must have been favored by the fact that Royall Junior was a Loyalist.[24] The case shows how from the very beginning the political context deeply oriented not only the demands of reparations for slavery but also the responses obtained by the petitioners. The petition had an impact in the public sphere. The Quakers widely disseminated Belinda's story. In 1783, the antislavery newspaper the *New Jersey Gazette* in the United States, as well as British newspapers and magazines published transcriptions of her first petition.[25] Although not advocating reparations to former slaves as a policy worth pursuing, upon freeing their slaves many Quakers provided them with financial restitutions.[26]

But Belinda's story did not end in 1783. After the first year, the estate suspended her allowances.[27] In 1785, she submitted a second petition to continue the payments authorized two years earlier. In 1787, she again petitioned the legislature and obtained the pension for only one year.[28] In 1788, she submitted another petition. Using for the first time her widow's last name (Sutton), she requested an annual pension of $52.[29] But as Royall's estate refused to pay the pension, on February 25, 1793, she once again petitioned the government, who determined that the payments should continue.[30] Up to this date, this is the last known petition submitted by Belinda Sutton, who may have died in the 1790s. Although only partially successful Sutton was the first known case of a freedperson who obtained financial reparations for slavery.

Reparations to former slaves were never seriously discussed in the public sphere during this early era of emancipation in North America. Yet, during the eighteenth century both in the North and in the upper South, masters who freed their slaves could award material compensation, such as land, as a reward for the services provided.[31] In the 1770s until the early nineteenth century, legislation mandating gradual abolition of slavery continued to prevail in northern states. After unsuccessful attempts to pass legislation to gradually abolish slavery before the end of the war, in March of 1784, Rhode Island adopted an Act that launched gradual emancipation. The children of enslaved women were to be freed, males after reaching twenty-one years old and females after completing eighteen years of age.[32] Likewise, in March 1784, Connecticut eventually passed the "Act Concerning Indian, Mulatto, and Negro Servants and Slaves." However, like the previous laws ratified in other northern states, the Act freed only the children of enslaved mothers born after the date of its passing and upon reaching twenty-five years of age.[33] Eventually, an additional Act enacted in May 1797 reduced the emancipation age to twenty-one.

Reparations to free men, unlawfully enslaved

In the northern states with large numbers of slaves, gradual abolition took even longer to be accomplished. New York, the northern state with the largest enslaved population, only passed legislation to end slavery gradually in 1799. Exactly as in Vermont, Pennsylvania, Rhode Island, and Connecticut, only the children born after the enactment of the law, on July 4, 1799, were to be freed. But in New York the law was more severe than in other states. It determined that freed male children had to serve the owners of their mothers until twenty-eight years old, and the freed female children until twenty-five years of age. The Act also established a mandatory register for all newborns.[34]

The enactment of gradual abolition legislation in the United States resulted from the efforts of black and white abolitionists who found a favorable context for the antislavery struggle after the end of the American Revolutionary War and the rupture with Britain. Yet, abolitionists constituted a heterogeneous group. Most of them were not willing to boldly attack the problem of property rights that justified the ownership of slaves, because such measures would hurt the interests of slave owners. Few of these early activists defended measures to redress the damage imposed on slaves, such as programs to provide education and land redistribution.[35] Moreover, whereas among white abolitionists there were former slave owners and individuals who still owned slaves, black radical abolitionists did not possess the necessary political strength to force the passing of immediate abolition. For the thousands of slaves living in the northern states, gradual abolition was an insufficient response, but to the slave owners gradual abolition was the only way to control the transition to free labor and consequently avoid any possible social unrest.

White abolitionists across North and South America consistently accepted the existing legislation that protected slave property and established mandatory financial compensation to the former masters of manumitted slaves.[36] Obviously, these important restrictions never prevented enslaved men and women from running away, resisting in various ways, and fighting for their freedom either collectively or individually. In states such as Vermont, Massachusetts, Connecticut, and Rhode Island, there are numerous examples of slaves who sued their masters and obtained freedom.[37] But despite freedom suits and self-emancipatory activity, it took several decades between the beginning of gradual abolition and the effective legal end of slavery in northern states.[38] In these so-called free states the lives of slaves and the newly freed population were in actuality not at all associated with the idealized notion of freedom. Moreover, as the internal slave trade and the illegal slave trade from Africa continued operating to Brazil and Cuba, free blacks could not move around the country or overseas without the risk of being kidnapped and sold into slavery. Yet, some black abolitionists such as Martin Delany (1812–1855) advocated emigration and the creation of a black nation outside the boundaries of the United States.[39] During a convention held in 1854, Delany and other members of the movement invoked the payment of reparations: "Nothing less than a national indemnity, indelibly fixed by virtue of our own sovereign potency, will satisfy us as a redress of grievances for the unparalleled wrongs, undisguised impositions, and unmitigated oppression, which we have suffered at the hands of this American people."[40]

Even in the north of the United States, blacks were constantly victims of racial discrimination and found themselves always in danger of being kidnapped and sold as slaves to the southern states. Since the early nineteenth century individuals unlawfully enslaved had sued those who held them in bondage and were successful in obtaining financial compensation.[41] In 1841, Solomon Northup (1808–1863), a free African American from New York was kidnapped in US national capital, Washington, DC.[42] After being sold to slave merchants, he was transported to Louisiana, where he remained enslaved for twelve years. The case narrated in the account *Twelve Years a Slave* gained worldwide attention with the award-winning film by the same name directed by the British filmmaker Steve McQueen.[43]

Northup was eventually freed, but his kidnappers were never convicted. Still, in 1854, congressmen Gerrit Smith (1797–1874) and Edward Wade (1802–1866) submitted several petitions demanding reparations for his illegal enslavement to the Congress of the United States. Northup's plea gained visibility and support among abolitionists, including Frederick Douglass (1818–1895).[44] One petition, dated February 20, 1854 and signed by dozens of citizens of Niagara County in New York requested "full compensation out of the Treasury of the Material Government to the said Solomon Northup for the loss and damage sustained by him in consequence of his abduction."[45]

Another petition of June 10, 1854, presented by citizens of Western New York to the House of Representatives of the United States made a similar demand. Arguing that if the General Government had the obligation to return "escaped slaves to Slavery at the public expense, provision should also be made to remunerate this kidnapped Freeman for the great loss he has unjustly sustained, by being deprived of his liberty." The petitioners insisted on equal rights: "If the oppressor has a claim on the National Treasury, to aid him in regaining his chattel, most surely the oppressed has at least an equal claim upon the public chest for being deprived of his liberty for twelve long years on a cotton plantation in the prime of life."[46]

Despite these calls, the Congress did not hear the petitions requesting financial reparations to Northup. In a letter addressed to William Lloyd Garrison (1805–1879), dated March 20, 1855, and published in *The Liberator*, abolitionist Henry Clarke Wright (1797–1870) narrated Northup's case. He concluded the letter, stating that to Northup the Union was a confederacy of kidnappers, and asked:

> Where is the Church or political party that will refuse to open the way to give this victim of slavery a hearing, and repay him for the suffering this Union has inflicted on him? But there are 4,000,000 of kidnapped men, women, and children still under the *American* lash. Who will help to redeem them, and pay for their sufferings?[47]

Although timidly, Northup's case encouraged US abolitionists to defend financial reparations to former slaves in several occasions before the beginning of the Civil War.[48]

Northup was not the only free African American unlawfully enslaved. In 1848, the case of John Lytle also gained public attention. Lytle was born free in Philadelphia approximately in 1817.[49] He worked on board of the ship *Jupiter* that sailed the Atlantic Ocean. After a shipwreck, he ended up in Sierra Leone. By 1837, slave merchants had sold him and transported him to Cuba, where for eleven years he was maintained under slavery in a plantation. In 1848, Lytle denounced his unlawful enslavement to journalist John L. O'Sullivan (1813–1895), who was visiting the island. Consequently, the Consul of the United States in Havana, Robert B. Campbell (1787–1862), supported Lytle's demand for freedom. The outcome of this incident is among the few cases of reparations to an individual illegally enslaved. In addition to be freed, the Cuban government paid Lytle $2,211.33 as reparations for the eleven years he was maintained in slavery. Liberated, he returned to the United States and joined the abolitionist cause in New York City.[50] Unfortunately, many other men and women unlawfully enslaved had not the same fate.

The great storm of Saint-Domingue

As gradual abolition followed its slow pace in the north of the United States, the climate of social unrest continued in continental France and its colonies in the Caribbean. In 1791, a great slave revolt broke out in Saint-Domingue, which eventually led to the decree of 1794 that abolished slavery in the French Caribbean and the Indian Ocean. But the taste of the victory did not last very long. Napoléon Bonaparte came to power in 1799 and reestablished slavery in the French colonies in 1802. This measure, however, intensified the rebellion, eventually causing the defeat of the French army and the abolition of slavery in Saint-Domingue.

The abolition of slavery in Saint-Domingue is inseparable from the broad Atlantic repercussions of the French Revolution. Unlike the United States, during the eighteenth century Saint-Domingue had significant freeborn and freed populations of color, among whom there were individuals who became slave owners. Situated between the group of white planters and slaveholders and the huge enslaved population, these colored freedmen and freedwomen occupied an ambiguous place in this colonial society. Despite these complications, white planters were aware that limiting the political rights of the free populations of color was critical to maintaining slavery in Saint-Domingue. Insisting on preserving racial distinctions, by the 1780s French colonial officials had already created legal barriers to limit the rights of its colored populations. These measures clearly established that emancipation could not erase the deep dark stain of African ancestry.[51]

On the eve of the French Revolution, an organized abolitionist movement emerged in France with the creation of the Société des Amis des Noirs. Led by Jacques-Pierre Brissot (1754–1793), this antislavery organization relied on the support of British abolitionists such as Thomas Clarkson (1760–1846). Yet, like in other regions of the Americas, white French abolitionists of this newly created society did not support the idea of immediate demise of slavery, but rather defended gradual abolition. Moreover, even those members who recognized the immorality of slavery accepted racist ideas such as the inferiority of Africans, perceived as barbaric, childlike, and in need of guidance.[52]

In 1788, when the Estates General was called in France, the newly created Société des Amis de Noirs seized the opportunity to intensify antislavery propaganda. Still, they faced opposition from the colonial delegates as well as from planters and merchants, who were all represented in the National Assembly. Benefiting from slavery, these representatives had reasons to fear the spread of abolitionist ideas in the French colonies. On the eve of the French Revolution about two-thirds of Saint-Domingue's enslaved population, estimated at 500,000 individuals, were born in Africa.[53] By August 1789, when France's National Constituent Assembly adopted the Declaration of the Rights of Man stating the equality of rights between all men, enslaved individuals from its colonies were being prevented from disembarking in continental France, a restriction intended to avoid the dissemination of ideas promoting insurrection and emancipation.[54]

As the French Revolution evolved it became clear that the establishment of equality of rights excluded the populations of color and was not intended to abolish slavery in the colonies, because the institution generated immense profits to France. Even after the fall of the Bastille in July 1789, the National Assembly granted only white planters the right to vote for the permanent assembly in Saint-Domingue's elections of 1790. White planters and French revolutionaries alike continued to deny political rights to the free population of color. Plantation owners and merchants, despite benefiting from the changes materializing in continental France, dreaded the abolition of slavery, and claimed the total control of colonial policies.

Saint-Domingue, unlike the United States, had a significant free population of color (*gens de couleur*). These freed coloreds were former slaves, or descended from slaves, who were able to purchase their own freedom at some point of their lives. Although many freed coloreds were people with modest means, a number of them became planters and slave owners. Still, their free status combined with their African ancestry placed these men and women in an intermediary category between slaves and white plantation owners. Therefore, among the white elites, there was still no consensus in giving political rights to the free coloreds. Some contemporaries, such as Médéric Louis Élie Moreau de Saint-Méry (1750–1819), supported the exclusion of the populations of color, because according to him they were accustomed to segregation. Julien Raimond (1744–1801) and Abbé Grégoire (1750–1831), for example, defended the idea that giving rights to the free populations of color would make them allies in preserving slavery. Yet, other contemporary commentators feared that granting rights to the coloreds would make them the ruling class in the colonies. Once in power, they could liberate their own slaves and the slaves owned by the white planters.

In March 1790, the French National Assembly approved the creation of a Colonial Committee that passed a law to regulate colonial affairs. However, the text of the law was vague. All those who owned property were enfranchised, but the law failed to specifically mention the free coloreds, giving them the ability to claim the right to vote. As the legal path did not seem to work, the populations of color decided to take up arms to fight for their rights in anti-colonial rebellion. In 1791, a decree by the National Assembly eventually gave voting rights to free coloreds who owned property and were born from two free parents. But affected by the news of rapid changes brought by the French Revolution, Saint-Domingue's enslaved population started struggling for freedom as well. At first, the populations of color were willing to fight the slave rebels. But as their demands for political rights from the French National Assembly were denied, they decided to take to arms to fight the white planters and took the slave rebels as their allies.[55]

In August 1791, the slave conspiracy erupted. Thousands of slaves marched through various estates in the northern plain of Saint-Domingue, burning down plantations, big houses, and slave quarters, slaughtering masters, refiners, and overseers, and attracting more insurgents. The turmoil continued for several months and progressively spread over the rest of the colony. On September 3, 1791, France adopted a new constitution that put an end to the Old Regime, by establishing a constitutional monarchy. However, despite an amnesty for revolutionary acts, there were disagreements whether or not the rebellious acts by free coloreds and slaves in colonies such as Saint-Domingue should be pardoned. Slaves had nothing to lose and were already engaged in destroying the slave system by freeing themselves and killing their masters.[56] During the amnesty negotiations, the rebel leaders formulated a series of demands, including better treatment for the slaves and other concessions. But except for the exchange of prisoners, the negotiations ultimately failed. The slave rebellion continued and acquired more violent contours. Slaves developed great military experience, as both free coloreds and whites recruited slaves to fight on their sides. In an attempt to neutralize the slave rebellion, on April 4, 1792, France's National Assembly enfranchised the free colored populations by awarding them the same political rights as the whites. This measure was intended to reinforce the gap between free coloreds and slaves and consequently to defeat the slave revolt. However, the slaves contributed to the victory of free coloreds and refused to accept returning to the plantations. Despite French efforts in gathering troops to fight the rebels, the revolt persisted and expanded.

After the suspension of the National Assembly and the establishment of a National Convention in France, King Louis XVI (1754–1793) was executed in January 1793. The end of the monarchy led the Spanish and the British to declare war against France, aggravating Saint-Domingue's situation. The Spanish started recruiting Saint-Domingue's slave rebels to join its troops in exchange for freedom, whereas the British gained support among the white planters and later also recruited African-born soldiers.[57] Moreover, to face the British and the Spanish interventions, the French also offered freedom and land to the slave rebels who joined the French army. French commissioners Étienne Polverel (1740–1795) and Léger Félicité Sonthonax (1763–1813), who had been in Saint-Domingue since 1792 to oversee the application of the decree giving political rights to the colored populations, started freeing the slaves during the year 1793 by gradually abolishing slavery in Saint-Domingue. This decision was eventually brought to Paris, where on February 4, 1794 the National Convention finally approved the abolition of slavery in the French colonies.

The newly freed slaves faced many constraints. Led by Toussaint Louverture (1743–1803) and André Rigaud (1761–1811), former slaves composed the forces that fought the British invaders until their defeat in 1798. But the specter of war and slavery continued to haunt Saint-Domingue. In 1799, Napoléon Bonaparte led a coup d'état that overthrew the Directory, and became the First Consul of France and leader of the Consulate. Meanwhile, the revolution continued in Saint-Domingue. In March 1801, seven years after the abolition of slavery by the National Convention, Louverture called a Constituent Assembly to draft Saint-Domingue's constitution. Promulgated in July 1801, the new constitution stated that the entire island of Hispaniola, including the Spanish portion by then controlled by Louverture, was part of the French empire. Establishing that henceforth the island was ruled by its own laws, the new constitution confirmed the prohibition of slavery in Saint-Domingue.

Relying on the military, Louverture named himself governor for life. But his rule was short. Napoléon Bonaparte rejected Saint-Domingue's autonomy. In February 1802, he sent an expedition of 22,000 soldiers to Saint-Domingue to fight Louverture. In May 1802, Bonaparte issued a decree reestablishing slavery in the French colonies. Although Louverture was imprisoned and deported to France, where he died one year later, the rebels continued fighting. As thousands of soldiers of Bonaparte's army succumbed to the epidemics of yellow fever, the slave rebels eventually defeated the French troops. On January 1, 1804, Jean-Jacques Dessalines (1758–1806) declared Saint-Domingue an independent nation. Saint-Domingue was the first colony in the Americas to abolish slavery altogether while simultaneously breaking its colonial ties with a European power. The new nation was renamed Haiti, and Dessalines was appointed lifetime governor general.[58]

No slave society in the Americas remained immune from the remnants of the slave rebellion that gave birth to Haiti. The new black nation became the symbol of freedom for the populations of African descent in the Atlantic world, and a reminder of the cruelties of slavery, as noted by David Walker, "Oh! my suffering brethren, remember the divisions and consequent sufferings of Carthage and of Hayti. Read the History particularly of Hayti, and see how they were butchered by the whites, and do you take the warning."[59] Yet, for white planters and slave owners in Europe and the Americas, the simple existence of Haiti was also a constant warning that a nightmare could become reality.

The years that followed the birth of Haiti were tragic ones. Destroyed by years of insurrection and French military intervention, the reconstruction of Haiti was an enormous task. Moreover, obtaining international recognition as an independent black nation, free of slavery, was among the greatest challenges faced by the new country. Former colonists and slave merchants from Bordeaux, Nantes, and La Rochelle scarcely accepted the independence of the former colony. Whereas planters pressured the French government to take action to recover Haiti, traders wanted the recognition of the independence in order to reestablish the trade relations.[60] With the rise of Haiti, the abolition of the Atlantic slave trade from Africa to the Americas, as well as the gradual abolition of slavery, dominated public and parliamentary debates. As discussed in the next chapter, Haiti eventually had to pay huge financial compensation to France in order to obtain international recognition. Yet, despite a growing antislavery movement in Europe and North America in the early nineteenth century, there were no public debates or collective demands to provide reparations to the newly freed populations.

Former masters win again

At the turn of the nineteenth century, international antislavery movements expanded. But, except for Haiti, slavery persisted in the Americas, including the north of the United States. In 1801, despite two decades of abolitionist activity supported by the New Jersey Society for Promoting the Abolition of Slavery and the Society for Friends led by the Quakers, New Jersey's enslaved population, estimated at 12,500, continued increasing.[61] In 1804, the same year Haiti became an independent country free of slavery, New Jersey eventually enacted legislation freeing newborns to enslaved mothers. On the ground, however, there was not much to celebrate.[62] The Act liberated the children of enslaved mothers born after July 4, 1804, and established age restrictions: twenty-five years old for males and twenty-one years old for females.[63]

In 1807, Napoléon Bonaparte crossed Spain to invade Portugal. In that same year the British Parliament abolished the international slave trade to the British colonies. Also in 1807, following the mandate of the Constitution of 1787, the United States Congress passed an Act, made effective in 1808, prohibiting the international slave trade to its territory. Moreover, in 1808, the French and Spanish alliance was dismantled. To resist French occupation, a series of *juntas* (councils) were created all over Spain, and eventually led to the establishment of the Cortes of Cádiz in 1810. Spain's first national assembly with representatives from its various colonies, the Cortes of Cádiz started discussing the abolition of the slave trade and slavery in the Spanish empire. But this was a period of crisis when the independence rebellions were emerging in the Spanish American mainland. Although the end of slavery was not near, Caribbean planters and slaveholders were anxious about its possible abolition, and emancipation hopes started growing among the enslaved population of Cuba and Puerto Rico.[64]

In 1808, the aftershocks of the Napoleonic Wars finally hit the Portuguese empire hard. Whereas Napoléon Bonaparte clearly threatened Portugal with invasion, British pressures to ban the imports of slaves from Africa to Brazil dramatically increased. In 1808, after escaping French occupation with the support of the British Navy, the Portuguese royal family settled in Brazil. As a result of this unusual move, in that same year, Portugal and Britain started signing a series of treaties intended to open the Brazilian markets to British manufactured products and to stop the slave trade.[65] In Britain, the abolition of the British slave trade was the first response to a powerful social movement gathering thousands of people who, for moral and religious reasons, condemned the continuity of the evil institution even though it still generated significant profits.[66] But at the international level, abolishing the slave trade to Brazil and Cuba would hinder the production of sugar, whose prices were lower than the sugar produced in the British Caribbean.[67]

In the first two decades of the nineteenth century, whereas the movement to abolish slavery in the Caribbean's British colonies grew, groups who

opposed emancipation publicly and systematically defended slavery.[68]
British Caribbean's slave owners were not able to unify their interests in
order to formulate formal demands for financial compensation in the event
of loss of slave property.

Starting in 1817, public registration of slaves was made mandatory in
most colonies of the British Caribbean, with the aim of controlling the
changes in the sizes of slave holdings. In the years that followed, the
movements for the abolition of slavery gained force on the one hand because
of the emergence of slave rebellions in Barbados, Guyana, and Jamaica, and
on the other hand through the activities of the Anti-Slavery Society. Created
in 1823, this society gathered hundreds of thousands of signatures petitioning
for the end of slavery. It also demanded better conditions for the enslaved
populations and gradual emancipation. As a result of this great popular
pressure, in 1823, George Canning (1770–1827), then Foreign Secretary,
presented a number of resolutions in the British Parliament intended to
improve the working and living conditions of slaves. Among others, the
resolutions encouraged formal marriage, the right of self-purchase, and the
end of whipping punishments.

As the issue of emancipation was introduced with the Canning's
Resolutions, the discussion on how to indemnify British slave owners
became the central element of the public debate on the abolition of slavery.
In a famous pamphlet, Augustus Hardin Beaumont (1798–1838) recognized
slavery as a national sin. He persuasively argued that slavery should be
abolished: "But is then Slavery to continue? Certainly not. Sacrifices must be
made to abrogate it. To ensure its safe abrogation, the co-operation of those
who are to make the Sacrifices must be ensured." Yet, he added: "How can
you ensure it? Why, by fairly compensating them for their Sacrifices, on the
same principle of all holders of other species of property are indemnified for
the loss or even *inconvenience* they incur for the public benefit."[69] In other
words, Beaumont defended that the state should compensate the slave
owners because of slave property loss.

Although different from Saint-Domingue's context, where the rebels
destroyed and expropriated plantations, slave owners made efforts to show
the "uniquely illiquid" character of slave property in the British Caribbean
with the goal of obtaining financial compensation from the government.[70]
With these arguments they sought to demonstrate and defend the chattel
nature of slaves. Moreover, the idea of financial compensation was not in
opposition to previous interventions of the British state that in the past had
provided emergency credit to planters and slave merchants.[71]

Despite differing views on the issue, for the planters and slaveholders in
Britain and everywhere else in the Americas slaves constituted a conventional
kind of asset. Even though this definition was contested by some British
abolitionists, several of them recognized the general principle of financial
compensation to slave owners. Indeed, the remaining point of divergence
between abolitionists and slave owners was rather how compensation

should be provided and what was financially viable.[72] However, like the abolitionist debates in other parts of the Americas, financial and material reparations to the former slaves, such as land redistribution and pensions to former slaves were mostly absent from these public exchanges.

Eventually, by 1833, the British government negotiated a compensation plan with the representatives of planters and slave owners. On May 14, 1833, Edward Smith Stanley (1799–1869), Lord Stanley, presented to the British Parliament five resolutions to end slavery. The resolutions encompassed the idea of gradual abolition manifested through a paternalistic system of apprenticeship that proposed to maintain former slaves as apprentice workers for a period of twelve years. Stanley also proposed financial compensations to the slave owners for the loss of slave property that would result from the abolition of slavery. In his proposal, the indemnities would be paid either by the British state or would be generated from the work provided by freedmen and freedwomen. In agreement with this paternalistic vision, his preferred option was nothing more than to require the enslaved population to pay installments toward their future freedom:

> I think that the negro is more likely to continue in a state of industry and exertion if he knows that a portion of the wages he earns will be set apart for the purpose of purchasing his freedom. Such a plan will be more likely to create in the negro habits of vigorous exertion, and patient self-denial, than if he were told—"You shall work three-fourths of the day for your master. For which you shall receive food and clothing, but for the other fourth part of the day you may work, or not, as you please, in order to obtain superfluities."[73]

After intense debates in the months that followed, the final Slavery Abolition Act of August 28, 1833, declared the end of slavery in the British colonies starting on August 1, 1834. In theory, the Act formally freed nearly 800,000 slaves. Except for Antigua, in all other British colonies of the Caribbean, slaves older than six were to follow a period of apprenticeship of four years if they worked as domestic servants and of six years if they were agricultural workers.[74] Moreover, the Abolition Act included a provision to compensate 46,000 slave owners with £20 million, with interest incurred from August 1, 1834.[75] Intended to control the former enslaved population, the apprenticeship system maintained intact most elements of the old relations between master and slaves. Still, apprentices had to be paid to any work provided beyond the agreed forty and one-half hours.[76]

Not only were former slaves required to continue working for their old masters. In addition, between 1834 and 1845, the Slave Compensation Commission indemnified former slave owners in the British Caribbean, Cape of Good Hope, and Mauritius for what was defined as loss of slave property. The comprehensive data gathered by this commission, and now made accessible through the project *Legacies of British Slave-Ownership*, includes the names of the individuals indemnified, the number of slaves, and the compensation amount. The registers show that slave-ownership was deeply rooted in Britain and widespread among a variety of individuals and groups.[77]

Unsurprisingly, former slaves and their descendants in British colonies such as Jamaica, Trinidad and Tobago, Bahamas, Barbados, Guyana, Antigua, and Bermuda were not compensated for the years in bondage, during which they were submitted to horrible working and living conditions, physical punishments, and sexual violence. Moreover, despite their new legal status and having some access to land ownership, in these Caribbean colonies former enslaved men, women, and children were forced to continue providing unpaid work to their former masters for a period between four and six years, until they obtained full emancipation.[78]

A lucrative institution in a nation divided

By the time slavery was outlawed in the British empire, the industries of tobacco, rice, and cotton had quickly expanded in the south of the United States, where slavery was central to the economy. As in other countries of the Americas, despite the ban of the international slave trade, the domestic slave trade continued to be very active in the United States. The process of legal abolition of slavery remained gradual, varying from state to state. In many states in the north, as a result of the legislation freeing newborns to enslaved mothers, existing slaves were kept in bondage until the middle of the nineteenth century: New York abolished slavery in 1827, Rhode Island in 1842, Pennsylvania in 1847, and Connecticut only in 1848. Although New Jersey legally abolished slavery in 1846, newly freed slaves became apprentices for life.[79] As the division between free states and slave states became clear in 1850, slaveholding states were willing to fight to keep the lucrative slavery institution alive.

In 1860 Abraham Lincoln (1809–1865) was eventually chosen to run as the presidential candidate of the Republican Party. In his early career as a politician, Lincoln conveyed his moral opposition to slavery. Yet, he neither challenged slavery, nor publicly defended its abolition.[80] Before the advent of the Civil War, Lincoln positioned himself against slavery only once, during the public debates regarding the Kansas-Nebraska Act of 1854, which gave the settlers the possibility of allowing slavery in the newly created territories, reversing the Missouri Compromise of 1820. As a presidential candidate, Lincoln opposed the expansion of slavery, but neither he nor his party advocated its end.

During the presidential electoral campaign, southerners increased a call for secession because, despite Lincoln's moderate positions regarding slavery, he was not a representative of the southern planters and slave owners. At the time of Lincoln's election as the president of the United States in November 1860, the abolitionist movement had been established in the country for almost a century. Additionally, the number of states where slavery had been abolished exceeded the number of slave states. Very quickly, the tensions between slave states and free states dramatically increased, especially among South Carolina's planters whose decline of political power became clear.[81] In December 1860, South Carolina General Assembly issued a proclamation announcing its secession from the United States, an action justified by the growing hostility to the institution of slavery by the free states.[82] During the four months after South Carolina's secession, six other states (Georgia, Florida, Alabama, Mississippi, Texas, and Louisiana) announced their separation from the Union, forming the Confederate States of America.

Lincoln sought to appease the doubts of the frantic southerners. In his inaugural address of March 4, 1861, he promised not to interfere in the states where slavery existed.[83] But the country was too divided to be soothed. The Civil War exploded five weeks later, when the Confederacy attacked federal Fort Sumter, in Charleston, South Carolina. In the three months that followed this event, Virginia, Arkansas, North Carolina, and Tennessee joined the confederacy, which later elected Jefferson Davis (1808–1889) as its president.

During the first months of the Civil War, emancipation became a central issue not only for Lincoln's presidency, but also for the Union's victory.[84] In 1861, most runaway slaves who joined the Union Army came from the four border slave states (Delaware, Kentucky, Maryland, and Missouri) that remained in the Union. As Eric Foner explains, Lincoln "drew on ideas he had long embraced, advancing a plan for gradual, compensated emancipation in these states, coupled with the colonization of the freed slaves outside the country."[85] To temporarily address the issue, on August 6, 1861 the US Congress passed a Confiscation Act allowing the Union Army to seize property, including slaves, employed by the Confederate armies. Although this Act did not officially emancipate any confiscated slave, three weeks later, Major General John C. Frémont (1813–1890) issued a proclamation seizing all property belonging to those rebelling against the federal government, including slaves, who therefore would be declared free. But Lincoln was hesitant. One month later, fearing the reaction of the slave owners who supported the Union, he ordered the decree's annulment. A similar situation repeated itself in the next year. On May 9, 1862, Major General David Hunter (1802–1886), then commander of the Department of the South, declared more than 900,000 enslaved men, women, and children of his department free and encouraged the recruitment of black soldiers. Lincoln revoked the measure ten days later, disregarding the increasing need to free enslaved men to enlist them as soldiers to fill the ranks of the Union Army.[86]

As the war continued and the Union Army moved toward the Confederate states, the unrest among the enslaved population was blatant.[87] The development of the Civil War transformed Washington, DC, accentuating racial inequalities. The Compromise of 1850 in the US Congress had already banned the slave trade, but slavery remained legal in the national capital. Additionally, although only 20 percent of the district's black population was enslaved, the remaining 80 percent of free black Washingtonians faced legal restrictions and discrimination.[88]

The persistence of slavery in Washington, DC became a concern among legislators in the years 1861 and 1862, especially when waves of escaped slaves from Virginia and Maryland arrived in the national capital.[89] Whereas fugitives from secessionist Virginia could not be claimed, federal fugitive laws were still in vigor. Consequently, Maryland fugitive slaves were sent to jail, creating an embarrassing situation that emphasized the contradiction of fighting a war over slavery when the federal government had not yet committed itself to abolishing slavery. As the fugitives issue gained public attention, it eventually contributed to the end of slavery in the national capital.

In December 1861, Senator and Vice-President Henry Wilson (1812–1875) proposed to Congress a Bill abolishing slavery in Washington, DC, which despite facing opposition, was approved. Lincoln signed the District of Columbia Emancipation Act on April 16, 1862, which later received a number of amendments. Yet, despite the particular context of war, as it happened with the British, this first Emancipation Act included a clause to compensate slave owners. But compensated emancipation was not a new proposal in the United States. In 1849, Lincoln had already proposed emancipation in Washington, DC in exchange for financial compensation to the slave owners. As in legal terms slaves were considered property, the principle of compensated emancipation was based on the Fifth Amendment of the US Constitution, which clearly established that government expropriation of property required providing indemnification.[90]

The District of Columbia Emancipation Act determined that slave owners would be compensated with an amount of up to $300 per slave. But evidently the indemnification would be paid only to the slave owners who confirmed loyalty to the Union. To this end, Lincoln appointed a board of commissioners, chaired by the North Carolina abolitionist politician Daniel Reaves Goodloe (1814–1902) to examine the petitions. The commission received 1,127 petitions claiming 3,100 slaves; 909 petitions were paid in full and 21 other petitions were partially paid, for a total of 2,989 slaves. In 1862, a supplemental Act allowed the submission of additional petitions; 161 petitions were submitted and 139 were approved.

As the Civil War evolved, many slaves ran away, whereas others were freed by the federal government to fight alongside the Union Army.[91] On July 17, 1862, the Congress of the United States passed a second Confiscation Act emancipating all slaves owned by Confederates. Although such a measure could only be enforced in the areas of the South occupied by the Union Army, it opened the path for the preliminary Emancipation Proclamation of the Confederate states of the South issued by Lincoln on

September 22, 1862, whose final version was issued on January 1, 1863. The proclamation was part of a strategy to fight the Confederate states and gain the support of freed slaves who would be able to join the Union's Army. Despite excluding 450,000 slaves in the border slave states of the Union (Delaware, Kentucky, Maryland, and Missouri) and 275,000 slaves in Tennessee, and many thousands in areas controlled by the Union Army in the states of Louisiana and Virginia, the decree freed more than three million enslaved men, women, and children, favoring the enlistment of black soldiers in the Union Army.[92] Eventually, after four years of a bloody Civil War, slavery was eventually abolished in the United States through the Thirteenth Amendment to the Constitution of December 1865. This time, slave owners were not financially compensated for the end of slavery. The abolition of slavery that followed the end of the Civil War in the United States was exceptional to some extent because it freed a much larger number of slaves (approximately four million), than previous emancipations and except for Washington, DC, slave owners were not paid indemnities.

Independence without emancipation

As in the United States, independences in Brazil and in the Spanish Americas did not lead to the immediate abolition of slavery. In the various countries of Latin America, the legal abolition of slavery was a gradual and painful process that started with the ban of the slave trade from Africa and continued with the enactment of free womb laws. Planter elites composed the core of the proslavery groups, whereas the free populations of color in rural and urban areas as well as urban middle groups were among those who joined the abolitionist cause.

The transatlantic slave trade to Mexico had been inactive since 1735, but its legal ban occurred after the end of the Mexican War of Independence (1810–1821). In 1810, when the uprising against Spanish colonial rule emerged, slavery remained legal and still existed in Mexico, even though its role in the economy was not as central as it was in Brazil, Cuba, or the United States.[93] During this period, the enslaved population of African descent in Mexico was estimated between 9,000 and 15,000 men, women, and children.[94] Although the creole elites never intended to include the abolition of slavery in their program to break Mexico's colonial ties with Spain, the early rebellion that gave birth to the Mexican War of Independence was a popular movement. This early movement for independence certainly lacked a clear agenda, but its leaders called attention to the problem of racial and social inequalities that separated white creole elites from the great majority of the poor colonial population of color.[95]

Led by the Catholic priest Miguel Hidalgo y Costilla (1753–1811), who initially started a rebellion to support the Spanish king deposed by the French, the movement developed fast and eventually gathered a popular army composed mostly of poor indigenous groups, mestizos, blacks, and mulattos to overthrow the Spanish colonial rule.[96] As the rebels took control of Guanajuato, Valladolid, and Guadalajara, Hidalgo and his officials issued a number of proclamations (*bandos*) ordering the emancipation of all slaves with no compensation for slave owners.[97]

On October 18, 1810, when passing through Valladolid, Hidalgo ordered the city's mayor José Maria Anzorena (1770–1811) to issue a decree ordering the slave owners to free all slaves.[98] The proclamation also punished slave owners who refused to follow the order, by establishing that those who failed in complying with the proclamation would "inevitably suffer the death penalty and have all their property confiscated."[99] As this declaration did not have the expected impact, on December 6, 1810, Hidalgo issued another similar decree in Guadalajara. This time, the first of the three articles established that slave owners had ten days to free their slaves and those who transgressed the order would be punished with the death penalty.[100]

The proclamations emancipating slaves issued by Hidalgo during the Mexican War of Independence did not actually abolish slavery. Yet, these acts encouraged the slaves to escape and claim their freedom. Moreover, even though in the cities controlled by Hidalgo's army the slave owners may have complied with the orders to avoid retaliation, the scope of these proclamations was limited.[101] Not only did Hidalgo not have legal authority to emancipate the slaves in Mexico, but also his popular army never controlled the whole territory. Less than one year after the proclamations were issued the rebels' army was defeated by the Spanish forces, who executed Hidalgo. As the problem of slavery remained unsolved, in the years that followed there were new attempts to abolish slavery, this time led by his successor José María Morelos (1765–1815), who was also eventually killed.[102]

After more than a decade of war, Mexico became independent in 1821. The provisional government created a slaves' commission which on October 24, 1821, presented a document with proposals to ban the international slave trade to Mexico and gradually abolish slavery. Two years later, on September 26, 1823, the Constituent Assembly passed a decree that prohibited the slave trade to Mexico, confiscated vessels transporting slaves into the country, and freed the slaves who entered the country after that date. Even though the Mexican Constitution of 1824 did not address the issue of slavery, constitutions of various Mexican states, enacted between 1824 and 1827, either abolished slavery or determined that newborns should be manumitted.[103] However, in the states of Chiapas, Michoacán, and Oaxaca the legislation included provisions to indemnify the masters. Moreover, at the states' level these laws faced opposition and were not properly enforced. Similarly to the United States and the British Caribbean, slavery remained a problematic topic of debate among Mexican elites because its abolition would engender property loss and hurt the interests of the slave owners.[104]

Eventually, after much resistance, President Vicente Guerrero (1782–1831) issued a decree on September 15, 1829 abolishing slavery in Mexico.[105] With this Act, Guerrero, a man of African descent himself, earned the reputation as the "Mexican Abraham Lincoln."[106] The text of the law succinctly declared slavery abolished and freed all those who until then were considered slaves. It also stated that "when the circumstances of the treasury allow the slave owners will be indemnified under the terms established by the law."[107] But even with the promise of financial compensation, the abolition decree faced opposition from slave owners in the south of Mexico where a sugar industry was growing, and also in the north, where cotton production was flourishing.

In the next few years, slave owners found ways to contravene the law when, for example, American citizens introduced slaves disguised as indentured workers in Texas. Moreover, after the deposition of Guerrero, his successor passed a law recognizing the legality of slavery in the places it still existed. Comparable to the historical narratives that celebrate the fact that by 1785 slavery was abolished in the north of the United States, the Mexican abolition of slavery in 1829 was not a reality on the ground. Indeed, slavery continued to be the object of decrees, and it was included in the articles of the next two Constitutions of Mexico, suggesting that it remained a crucial problem until the eve of the Mexican Revolution.[108]

Other former Spanish colonies in the Americas did not abolish slavery immediately after they attained independence from Spain. As in Brazil and in the Spanish colonies of Cuba and Puerto Rico, and the United States, most newly independent countries in the Americas adopted a gradualist approach that protected the interests of the slaveholders. This reluctance in ending slavery showed how the institution remained important for their economies. Between 1811 and 1842, the Atlantic slave trade to the various former Spanish colonies in Central America and South America was legally abolished. Yet from 1843 to 1847 it reopened in Peru, as well as in Argentina and Uruguay between the 1820s and the early 1830s.[109]

Except for the Dominican Republic, which abolished both the slave trade and slavery in 1822, all the other former Spanish colonies adopted gradual abolition by first enacting free womb legislation and only later abolishing slavery. New nations that enacted early free womb legislation were seeking support of the populations of color during the wars of independence. In the areas where these laws were passed subsequently, governments and other factions fighting various wars freed enslaved men to have them joining armed forces.[110]

South American regions such as Chile and the Río de La Plata respectively enacted free womb laws on October 15, 1811 and on January 31, 1813.[111] Whereas in Chile the free womb legislation did not impose any restrictions to the newly free population, in the region of Buenos Aires young freedmen and freedwomen had to provide unpaid work to the master until fifteen years old. After this age, they were entitled to receive the amount of one *peso* per month, but would be free only when they married or reached majority age, twenty years old for males and sixteen years old for females.[112] The regions of present-day Ecuador, Colombia, Peru, and Venezuela passed free womb legislation in 1821; Uruguay in 1825; whereas Bolivia and Paraguay passed laws freeing newborns both in 1831 and 1842. In all these countries, despite the varied size of enslaved populations, slave owners resisted the new legislation and found numerous ways to avoid registering the newborns. Moreover, when time approached to effectively free the slaves who benefited from these laws, the owners found ways to extend the age of majority to twenty-five years old and even until fifty years old.[113]

Despite free womb legislation, the demise of slavery was a lengthy process in Latin America. Chile, whose slave population was very small, was the first country in South America to abolish slavery. But after the first decree of July 24, 1823, declaring that "those who until today had been slaves, are absolutely free since the publication of this agreement," the slave owners continued putting pressures on the government in order to obtain financial compensation, and three days later another decree established a series of restrictions to the legal award of free status to the former enslaved men and women.[114] Eventually the new Chilean Constitution enacted on December 29, 1823 permanently abolished slavery by declaring: "In Chile there are no slaves: whoever set foot on its territory for one calendar day will be free. Whoever has this trade cannot live here more than one month, and can never be naturalized."[115] It took Uruguay two decades after this to enact a law abolishing slavery, on December 12, 1842. But despite this abolition, enacted during the Uruguayan Civil War (1839–1851), a system of appren-ticeship was established for women and children and then reversed only with the end of the war in 1853.[116] During the next two decades, except for Brazil, Puerto Rico, and Cuba, slavery was abolished all over the Americas. In 1848, slavery was abolished in Martinique, Guadeloupe, and French Guiana.[117] The regions of present-day Ecuador, Colombia, and Panama passed legislation abolishing slavery in 1851 (effective in January 1, 1852), most of Argentina in 1853, Peru and Venezuela in 1854, Bolivia in 1861, and Paraguay in 1869.[118]

The slave trade is alive and profitable

In spite of the death of slavery in Spanish South America, the echoes of gradual abolition of slavery took much longer to be heard in Brazil. At the end of the eighteenth century, the Portuguese colony witnessed a decline in the gold production. During the early nineteenth century, a new coffee industry emerged in the southeast region, encouraging the continuity of the slave trade to the country. But since 1808, when the Portuguese royal family moved to Rio de Janeiro, opening the Brazilian market to the importation of British manufactured goods, Britain increasingly pressured Portugal to end the slave trade to Brazil. On February 19, 1810, Portugal and Britain signed two crucial treaties. Article 9 of the Treaty of Navigation and Commerce gave Britain an advantageous tariff of 15 percent of the value on British goods imported to Brazil. Moreover, in Article 10 of the Treaty of Alliance and Friendship, Portugal agreed to gradually end the slave trade to Brazil and to restrict it to its territories in Africa. In other words, the treaties of 1810 ended the colonial pact that provided to Portugal the trade monopoly with Brazil, a step that favored Brazilian independence, which like other independences in Latin America was supported by Britain.

In 1815 a treaty signed between Portugal and Britain banned the slave trade north of the equator. But even though this treaty made illegal the slave trade from West Africa to Brazil, its provisions were never fully enforced. British pressures on Brazil continued after the country became independent from Portugal in 1822. Henceforth, led by the son of the Portuguese King, Dom Pedro I (1798–1834), Brazil became an empire and the only Latin American independent nation to maintain a long-term monarchical system. In this new context, neither slavery, nor the slave trade were abolished, despite the existence of early proposals for gradual abolition.

In 1823, following the independence, the new emperor called a Constituent Assembly to write the first Constitution of Brazil. José Bonifácio d'Andrada e Silva (1763–1838), Brazil's first Prime Minister, and deputy representing São Paulo, authored a Bill proposing the gradual abolition of the slave trade and slavery to be presented to the assembly. In the introduction of his groundbreaking Bill, he blamed the Portuguese for being the pioneers in developing a "legal trade of hunting free men and selling them as slaves in the European and American markets."[119] He defended the notion that plantations worked by slaves were not profitable, and also contested the idea that slaves were property: "If the law should defend property, it must defend much more the personal freedom of men, who must not be the property of anybody without attacking Providence."[120] Among others, the Bill proposed the end of slave imports within a period of four to five years. It also proposed the creation of a register of slaves, restricted physical punishments, and even established emancipation of children of slave owners with enslaved women. Unfortunately, the innovative Bill was never presented to the deputies. After a series of political conflicts, the emperor dissolved the assembly on November 12, 1823, and Silva was arrested and sent into exile. As a result, a law establishing the end of the slave trade would have to wait almost a decade to be enacted, even though in 1826, Brazil signed a treaty with Britain, reinforcing the terms of the treaty of 1815, this time agreeing to halt the slave trade from Africa within three years.[121]

Despite British pressure to stop the international slave trade to Brazil, in the ten years that followed Brazilian independence, approximately 495,000 enslaved Africans disembarked in the new nation. Even though the Brazilian empire and its planter elites continued fully supporting the slave trade they showed signs of division.[122] When the deadline to stop the slave trade, as established in the treaty of 1826, arrived in March 1830, the slave trade continued as usual. Eventually, British pressure, along with the increasing international opposition to the slave trade, produced results. On November 7, 1831, after lengthy debates, the Brazilian Congress passed the Feijó Law, prohibiting the imports of enslaved Africans to Brazil.[123] Although there was no organized abolitionist movement in Brazil, stopping the slave trade was the first step to abolish slavery over the next several decades. Yet, in a country such as Brazil, there was a huge distance between law and reality.

The first article of the new law mandated the freeing of all slaves who entered Brazilian ports coming from outside after the date of its enactment. Yet the law exempted the slaves registered in the service of vessels from countries where slavery was permitted. The law also did not included slaves who escaped the Brazilian territory or foreign vessels, which were to be "delivered to their masters who claim them, and reexported outside Brazil."[124] Even though the law was never effectively enforced, its enactment allowed British authorities to seize vessels transporting enslaved Africans to Brazil. It also made possible the apprehension of enslaved Africans, by Brazilian authorities, after their arrival in Brazilian shores. Moreover, it established that Africans who were illegally brought to the country after the passing of the law would be freed and reexported, a provision that was never applied successfully. Consequently, the law originated a new category of "liberated Africans" in Brazil, whose legal statuses were similar to the Africans liberated by the British squadrons in other parts of the Atlantic world.[125] Once their status was confirmed, liberated Africans were employed by the Brazilian state to perform public works or by private individuals for whom they should work as servants or free workers for a period of fourteen years.[126] During the three decades after its passing, the Law of 1831 served as basis for freedom suits filed by individuals who after reaching free soil, by entering neighboring countries where slavery had been abolished, such as Uruguay, Argentina, and Peru, claimed free status once they returned to Brazil either voluntarily or by force.[127]

The Spanish empire also took measures to stop the slave trade. In 1835, Spain signed a treaty with Britain that prohibited the slave trade to Cuba and Puerto Rico, replacing the previous Anglo–Spanish treaty signed in 1817, which established that the slave trade to the remaining Spanish colonies should end in 1820. Britain, as it did with Brazil, also pressured Spain to free the slaves who entered its colonies after 1820, but evidently the efforts to enforce these treaties were not successful.[128] In 1845, a law prohibiting the slave trade to Cuba and Puerto Rico passed in the Spanish Cortes, adding to the previous treaties of 1817 and 1835.[129] Despite legal prohibitions, the slave trade from Africa continued. Between 1820 and 1867, when the ban of the Cuban slave trade was effectively enforced, approximately 551,911 enslaved Africans disembarked in Cuba, whereas between 1820 and 1842, Puerto Rico imported nearly 14,178 slaves.[130] Between 1832, after the first legal ban to the slave trade, and the passing of the Eusébio de Queirós Law (Law no. 581 of September 4, 1850) that outlawed slave imports for a second time, slave merchants illegally introduced nearly 737,000 enslaved Africans to the Brazilian empire.[131] The slave trade persisted because despite the risks, for many slave merchants operating in Cuba and Brazil, including the notorious Julián Zulueta (1814–1878), Pedro Blanco (1795–1854), Francisco Félix de Souza (1754–1849), and Joaquim Pereira Marinho (1816–1887), it was a business that allowed them to make extraordinary profits.[132] For slave owners in these two areas where the sugar and coffee industry were expanding, the use of a slave workforce was still the most lucrative and accessible option.

After the legal ban of the slave trade to the country, Brazilian government and elites started debating the paths to the end of slavery. Still a monarchy, the Brazilian empire was already engaged in a process of modernization and urbanization. The expansion of the coffee industry in the southeast had weakened the northeast planter class, the monarchy's main supporter. Brazil had large freeborn and freed black populations. The high rate of manumissions, especially through self-purchase, the low natural growth of the slave population due to gender imbalance and death rate, and the ban of the slave trade from Africa, led to the decline of the number of available slaves.[133] In order to offset the diminished number of slaves, southeastern planters started employing European immigrants on coffee plantations. Nevertheless, enslaved men, women, and children remained the main workforce in the rural areas until the 1880s. As the prices of slaves increased, the domestic slave trade from the northeast to the southeast region, zone of the rich coffee industry, intensified.

As in several societies of the Americas, one of the main arguments that continued supporting the existence of slavery relied on the old principle that slaves were property, which could not be confiscated without indemnification. In 1869, an article appeared in *Radical Paulistano*, a newspaper published by the radical wing of the Liberal Party, denounced the imperial government for failing to enforce the Law of 1831 that banned the slave trade to Brazil:

> The voices of abolitionists have emphasized a highly criminal act, and for many years greatly supported by our unworthy authorities. It is the fact that most of the existing African slaves in Brazil were imported after the law forbidding the trafficking enacted in 1831. Fearing the public opinion, the owners of free Africans start selling them to places distant from their residences [. . .] We can state that many Africans are living in this city in identical circumstances, with the knowledge of the authorities, who are the main protectors of this horrible crime.[134]

The article is attributed to black abolitionist, journalist, lawyer, and poet, Luiz Gama (1830–1882). Born free, he was the son of an African freedwoman and a well-to-do individual man of Portuguese origin, who illegally sold him into slavery, when he was ten years old. In the household of his master, he learned how to read and write, and by 1848 he obtained his freedom.[135] During the 1860s, Gama became one of the greatest Brazilian abolitionists. His articles are a good example of how Brazilian abolitionists convincingly utilized legal arguments to oppose the claims of slave owners and public authorities who defended slavery. He overtly denounced the illegal enslavement of Africans who had arrived in Brazil after the legal ban of the slave trade of 1831. Indeed, the Anglo–Brazilian mixed commission courts and other Brazilian authorities liberated approximately 11,000 of the 786,000 enslaved Africans illegally introduced in Brazil between 1831 and 1856.[136]

Property rights above all rights

After the end of the Civil War and the abolition of slavery in the United States, Brazil and the Spanish colonies of Cuba and Puerto Rico were the only societies in the Americas where slavery continued. As part of the wave of liberal reforms in Spain and its colonies and responding to the context of the Civil War in the United States, discussions on how to replace the slave workforce also emerged in Spain and its Caribbean colonies. Bringing together Cubans and Spanish citizens, the first campaigns to abolish slavery and stop the slave trade culminated with the creation of the Spanish Abolitionist Society in 1865.[137] However, the importance of slavery in the two Spanish islands in the Caribbean differed. Whereas slavery declined in Puerto Rico, it expanded in Cuba.[138] Although Cuban slave owners and planters recognized that the end of slavery was near, exactly like in the United States and Brazil they continued subscribing to the idea that emancipation should be gradual, by relying on two main points. First, slave owners should receive financial compensation. Second, embodying a paternalistic view regarding the slave population, masters should continue to take advantage of the work of former slaves, through a system of apprenticeship.

As in other societies of the Americas where gradual abolition prevailed, in Cuba and Puerto Rico the ruling classes managed to control the entire negotiated process that led to the end of slavery. Things changed particularly fast after the end of the Civil War and the abolition of slavery in the United States, which put additional pressures on stopping Cuban slave trade activity. In 1866, the Spanish government called a meeting with representatives from the colonies of Puerto Rico and Cuba to discuss political and economic reforms.[139] Differences between the two colonies were evident. Although slave labor was important in Puerto Rico, Cuban slave population was much larger and central for its lucrative sugar industry. During the debates on abolition, whereas Puerto Rican deputies agreed with the idea of suppressing slavery, delegates from Cuba rather emphasized gradual emancipation. But Cuban elites continued to be increasingly unhappy with the Spanish administration. Despite proposing reforms, the Spanish Crown created new income taxes and continued excluding the creoles from important positions. Once the meetings were concluded, planters rejected the prospect of gradual emancipation. Yet, whereas in Spain the debates about gradual emancipation intensified after the deposition of Queen Isabella II in 1868, in Cuba, the colonists from the eastern part of the island embraced the idea of independence in an uprising that gave origin to the Ten Years War (1868–1878).[140] Slave rebels and free coloreds, who were also discriminated against by colonial policies, joined forces with the elite groups to fight for the abolition of slavery and independence from Spain.[141]

In December 1870, the colored rebels were eventually successful in pushing the rebellious colonists to declare the abolition of slavery in eastern Cuba.[142] But during a period of war, newly freedmen and freedwomen were assigned with ambiguous positions that kept them subordinated to the white elites.[143] Additionally, this first emancipation did not really affect Cuba's entire slave system, because most slaves resided and worked in the western portion of the island, the region responsible for the largest production of sugar and which was not affected by the war.[144]

Spain feared that the US support of the rebellion in the eastern region of the island could lead to Cuban independence. Despite risking the loss of its colony, in order to face the rebels who had abolished slavery in that part of the island Spain accelerated the discussion about the gradual abolition of slavery in its colonies. On July 4, 1870, the Spanish Parliament passed the Moret Law, which, similarly to the US Emancipation Proclamation, was conceived as a wartime response. Authored by Segismundo Moret y Prendergast (1833–1913), an economist and abolitionist, who was by then the Minister of Overseas in the cabinet of the provisional government of Juan Prim (1814–1870), the law launched gradual compensated emancipation in the colonies of Cuba and Puerto Rico.

The Moret Law's first article emancipated all children born to enslaved mothers after its publication. Its second article also freed all slaves born after September 17, 1868. The third article declared free "all slaves who had served under the Spanish flag or who in any capacity have helped the troops during the current insurrection in Cuba."[145] In addition, this article determined that the masters of the newly freed slaves who had remained loyal to Spain would receive financial compensation equivalent to the value of the slaves they owned. As expected, however, insurgent masters received no financial reward.[146] The fourth article of the Moret Law emancipated the slaves older than sixty years old as well. The law also included a series of restrictions. On the one hand, it created a system of *patronato* for the slaves freed under its first and second articles. This system established that *libertos* (recently freed slaves) were to remain under the custody of the enslaved mother's master, who could use their workforce for free. It also determined that when the newly freed individuals reached eighteen years old, they were entitled to receive a wage in the amount equivalent to the half of the salary of a free person, according to class and profession. Still, half of these earnings would be reserved to a fund for each individual. Upon reaching twenty-two years of age the *patronato* system would end and the *liberto* would receive the funds saved during the last four years. The law also established that free fathers of *libertos* could claim their children if they indemnified the masters with the amount corresponding to the expenses made on behalf of them. Moreover, as the law included the creation of a national slave register, unregistered slaves were to be declared free by the state. In the decade after the passing of the Moret Law, the number of slaves in Cuba decreased from nearly 300,000 to 200,000. Still, few of the emancipated slaves were individuals in working age.[147]

While eastern Cubans fought to abolish slavery, antislavery ideas gained additional force and visibility in Brazil. Favored by international and domestic factors, by the end of the 1860s the country witnessed the emergence of an organized abolitionist movement. The approaching end of the Paraguayan War (1864–1870) contributed to the discussion about the gradual abolition of slavery in the Brazilian Congress and in the public sphere. During the early years of the war, fought between Paraguay and the alliance formed by Brazil, Argentina, and Uruguay, as had occurred during the American Revolutionary War in the previous century, Brazilian masters either donated their slaves to the army or navy or freed their slaves "to serve in their place or in the place of a son."[148] However, between 1867 and 1868, in order to encourage this practice the imperial government started compensating the masters to free their slaves to fight, contributing to fueling the debate on the abolition of slavery.[149]

Brazil could not escape the cycle of abolitions that started in Saint-Domingue at the end of the eighteenth century and culminated with emancipation in the United States in 1865. At the domestic level, the country was witnessing a process of urbanization that propelled the discussion about modernization among the emergent urban groups. Slavery, once understood as a given, was now perceived as a horrible and inhumane institution that could not fit the modernization project promoted by these groups. The division among urban and rural elites embodied in the disputes between the Liberal Party and the Conservative Party that governed the country eventually led to the approval of gradual emancipation legislation.[150]

Yet, as in other parts of the Americas, influential Brazilian slave owners and planters opposed the abolition of slavery by arguing that its suppression would put in danger the country's agricultural economy.[151] Elites embraced the idea of gradual and compensated abolition as a path to end slavery while at the same time avoiding hurting the interests of slave owners and preventing possible violent outcomes. In 1863, Agostinho Marques Perdigão Malheiro (1824–1881), attorney and general deputy for the Conservative Party supported this gradualist vision, by invoking the idea of a free womb law, in a public speech at the Brazilian Attorneys Institute of which he was the president.[152] Familiar with the British and French literature, Malheiro endorsed gradual and compensated abolition of slavery in his three-volume book *A escravidão no Brasil* (Slavery in Brazil), published in 1866. He argued that although illegitimate, slavery was a legal institution, reason why only a positive law could end slavery and slave owners should be compensated.[153] The jurist emphasized the need to protect the rights of slave owners in order to avoid a possible violent outcome as it had occurred in the United States, where the war consumed a great amount of money, "killed hundreds of thousands of people, disabled and made suffer millions of others, flooded with blood the fields of numerous battles [. . .] and brought the public murder of Abraham Lincoln," whom he described as the "first elected [. . .] representative of the abolitionist opinion."[154]

In the 1870s, the debates about the gradual abolition of slavery in the Brazilian Congress revealed the ways Liberals and Conservatives supported slave owners, and their concern with the potential financial losses that emancipation would generate. In various speeches, congressmen constantly referred to slaves as "rude, stupid, uneducated, fanatic, and believers of mysterious deities, in fetishism."[155] As elsewhere in the Americas, proposals of reparations to the future freed population were absent from their speeches. Instead, these politicians constantly expressed the fears and anxieties of Brazilian elites: "And what should we wait of these brutish spirits? The police will take care of them, forcing them into work, but they, judging themselves free as any other citizen, will revolt even more, and all will be worse."[156] Similar to Mexico, Cuba, and the United States, these early debates reveal the concerns of both Liberals and Conservatives about how to compensate the masters for the loss of slave property, and how to get rid of the populations of African descent by either introducing more European immigrants or sending them outside national borders.[157]

On May 12, 1871 a Bill freeing the newborns to enslaved mothers was presented to the Brazilian Chamber of Deputies. Although it is impossible to precisely determine the free and enslaved population for that year, based on the numbers of the first Brazilian Census of 1872, there were approximately 1,510,806 slaves in Brazil, representing 15.2 percent of the country's total population, estimated at 9,930,478.[158] The Bill led to several months of public debates between abolitionists and the supporters of the large landowners, which were vastly disseminated by the press. Notwithstanding the divergences, Liberals and Conservatives agreed to establish the guidelines to preserve the interests of the slave owners and to determine how the Brazilian state would compensate them. Both parties obviously disregarded any possible measures to support the future freed population.[159]

Eventually, the Rio Branco Law or Free Womb Law (Law no. 20140) passed in the Brazilian Congress and was enacted on September 28, 1871.[160] Despite recognizing its gaps, the white abolitionist deputy of the Liberal Party, Joaquim Nabuco (1849–1910), praised the law as a great achievement: "imperfect, incomplete, ill-conceived, unjust, and even absurd as it looks to us today, that law was nothing less than a moral blockade of slavery. Its only decisive and irreversible part was this principle: 'No one again will be born a *slave*'."[161] This statement, though, was not totally accurate. Unsurprisingly, like all legislation emancipating newborns to enslaved mothers enacted in other parts of the Americas, the first article of the law established that although freed, the child would remain the property of the enslaved mother's master until the age of eight years. Then, the owner could decide either to free the child and receive a financial compensation of 600 *mil-réis* (in thirty-year bonds of 6 percent) from the Brazilian state or to continue using the child's workforce for free until twenty-one years old.[162] According to slave registries of São Paulo's province, slave owners who freed 158,093 slaves as a result of the law of 1871 obtained approximately 414 *contos* and 882 *mil-réis* in financial compensation.[163]

The Free Womb Law also created an emancipation fund to manumit slaves in the various Brazilian provinces. Moreover, as previously implemented in the states of Vermont and New York, the law also mandated for the first time the general registration of the entire Brazilian slave population, which should include information such as name, sex, state, aptitude to work, and filiation.[164] The law also mandated that slaves who were not registered within an one-year period would be considered freed.[165] Even if slave owners found numerous ways to avoid the new requirement, at the time of its enactment, the law did not emancipate any living slaves. Still, the register became an important instrument to identify Africans brought to Brazil illegally after 1831, as well as their descendants, and the individuals enslaved unlawfully.

As Brazil passed its Free Womb Law, debates on emancipation continued in Cuba and Puerto Rico. Following popular demonstrations in several Spanish cities, on December 23, 1872, Minister of Overseas Tomás Maria Mosquera (1823–1890) eventually introduced in the Spanish Parliament a Bill abolishing slavery.[166] On March 22, 1873, the Spanish Parliament passed a law ending slavery in Puerto Rico, which freed around 29,335 slaves.[167] Yet, as in the British Caribbean, the law established that newly freed slaves would have to work under three-year labor contracts to their former masters. Moreover, slave owners obtained financial compensation of 200 pesos per slave, and excluded any form of reparations to the freed population.

After Puerto Rico's emancipation, Cuba maintained slavery for seven more years. Eventually, on February 13, 1880, the Patronato Law passed in the Spanish Parliament. In theory, the new law abolished slavery and established an eight-year period of apprenticeship, by renaming the newly freed slaves *patrocinados* whereas the former masters were now called *patronos*. Despite the change of names, as Rebecca J. Scott explains, the relations between former masters and slaves remained untouched. Under the new system, a *patrocinado* was not legally free, whereas a *patrono* maintained the right to use the labor of his *patrocinados* and to transfer ownership to another master.[168] According to the new law, depending on age, *patrocinados* would receive an amount of one to three pesos per month, and *patronos* also had to pay for food, clothing, and provide the *patrocinados* with instruction. The law also introduced a decreasing scale of prices for slaves wishing to purchase their freedom. Finally, every year the *patronos* had to free one-quarter of their *patrocinados*.[169]

The Patronato Law included the creation of *juntas de patronato*, councils charged of enforcing the new *patronato* system. It also established *juntas protectoras de libertos*, whose official mission was to protect both the interests of *patronos* and *patrocinados*, as if such a feat were possible. In addition to having among its members notorious slaveholders and slave merchants such as the infamous Julián Zulueta, the new ambiguous system had gaps and was not effectively enforced all over the island.[170] Thus, despite the absence of an organized abolitionist movement, about two years after the implementation of the *patronato* system, Cuban elites and a few politicians opposed to the colonial government started proposing its end.[171] Eventually, the *patronato* ended on October 7, 1886, two years prior the established date of 1888. As many *patrocinados* obtained their freedom in the five years that followed the creation of *patronato*, at the final demise of this system, Cuban registers included approximately 99,566 *patrocinados*.[172]

The last bastion of slavery

After the end of slavery in Cuba, Brazil remained the only slave society in the Americas. Since the abolition of the slave trade from Africa to Brazil in 1850, large-slaveholding Brazilian elites started defending policies to encourage the immigration of European workers to replace the slave workforce. During these years, as in other societies that heavily relied on slave labor like Cuba and the United States, elite groups, including politicians, intellectuals, and slave owners debated what future they envisioned for the future freed populations, and how they could be integrated or not in Brazilian society. Yet, as underscored by Robert Conrad, most Brazilians and also many abolitionists failed to envision what kind of society they wanted after the end of slavery.[173] This moderate position can be explained by the fact that except for a few exceptions such as Luiz Gama and black journalist José do Patrocínio (1854–1905), whose mother was an enslaved woman, most abolitionists were whites and members of economic and political elite circles.

Until the middle of the 1870s, most Brazilian abolitionists accepted the principle of property rights and the idea of gradual abolition. Although foreseeing the end of slavery, they rarely publicly opposed the idea of financial compensation to slave owners. As they rather viewed the end of slavery as a simple transition from slave labor to free labor, they could hardly start any kind of discussion addressing the need of financial and material reparations to former slaves. Despite these limitations, by the middle of the 1870s, Brazilian abolitionists brought to the public debate for the first time the issue of land distribution to the future freed population. In the context of a country where land was highly concentrated in the hands of few very wealthy individuals, redistributing land could certainly be conceived as a form of reparations for slavery.

In 1875, black abolitionist André Rebouças (1838–1898) was the first to emphasize the need to grant land to freed populations in his book *Á Democracia Rural Brazileira* (The Brazilian Rural Democracy).[174] Although addressed to planters and slave owners and not to the slaves or the freed population who were not able to read, the book contained numerous proposals which to some extent could be understood as material reparations to the freed population. Among others, Rebouças defended the need to distribute land and provide education not only to the freed population, but also to the European immigrants (*colonos*).[175] Using examples from French colonies in the Caribbean, the United States, and even Mexico, Rebouças attempted to convince readers that by replacing slaves with free workers agriculture would be more productive and profitable to landowners. His proposal had some influence on the works of other politicians. Three years later, the white Liberal politician, Viscount and Field Marshall Henrique Pedro Carlos de Beaurepaire-Rohan (1812–1894), also wrote an essay proposing land redistribution to former slaves in order to transform freedmen and freedwomen into *foreiros* (tenant farmers).[176] However, neither of these authors considered that in order to distribute land among the freed populations and colonists, it would be necessary to attack the interests of large landowners, first by emancipating their slaves, and second by expropriating and dividing their large estates, proposals that no large landowner would ever accept.

During the 1880s, proslavery elites continued to defend the idea that slaves were property and consequently slavery could not end without compensation to slave owners. Brazilian abolitionists, now opposed to the idea of indemnifying the slave owners, responded to these objections by using legal arguments. Created on October 30, 1880, the Sociedade Brasileira Contra a Escravidão (Brazilian Society Against Slavery) was presided over by Joaquim Nabuco, and gathered in its ranks important public figures, including intellectuals, lawyers, politicians, journalists, and artists, and a few black abolitionists such as Gama and Rebouças. In its first public manifesto the society attacked the legality of Brazilian slavery by reminding the reader:

> that it is false that most of the slaves in the country are legally owned; the register, even produced with visible bad faith, would have by itself denounced the violation of the Law of October 7 1831. After the prohibition of the slave trade, the country's slavery was still renovated through it. Numerous Africans who are employed in agriculture, were criminally imported, and the children of these enslaved constituted the new generation of slaves. Not even the excuse that slavery is legal property

is in its favor: on the contrary it is illegal and criminal in such a large degree that the simple revision of the titles of slave property would suffice to extinguish it.[177]

Articles with similar arguments also appeared in the various numbers of the society's newspaper *O Abolicionista* (The Abolitionist), whose aim was to disseminate abolitionist propaganda among Brazilian elite circles. On its pages the newspaper reproduced letters of support to the abolitionist cause by prominent individuals and even letters from slave owners announcing the emancipation of their slaves. Among the most intriguing supporters of the group was the former Confederate and slave owner Henry Washington Hilliard (1808–1892), who represented the United States in Brazil from 1877 to 1881. Despite his recent proslavery past, at that point Hilliard had changed his mind and claimed the economic benefits of the end of slavery in the south of the United States. In Brazil, he became a supporter of gradual emancipation. On their end, the members of the Brazilian Society Against Slavery praised him and apparently did not mind having among them a former Confederate. Hilliard's support was so appreciated by the society that in 1880, the organization offered a banquet in his honor at an elite club in Rio de Janeiro. Contemporary observers reported that the ballroom was decorated with pictures of the Confederates' enemy, Abraham Lincoln, an event that apparently irritated Brazilian slaveholding elites.[178]

O *Abolicionista* also reported on Nabuco's travels in Europe and the United States, where he campaigned for the end of slavery in Brazil. It also disseminated letters of support from international antislavery groups from France and Britain, including the British and Foreign Anti-Slavery Society, that supported the abolitionist cause in Brazil.[179] As in its inaugural manifesto, several articles of *O Abolicionista* defended the idea that slavery kept Brazil backward and only free labor could bring progress to the country. In its first number of November 1, 1880, an article stated that "slavery was publicly exposed as reducing free persons into captivity; because the current slaves are the children of those imported, or the African themselves, which the law, forty-nine years ago, declared free."[180] Another article reported Nabuco's words who as early as in 1880, claimed that "Brazil was the only country that today prevents slavery from being declared a crime against humanity, subjected such as piracy and the traffic of slaves, to the action of the international law."[181]

Likewise, the next number of *O Abolicionista* reproduced an article by Luiz Gama, in which he denounced public auctions of slaves, whose announcements contained the ages and the regions of provenance of Africans to be sold, showing not only that the men and women on sale were born in Africa, but that they were illegally brought to Brazil after the first legal ban of 1831.[182] In one article entitled "Legal Question" published over three numbers of *O Abolicionista*, Gama explored in detail the legal history of the abolition of the Atlantic slave trade to Brazil. Once again, he focused on the illegal ownership of Africans who were illegally introduced in the country. These recurrent complaints evidently underscored that most of the two last generations of Africans transported to Brazil, after the enactment of the Law of 1831 which banned the slave trade from Africa to Brazil, along with their descendants were being illegally held in bondage. Moreover, as in the United States, numerous free and freed individuals unlawfully enslaved had been brought to the country through the southern borders of the Brazilian empire.[183] Yet, neither Gama, nor Nabuco, discussed in *O Abolicionista* how to provide reparations to the future freed population.[184] Eventually, although these grievances had some repercussion in the public sphere, the majority of Africans illegally imported to Brazil remained slaves. Slavery persisted in Brazil as a strong institution.[185]

On May 9, 1883, when even Cuba had already started the process of ending slavery with the creation of the *patronato* system, the Confederação Abolicionista (Abolitionist Confederation) was created. Led by José do Patrocínio, the new confederation gathered all Brazilian abolitionists organizations under its umbrella. Its manifesto, written by Rebouças and Patrocínio, presented a more radical view of emancipation by rejecting gradualism and voicing the idea of immediate emancipation without payment of indemnifications to the masters. The document denounced slave owners who established prices for their slaves that were much higher than their original value, in order to obtain the maximum possible amounts from the newly created emancipation funds established all over the country.[186] By explaining these cases, abolitionists demonstrated that in practice, in manumitting slaves by using the emancipation funds, slave owners were obtaining financial compensation: "immoral industry has no right to compensation [...]. Abolition should be immediate, instantaneous and without any compensation."[187]

In contrast with previous moderate and gradualist views of emancipation that considered the possibility of compensating slave owners, the manifesto argued toward the opposite direction, by calculating the sums due by the slave owners to the enslaved population:

> Do they have, by any chance, an idea of the sum they owe in salary to the generations that succeeded in captivity for three centuries? [...] Let's take the number of 1,500,000 slaves with a salary of 1$000, during 300 years, or 90,000 business days, and we will arrive to the prodigious number of 135,000,000 *contos de réis*. [...] In the twelve years that followed after the Rio Branco Law [Free Womb Law], you have usurped from the slave, only in salaries: 5,400,00 *contos de réis*![188]

By bringing the discussion around to the amount due to the slaves and not to the slave owners, these abolitionists invoked reparations for slavery in the public sphere, perhaps for the first time in Brazil. The document stated that the abolition of slavery should be conceived "as reparation for the spoliations, atrocities, and crimes committed by the slaveholders, since the colonial times."[189] Condemning the idea of compensating slave owners and planters and emphasizing their debt toward the enslaved population, this document shows that although rarely, even before the abolition of slavery in Brazil, the issue of financial reparations to the enslaved population appeared in the discourses of some abolitionists.

In 1884, as the abolitionist movement grew all over Brazil, the question of material reparations to former slaves through land redistribution emerged with the proposal of a new Bill by Manuel Pinto de Sousa Dantas (1831–1894), Senator of the Liberal Party and president of the cabinet of ministers. The Dantas Bill or Bill No. 48 established not only the emancipation of enslaved men and women greater than sixty years old, but also a series of other measures envisioning the future of the newly freed populations. As formulated by André Rebouças ten years before in his book *Á Democracial Rural Brazileira*, the Bill proposed the awarding land to European immigrants and to former slaves.[190]

In addition, following a similar orientation, on March 25, 1884, the positivists of Rio de Janeiro released a manifesto dedicated to "the sainted memory of the first of the blacks, Toussaint Louverture (1746–1803), Dictator of Haiti, promoter and martyr of the freedom of his race."[191] The document, authored by Miguel Lemos (1854–1917), argued that the "man cannot be considered *property* of anybody: the *producer* of human capital, in no way can be confused with the product of his work."[192] Defending the necessity of establishing a Republican dictatorship, the manifesto called for the immediate abolition of slavery with no indemnification to the slaveholders. Despite advocating the need to attach ex-slaves to the land, the document also suggested that these properties should remain under the masters' control.[193] Still, the manifesto also recommended the creation of schools of primary instruction to be maintained by landowners, the regulation of working hours, and decent salaries to the freed population, proposals which, in the Brazilian situation, could be understood as a form of reparation to the future emancipated population.

Proslavery groups submitted twenty-four petitions against the Dantas Bill. Emulating the abolitionist model, they organized a confederation to oppose the end of slavery.[194] Eventually, when the Bill was introduced to the Brazilian Chamber of Deputies on July 15, 1884, there was enormous opposition by proslavery groups, and great division among the deputies. During the congressional debates, slaveholders accused their opponents, including the well-known jurist and abolitionist Rui Barbosa (1849–1823), of spreading communist ideas. According to the proslavery group, abolition would put land ownership at risk.[195] With the house divided, a no-confidence vote was called, and the proslavery group won the vote. Because of this division, the cabinet of ministers was summoned to take a position, which essentially reproduced the vote of the Chamber of Deputies.

On July 30, 1884, to avoid a defeat and using its special powers, emperor Dom Pedro II (1825–1891) decided to dissolve the Chamber of Deputies, and call new elections.[196] Meanwhile in the context of a more radicalized abolitionist movement, Nabuco, Rebouças, and Patrocínio along with their supporters, organized massive street demonstrations in various capitals of Brazil. As the electoral campaign evolved in 1884, the provinces of Ceará and Amazonas emancipated their slaves. The capital of Rio Grande do Sul, Porto Alegre, also emancipated its slaves. The abolitionists now defended an agrarian reform that would award land to the freed population. Other politicians associated with the positivist doctrine and who defended the establishment of a Republic system welcomed these proposals and campaigned for the candidates who opposed slavery.[197]

In 1885, the Congressman João Maurício Wanderley (1815–1889), known as Baron of Cotegipe, introduced a new Bill authored by the senator José Antônio Saraiva (1823–1895), Conservative Party, to replace the Dantas Bill. The new Bill offered the possibility to declare the slave's filiation as "unknown" thereby eliminating the problem of exposing the owners who illegally purchased enslaved Africans imported after 1831. Moreover, this new version dropped several articles of the previous Bill, and increased the established prices for the slaves. More importantly, it introduced financial compensation to the slave owners.[198]

In 1885, the Sexagenarian Law (or Law Saraiva-Cotegipe) freed enslaved individuals older than sixty years. But the new legislation also determined that in order to compensate the masters the newly emancipated slaves should work three additional years at no cost or until the age of sixty-five.[199] Similarly to the Free Womb Law, the Sexagenarian Law established a mandatory register of all slaves and compensation to the masters. Unsurprisingly, the new law did not contain any provisions with reparations to elderly former slaves.[200]

The growth of the abolitionist movement and the ineffectiveness of the two emancipationist laws were evident. But starting in the 1870s, and especially during the 1880s, slaves led protests as well as massive flights in urban and rural areas.[201] Slave insurgency along with widespread demands to end slavery contributed to deepening the crisis of the Brazilian slave system.[202] In 1886, the year that slavery was abolished in Cuba, Law no. 3.310 revoked the article 60 of the Criminal Code of 1830 and Law no. 4 of June 10, 1835 that imposed whipping sentences on slaves. The final collapse of slavery seemed to be near in Brazil.

On the eve of the abolition of slavery in Brazil, enslaved men and women led massive manumission campaigns.[203] Fearing revolts, masters freed thousands of slaves. Meanwhile, men and women who remained enslaved ran away in great numbers, in the coffee zones of Brazil's southeast. Still, slaveholders counted on their representatives in the Chamber of Deputies to obtain financial compensation, or at least some kind of measure allowing them to maintain relations of dominance with the future freed population.[204]

After passing in the Chamber of Deputies on May 8, and in the Senate, on May 13, 1888, Princess Isabel (1846–1921), the regent, eventually signed the Golden Law, which freed nearly 700,000 slaves, most of them in the southeast region, where the coffee industry was located.[205] Although the newly freed population was numerically significant, it was small in comparison to the existing black Brazilian population, who obtained freedom in the previous decades through other available means.[206]

A pending debt

From 1517 to 1888, wherever slavery existed in the Americas, slaves were legally recognized as property. Only in the most extreme cases did abolitionists challenge this fact. So it was that wherever slavery ended through gradual abolition, slave owners either obtained funds and loans to compensate for their alleged financial losses or to continue using the work of the freedmen and freedwomen. Despite different contexts during the era of emancipation, the issue of financial and material reparations to the former slaves seldom surfaced in the abolitionist debates. Rare were the examples of former slaves like Belinda Sutton from Massachusetts who either demanded or were successful in obtaining reparations for the period they lived in bondage. The plea to redress the years of abuse to which enslaved men, women, and children were submitted during slavery remained largely ignored. Most abolitionists neglected the need to draw a plan to provide the newly freed population with better living and work conditions as well as with decent wages, access to land, and education. Although there were isolated cases of demands for reparations to former slaves or to individuals who were unlawfully enslaved, the real fight for reparations for slavery and the Atlantic slave trade was about to begin.

3

"We Helped to Pay This Cost"

In the decades that followed the abolition of slavery in the Americas, former slaves and their descendants started fighting either collectively or individually for material and financial reparations for slavery. During this time, slaves requested, from the governments and former masters, land and pensions to cover the period during which they provided unpaid labor. Yet, they met many hurdles. Haiti, the first country to abolish slavery in the American continent, faced enormous obstacles to the construction of a new society free from human bondage. To obtain the recognition of its independence, the leaders of the slave revolt who ruled the new nation, most of whom were either former slaves or descendants of slaves, agreed to pay a huge financial indemnity to France. In the British and French Caribbean, economies where the workforce became scarce, former planters and government officers often coerced freedmen and freedwomen to continue performing agricultural work in very precarious conditions. In most of these societies, newly freedpeople competed for wages with newly arrived immigrants and indentured workers.

In the decade after the legal abolition of slavery in the United States, during the Reconstruction Era (1865–1877), former slaves had access to full citizenship. Therefore, at least initially, most educated African Americans focused their efforts, not on demanding financial and material reparations for slavery, but rather on securing the newly acquired civil rights. Yet, this new era did not last long. White southerners opposed these rights through a variety of legal artifices and growing racial violence, by impeding African Americans from effectively achieving equal rights. Moreover, despite the creation of the Freedmen's Bureau at the end of the Civil War in the United States, by the end of the nineteenth century all attempts to redistribute land to former slaves had failed.

In this context of unachieved citizenship and growing racial hatred, thousands of US freedmen and freedwomen fought for resources which they understood were owed to them by the government and former masters. Led by an elderly black woman, and supported by hundreds of aged former slaves, the National Ex-Slave Mutual Relief, Bounty and Pension Association of the United States of America gathered together freedpeople to petition Congress to pass legislation providing them with pensions. In their written discourses, correspondence, and other written materials, the leaders of this movement clearly showed that pensions for the work they performed during bondage, which by nature consisted of unpaid labor, was a form of restitution for what was stolen from them. The ex-slaves pension movement became the first, the largest, and the most enduring initiative demanding payment for the years during which enslaved men and women provided unpaid labor to their masters. This movement constituted the first movement requesting reparations for slavery in the Americas.

To a lesser or greater extent, former slave owners were always successful in obtaining indemnities for the loss of slave property. Haiti had to pay huge amounts of financial compensation to France to obtain recognition for its independence. Following the abolition of slavery in the British and the French Caribbean as well as in the American colonies of Sweden (1846), Denmark (1848), and of the Netherlands (1863), slaves did not obtain reparations, but the governments of these European powers paid indemnities to former slave owners. In Cuba, Puerto Rico, and Brazil free womb laws provided compensation to the masters as well.

Still, after emancipation these large slave societies in the Americas had not witnessed any collective demands of financial reparations. Providing reparations to former slaves was never a central concern for white abolitionists and legislators in the Americas, but at least in Cuba, and for a short period of time in the United States, former slaves succeeded in obtaining some civil rights, including the right to vote. Individually and in very small groups, freedmen and freedwomen used the judicial system to attempt to obtain reparations for slavery. Although these claims were not successful, they demonstrate that calls for financial, material, and symbolic reparations for slavery have an established history.

This chapter shows that after the abolition of slavery, demands of reparations for slavery were entangled with broader debates about the future of former slave societies. Whether in the United States, Cuba or Brazil, freedpeople fought to have access not only to civil rights but also to material resources. Individually or gathered in associations, former slaves addressed demands for reparations to the governments and to their former masters. What elements motivated these requests? What arguments did these social actors sustain when calling for reparations for the time they lived in bondage? Combining macro-history and micro-history, this chapter looks at how the broader contexts and the actions led by individuals and groups, especially freedwomen, favored or prevented the emergence of demands of reparations between the end of the nineteenth century and the three first decades of the twentieth century.

Paying the huge price

Following its Declaration of Independence, Haiti continued dealing with great social and economic instability. In 1806, Dessalines was assassinated and left the nation divided: Alexandre Pétion (1770–1818) ruled the southern Republic of Haiti, whereas Henri Christophe (1767–1820) proclaimed himself sovereign of the Northern Kingdom of Haiti. Meanwhile, France persisted in its retaliations against the young black nation. By refusing to recognize the new country's independence, the French nourished fruitless hopes of regaining control of its former colony. Between 1804 and 1806, the French were successful in obtaining embargoes from the Danish West Indies and the United States against Haiti, even though the trade with the new black nation never really came to an end.[1] France also pressured European countries and the United States to prevent them from officially recognizing Haitian independence.

After the defeat of Napoleon Bonaparte and the Treaty of Paris of May 1814, the obstacles to the recognition of Haiti as a sovereign nation persisted. During the Congress of Vienna in 1815, European powers gave back to France its boundaries of 1792, therefore acknowledging its rights over Haiti.[2] Despite these hindrances, the new nation never remained completely isolated.[3] King Christophe developed close relations with British merchants and abolitionists, especially with Thomas Clarkson, who served as his ambassador of sorts in Europe. Still, the British government, in agreement with France, refused to recognize Haitian liberation or to cultivate formal diplomatic relations with the new independent country.[4] The justification for this refusal was clear. Although Britain outlawed its slave trade in 1807, the institution of slavery was fully preserved in the British Caribbean. As the very existence of Haiti was a threat to the preservation of slavery in the neighboring colonies, Britain sought to establish the terms of official relations with the young nation.

As the Bourbon Restoration (1814–1830) started, former French colonists renewed their attempts to foster lucrative trade relations with Haiti. In 1814, French representatives came to the island to negotiate with Pétion and Christophe. They had the clear intent of regaining control of the former colony. These delegates proposed that Haiti pay financial compensation to France in exchange for the recognition of its independence. In his correspondence with Christophe, Thomas Clarkson advised the king to pay the requested indemnification, but only if doing so proved "reasonable and moderate, and such as you can pay without any great sacrifice, either at once or by installments in a course of years."[5]

The article 12 of the "General Provisions" of the Constitution of Haiti (1805) established that "all property which formerly belonged to any white Frenchmen is incontestably and of right confiscated to the use of the state."[6] Even though the French government had already provided slaveholders and planters who fled Saint-Domingue with financial assistance, they persisted in their requests for indemnifications to cover property losses incurred during the revolution. Avid to reestablish business relations with the old colony, French merchants also demanded that the government solve the impasse by recognizing the independence of the new nation.

In this "tug-of-war" context, Pétion was more inclined to pay financial compensation to France. But Christophe never accepted such a suggestion. In a letter, dated November 20, 1819, Minister of Foreign Affairs, Julien Prévost (Duke of Limonade) expressed to Clarkson his profound opposition to the idea of paying indemnities to France: "Is it conceivable that Haitians who have escaped torture and massacre at the hands of these men, Haitians who have conquered their own country by the force of their arms and at the cost of their blood, that these same free Haitians should now purchase their property and persons once again with money paid to their former oppressors?"[7] Following failed attempts to obtain payment of financial compensation, France and consequently other European nations along with the United States continued denying recognition to Haiti. This obstruction restricting trade affected the new nation's recovery and development, and limited its political power in the international arena.

After Pétion's death in 1818, his protégé Jean-Pierre Boyer (c. 1776–1850) was appointed president of Haiti. Two years later, with Christophe's death, Boyer was free to undertake the reintegration of the north and the south. The new president ruled the nation with a despotic hand. In 1822, one year after Santo Domingo's independence from Spain, he unified the island under his government, and issued a decree abolishing slavery in its eastern part as well. During Boyer's term, the discussions with France on the recognition of Haiti's independence continued but the amount of the indemnity requested by the French remained contentious.[8] In 1825, when there was no hope that France would ever recover Haiti, King Charles X proposed an agreement to Boyer. The deal included advantageous duties for French imports and the payment of financial compensation to France for the loss of plantations and slave property during the slave revolt. In exchange, France would finally recognize Haiti's independence.[9]

To seal the agreement, the King of France issued a royal ordinance dated April 17, 1825. A squadron of fourteen vessels carrying 528 cannon delivered the decree at Port-au-Prince. Written in a clear colonial tone, the document ordered opening Haitian ports to all nations. It also determined that duties for ships and products that either entered or left these ports were equal for all countries, except for the French, whose duties would cost half of the amount charged to other nations. It also stipulated that Haiti would pay 150 million francs in five installments in order to allow France to compensate the former colonists.[10] The calculation of this amount was based on the annual revenues obtained by Saint-Domingue's planters from sugar, coffee, cotton, indigo, and other commodities during the colonial period, and also included the value of the urban properties they lost in 1789.[11] Although not included in the initial calculations, historians agree that slave property was considered in the evaluation and the distribution of the indemnity to the French planters and slaveholders.[12]

Boyer accepted the proposal in a public announcement in which he stated that through the recognition of Haiti's independence France consecrated the legitimacy of the Haitian people's emancipation.[13] Following the first French ordinance imposed on Haiti, a new royal decree of September 1, 1825, created a commission mandated with establishing the modalities of indemnity claims and the basis for their distribution.[14] Among those eligible to receive financial compensation were not only white French colonists, but also planters and slave owners of color who remained loyal to France and had gone into exile.[15] Eventually, the law of April 30, 1826 created a commission to receive the applications submitted by the colonists and to establish the values of their properties.[16] Of 27,000 applications for financial compensation submitted to the commission, 12,000 were retained.[17] Unlike other postemancipation societies whose governments also indemnified former slave owners, Haiti's example was singular. It was the only case that former slaves provided financial indemnities to the slaveholders. Moreover, French slaveholding elites were reimbursed not only for the loss of slave property but also for the costs of all properties they owned in the former colony.[18] In addition, white richest planters constituted the majority of those who obtained financial compensation from the French state.[19]

Without available funds, Haiti had to take loans from various European banks to pay the first amount of 30 million francs.[20] In 1838, as it became impossible to disburse the next installments, Haiti and France signed a treaty that reduced the expected balance from 120 million to 90 million francs. The agreement also extended the payments to over thirty years, until 1867.[21] But the lack of recognition from other countries also hindered Haiti's future. The United States waited until June 2, 1862 to recognize the new independent nation.[22] This late recognition of the Haitian nation during the presidency of Abraham Lincoln, when the United States was divided by a Civil War fought because of slavery, was not a charitable measure, but rather intended to incentivize trade between the two countries. Moreover, it was also linked to the hopes that the young Caribbean country would be able to accept African American immigrants after an eventual abolition of slavery in the United States.

It was not until 1883 that Haiti eventually finished paying the debt contracted with European financial institutions. The various loans taken from foreign banks to consolidate other local loans created a cycle of debt that put the country near bankruptcy.[23] Despite these enormous obstacles, much of Haiti's population obtained political rights. Many citizens became landowners. Moreover, many men, especially those who actively participated in the revolution, obtained positions of leadership. Several of these leaders became kings, presidents, and ministers of the new black nation.

The very existence of Haiti could be envisioned as an example of reparations to a whole population that for many years was kept in bondage. Yet, such an idea was seriously compromised after former slaves themselves paid France for their freedom. The payment of financial compensation to French slaveholding elites contributed to the exacerbation of the external and internal debts that ultimately deepened the young country's social inequalities, undermining its future political autonomy and material prosperity. Despite the early end of slavery, the agreements that stipulated the disbursement of indemnities to France kept Haiti under French control until the end of the nineteenth century, when the country entered the zone of influence of the United States.[24] Also, in the decades that followed the new ruling elites of Haiti promoted their own interests and enriched themselves mainly through systematic corruption.[25] The great majority of the descendants of freedpeople of Haiti remained socially and economically excluded. In this complex context that persisted over the next two centuries, reparations for slavery continued to be an unachieved project at least to the great majority of Haiti's descendants of slaves.

Fighting for citizenship in precarious conditions

Freedpeople also struggled in the British Caribbean colonies. Following the abolition of slavery, the British government did not redistribute land to former slaves or pay them any kind of financial reparations. The end of slavery contributed to the decline of sugar and coffee production in the region, which had to compete with their Brazilian and Cuban counterparts, whose industries relied on slave labor and where planters still profited from the work provided by enslaved men, women, and children. Without slaves, British planters faced the problem of a decrease in the available workforce. In the new postemancipation context, freed blacks sought better salaries and working conditions, and rejected laboring for meager wages. Freedmen and freedwomen who succeeded in purchasing land, invested their time working on their own newly acquired plots.[26] They expressed autonomy by refusing to work for the large landowners on a regular basis. In response, planters reinforced old stereotypes of black populations as lazy and unapt to work.[27]

In colonies like Jamaica, planters and colonial officials attempted to control the freed population. Initially, they made unsuccessful attempts to attract whites from England and Ireland, but eventually they addressed the problem of lack of labor force with the introduction of indentured workers, especially from the British colony of India, and in lesser extent from Africa as well. The arrival of these new recruits increased the available workforce, allowing planters to decrease the wages of former slaves.[28] Housing conditions for freedpeople also became more precarious. To cover the losses caused by the declining profitability of agricultural production, many planters seized dwellings and plots of land, which in the past slaves and apprentices had occupied for free, and started imposing rent charges.[29] But despite these enormous hardships, over the nineteenth century freedpeople attempted to acquire land in order to achieve economic and political autonomy, as well as social mobility. Several individuals and families amassed funds that allowed them to purchase smaller or bigger plots. When buying land was not possible, freedpeople were willing to fight for their rights and occupy abandoned estates.

Although black and brown former slaves and their descendants formed the majority of the population of Jamaica, the island remained a British colony and political power continued in the hands of white elites. After the legal abolition of slavery, voting restrictions based on property ownership restricted the pool of voters to only 1 percent of the population.[30] The persistence of these social, economic, and racial disparities in Jamaica led to the rise of the Morant Bay Rebellion in 1865, six months after the end of the Civil War in the United States. Black rebels, most of them peasants, denounced their working and living conditions as resembling slavery. In addition to an outcry over taxation, the insurgents demanded land, jobs, and higher wages for the formerly enslaved population and their descendants.[31]

British colonial authorities violently repressed the insurgents. Still, the revolt's aftermath created a period of change, as important public debates about the living and working conditions of freed populations emerged. In the decades after the rebellion, peasant landownership increased. But such a growth was not associated with new official policies. It rather resulted from the development of the fruit export industry. Despite this improvement, toward the end of the nineteenth century, the ability of black peasants to own land decreased because of the growing monopoly of the United Fruit Company, a US corporation which produced and exported bananas, mainly to the United States.[32] During the 1930s, even though peasant families constituted between 60 percent and 80 percent of Jamaica's population, most blacks remained living in poverty.[33]

On April 27, 1848, France passed a decree abolishing slavery in its colonies, to be effective two months later. But slaves did not wait. In colonies like Martinique, enslaved men and women organized a powerful uprising that anticipated the end of slavery, to May 23. Although until then French support to slavery was based on the institution's legality, the decree's language was clear in declaring slavery "an attack on human dignity."[34] However, as occurred in the British Caribbean colonies, freedmen and freedwomen were denied financial and material reparations. Moreover, the French state compensated former slaveholders. In its article 5, the law of April 27, 1848, that abolished slavery ordered the National Assembly to establish the amount of financial compensation to be awarded to the old slave owners. Eventually, the law of April 30, 1849, mandated the colonists should receive 12 million francs for the loss of 247,810 slaves in all its colonies, including Reunion Island and Senegal. Half of this amount was to be paid in cash within the thirty days that followed emancipation. In French Guiana, where there were 12,525 slaves, masters obtained 29.74 francs for each slave; Guadeloupe, which had an estimated population of 87,087 slaves, slave owners were paid 22.35 francs per slave. In Martinique, there were 74,447 slaves, former masters received the amount of 20.25 francs per slave.[35] The French state paid the other six million francs to the colonists in twenty annuities with an interest of 5 percent.[36] ✓

The postemancipation period in French Caribbean colonies carried similarities with the British Caribbean context. In Martinique, Guadeloupe, and French Guiana, several former slaves left the plantations. Yet, there were no measures for land redistribution to former slaves and few were successful in acquiring their own plots.[37] As in other former slave societies, the colonial government put in place repressive measures allegedly designed to avoid vagrancy. In reality, by restraining the mobility of freed population the small white planter elite sought to compel freedmen and freedwomen to remain working on the plantations.[38] ✓

To solve the scarcity of workers brought on with the end of slavery, the French government also introduced indentured laborers from Africa and Asia in its Caribbean colonies. Between 1854 and 1862, 18,520 Africans arrived in Martinique, Guadeloupe, and French Guiana.[39] Ostensibly free, most of these men and women were in fact captives repurchased by French recruiters in the West Central African slave markets, who were forced into ten-year labor contracts. French colonies also imported approximately 82,000 workers from India, China, and Madeira Islands.[40] Old and new Africans and their descendants continued to be dominated by oppressive labor regimes. Over the next century, the government of France subjugated the population of its colonies in the Americas. In Martinique, Guadeloupe, and French Guiana, former slaves and their descendants were disenfranchised, and denied access to full citizenship. In these societies, as in the British Caribbean colonies, freedpeople were not provided with reparations for slavery.

Aborted citizenship and land redistribution

Toward the end of the US Civil War, on March 3, 1865, an Act of the US Congress created the Bureau of Refugees, Freedmen and Abandoned Lands. Later known as the Freedmen's Bureau, this institution was designed to support former slaves and the poor white populations affected by wartime problems.[41] With the end of the Civil War and the ratification of the Thirteenth Amendment to the Constitution on December 6, 1865, slavery was legally abolished in the United States.[42] Political and social unrest characterized the years that followed emancipation. The Reconstruction Era had the enormous challenge of reuniting a nation marked by the traces of a bloody war and the deep scars of slavery.

Freed at last, African Americans fought for the civil rights that should follow emancipation. They sought financial and material resources to rebuild their lives as free individuals. But, as in other former slave societies, planters and government officials were concerned about the workforce shortfall generated by the end of slavery. From 1865 to 1866, southern states passed Black Codes as a solution to this problem. Based on older slave codes, this series of laws, intended to restrain freed African Americans workers, included provisions to punish black mobility with criminal charges of vagrancy. With the south destroyed by the war and because of the workforce shortage occasioned by the end of slavery, this dynamics contributed to expand the existing system of convict leasing. The imposition of penal labor on individuals serving time in prison expanded in southern states such as Georgia, Mississippi, Florida, and North Carolina. The legislation punishing vagrancy supported the growing incarceration of freed individuals, who hence provided unpaid work in plantations and factories. Over the next decades, this new dynamic led to the growth of the country's black prison population.

US former masters expected freedpeople to continue working for them without any compensation. Yet, former slaves were aware they were entitled to be paid for their work and clearly stated their rights in their exchanges with their former owners. In an unusual letter dated August 7, 1865, published in the *New-York Daily Tribune*, Jourdon Anderson (1825–1907), from Tennessee, answered his old owner, Colonel P. H. Anderson, who after the end of the war appealed to Anderson to bring his family and return to work for him. Living in Dayton, Ohio, Anderson explained to his old master that as a freedman he was living in a comfortable home and getting a monthly salary of $25 in addition to clothing and food. Moreover, his three children were attending school and performing well. Not only did the freedman not express any desire to work for his former master, but in an individual request, he asked Colonel Anderson to retroactively pay for the services provided when he was living in bondage:

> we have concluded to test your sincerity by asking you to send us our wages for the time we served you. This will make us forget and forgive old scores, and rely on your justice and friendship in the future. I served you faithfully for thirty-two years and Mandy twenty years. At $25 a month for me, and $2 a week for Mandy our earnings would amount to $11,680. Add to this the interest for the time our wages has been kept back and deduct what you paid for our clothing and three doctor's visits to me, and pulling a tooth for Mandy, and the balance will show what we are in justice entitled to.[43]

Former slaves like Jourdon Anderson were not successful in being paid retroactively and few of them, especially the elders, were able to afford decent work and living conditions. The newly freed population continued to face numerous difficulties. In a society where white supremacy and deeply rooted racism ruled, many former slaves remained in a position of social and economic exclusion.

Despite these significant obstacles, the Reconstruction Act of March 2, 1867 promised an unprecedented new era of civil rights to the freed population of the United States. The Act gave African American males right to vote. Black men were also allowed to run for office. State constitutions approved by the Reconstruction conventions abolished the property qualification for voting and holding office, and some states ended imprisonment for debt.[44] Moreover, the Fourteenth Amendment to the US Constitution, approved on July 9, 1868, instituted birthright citizenship and established equal legal protection. Likewise, the Fifteenth Amendment, ratified in 1870, prohibited disenfranchisement based on "race, color, or previous condition of servitude."[45] In this brief period that followed emancipation, former slaves used their citizenship rights to transform local and state governance. Yet, southern whites and northern conservatives fiercely opposed these measures. Soon this progressive period was drawn to a close in southern states through retrogressive Supreme Court decisions and the withdrawal of federal oversight. Therefore, local administrations employed explicit violence, fraud, poll taxes, literacy tests, and other mechanisms that limited the ability of black citizens to register and vote.

After the end of slavery, some former abolitionists supported the idea of providing former slaves with land. Still, the US government never designed any proposal to grant free land to the newly emancipated populations as a form of material reparations for slavery.[46] Instead, all initiatives implemented were rather intended to afford access to land through purchase or leasing contracts. During the first two years of the Civil War, the federal government had already taken official measures to confiscate property from the Confederates, including land. Nonetheless, all these measures failed.[47]

On January 16, 1865, when the Civil War approached its end, General William T. Sherman (1820–1891) issued the Special Field Order No. 15. The order confiscated land corresponding to an area of approximately 400,000 acres along the Atlantic coast from Charleston, South Carolina, to Florida's St. John's River. Intended to benefit freed black families, the measure also called freed men to join the Union Army. An additional order allowed the army to rent mules to the new land owners. Sherman's order gave origin to the slogan "Forty acres and a mule," which still today is invoked to illustrate the hopes and the subsequent failure of the attempts of land redistribution that followed emancipation.

In addition, before the final abolition of slavery in 1865, the fourth section of the "Act to Establish a Bureau for the Relief of Freedmen and Refugees," which created the institution later known as Freedmen's Bureau, proposed the distribution of abandoned lands to freed populations. According to the decree, the appointed commissioner of the newly created bureau had the authority to provide "tracts of land within the insurrectionary states as shall have been abandoned, or to which the United States shall have acquired title by confiscation or sale, or otherwise, and to every male citizen, whether refugee or freedman, as aforesaid, there shall be assigned not more than forty acres of such land."[48] The government limited the use of these plots to a period of three years, during which tenants were required to pay an annual rent. By June 1865, 40,000 freedmen settled on these lands and started growing crops. But there was no expansion to this policy.

Months later, hopes of land distribution to the freed population were cut short. In 1865 President Andrew Johnson (1808–1875), who replaced Lincoln after his assassination, revoked the bureau's order redistributing land confiscated during the war to former slaves.[49] Despite the resistance of abolitionists, he issued an amnesty proclamation on May 29, 1865 pardoning the rebels and restoring their lands. Although freedmen and freedwomen strongly reacted against this measure, eventually former slaveholders expelled thousands of families of freedpeople from the lands previously confiscated.

However, other attempts followed. After the federal government's failure in fulfilling the promise of land distribution in the South Carolina and Georgia sea islands, middle Tennessee, and other places in the South, the chief of the Freedmen's Bureau, General Oliver O. Howard (1830–1909), introduced a new Bill in the US Congress. The Southern Homestead Act passed on June 21, 1866. It made available for sale approximately 47 million acres of public land in the states of Alabama, Arkansas, Florida, Louisiana, and Mississippi. The law established that the land would be sold, not given, to freedpeople and loyal whites in parcels of eighty acres until 1867. Yet, the land accessible for purchase was of inferior quality, and most former slaves lacked resources to acquire the existing land. In 1869, only 4,000 families attempted to secure land, especially in Florida. Despite some exceptions, most land went to whites, and in subsequent years many freedmen and freedwomen lost the lands they had originally succeeded in purchasing.[50]

In areas such as Louisiana, similarly to the British and French Caribbean, planters refused to either sell or rent land to the freed population, with the intent of giving freedpeople no other choice than to work for low wages. In some cases, freedmen and freedwomen claimed the land formerly used to cultivate their own gardens, but these plots only yielded limited sustenance to feed their families. When former slaves became small landowners, landownership was not the result of a land reform to redress inequalities developed during slavery, but acquired through their own abilities to fight for it and negotiate working conditions. Ultimately, these hindrances prevented the social ascension of freed populations, and contributed to perpetuate two distinct groups. Freed African Americans, with limited mobility, became wage workers in sugarcane plantations, whereas whites, with access to landownership, became farmers.[51]

As freedpeople's expectations of land ownership and access to full citizenship vanished into thin air, new projects to settle African Americans in particular regions of the United States and in Africa resurfaced. By 1868, the American Colonization Society sent to Liberia 2,232 African Americans from the South, including Nashville and other parts of Tennessee. By this time former slaves and black abolitionists, such as Sojourner Truth, defended land redistribution to former slaves as a form of reparation for slavery. Her arguments were clear: enslaved men and women helped to build the nation's wealth and therefore should be compensated:

> We helped to pay this cost. We have been a source of wealth to this republic. Our labor supplied the country with cotton, until villages and cities dotted the enterprising North for its manufacture, and furnished employment and support for a multitude, thereby becoming a revenue to the government. Beneath a burning southern sun have we toiled, in the canebrake and the rice swamp, urged on by the merciless driver's lash, earning millions of money[52]

Truth took concrete measures to fight for land redistribution to the freed population. In 1870, she circulated a petition requesting the US Senate and House of Representatives to provide land to the "freed colored people in and about Washington" to allow them "to support themselves."[53] However, her efforts were ineffective.

Following the shutdown of the Freedmen's Bureau in 1872, Benjamin Singleton (1809–1900), a former slave from Tennessee who became a leading figure of black nationalism, created a company to acquire public land with the purpose of creating a black territory in Kansas. Between 1873 and 1881, he helped African American groups from Tennessee, Kentucky, Louisiana, Mississippi, and Arkansas relocate to Kansas. But as discrimination continued to grow in the country in the following years, Singleton started promoting the emigration of African Americans to Canada and Liberia. In 1879–1880, it is estimated that approximately 25,000 African Americans may have emigrated to Kansas, whereas during the period after the Civil War approximately 4,000 managed to reach Liberia.[54] In the ensuing years other similar emigration initiatives emerged. In 1885, Singleton and his followers created the United Trans-Atlantic Society to promote the migration of African Americans to Africa.[55]

Likewise, Henry McNeal Turner (1834–1815), Bishop of the African Methodist Episcopal Church, promoted emigration to Africa as the only solution for African Americans to escape racism and racial hatred. Turner was also an advocate of financial reparations.[56] In a speech delivered during a meeting of the National Council of Colored Men held in Cincinnati in November 1893, Turner not only denounced racism, but also the working and living conditions of freedmen and freedwomen after emancipation, by asking what would have happened to Anglo-Saxons if they had been enslaved for more than two centuries:

> For this Anglo-Saxon, I grant, is a powerful race; but put him in our stead, enslave him for 250 years, emancipate him and turn him loose upon the world, without education, without money, without horse or mule or a foot of land [. . .] The mule and forty acres of land, which has

been so often ridiculed for being expected by the black man, was a just and righteous expectation[57]

In addition to denouncing how former slaves were deprived of material resources, Turner went further and made a clear call for financial reparations:

> And seeing that this is our status in the United States today, it devolves upon us to project a remedy for our condition if such remedy is obtainable, or demand of this nation, which owes us billions of dollars for work done and services rendered, five hundred million dollars to commence leaving it. [. . .] For I can prove, by mathematical calculation, that this nation owes us forty billion dollars for daily work performed.[58]

Although none of these proposals resulted in any official measure granting free land or other forms of financial and material reparations to former slaves, they suggest how African Americans continued debating and demanding redress for slavery.

Fighting for pensions as reparations for slavery

Reconstruction was a failure in providing financial and material resources to freedpeople. Although some freedmen and freedwomen were able to purchase land with their own resources, most remained living in poverty, without access to decent jobs. In 1883, the Supreme Court invalidated the Civil Rights Act of 1875, which prohibited racial discrimination by private parties. In 1896, this decision was reinforced when the *Plessy vs. Ferguson* decision by the Supreme Court confirmed the constitutionality of racial segregation. Therefore, southern states continued the segregation of blacks and whites in public spaces, schools, transportation, and the military. In the northern states, white supremacy and racism prevailed in various spheres as well. African Americans faced growing civil rights restrictions and continuous racial hatred, through lynching and other forms of racial violence. In this context, thousands of freed individuals along with their descendants organized themselves to obtain pensions for the period they lived and worked in bondage in the United States. This movement became the largest organized effort requesting demands of reparations for slavery.[59]

Toward the end of the nineteenth century, when most former slaves were very old and no longer able to work for wages, Walter R. Vaughan (1848–1915) drafted a Bill to provide pensions to former slaves. He became one of the leaders of the movement demanding pensions to freed people. Yet, he was neither an African American, nor a former slave. He was a white man born in Virginia, who lived most part of his life in Alabama. An attorney, businessman, and editor, Vaughan was a member of the Democratic Party, who had served two terms as the mayor of Council Bluffs, in the state of Iowa. He had also lived in Omaha, Nebraska, where he edited the Democratic newspaper *Omaha Daily Democrat*, and later moved to Washington, DC, where he created another newspaper, the *US Department News Eagle*.

The idea of pensions to former slaves liberated by the Emancipation Proclamation of 1863 and by the Thirteenth Amendment of the Constitution of the United States of 1865, as well as other state decrees and amendments, was modeled after the programs that provided pensions to disabled veterans of the Civil War and their families, including African Americans. On June 24, 1890, the Republican Congressman William James Connell (1846–1924) of Nebraska introduced the Bill to Congress. Without any mention of former slave owners, the Bill proposed that the Department of the Treasury of the United States grant pensions to freedmen and freedwomen. The proposal was based on age, assuming that older individuals would have more difficulty in finding employment. According to the Bill, former slaves older than seventy years were entitled to receive a sum of $500 and an amount of $15 per month until the end of their lives. Freed individuals less than seventy years of age and older than sixty would receive $300, and a monthly amount of $12. Freedpeople between fifty and sixty years of age would obtain $100 and a monthly stipend of $8. Freed individuals younger than fifty years were entitled to an amount of $4 per month until reaching fifty years old.[60]

Despite having received support from both black and white individuals, the Bill failed to pass. But the campaign continued. In the next year, Vaughan published a small book defending the payment of pensions to former slaves, which sold several thousand copies.[61] The publication explained the history of slavery in the United States and drew a portrait of several African Americans who fought for the abolition of slavery. Yet, as a white man of his time, his views of slavery and of freedpeople were racially paternalistic. According to him former slaves "have gone forth from homes of comparative comfort into circumstances of absolute penury," and as a result, the federal government should provide them with pensions.[62] His descriptions reproduced the image of slave owners as beneficent providers to their human property. Whereas Vaughan subscribed to the stereotype of African Americans as obedient and even submissive citizens, he described Native Americans as rebellious and ungrateful. To him, the "negro is a progressive, honorable citizen" whereas the Indian, who "has cost the government millions of dollars and has been a murderer of the race for hundreds of years" is provided with food, clothing, and money.[63] Curiously, in order to argue that former slaves deserved pensions, Vaughan also explored the history of the African continent, by, among others, underscoring that great black men constructed the pyramids of Egypt. Such thoughts, which at the time were rejected by the adherents of scientific racism, in some ways anticipated ideas that were later promoted by Afrocentrism.[64]

But more importantly, Vaughan's book reproduced the Bill proposing a pension for former slaves. It also contained several letters written by US citizens and politicians who supported the project. In one letter addressed to Congressman Connell, a white man from Kentucky, stated that the condition of former slaves "was made wretched by the act of emancipation." He wrote that because the slaves "helped to develop the resources and wealth" of the United States, freedmen and freedwomen deserved to get pensions.[65] Another letter to Vaughan was written by an African American man from Arkansas, who identified himself as a "true blue republican," who was freed when he was young. In the letter, the author praised the Bill because, according to him, "justice should be done to the elder ones, at least, who were turned loose at an old age, without education, homes, or money, and broken down in health, unable to make a support."[66]

Vaughan's booklet also included a copy of a handwritten letter by Frederick Douglass supporting the Bill and financial reparations. In the words of the famous African American abolitionist: "the nation has sinned against the Negro. It robbed him of the rewards of his labor during more than two hundred years, and its repentance will not be genuine and complete till according to the measure of its ability, it shall have made restitution." Douglass also added that the living and working conditions of freedpeople remained similar to the ones they had under slavery. To him, "the Negro had neither spoils, implements nor lands, and to the day he is practically a slave on the very plantation where formerly he was driven to toil under the lash." Douglass concluded praising Vaughan's initiative: "Your bill is just and I thank God that you have the head and heart to press it upon the attention of the nation."[67]

In 1892, as part of the project to pass legislation to allocate pensions to former slaves, Vaughan created the Ex-Slave National Pension Club Association, a secret and fraternal society. Only African Americans could join the organization. Membership consisted of a fee of 25 cents and the payment of a monthly amount of 10 cents.[68] Still at this point, his motivations to defend pensions to former slaves were ambiguous. Was Vaughan attempting to take profit from the financial contributions of freedpeople? Whereas an early author sustained that he was an eccentric and mentally ill individual, Berry's hypothesis is more plausible. According to her, Vaughan believed that pensions to former slaves would inject money into the economy of the South, helping white entrepreneurs to recover from wartime crisis.[69] In other words, his main concern was not the faith of freedmen and freedwomen, but rather how freedpeople would contribute to reviving the southern economy.

Vaughan circulated the text of the Bill for publication in newspapers and also collected signatures on petitions addressed to the US Congress in support of the Bill. In Vaughan's arguments, the payment of pensions to former slaves was described as financial reparations for the past wrong of slavery: "Is it the right of the ex-slaves that they have compensation for wrongs endured? Can a great and beneficent government deliberately sanction a cruelty and a wrong without making reasonable indemnity for the wrong afflicted?"[70] To him, financial reparations were more important than any other forms of restitution: "Put money in your purses and respectability will ensue just as certainly as that water escaping from a gathered reservoir will run down hill, pursuant to the established laws of gravitation."[71]

Despite its significance, upper-class African Americans, including most clergymen, scholars, and politicians opposed the movement for pensions to ex-slaves. Even African American congressmen such as John Mercer Langston (1829–1897), Thomas E. Miller (1848–1938), and Henry P. Cheatham (1857–1935) dismissed these demands for financial reparations. Instead, they attempted, with no success, to pass legislation supporting voting rights and education.[72] After the end of the activities of the Freedmen's Bureau, which had fomented the creation of schools and historically black colleges that allowed freedpeople, or at least their descendants, to have access to education, these prominent figures continued giving priority to projects which they understood would uplift African Americans, including "the establishment of schools, colleges, churches, and the like for the education of the young generation of negroes and for the moral culture of the black people, young and old alike."[73] However, many former slaves belonging to the working class did not support this view. According to them education could not solve the immediate survival needs of elderly freedmen and freedwomen.

The campaign promoting the payment of pensions to ex-slaves had an impact in the public sphere, even though black and white press rarely provided news about the movement. In the scarce articles published about the campaign, most newspapers described the associations that promoted the project of reparations as fraudulent initiatives.[74] Between 1896 and 1903, congressmen introduced eight other almost identical ex-slave pensions Bills in the US Congress. In 1896, Senator Shelby Moore Cullom (1829–1914) from Illinois and Senator John Mellen Thurston (1847–1916), from Nebraska, both from the Republican Party, presented the Bill for consideration by the Congress. Two years later, in 1898, William Ernest Mason (1850–1921), a Senator of the Republican Party from Illinois introduced the Bill one more time. In 1899, Charles Curtis (1860–1936), by the time a Representative of the Republican Party from Kansas, and Edmund Pettus (1821–1907), a Senator of the Democratic Party from Alabama, who was also a Grand Dragon of the Ku Klux Klan, presented the Bill again. Despite agreeing to present the Bill, these congressmen were very far from being dedicated supporters of the movement demanding pensions to former slaves.[75]

Later on, as the Bills failed to pass, Vaughan attempted to gain support from southern whites by presenting the subsequent versions of the Bill as a "Southern-tax relief bill."[76] Yet, other emerging associations promoting the passage of legislation providing pensions as reparations to former slaves continued to employ the original Bill's title.[77] Eventually, in 1903, Edmond Spencer Blackburn (1868–1912), a Representative of the Republican Party from North Carolina, and Marcus Alonzo "Mark" Hanna (1837–1904), a Senator of the Republican Party from Ohio, introduced the Bill in Congress one last time. But as expected, the large majority of the white Congress opposed the Bill, and once again it failed to pass.

A movement led by former slaves

At the end the nineteenth century and during the early twentieth century, freedpeople took control of the movement demanding pensions for former slaves, through the creation of organizations that challenged the hegemony of Vaughan's club.[78] Among these groups were the Ex-Slave Petitioner's Assembly, the Great National Ex-Slave Union, Congressional, Legislative, and Pension Association of the United States of America, and the Ex-Slave Pension Association. However, among them, the National Ex-Slave Mutual Relief, Bounty and Pension Association of the United States of America was the most important. Led by African Americans, the association was incorporated in 1897. It centered its activities around the defense of financial reparations to former slaves.[79] Unlike Vaughan's club, the association was not a secret society, but an entity opened to "any ex-slave or friend of color who is eighteen years old or older, male or female" who wanted to join it.[80]

This new association justified the demand of pensions as reparations for slavery because "[m]illions of our deceased people besides those who survive, worked as slaves for the development of the great resources of this country."[81] Between 1897 and 1898, the organization attracted at least 34,000 new members. In 1899 the association's president claimed 600,000 members.[82] Created to support the passage of legislation providing pensions to former slaves, its agents collected petition signatures supporting the Mason Bill (4718), introduced in the Congress of the United States in 1898. In the five years that followed, the organization also supported several other nearly identical Bills. Moreover, its various chapters and branches labored to provide older members with medical and burial assistance. To promote its cause, the association also published its own newspaper titled *National Industrial Advocate*, reflecting the working-class profile of some of its members.

The National Ex-Slave Mutual Relief, Bounty and Pension Association was led by Isaiah H. Dickerson (1858–1902) and Callie D. House (1861–1928). Dickerson was an African American teacher and minister. Prior to joining the association and becoming its general manager, he had worked for Vaughan's organization as a travel agent, but left this position after a disagreement. House was a former slave who resided in Nashville, Tennessee.

A widower, she was the mother of five children, and worked as a washerwoman. As in Vaughan's organization, to join the association, freedmen and freedwomen had to pay a membership fee of 25 cents and a monthly amount of 10 cents. These fees supported the various organization's meetings and campaigns promoting the passage of legislation establishing pensions to ex-slaves.

Since the creation of the National Ex-Slave Mutual Relief, Bounty and Pension Association, Vaughan denounced it as a fraudulent initiative in an attempt to keep control of the cause defined according to his own terms. As word about legislation providing pensions to former slaves started circulating, freedmen and freedwomen wrote numerous letters to the Bureau of Pensions requesting information about it. In this correspondence, former slaves usually provided their place of residence, age, and names of their former masters. Many authors of these letters were elderly men and women. Their correspondence reveals their hard living conditions after the end of slavery.

Although federal agents responded to the inquiries by denying the existence of any provisions aimed at paying pensions to ex-slaves, more letters continued to arrive. Sometimes, former slaves addressed themselves directly to the President of the United States, and this mail was occasionally redirected to the Bureau of Pensions.[83] In one of these letters, an old freedman named Anderson Dillon from Sparta, Illinois, wrote to President William McKinley (1843–1901) requesting details about possible pensions to former slaves:

I am old and am not work now and no one help me and cripple with the rheumatism and I am 84 years old now and have no horses no cows no hogs either and nothing to get with and if I was just able to work I would be glad but any working days is all over with now but the slave holders had got the best of us old colored folks and then sent us out with out any thing. I think if they would have given us a home they would have done well one and my wife both was in slavery and neither one is able to do any thing much I try all the time to work but looks like I don't get along very good Mr. McKinley you might send me a little money if it was a couple of dollars I would be very thankful to get that they all tell me you are a good Christian man and I know you would not suffer to know of one getting a long so poor and you doing so well I have done all in my power to get you elected and will do all I can again if I am living until then for times is hard and I think if the democrats gets in it will be worse and I don't want to see any harder times then they are now I am living in a little old cabin and when it rains it comes in as same as if their was no roof on it the boards is all coming of and I can't do any good with it and I have no kitchen nothing but the one room but poor folks [illegible] broke up and stone up with old age and rheumatism that gets a way with me and I wish you would please tell me whether that is so are not about the slave money I would like to know.[84]

Anderson Dillon was conscious that after being usurped by his owners for many years, he was now abandoned to himself. Like him, numerous former slaves continued living in precarious material conditions, which objectively were not very different from slavery. Without access to land and income, elderly freedmen and freedwomen could barely survive. Despite the atrocious context, Dillon attempted to show the Republican President that freedpeople had a voice, and because they voted for him, they expected his support in return. Ultimately, he indicated that he and other fellow former slaves were ready to fight for the pensions.

The federal government perceived these associations negatively. On the one hand, official agents suspected these groups of leading a fraud scheme. On the other hand, the government feared the consequences if thousands of freedmen and freedwomen organized themselves to demand reparations for slavery. By the end of the 1890s, the Department of Justice, the Bureau of Pensions, and the Post Office Department started investigating the National Ex-Slave Mutual Relief, Bounty and Pension Association for fraudulent activity. Government officials argued that its leaders were misrepresenting themselves as federal agents. They claimed that after convincing former slaves that pension legislation had been enacted, the association's officers illegally used mail services to collect financial contributions.[85]

Although in the various organizations promoting the pension Bills to former slaves there were individuals involved in dishonest dealings, for the federal agents it remained a difficult task to demonstrate that organizing freedpeople to demand pensions was an illegal act. An agent who attended an assembly of the National Ex-Slave Mutual Relief, Bounty and Pension Association in January 1898 reported to the Commissioner of Pensions that during the meeting he "heard nothing that violated the law."[86] Although some individuals may have given wrong information in order to take financial advantage of former slaves, official documentation clearly shows that the mission of the National Ex-Slave Mutual Relief, Bounty and Pension Association was to promote campaigns to pass legislation creating pensions to freedmen and freedwomen.

As the investigation about fraudulent activity expanded, federal agents persecuted the leaders of the association and its members, who defended themselves and explained the organization's endeavors. On December 2, 1897, a freedman man named J. L. Walton from Madison, Arkansas, responded to an inquiry by the Commissioner of Pensions. According to him, a gentleman persuaded him and other former slaves "to come together as a race, and ask this great common wealth" to grant them with a pension for "past services" to help them to care for their "old and infirm parents."[87] In another letter by the members of an ex-slave club of North Carolina, a religious leader reminded the federal agent that former slaves were living a Christian life and "keeping out of disobeying the laws," but also underscored their "quite needful condition."[88]

The association's officers explained to government officials how collecting petition signatures to pass legislation benefiting former slaves and requesting membership fees to run the organization were not unlawful actions. In 1899, Isaiah H. Dickerson responded to a letter from the assistant attorney general for the Post Office Department. He detailed the activities of the National Ex-Slave Mutual Relief, Bounty and Pension Association and clarified that their goals were the "relief of the suffering ex-slaves who are bent up with Rheumatism from the hardship of slavery" and who were no longer able to perform manual labor to support themselves.[89] Likewise, in that same month Callie House sent a letter to the same agent. Once again, she expounded on the objectives of the movement by insisting that their goal was to obtain redress for a historical wrong: "we are organizing our selves together as a Race of people who feel that they have been wronged."[90] More incisively than Dickerson, she insisted on the fact that former slaves were left with no resources and therefore they had the right to organize themselves to demand restitutions:

> turn loose ignorant[s,] bare footed and naked without a dollar in their pockets without a shelter to go under out of the falling rain but was force to look the man in the face for something to eat who once had the power to whip them to death but now have the power to starve them to death. We the Ex-Slave feel that if the government had a right to free us she had a right to make some provisions for us as she did make it soon after our Emancipation she ought to make it now. I insure you that the officers of this organization have not promise its members any thing or have we insured them that they will get any thing. [. . .] We have perfect Right as Ex Slave to assemble our selves together and organized our selves and elect men and women to organize our Race together to petition the Government for a Compensation to alleviate our old decrepit men and women who are bent up with Rheumatism from the exposure they under gone in the dark days of Slavery.[91]

In another letter to the Commissioner of Pensions, House explained the objectives of her organization. By using the term "redress," she described the demands for pensions to former slaves as financial reparations for slavery, underscoring that petitioning the government was a constitutional right of all citizens of the United States. House insisted that the goals of the association included taking care of the ill, burying the dead, and petitioning the US Congress to pass legislation awarding pensions to ex-slaves. According to her, the federal government owed the ex-slaves an indemnity for the labor stolen from them after the adoption of the Declaration of Independence. By doing so, she appropriated the same arguments employed by abolitionists since the end of the eighteenth century and asserted in several slave narratives.[92] House also reminded the Commissioner that although the declaration stated that all were men born equal, slaves had to work and were taxed like chattels in "the land of the free and home of the [b]rave. [N]ow since we have been freed and made citizen[s] we can read for our selves that we ought to have been free nearly 100 years before we was." She also contended that the members and officers of the National Ex-Slave Mutual Relief, Bounty and Pension Association were "working by the laws that the white man north and south made" and concluded by noting that "the Constitution of the United States grants it citizen[s] the priviledge to petition congress for a redress of grievance therefore I can't see where we have violated any law what ever the monthly dues."[93]

The leaders of the association sent several other letters to government authorities. They stated that their members were informed that their sole goal was petitioning Congress for the passage of a pensions Bill that was not yet a law. But in 1899, the federal government took additional measures to stop the activities of the various associations, by imposing a postal ban on the National Ex-Slave Mutual Relief, Bounty and Pension Association. Therefore, the Post Office Department intercepted the leaders' correspondence, whether or not it was related to the association. Moreover, the organization was prevented from using mail services.[94] To circumvent the ban, the officers changed the name of the association by replacing the terms "bounty and pension" with "benevolent, and aid" as reported in a memo sent to the various branches and chapters of the organization: "Owing to the fact that the Government of these United States feel we are misleading in our phraseology and was do not desire to mislead our Brother and Sister We do now name this great organization the National Ex-Slave Mutual Relief Benevolent and Aid Association of the United States of America." The document also highlighted that "this name does not destroy our aim and purpose of work in the assistance to one another."[95]

None of these measures succeeded in stopping the government from persecuting the organization. Soon afterward, the Post Office Department issued a fraud order against the association's administrators, which led newspapers around the country to publish their portraits. In response to the accusations of fraudulent activities, the leaders defended themselves in written exchanges with the government's officials. In a letter sent to an agent of the Post Office Department, House denounced that government persecution was indeed motivated by racial discrimination against black people:

I am American born woman and was Born in the Proud old state of Tennessee and I am considered as a law abiding citizen of that state [.] Any one that work[s] honestly and earnestly for the up building of there own Race would like for it to be Recognize that way [.] let it be a white man or white woman or a black man or a black woman[.] My face is black as true but it's not my fault[.] But I love my name and my honesty in dealing with my fellow man.[96]

In the next year, House sent another letter to the same agent, insisting that the association's mission was to fight to redress past wrongs: "tell the people to unite and ask the Congress of the United States to pass same measure to help them in their old declining age in the way as an indemnity for pass wrongs." Once again, she argued that the charges against her were based on racial prejudice: "I believed the evidence [. . .] are pregidice against the Negro for the Charges are no true and I believed they are made against us simply because we are Negroes and helpless."[97] Although House defended herself, as the only black woman leader of the movement, she was aware of her fragile position in relation to the accusations of fraud orders.

Despite all these hindrances, during the next decade the association continued campaigning to pass legislation providing pensions to former slaves. It also maintained its local and national meetings. In 1915, the organization hired Cornelius J. Jones (1858–1931), the famous lawyer and political figure, who was already one of its prominent members. In 1896, Jones was the first African American attorney to present an oral argument before the Supreme Court of the United States, in *Gibson vs. Mississippi* case. He defended John Gibson, a black worker who killed a white overseer on a Mississippi plantation. As the subsequent Bills demanding pensions to ex-slaves failed to pass, by relying on Jones's assistance, the National Ex-Slave Mutual, Relief, Benevolent, and Aid Association made a last move.

In 1915, they filed a class action lawsuit in the federal court of the District of Columbia against the Secretary of the US Department of the Treasury, William Gibbs McAdoo (1863–1941), claiming the amount of $68,073,388.99 collected in cotton taxes by the Treasury between 1862 and 1868. The origin of these funds dated back to 1862, when the federal government created the first cotton tax to offset the war's financial burden on the Union. When, after the war, southern senators attempted to recover and return the money to the former slave owners, the existence of the tax income was made public and largely disseminated in the black press. By the beginning of the Civil War, slaves had already picked and stored the cotton and the taxes paid for it remained retraceable in the Department of the Treasury. The claim stated that the federal government owed the entire amount of taxes collected from 1862 to 1868 to former slaves, who cultivated and harvested the taxed cotton without any remuneration. This litigation became the first class action demanding reparations for slavery in the United States.[98]

Soon the news about the lawsuit spread among former slaves. On October 15, 1915, the Department of the Treasury responded to the association's claim in a press statement. The government not only asserted its right to keep the money, but also urged the claimants to turn to their old masters to demand financial reparations. Later on, the Secretary of the Treasury went further, and even denied the existence of the funds.[99] Eventually, the District of Columbia Court of Appeals rejected the cotton tax case's claim due to governmental legal immunity. According to this doctrine the government of the United States may not be sued unless it gives consent.[100]

As late as in April 1917, a former slave sent a letter to the Commissioner of Pensions inquiring about the taxes funds: "I am told that the United States has appropriated $68 072 388, 97/100 to pension or to reimburse all ex-slaves for services rendered the US or for cotton seized by the government prior to or during the civil war."[101] The counter to this letter was clearly negative: "the government of the United States has not appropriated the sum of $68,072,388.97 to pension ex-slaves or to reimburse them for services rendered in the raising of cotton which was seized by the Government during the Civil War. There is no provision of law under which an ex-slave can be pensioned as such."[102]

But the federal government had yet to execute the final coup against the movement for reparations. While Cornelius Jones was appealing the cotton tax case in the Supreme Court, the Post Office Department charged him and Callie House for using the US mail to defraud. Notable members of the African American community publicly defended Jones. After two trials, federal officials feared convicting the very same lawyer who had filed a lawsuit against the government. Eventually the federal prosecutor dropped the case against Jones.[103]

Jones escaped further persecution, but the charges against House, who did not enjoy his same social position, were pursued. In March, 1916, the federal prosecutor presented the case against her to a grand jury in Nashville, Tennessee. House was indicted with violating postal laws of the United States for obtaining money from freedpeople through false pretenses, even though according to the accusation she was aware that no pensions would ever be awarded to former slaves. Without identifying any individuals victimized by the association, the accusation maintained that most of the funds amassed were collected by House for her personal use.[104] On August 3, 1916, the police arrested House at her modest home in Nashville, where she had been living with her family for more than twenty-five years. She pled not guilty, and eventually the judge scheduled a three-day trial for the next year. By this time, federal prosecutors assessed that 300,000 individuals were members of the organization.[105]

Subsequent to House's first arrest, a number of signs indicated the nearing of the end of the movement for pensions to former slaves. While the federal government persecuted the association's officers, newspapers reported on the quick progression in the construction of the Lincoln Memorial in Washington, DC.[106] More than fifty years after the abolition of slavery, Lincoln was memorialized in marble and stone, while former slaves remained living in poverty.[107] Moreover, another event also held in the national capital was a revealing example of this situation. From October 23 to November 6, 1916, the 54th Convention and Reunion of Ex-Slaves and Former Owners took place in the Cosmopolitan Baptist Church in Washington, DC.[108] The National Evangelistic Ministers' Alliance of America and the White Cross National Colored Old Folks' Home Association of America, presided by Reverend Simon P. W. Drew (1873–1934), sponsored the convention.[109]

Drew had a positive reputation as a local leader of the African American community. Newspapers described him as "an able pulpit orator," who possessed "that kind of magnetism which draws out large crowds to hear him."[110] Politically engaged in denouncing racism, under his leadership, his association launched a movement to create a memorial honoring Brooker T. Washington (1856–1915) in the national capital.[111] On April 14, 1916, Drew also participated in a public meeting protesting the presentation of the racist film *The Birth of a Nation* (1915).[112] ✓

Although former slaves preserved their mutual connections, the convention of former slaves was not intended to discuss questions related to reparations. Congregated to socialize and pray, several of its participants were aged men and women, and several were nearly one hundred years of age (Figure 3.1). The organizers distributed 5,000 free dinner tickets to be provided to the attendees for the entire period of the reunion, suggesting that many participants were in need. Unable to work and without any income, these former slaves, including many elderly women (Figure 3.2), remained living in precarious conditions and depending on charity to survive.[113] ✓

✓ FIGURE 3.1 *Slaves Reunion.* In the picture: Lewis Martin, age 100; Martha Elizabeth Banks, age 104; Amy Ware, age 103, Reverend Simon P. W. Drew, born free. Washington, DC, United States, 1916. Photographer Harris & Wing. Courtesy: Library of Congress Prints and Photographs Division, Washington, DC, United States.

FIGURE 3.2 *Slaves Reunion*. In the picture: Annie Parram, age 104; Anna Angales, age 105; Elizabeth Berkeley, age 125; Sadie Thompson, age 110. Washington, DC, United States, 1916. Photographer Harris & Wing. Courtesy: Library of Congress Prints and Photographs Division, Washington, DC, United States.

The year of 1917 was not any better for the movement demanding reparations to former slaves. In April, the United States eventually entered the First World War (1914–1918). The country sent thousands of soldiers to the western front, including more than 350,000 African Americans, who served in segregated units under the command of white military officers. Black soldiers fought the war for a country where they were submitted to racial hatred, denied civil rights, and where they were socially and economically excluded. Meanwhile, House's activities in the National Ex-Slave Mutual, Relief, Benevolent, and Aid, Association were close to the end. On September, 17, 1917, an all-white male jury found her guilty of using mail services to defraud. She was sentenced to spend one year in prison. Two months later, she started serving her time at the Missouri State Prison at Jefferson City.

Some chapters of the association continued working after House went to prison but now they operated as mutual aid societies and no longer requested reparations for slavery. Approximately ten years later, Reverend Drew, the man who convened the convention of former slaves in Washington, DC in 1916 had a similar sad fate. In the presidential elections of 1928, Drew ran for vice-president of the United States along with Jacob Sechler Coxey

(1854–1951), candidate for president for the Interracial Independent Political Party. But two years later, in May, 1930, exactly like House, Drew was indicted for using mail to defraud. A jury accused him of collecting funds, without authorization, for the Boydton Industrial Institute at Boydton, in Virginia, which had been closed for more than two years. In his defense, he explained that his efforts were genuine because the funds collected were intended to reopen the institution. Nevertheless, he was sentenced to spend one year in prison. He suddenly died three years later.[114] The fates of Jones and House, and to some extent of Drew, anticipated the treatment that federal authorities inflicted on the future leaders who fought for reparations for slavery. The persecution and criminalization of early organizations advocating reparations demonstrate that official agents took the work of these activists very seriously, and for this reason they did not hesitate in taking all necessary measures to impede their activities.

Requesting the former masters to pay back

No other country in the western hemisphere witnessed movements requesting reparations for slavery like Vaughan's Ex-Slave National Pension Club Association and the National Ex-Slave Mutual Relief, Bounty and Pension Association. Similarly, only the United States knew the creation of an institution like the Freedmen's Bureau, which despite being unsuccessful in securing land for former slaves, nevertheless for a limited time succeeded in establishing a record in assisting freedpeople against discrimination and violence. After the end of slavery in the Spanish colonies of Cuba and Puerto Rico, and in Brazil, no organized groups pursued claims for restitution. Yet, in Latin America and the Caribbean, although rare and very sparse, some former slaves individually addressed demands for reparations to their former masters and to the federal government.

In Cuba, the transition to a free labor society presented several similarities with the postemancipation period in the French and the British Caribbean. As in other parts of the Americas, the end of slavery in Cuba was not followed by financial and material reparations to former slaves. After emancipation, former slaves fought for equal citizenship in a society that remained racially divided. Still segregated, Afro-Cubans faced discrimination in various spheres of social life, including employment and education.[115] During this time, the sugarcane industry expanded and was oriented toward the North American market. Land became increasingly concentrated in the hands of large landowners, preventing former slaves from having access to the small plots that both they and their ancestors had used for subsistence agriculture. Forced to compete with Spaniards and Chinese indentured workers, freedpeople were offered low wages which only permitted them to fulfill their basic needs.[116] Some freedmen and freedwomen continued cultivating sugar on their old plantations, whereas others moved to new estates. Yet, many former slaves started growing sugar and became wage laborers on a part-time basis. Many others migrated from the sugar regions to other rural areas or to the cities.[117] Indeed, few recently emancipated individuals became *colonos*, a category that included tenant farmers, sharecroppers, and small landowners, but most of them were indeed descendants of free Cubans of African descent and not newly freed individuals. Ultimately, access to land ownership remained precarious for former slaves.

A few freed male individuals, who served in the rebel army, as well as their descendants were able to obtain financial rewards that enabled them to rent or to purchase land. Yet, as Rebecca J. Scott explains "rural Cubans helped to create the political conditions for opening up broader claims to resources, whether as wages, as land or, in one exceptional case, as reparations."[118] Here, the historian refers to the case of Andrea Quesada y Acevedo, a former enslaved woman who lived in the Santa Rosalía plantation in the coastal city of Cienfuegos, in southern Cuba.[119] In 1906, when Quesada was an old woman of sixty-two, she demanded reparations for the time she lived in bondage.[120]

Andrea Quesada y Acevedo did not lobby for restitutions from the Cuban government, but rather from the heirs of her previous owner. She claimed that on July 24, 1870, her then owner José Quesada y Sada had freed her in a document (*memoria*) that was to be attached to his testament upon his death.[121] But after the testator's death on February 21, 1876, his heir Manuel Blanco y Ramos not only kept the document secret but never fulfilled the *memoria*'s directions. Instead, he kept all the deceased's properties, including his slaves, until 1886, when slavery was legally abolished in Cuba.[122] Quesada y Acevedo claimed that she was illegally kept under slavery for one decade and that she was named as a beneficiary in her former owner's testament. Based on these claims, she filed a lawsuit demanding part of Blanco y Ramos's inheritance as financial reparations. Although she individually started the claim for restitution, the news about the lawsuit spread among other former slaves, including African-born individuals, once owned by Quesada y Sada.[123] By April 1907, there were fifty-two other men and women who also filed lawsuits making the same demands of the heirs of Blanco y Ramos.[124]

The attorney for defense, Emilio Menéndez, responded to Quesada y Acevedo and the other plaintiffs. He asserted that his clients, the heirs of Blanco y Ramos, were not aware of the existence of any document left by Quesada y Sada affirming neither the freeing of his slaves nor making them his heirs. On the one hand, he claimed that thirty years had passed. On the other hand, he sustained that the litigant had to prove the existence of such a deed. He also insisted that she had to demonstrate that she was "one of the beneficiaries to which said *memoria* makes reference" and that "the favor or bequest that the testator made to the plaintiff was that of granting her liberty."[125] Menéndez denied the charges and requested the judge dismiss the case. To this defense, the litigant's lawyer responded that the "burden of proof" was the responsibility of Blanco y Ramos and his successors and not of his client. He also contested the claim that his client's mandate was invalid because thirty years had passed. Finally, the judge Antonio J. Varona, ruled the case on April 12, 1907. He declared the lawsuit inadmissible, justifying that the "testator's declaration of intention does not mean that he carried it out."[126]

Quesada y Acevedo and her legal representatives appealed the case, but the appeal was rejected and the case closed on December 8, 1908. Although rejected, the demand of reparations formulated by Quesada y Acevedo and followed by other former slaves owned by her previous master indicate that beyond the United States, freedmen and freedwomen were not only aware that former masters and the government owed them reparations for the years they remained in bondage, but were also willing to use various means to obtain restitution. Both in Cuba and in the United States, despite being deprived of political and economic power, former enslaved elderly women, like Andrea Quesada y Acevedo and Callie House, played a leading role in voicing demands for reparations for slavery.

The Republican backlash

Political instability marked the period that followed the end of slavery in Brazil. The monarchy collapsed and a Republican government replaced it in November 1889. Despite the lack of segregation laws, similarly to other postemancipation societies, the Brazilian government authorities feared that the newly emancipated slaves would cause social unrest.[127] Both the press and public authorities portrayed the freed population as dangerous and unfit to live in freedom.[128] In the urban areas, white newspapers denied the existence of racism. Promoting the idea of integration and propagating white values of respectability, these publications characterized African traditions as barbarian and black culture as inferior.[129]

In Brazil, the majority of former slaves remained deprived of access to landownership and to basic education through policies that had the explicit goal of reinforcing freedpeople's social exclusion.[130] In São Paulo, Rio de Janeiro, and Bahia, many freedmen and freedwomen continued working on the estates of their old owners in exchange for food and dilapidated accommodations, whereas those who gradually moved to other plantations became either sharecroppers or day laborers.[131] Others moved to the cities expecting better working conditions. As the workforce was scarce, the police in complicity with landowners intimidated former slaves who were not willing to work under the newly imposed unstable conditions. In order to avoid being sent to prison for vagrancy, freed individuals were forced to take work contracts.

In Brazil, despite the hardships of the postemancipation period, a small number of former slaves invoked symbolic reparations for slavery in their exchanges with government officials. In a letter of April 19, 1889, a commission of freedmen from several plantations of Vassouras, a municipality in the coffee zone industry of the Paraíba River Valley, sent a letter to then General Deputy Rui Barbosa. Although addressing Barbosa as a "great citizen," and as a man who "greatly influenced our emancipation," the group made clear that the abolition of slavery had not been a gift from the monarchy and white abolitionists, but the result of their own struggle:

> we perfectly understand that the emancipation came from the people who forced the Crown and the Parliament to decree it and that our freedom was signed in Cubatão [a *quilombo* or runaway slave community] and therefore we will not raise arms against our Brothers, despite having being advised to do so by the courtiers of the palace, our greatest torturers in the past.[132]

In the letter, the commission composed by Quintiliano Avellar, Ambrosio Teixeira, João Gomes Batista, Francisco de Salles Avellar, José dos Santos Pereira, Ricardo Leopoldino de Almeida, and Sergio Barboza dos Santos, argued that the Free Womb Law of 1871 was cheated because the clause that mandated investment in freedchildren's education was never put into practice. According to them:

> Our children rest in deep darkness. It is necessary to enlighten them and guide them through the means of instruction. Slavery has always been the mainstay of the throne in this vast and dear country; now that the law of May 13, 1888, abolished it, the ministers of the "Queen" want to make the freedmen, our unconscious comrades, the basis for lifting the foundation of the third empire. The freedmen of Paty de Alferes, represented by us, protest against the indecent means that the government wants to take hold of it and by taking advantage of this occasion declare that they do not adhere to such a collusion and that until today, sucked by the empire's government, they want education and instruction that the law of September 28, 1871 granted them.[133]

The freedmen also reminded Barbosa that the imperial government was still collecting an additional tax of 5 percent established by the Free Womb Law to create the emancipation fund. Although they claimed to obtain these funds as financial reparations, they insisted those funds be invested in the education of freedpeople's children.[134]

The answer to this letter is unknown, but Barbosa's positions regarding the need to educate the illiterate freed masses were quite contradictory. During the abolitionist campaign his speeches emphasized education as the only instrument to secure a prosperous future for freedmen and freedwomen and their children. But after the abolition of slavery his paternalistic vision of the newly freed black population, seen as barbarian, childish, and needing guidance from the white elite, led him to defend positions that denied the black population in Brazil the right to citizenship.[135] Although this vision was not unanimous among abolitionists, it was dominant among Brazilian planter elites and their representatives in the Chamber of Deputies.[136]

In the decades that followed emancipation, Brazil's freedpeople did not receive any kind of financial and material reparations. Moreover, unlike in the United States and Cuba, former planters and slave owners avidly persisted in seeking claims for their alleged moral and material losses. Even though the new unstable context scarcely favored attempts to obtain indemnities, along with their representatives these groups continued demanding financial compensation from the Brazilian state.[137]

Three Bills, presented by Antônio Coelho Rodrigues (1846–1912), João Maurício Wanderley, and even by the abolitionist João Alfredo Correia de Oliveira (1835–1919), focused on indemnifying former slave owners. In 1890, the Republican Anfriso Fialho (1839–19?) launched a campaign proposing the creation of a bank to provide lines of credit to Brazilian planters and old slaveholders. Rui Barbosa, who by then had become Minister of Finance of the new Republican government, rejected the proposal. He declared that instead of compensating the former masters, "it would be more just, and it would better correspond to the national sentiment, if it was possible to find out a way to compensate the former slaves, without burdening the treasury."[138] Despite this statement, neither the national sentiment, nor the government's initiatives pointed toward any kind of financial reparations to former slaves.

Yet, these requests to compensate the former slave owners and planters propelled one of the most controversial episodes of the Brazilian postemancipation period. On December 14, 1890, Barbosa issued a decree ordering the burning of all "papers, books of register, and documents related to slavery, housed in the offices of the Ministry of Finance."[139] For decades this ministerial decision led many scholars to believe that all documents related to slavery in Brazil were destroyed. But the order only included the documents housed in the Ministry of Finance.

Barbosa's decision was interpreted as an attempt to erase the traces of slavery in Brazil. With the approach of the centennial of the abolition of slavery in 1988, a number of publications engaged in rehabilitating Barbosa's memory. These works explained that not all existing documents were destroyed as a result of the minister's decision. Moreover, because of bureaucratic slowness, many offices around the country did not follow his order, and in some cases copies of the documents were stored elsewhere as well. At the same time, these studies highlight that Barbosa indeed intended to prevent the former slave owners from requesting financial compensation for the losses of slave property after the abolition of slavery.[140]

Today, it is largely accepted that the decree ordering the burning of the slave registries was a measure to prevent the slave owners from succeeding in obtaining financial compensation from the Brazilian state. But it is worth emphasizing that preserving the records could also cause future legal problems for the old slave owners. First, some of these registries probably contained evidence of the illegal importation of Africans after 1831, when the slave trade to Brazil was first abolished. Second, despite Barbosa's good intentions, scholars failed to emphasize that the decision to scorch the register and other documents housed in the Ministry of Finance would also prevent possible future demands for financial reparations from the freed population to their former masters.

Once the issue of compensating the former masters was apparently solved, it became even clearer that the new Brazilian Republican government did not intend to put in place an official plan to support the newly freed population as was at least attempted during the Reconstruction period in the United States, through the work of the Freedmen's Bureau. Moreover, there were no measures put in place to pay financial reparations and distribute land to the freed populations. No programs were ever established to supply basic education and professional training to the newly freedmen and freedwomen.[141]

In the first decades of the twentieth century, the idea of the abolition of slavery as a gift given by the redeemer Princess Isabel to the enslaved population remained present in the public and official memory, as well as in the collective memory of elderly Afro-Brazilians.[142] But over the second half of the twentieth century, the Brazilian black movement increasingly questioned the narrative of the abolition of slavery as a gift, by replacing the celebration of May 13 (date of the signature of the Golden Law) with the commemoration of November 20, date of the death of Zumbi of Palmares, the leader of Brazil's seventeenth-century largest and longest-lasting *quilombo*. Despite this shift, recent scholarship started rehabilitating Princess Isabel's importance, by emphasizing her contribution to the late abolitionist movement, including her support to slave escapes and the *Quilombo* of Leblon, in Rio de Janeiro.[143] Historians recovered a letter written by Princess Isabel before the abolition of slavery, in which she suggested her intention to purchase and distribute land to the new freed population.[144] In the letter, dated August 11, 1889 and addressed to Manuel Afonso de Freitas Amorim (1831–1906), the Viscount of Santa Vitória, the princess reacted positively to the viscount's intention to donate funds from his bank to purchase and donate land to the former slaves. The princess believed that this proposal would allow the freed population to own land where they would be able to develop agricultural activities and livestock production.

Taken out of context, Isabel's letter could suggest that she and some of the monarchy's supporters defended reparations for slavery. In this interpretation, her project was not achieved because three months after the signature of the Golden Law a republican military coup put an end to the monarchy and sent the royal family into exile in Europe. It can also be argued that the letter was part of a political plan to put in place a third reign led by Isabel. After all, among the Brazilian population of color, her popularity as the great redeemer increased after the signature of the Golden Law. Moreover, her support to *quilombo* of Leblon is not in contradiction with possible measures to assist freedpeople. Yet, the Brazilian landowning elite would never accept offering land as material reparations to former slaves.

Losing voting rights

The new Republican government that took control of Brazil in November 1889 continued denying full citizenship to the freed population. With the approval of the Constitution of 1891, which replaced the previous Constitution of 1824, only male individuals older than twenty-one years and with a high income had the right to vote. However, the plan to restrict the right to vote had been in progress for more than a decade. In 1879, when Rui Barbosa was still a congressman, he authored and introduced the Sinimbu Bill to the Chamber of Deputies.[145] In debates in the Chamber of Deputies, Barbosa enthusiastically supported the proposal to deny illiterate people the right to vote.[146] His defense relied on the example of the United States, which at that point denied civil rights to African Americans, by insisting that in the North American country although a minority, illiterates were not allowed to vote.[147] In Brazil, however, more than 80 percent of the population was illiterate.[148] In Barbosa's own words, "political judgment is achieved through the knowledge of the state's affairs, and as this knowledge is achieved through reading; and as reading is impossible to the illiterates, it is a general assumption that the illiterate does not have this social aptitude."[149] Ultimately, despite being an abolitionist, Barbosa perceived the uneducated black population as infantile and incapable of making its own political choices.[150]

The Sinimbu Bill passed in the Chamber of Deputies, but the Senate rejected it. Thus, in April 1880, the leader of the new cabinet introduced a new Bill to the Chamber of Deputies, which once again generated intensive debates. Yet, like the previous one, the new Bill kept income restrictions and eventually established that only male individuals older than twenty-one years who could read and write were allowed to vote. The Chamber of Deputies and the Senate eventually approved the Bill no. 3.029 of January 9, 1881, also known as Law Saraiva. The law had the pernicious effect of limiting the Brazilian's population right to vote from 10 percent to 1 percent. In particular, this change dramatically restricted the right to vote of freed and free black populations.[151] In the years that followed other decrees adjusted the law. Decree no. 3122 of October 7, 1882 ascertained that in order to vote, citizens should handwrite and sign a request. It also mandated that if an attorney presented the request on behalf of a given citizen, the notary should compare the handwriting and the signature to previous documents. Later, Decree no. 200A of February 8, 1890 established that a citizen could verbally request to be included in the electoral list, but in this case a quick literacy exam would be applied. This legislation and the Constitution of 1891 ostracized the illiterate population, of whom the majority were black.[152]

Over the next decades scarcely any black citizens ran as candidates for the elections. Voters also elected very few black candidates for political offices. This context greatly contrasted with Cuba. At the end of the nineteenth century, black and brown males fully participated in a multiracial rebel army that fought for the colony's independence from Spain.[153] More importantly, the Cuban Constitution of 1901 gave equal voting rights to all male citizens older than twenty-one years.[154] Broad voting rights did not remain only on paper. In 1907, an electoral census showed that Cuban eligible voters included "virtually every male citizen over the age of twenty-one," including several former slaves.[155] In 1908 Cuban presidential elections, 71 percent of adult males voted, whereas in the US South, 30 percent of eligible males voted in elections of 1910. This disparity is also visible between Cuba and Brazil. In 1906, voters represented 2 percent of Brazilian population, whereas in Cuba voters corresponded to 21 percent of the country's total population.[156]

In Brazil, although many blacks remained excluded from occupying elected positions, some black citizens were elected for office in the early twentieth century. In 1903, Manuel da Motta Monteiro Lopes (1867–1910), referred to as "defender of the workers" and "leader of the blacks" was elected councilman in Rio de Janeiro.[157] Six years later, in 1909, he was elected congressman for the Federal District (by then the city of Rio de Janeiro). But according to the procedures in place, before taking office, the list of all elected senators and congressmen should be approved at various levels and then recognized by a special committee in the National Congress, which usually only confirmed the candidates who represented the groups in power. Because he was a black political leader, Lopes faced a great campaign of opposition, which became visible in Rio de Janeiro's press. He succeeded in taking office only after great popular demonstrations led by black and white supporters.[158] During his term, first as a councilman and later as a congressman, he defended labor rights and equality among blacks and whites.[159]

Still, during the debates about the abolition of slavery, both in Cuba and Brazil, planter elites and the government started discussing proposals to favor European immigration to replace the slave workforce. According to their views, the introduction of European immigrants would favor racial mixture (*mestiçagem* or *mestizaje*) and the gradual whitening of the predominantly black Cuban and Brazilian populations. By 1885, subsidized European immigration had increased in Brazil, and attained its height after 1888. From 1875 to 1885, 42,000 immigrants arrived in São Paulo alone; in 1888, more than 92,000 and between 1888 and 1900, more than 800,000 immigrants reached the region. Moreover, from 1884 to 1887, nearly 60,000 rising to 70,000 immigrants had been employed in the agricultural industry of São Paulo, exceeding the number of 50,000 slaves who worked in the plantations of the area in 1885.[160]

Restrictive immigration legislation supported Brazil's whitening project. On June 28, 1890, Decree no. 528 drastically limited immigration from Africa and Asia. Therefore, immigrants from these continents had to be approved by the National Congress. These restrictions contrasted with the British Caribbean and Cuban contexts. Britain, after 1834, and Spain, between 1840 and 1878 (still during slavery), introduced Chinese indentured servants in their colonies in the Caribbean to replace enslaved Africans in agricultural activities.[161] Likewise, because of the workforce shortage, Brazil eventually had to consent to the entry of immigrants from Asia. Law no. 97 of October 5, 1892 allowed the admission of Chinese and Japanese immigrants, most of whom came to the country to work in the southeast coffee industry.

As for the freed population, like the United States, Brazil witnessed the emergence of numerous black mutual aid societies. These organizations included Catholic lay brotherhoods and other lay associations like the Sociedade Protetora dos Desvalidos (Humane Society of Underprivileged) created in 1832 in Salvador, Bahia.[162] During the period of slavery these groups helped slaves to purchase manumission. They also provided assistance to integrate freed individuals in Brazilian society, a role they continued playing after emancipation. During the early twentieth century in São Paulo, several mutual aid black organizations focused their activities around voting rights and access to education. The Centro Cívico Palmares (Palmares Civic Center), created by Major Antônio Carlos from Minas Gerais, was São Paulo's first Afro-Brazilian activist organization.[163] With 100 to 150 members, the group's name invoked the largest and longest-lasting Brazilian runaway slave community, the *quilombo* of Palmares. The society developed a series of projects, including the creation of a library, a theater, a medical clinic, and secondary school courses. All over the country, black groups created newspapers as well as clubs and societies carrying the name May 13 (date of abolition of slavery) to promote social activities and support the rights of black Brazilians. These various organizations sought to fight against discrimination, to improve social and cultural ties among black citizens, and to resource them with social services.

Yet, of all associations that emerged during the postemancipation period, the Frente Negra Brasileira (Brazilian Black Front), created in 1931 in São Paulo, was the first national black organization. The group aimed at promoting the "political and social union of national black people for the affirmation of its historical rights by virtue of their material and moral activity in the past and to claim their current social and political rights, in the Brazilian Communion."[164] Still, this association and its leaders advocated integration, by barely challenging the idea of whitening.[165] Other groups often embraced respectability politics. By condemning alcoholism and behaviors perceived as immoral, they often encouraged black men and women to project an image of honorability and politeness.[166] Despite their particularities, from the 1920s to the 1960s Brazilian black organizations failed to make any demands for material and financial reparations as the movement for pensions to former slaves did in the United States.

Although in Brazil land ownership remained concentrated in the hands of few families of large landowners, during the rule of President Getúlio Vargas (1882–1954) black Brazilians in rural and urban areas started obtaining better working conditions.[167] Vargas was a populist leader, whose political support relied both on the rural elites and on the growing working class and union leaders. After taking control of the government after a military coup in 1930, the new president suspended the Constitution of 1891. Following pressures from his opponents who organized an armed uprising in the state of São Paulo in 1932, Vargas eventually called the election of a Constituent Assembly. The new Brazilian Constitution of 1934 established the eight-hour workday as well as the weekly rest-day. After creating the Labor Court in 1939, Vargas eventually signed Decree no. 5.452 of May 1, 1943, commonly known as the Consolidation of Labor Laws, ratifying a unified system of social welfare that included minimum wage, mandatory vacation, unemployment insurance, and retirement benefits.

A controversial political figure, Vargas was a populist president, who also became a dictator. As the creator of the system of social welfare, he acquired the status of "father of the poor," reason why many Afro-Brazilians considered him as the true Great Emancipator.[168] Until recently aged black men and women stated in oral interviews that Princess Isabel only signed the Golden Law, but it was Vargas who really freed the slaves.[169] Contradictorily, although Vargas introduced welfare, during the Estado Novo (New State) dictatorship (1937–1945), he also suppressed civil rights, including closing organizations like the Brazilian Black Front, which by then had recently became a political party. These progressive changes during the first four decades of the twentieth century positively affected the elder urban black population, among whom there were former slaves, and their descendants. Yet, in a country where only one-third of the population lived in the urban areas, working and living conditions of rural workers remained extremely precarious.

Although Afro-Brazilian populations continued to face enormous social and economic exclusion, most black organizations failed to question the ideology of racial democracy. During the 1930s, this ideology, which also emerged in varied forms in other parts of Latin America as the idea of mestizaje, gained strength in the public sphere. Because legal racial segregation never existed in Brazil, many intellectuals and a number of black activists embraced the view that harmonious racial relations prevailed in the country, which unlike the United States did not experience the problem of racial hatred and racism. But even though legal segregation did not exist, there was recognition that disguised forms of white supremacy ruled in Brazil, informally preventing black Brazilians from having access to schools, clubs, and other social spaces. For this reason, on July 3, 1951, Vargas signed

Law 1390 (known as Law Afonso Arinos), which criminalized racial discrimination in the country. The law included prison sentences and established fines to be imposed on the offenders. Until the 1960s, the deception of racial democracy contributed to preventing the emergence of public demands of financial and symbolic reparations for slavery in Brazil.

Reparations postponed

This chapter showed that although thousands of former slaves demanded financial and material reparations for slavery through the end of the nineteenth century and the early twentieth century in the United States, none of these attempts were successful. In Haiti, despite having dominated the land and others means of production that were once controlled by the French colonizers, the leaders of the new black country agreed to pay an enormous indemnity to the old metropole in order to be officially recognized as an independent nation. Destroyed by years of war, the colossal new debt seriously harmed the largest part of its population, which continued living in poverty. In the neighboring Jamaica, Barbados, Martinique, Guadeloupe, and French Guyana, which remained British and French colonies, former slaves faced similar problems and did not benefit from any program redistributing land.

In the United States, where Reconstruction had already proved to be a failure, hopes of citizenship and integration faded. Legal segregation and extreme racial violence were consolidated in the South. In addition, African Americans were marginalized through a series of state measures that included poll taxes and literacy tests. In this hopeless context, combining on the one hand the lack of civil rights, and on the other the persistence of poverty among thousands of elderly former slaves, who remained without access to material resources allowing them to survive, a powerful movement demanding pensions for former slaves surfaced and gained support among former slaves in several states. Although the attempts to pass legislation providing pensions to former slaves failed and despite the federal government persecution of the leaders of this movement, its very existence shows that former slaves, and especially those in more vulnerable conditions like old freedwomen, understood that they deserved redress for the unpaid work provided during the period of slavery. Likewise, the end of slavery in Latin America did not offer many hopes of social and economic inclusion to former slaves. In Cuba, a freedwoman like Andrea Quesada y Acevedo and her old slave mates proved that they were aware that their old owners owed them material and financial reparations for the unpaid work they performed. Although their attempts to obtain the inheritance of their master failed, white lawyers recognized that their demands were worth pursuing. In Brazil, the Republican government that replaced the monarchy at the end of the nineteenth century, disenfranchised the great majority of illiterate black

Brazilians. Without land, education, and voting rights, former slaves and their descendants continued living in material conditions that were very close to what existed in the period of slavery. In both Cuba and Brazil, as well as in other parts of Latin America, the absence of legal segregation combined to the powerful ideologies of racial democracy and *mestizaje* contributed to disguising racism and racial inequalities, ultimately preventing the emergence of organized movements demanding reparations for slavery. In these regions, demands for reparations emerged at different rhythms only after the end of the Second World War.

4

"What Else Will the Negro Expect?"

The years between the two world wars were characterized by sparse mentions of reparations for slavery. Until the end of the First World War, individuals and groups who advocated material and financial restitutions to former slaves did not employ the term "reparations" to refer to these requests. After the end of the war, for the first time in history, the term "reparations" was popularized as the payment of financial wartime indemnities by a nation, leading African Americans to embrace the term when demanding restitutions for slavery. Although black nationalist activists such as Marcus Garvey invoked the need for reparations in some of his speeches, these demands were not central elements in the programs of the organizations he created.

This landscape of isolated demands of reparations for slavery and the Atlantic slave trade dramatically changed after the end of the Second World War. The fall of the Nazi regime in Germany and the revelation of the Holocaust atrocities contributed to the intensification of the debates on human atrocities and racism. German reparations to the Jewish victims of the Holocaust, along with the recognition of the brutalities committed against Japanese Americans during wartime, encouraged African American activists to request reparations for more than three centuries of slavery. Likewise, the rise of the Cold War shifted the ways black militants and political leaders conceived the problem of the social and economic legacies of slavery and the Atlantic slave trade in the Americas and Africa.

Reparations were not the central element of the Civil Rights Movement's agenda. But several prominent African American leaders challenged the US government to address the problem of racial inequalities associated with the legacies of slavery and Jim Crow. Their demands included the creation of legal mechanisms to fight against social and economic inequalities, racism, and segregation, and for access to full citizenship. Despite this focus on civil rights, during the 1960s black nationalist groups gave new life to the reparations cause. Along with many supporters, they led public campaigns calling for reparations for slavery and the Atlantic slave trade.

This chapter discusses the contrasting ways Brazil, Cuba, and the United States dealt with the problem of symbolic, material, and financial reparations for slavery from the Great Depression and continuing through the Cold War era. In 1959, a revolutionary movement deposed the dictator Fulgencio Batista (1901–1973) in Cuba. The new revolutionary government conducted a large agrarian reform, which redistributed land to peasants, thereby benefiting black Cubans. Brazil, however, took a very different path. On April 1, 1964, a military junta deposed the country's president and took control of the country. Over the next twenty-one years, the dictatorship prevented the public organization of the black movement, thus hindering any attempts to demand reparations for slavery. Despite these varied paths, this chapter illustrates how the era of the Civil Rights Movement opened an enormous space to reintroduce the issue of restitutions for slavery in the public debate, especially in the United States but also in other parts of the Americas.

"America claims she has nothing for us"

On the eve of the First World War, as the movement demanding pensions for former slaves declined, Marcus Mosiah Garvey (1887–1940) launched the Universal Negro Improvement Association (UNIA) as well as other related initiatives gathering black men and women in the United States, Canada, South America, and Central America, as well as in English-speaking countries of the Caribbean and Africa. Although demands for symbolic and material reparations for slavery and the Atlantic slave trade were not central elements of the programs of Garvey's organizations, his speeches calling the sons of the African diaspora to return to Africa invoked the need for restitution, attracting countless followers in different countries.

Born in Jamaica, Garvey was a descendant of slaves and publicly claimed this identity: "We are the descendants of the men and women who suffered in this country for two hundred and fifty years under that barbarous, that brutal institution, known as slavery."[1] Whereas his grandfather, William Garvey (c. 1805–1891), was an enslaved man, his father Mosiah Garvey (1837–1920) was born during the apprenticeship period in Jamaica.[2] As a young man, Garvey left school to work as a printer in Kingston. In 1910, when he was already invested in becoming a young political leader and orator, he moved to Central America, where he spent time working for a small newspaper in Costa Rica. He also spent time in Belize, Honduras, and Panama, and then moved to England. Back in Jamaica in 1914, Garvey maintained a correspondence with African American educator and author Booker T. Washington (1856–1915) with whom he discussed the creation of an industrial and agricultural school in Jamaica inspired by the model of the Tuskegee Institute in Alabama. Unfortunately, Washington died one year before Garvey was finally able to come to the United States in 1916.

Garvey created UNIA as a benevolent association in 1914 when he was still in Jamaica, but the organization only acquired its international dimension when he moved to the United States. Once in the new country, he soon realized that the early educational projects he had in mind, once also advocated by Washington, were indeed facing enormous obstacles, preventing black integration into white American society. As African American soldiers returned from the war and migrated to urban centers, racial violence and segregation increased. Disenfranchisement continued, destroying hopes of assimilation among many black activists and ordinary citizens. This new context led Garvey to become the most prominent promoter of black nationalism. By centering UNIA's program on the empowerment of populations of African descent in the United States, and in the African diaspora, Garvey promoted the movement back to Africa as a response to the persistent exclusion and racial violence faced by black populations in the Americas. Garvey led numerous initiatives. He created the weekly newspaper *Negro World* and the Universal Printing House. He also launched the Black Star Line, a steamship company to facilitate commercial exchanges between black populations in the United States, the Caribbean, and Africa. In just a few years, hundreds of chapters of UNIA emerged around the world. Very visible with its public meetings and parades, the organization's membership numbers are hard to assess. But it would not be an exaggeration to state that hundreds of thousands of black men and women across the Americas and the African continent either joined or admired the association.

During the rise of UNIA, the notion of "reparations" gained attention with the end of the First World War. In 1919, the Treaty of Versailles mandated Germany to pay U$33 billion in compensation for war damages to the Allied and Associated Powers (United States, Britain, France, Italy, and Japan).[3] That same year, Garvey purchased the Liberty Hall building in Harlem, New York City, which became UNIA's headquarters. From August 1 to August 31, 1920, UNIA's first international convention gathered approximately two thousand attendees at Liberty Hall. That meeting approved the "Declaration of the Rights of the Negro Peoples of the World," a document with guiding principles of the association demanding civil rights and the end of racial segregation.

But very soon Garvey started facing hostility by both African American leaders and the US federal government. NAACP (National Association for the Advancement of Colored People) and its co-founder W. E. B. Du Bois (1868–1963) fought Garvey's views advocating black separatism. On his end Garvey disapproved NAACP's integrationist program. Opposition from African American intellectuals only increased.

In February 1922, exactly as happened with the leaders of the movement requesting pensions for former slaves, such as Callie House, Garvey was indicted for mail fraud originating from the sale of Black Star Line stock, including the announcement of the transatlantic voyage of SS *Phyllis Wheatley*, a ship which UNIA did not yet own. In June 1922, with the hope of obtaining support to his black nationalist agenda, Garvey met in Atlanta Edward Young Clarke (1877–1950), the leader of the white supremacist Ku Klux Klan, whose number of members around the country by the time was estimated at between four and seven million. Garvey's goal was to negotiate racial separatist lines. African American activists perceived the meeting as betrayal, and the resulting conflicts often ended with physical violence.[4]

On May 18, 1923, Garvey's trial began. On June 21 of the same year, the jury sentenced him to spend five years in prison. Yet, on September 10, 1923, after staying three months in prison, he was released on bail. On that occasion, he delivered an important speech in Liberty Hall wherein he called for both material and symbolic reparations for slavery and colonization:

> America claims she has nothing for us; and England says she has nothing for us; France says so, and the different European governments say they have nothing for us, and we hear some talk now that they have nothing for us in these parts; but we have decided that we have something for ourselves, and we have understood that somebody has been keeping it for us. Now we are just about thanking them for being so good in keeping that which was belonging to us, and we are just asking to us. [. . .] We are asking England to hand it back; we are asking France to hand it back; we are asking Italy to hand it back; we are asking Belgium to hand it back; we are asking Portugal to hand it back; we are asking Spain to hand it back.[5]

Despite these rhetorical demands for reparations, the period that followed Garvey's first arrest in the United States marked UNIA's decline. Garvey was under continued scrutiny by the Federal Bureau of Investigation and by 1923 the federal government, through its Immigration and Naturalization Service, initiated measures to deport him to Jamaica. In the following year, Du Bois published an article describing Garvey as "without doubt, the most dangerous enemy of the Negro race in America and in the world" because of his black nationalist positions.[6] On February 8, 1925, Garvey was arrested and resumed serving his sentence in prison. After several appeals, President John Calvin Coolidge Jr. (1872–1933) commuted his sentence. Garvey was deported from the United States, and settled in London, England, where he died in 1940.

Between the two world wars, UNIA acquired visibility in various countries with significant populations of African descent. Meanwhile, the legacies of slavery persisted in the Americas. In the United States, even though the prospects of obtaining restitutions for the living former slaves and their descendants looked unlikely, the idea of pensions for former slaves as a form of reparations remained alive among old ex-slaves.

"Never knowed any what got land or mules nor nothing"

From 1933 to 1938, President Franklin Delano Roosevelt (1882–1945) created federal programs to provide relief to the populations affected by the nefarious effects of the Great Depression that ravaged the United States after the Stock Market Crash of 1929. These initiatives usually referred to as the New Deal, included the Works Progress Administration, which employed more than eight million people. As part of this relief package, in 1935, Roosevelt launched the Federal Writers' Project, an initiative aimed at funding written works and supporting writers. Between 1936 and 1938, men and women employed in this project were assigned to interview former slaves in seventeen southern states. Despite the biases of the interviewers and the limitations of the material collected, these hundreds of testimonies of elderly former slaves provide glimpses on their living and working conditions. More importantly, these narratives also reveal their expectations and views regarding restitution for slavery.

In their accounts, several interviewees, although very old, were also too young when slavery was abolished. Yet, former slaves remembered the days they lived in bondage, the Civil War, and the years that followed emancipation. At first sight, several testimonies suggest that former slaves preferred their working and living conditions during slavery, rather than after emancipation. Yet, as in other oral narratives, such statements, made almost seventy years after the legal abolition of slavery in the United States, reflected not on the realities of the past, but rather their precarious economic position at the time of the interview.

Still, in the 1930s, several of the former slaves lived in extreme poverty. Unassisted by the government, their living conditions were similar to the elderly freedmen and freedwomen who in previous decades petitioned the US Congress to obtain pensions. Although one could argue that during this period there were poor whites who were facing similar hardships, for most former enslaved men and women, extreme poverty was the only reality they had experienced for generations. Yet, several former slaves interviewed in the context of the Federal Writers' Project stated that after emancipation through different means they were successful in becoming owners of a small parcel of land and a house. Aunt Adeline, an elderly woman eighty-nine years old and resident of Fayetteville, Arkansas, provided one example from her family. She explained that after the end of the Civil War her former master, in an exceptional gesture, gave money to his former slaves:

When the war was over, Mr. Parks was still in the South and gave to each of his slaves who did not want to come back to Arkansas so much money. My uncle George came back with Mr. Parks and was given a good mountain farm of forty acres, which he put in cultivation and one of my uncle's descendants still lives on the place.[7]

Other former slaves also declared that after emancipation they remained living on the same plantation they used to work during slavery times.[8]

However, several interviewees testified that they were never able to obtain any land: "It seem like it tuck a long time fer freedom to come. Everything jest kept on like it was. We heard that lots of slaves was getting land and some mules to set up theirselves; I never knowed any what got land or mules nor nothing."[9] Despite their old age, freedmen and freedwomen clearly knew that land distribution as reparations for slavery was a myth. Boston Blackwell, a former slave ninety-eight years old, and resident of North Little Rock, Arkansas, illustrated with humor the tale of "forty acres and a mule": "That old story 'bout 40 acres and a mule, it make me laugh. Yessum they sure did tell us that, but I never knowed any pusson which got it." Curiously, by the time of his interview he still recalled the campaigns to provide pensions to former slaves: "The officers told us we would all get slave pension. That just exactly what they tell. They sure did tell me I would get a passel (parcel) of ground to farm. Nothing ever hatched out of that, neither."[10] Thomas John, a resident of St. Cleburne, Texas, born in 1847, was near ninety years old by the time of the interview. He also remembered the myth of land distribution and ironically associated it to the small old age pension, which he had recently started receiving:

De Yankees told us niggers when they freed us after de war dat dey would give each one of us 40 acres of land and a mule. De nearest I'se ever come to dat is de pension of 'leven dollars I gets now. But I'se jus' as thankful for that as I can be. In fac', I don't see how I could be any more thankful it 'twas a hun'erd and 'leven dollars.[11]

These testimonies show that during the Great Depression, several former slaves who at some point had access to land ownership or who were able to purchase a house had lost their properties in the decades that followed. Like the previous generations who fought for pensions for former slaves, many men and women were living their old days in extreme poverty. Maria Sutton Clemments, an elderly resident of DeValls Bluff, Arkansas, was between eighty-five and ninety years old when she was interviewed. She related to the interviewer her life with her husband in the period after the end of slavery. Although initially they were able to purchase a house and some land, eventually they lost everything:

When we got so we not able to work hard he come to town and carpentered, right here, and I cooked fo Mr. Hopkins seven years and fo Mr. Gust Thweatt and fo Mr. Nick Thweatt. We got a little ahead then by the hardest. I carried my money right [bag on a string tied around her waist]. We bought a house and five acres of land. No mum I don't own it now. We got in hard luck and give a mortgage. They closed us out. Mr. Sanders. They say I can live there long as I lives. But they owns it.[12]

Likewise, Lewis Chase, an elderly man of approximately ninety years of age and resident of Des Arc, Arkansas, told his interviewer that he never had access to land ownership. Probably a matter of dignity, he avoided complaining during the interview by tempering that his employers housed him, like in the times of slavery: "Noom I never owned no land, noom no home neither. I didn't need no home. The man I worked for give me a house on his place. I work for another man and he give me a house on his land. I owned a horse one time. I rode her."[13]

These former slaves recollected periods of hunger, as well as lack of access to land and house ownership. Moreover, several elderly men and women voiced the need to obtain pensions, which had just been recently created by the Social Security Act of 1935. Mary Minus Biddie, 105 years old, and resident of Eatonville, Florida, praised Roosevelt for giving her a pension, which she had anticipated for a very long time. But although former slaves appreciated the new social programs, they did not see old age pensions as gifts from the federal government, but rather as payment to what was due to them since emancipation: "Roosevelt has don' mo' than any other president, why you know ever since freedom they been talkin' 'bout dis pension, talking' bout it that's all, but you see Mr. Roosevelt he don' com' an' gived it tu us. What? I'll say he's a good rightus man, an' um sho' go' vot' fo' him."[14] Biddie's interviewer interpreted this statement as an indication of gratitude and resignation: "Residing in her little cabin in Eatonville, Florida, she is able to smile because she has some means of security, the Old Age Pension."[15] Yet, despite the biased comment by the interviewer, the daily reality of most former slaves was quite different, and in several states they did not have much reason to smile. In Arkansas especially, several elderly men and women described their difficult living conditions. Despite having worked until their seventies, most of them were still fighting to obtain a pension.[16]

The interviews show that the movement to provide pensions to former slaves, discussed in Chapter 3, remained alive in the memory of freedpeople as late as the period of the Great Depression. Richard Grump of Little Rock, Arkansas, was eighty-two years old when he was interviewed. Like other former slaves, he worked until reaching the age of seventy-five years. Although by the time of the interview he was receiving an old age pension, he still expected to obtain an ex-slave pension as a form of reparations for the years he lived in bondage: "Whatever they want to give me, I'll take it and make out with it. If there's any chance for me to git a slave's pension, I wish they would send it to me. For I need it awful bad. They done cut me way down now. I got heart trouble and high blood pressure but I don't give up."[17]

Another interviewee, Louisa Davis, a resident of Winnsboro, South Carolina, declared her age as 106 years. Although in her testimony she made sure to make positive comments about white people, certainly in order to avoid any trouble, she also emphasized that her husband's former owners refused to provide him with any kind of financial compensation for slavery times:

When de war come on, Sam went wid young Marster Tom Sloan as bodyguard, and attended to him, and learned to steal chickens, geese, and turkeys for his young marster, just to tell 'bout it. He dead now; and what I blames de white folks for, they never would give him a pension, though he spend so much of his time and labor in their service. I ain't bearin' down on my kind of white folks, for I'd jump wid joy if I could just git back into slavery and have de same white folks to serve and be wid them, day in and day out.[18]

Other elderly men and women also referenced the pensions to former slaves during their interviews, even though sometimes it was not clear if they were indeed referring to the old age pensions. For example, Boston Blackwell, ninety-eight years old, and resident of North Little Rock, Arkansas, told his interviewer he still expected to get an ex-slave pension:

Always I was a watching for my slave pension to begin coming. 'Fore I left the army my captain, he told me to file. [. . .] My file number, it is 1,115,857. After I keeped them papers for so many years, white and black folks bofe told me it ain't never coming—my slave pension—and I reckon the chilren tored up the papers. Lady, that number for me is filed in Washington. Iffen you go there, see can you get my pension.[19]

Likewise, Laura Thornton, a 105-year-old woman from Little Rock, Arkansas, still remembered the proposals to award pensions to ex-slaves at the time of her interview: "They made like they was goin' to give old slave folks a pension." Despite her hopes, she was not receiving any old age pension and depended on her grandchildren to survive:

They ain't gimme none yit. I'm just livin' on the mercy of the people. I can't keep up the taxes now. I wish I could git a pension. It would help keep me up till I died. They won't even as much as give me nothin' on the relief. They say these grandchildren ought to keep me up. I have to depend on them and they can't hardly keep up theirselves.[20]

The struggle for reparations under the Communist threat

Whereas some former slaves conveyed their expectations regarding a possible form of reparations for slavery, during the period between the two world wars, debates on the general notion of material and symbolic reparations continued at the international level. In 1928, the Permanent Court of International Justice responded to an international court case by requesting states to provide restitution for unlawful acts. Through this measure, reparations became a principle of international law.[21]

Near the end of the Second World War, during the Yalta Conference of 1945, the Western Allied Powers (United States, Britain, and France) discussed again the terms through which Germany would pay postwar reparations. After the end of the war, during the Potsdam Conference, intensive negotiations on German reparations for war damages to specific states continued. During the second half of the twentieth century, while the fight against European colonial rule in Africa, the Caribbean, and Asia intensified, the struggle for civil rights in the United States carried on as well. In this period, organizations representing the interests of groups victimized during the Second World War embraced the concept of reparations.

Jewish Holocaust survivors succeeded in obtaining official apologies and financial compensation from Germany. Just after the end of the war, the Jewish Agency submitted demands for reparations to the Allied Powers.[22] In 1951, the newly created state of Israel requested reparations of $6 billion from West Germany for Jewish property stolen by the Nazis. The requests also included an additional amount of $1.5 billion to cover the costs of the resettlement of approximately 500,000 Holocaust survivors in Israel. Several Jewish organizations supported these enterprises which culminated with the creation of the Conference on Jewish Material Claims Against Germany.[23] Yet, several Holocaust survivors opposed the idea of receiving indemnifications. They considered that material and financial reparations would not redress the persecution and genocide of millions of Jews.

On February 19, 1942, almost three months after the Japanese attacked Pearl Harbor, US President Franklin Delano Roosevelt signed the Executive Order 9066. The order established that the "Military Commander may determine from which any or all persons could be excluded" from particular designated areas without trial or hearing.[24] Without any warning to the Japanese American population, the order allowed the issuing of exclusion orders to be posted in 108 areas from where men, women, and children of Japanese descent should be removed.[25] Approximately 120,000 US citizens and permanent resident aliens of Japanese ancestry were relocated under the War Relocation Authority in ten concentration camps in various parts of the United States.[26] On December 18, 1944, the US Supreme Court ruled that the War Relocation Authority was not authorized to confine Japanese American citizens who were not charged with disloyalty. Despite this decision, it was not until January 2, 1945 that the internees started leaving the camps. Eventually, on July 2, 1948, President Harry S. Truman signed the Japanese American Evacuation Claims Act allowing Japanese Americans sent to internment camps to submit financial claims for property loss that resulted from relocation.[27]

In the years that followed the Act's signature, former internees submitted thousands of claims to the federal government. Between 1948 and 1978, the Congress of the United States issued eight other Acts to amend the original legislation. Meanwhile, in 1980, another victorious case of reparations was concluded when the US Supreme Court ordered the federal government to pay $17.1 million in damages to eight Sioux tribes for South Dakota's land seized in 1877.[28] Likewise, in 1988, after decades of public debates, as well as pressures by associations of Japanese Americans, President Ronald Reagan (1911–2004) eventually signed the Civil Liberties Act. The Act acknowledged the "injustice of evacuation, relocation, and internment of United States citizens and permanent resident aliens of Japanese ancestry" during the Second World War. The Act also addressed a formal apology to the victims for the "evacuation, relocation, and internment."[29] Moreover, the law established a public fund to teach the population about the wrongful act in order to avoid a similar event from occurring in the future. Finally, it mandated compensation of $20,000 to each victim confined in internment camps. By the time the law passed, approximately 60,000 former internees of the 120,000 interned were still alive. In 1998, Canada also issued an apology to Japanese Canadians who were confined in internment camps during the Second World War, and provided to each survivor financial reparations of US$17,325.[30]

As the international struggle against Nazism and Fascism evolved during the Second World War, the issue of reparations for slavery barely reached the public sphere. But the awards of restitution to groups victimized during the war encouraged black activists to demand reparations. The end of the war highlighted again the situation of social and economic exclusion of black populations in the Americas and Africa. Although the United States battled dictatorial regimes abroad, at the domestic level, African Americans remained segregated, with their voting rights denied, and as victims of racial hatred. Likewise, even though African soldiers had fought the Axis powers along with the Allies during the war, in their home countries African populations remained submitted to oppressive European colonial regimes. African American public figures who identified themselves as descendants of slaves vaguely mentioned restitutions for slavery in their discourses. However, despite their visibility, these social actors did not have and did not seek the necessary popular support to address formal demands of reparations either to governments or to descendants of former slave owners. Thus, although important, their rhetorical and individual calls for reparations remained isolated endeavors.

During the first half of the twentieth century, racism and precarious living conditions continued as overarching concerns for most African Americans. Yet, many men and women from the second generation up from slavery succeeded in getting access to education, which allowed them to obtain better material conditions. The example of the athlete, celebrated actor, singer, and civil rights activist Paul Robeson (1898–1976) illustrates this new social mobility. Robeson was born in Princeton, New Jersey. His father was an enslaved man, who escaped slavery running away from a North Carolina plantation.[31]

Through his work and political activity, Robeson advocated the rights of black populations not only in the United States, but also in Africa and the African diaspora. In the 1930s, Robeson became a friend of the Soviet Union. By that time, the Communist Party of the United States (CPUSA), founded in 1919, had gained influence among African Americans. Between 1923 and 1924, several members of the African Blood Brotherhood joined the party.[32] Among them, was Harry Haywood (1898–1985), who became one of its prominent leaders. In 1928, during the congress of the Third International (Comintern), an organization gathering all national communist parties, he developed the "Resolutions on the Negro Question."[33] Sustaining the thesis that African Americans formed a nation within a nation, he defended self-determination through the formation of a Black Belt Republic in the South. In the context of this growing influence of the CPUSA among African Americans, Paul Robeson visited the Soviet Union for the first time in 1934. But with the rise of the Cold War, the US Federal Bureau of Investigation (FBI) and Central Intelligence Agency (CIA) became increasingly interested in his political activities. Federal officials suspected that Robeson had become a member of the CPUSA, and kept him under close surveillance.

As the Second World War evolved, Robeson brought to light in his speeches the social and economic exclusion of African Americans. To Robeson their situation of economic insecurity resulted from "continuing discrimination in employment [. . .], coupled with other forms of economic exploitation and social discrimination in urban areas." He opposed black enlistment in the US military because of "segregation and inferior status assigned to Negroes in the armed forces." Robeson also denounced "the poll-tax system of the South, which operates to maintain undemocratic elements in places of authority not only below the Mason-Dixon line but in our national life as a whole."[34] Moreover, he also fought against the participation of African Americans as soldiers during the Korean War (1950–1953).

In his speeches and writings, Robeson not only claimed his identity as the descendant of a slave, but also nurtured the idea of reparations for slavery. After the end of the Second World War, he became a strong supporter of the independence of African countries and also of the US labor movement. In a public address delivered during a meeting of the National Labor Conference for Negro Rights held in Chicago on June 10, 1950, Robeson reminded his audience that it was "*the Negro people, upon whose unpaid toil as slaves the basic wealth of this nation was built!*"[35] In that same year, in a speech delivered during the Trade Union Convention, he expressed a similar argument: "On the backs of my forebears [. . .], in the cotton fields, in the mines and mills, on the rivers and streams, providing wealth of every kind, was much of the South—Way of whole United States built. This is so today."[36]

In his notes for another public speech, he emphasized the fact that until that day, former slaves and their descendants had not received any kind of restitution. Even worse, they were still denied civil rights: "For we are still fighting to get our 40 acres & a mule in the South, still fighting for right to a decent job, all opportunities of upgrading & advancement, still fighting for a chance to gain decent homes, to have decent food at reasonable prices, still fighting to vote to stay alive—not be lynched by."[37] As an activist of international reputation, Robeson's defense of African American civil rights was also related to the emergence of the demands for reparations for the Jewish victims of the Holocaust. In 1952, he published an article in the *New World Review* supporting the petition "We Charge Genocide," which he helped to write, and presented by William L. Patterson (1891–1980) to the United Nations.[38] In this essay, Robeson referred to the "tens of millions sacrificed in the slave ships and on the plantations," by comparing slavery to the Holocaust.[39] Based on the Genocide Convention adopted by the General Assembly of the United Nations on December 9, 1948, the article maintained the official definition of genocide as "acts committed with intent to destroy, in whole or in part, a national, racial, ethnic or religious group," which comprised "causing serious bodily or mental harm to members of the group."[40] Robeson stated that segregation and Jim Crown constituted "genocidal policy of government against Negro people."[41] Although addressing an urgent need, African American activists certainly knew that the possible recognition of Jim Crow as genocide, to the same degree acknowledged for the Holocaust, could favor formal demands for reparations for slavery in the future.

Likewise, in his occasional contributions to the progressive magazine *Jewish Life*, Robeson drew attention to the historic alliance of Jews and African Americans against racism and discrimination in the United States. He underscored that "the rights of all other minorities, are inseparably linked with the liberation struggles of the Negro people."[42] Unlike previous activists who voiced the need for reparations for slavery, Robeson was not arrested or convicted of mail fraud by federal authorities. Yet, the passing of the Internal Security Act of 1950 increased the persecution of individuals suspected of being communists. Consequently, in that same year, the US Department of State confiscated Robeson's passport on the grounds that he was a member of the CPUSA, which four years later was outlawed through the Communist Control Act.[43] Despite this major restriction, he continued his political activities in the United States. On September 23, 1953, he received the Stalin Prize for Strengthening Peace, an award named after the controversial Soviet dictator. Prevented from traveling to Moscow, he was conferred the prize during a ceremony held in Harlem's iconic Hotel Theresa in New York City.[44] In 1958, Robeson's passport was eventually restored.

Reparations for slavery and the agrarian issue

As the Civil Rights Movement and the struggle for emancipation in Africa and the Caribbean evolved, former slave societies in the Americas debated the problem of social and economic inequalities. Yet, these debates failed to identify the populations of African descent as the greatest victims of social exclusion. With the rise of the Cold War, Cuba and Brazil had to deal with the need for agrarian reform to provide land to the enormous majority of their populations still living in rural areas without access to landownership. Yet, the two nations took dramatically different paths.

The United States continued to exert great political and economic influence on Cuba in the five decades after its independence from Spain. Free from colonial rule, the race problem persisted on the island. Afro-Cubans who fought the wars of independence continued fighting for civil rights. This long battle culminated with the 1912 uprising which mainly spread in Oriente province. Led by the Partido Independiente de Color (Independent Party of Color), the revolt was harshly suppressed by the armies of Cuba and the United States, making hundreds of Afro-Cuban victims.[45] In the years that followed, the racial problem persisted, and access to landownership remained a major problem. As the land concentrated in the hands of large landowners, black peasants, who remained illiterate and living in poverty, became wage workers. Afro-Cubans who owned plots of lands (realengos), which their ancestors received as a reward for their participation in the wars of independence, had then to fight companies and landlords who threatened to take their lands.

During the 1930s, Cuban peasants did not voice demands for reparations for slavery. But under the leadership of black veteran Lino de las Mercedes Álvarez (1877–1954), they fought to keep possession of realengos.[46] As these movements emerged, the Communist Party of Cuba (PCC) attempted to obtain support from black peasants in areas such as the sugar and mining region of the province of Oriente, where blacks still outnumbered the white population.[47] Advocating self-determination and the creation of a multinational "black nation" within Cuba, similarly to the CPUSA, the PCC defended a Cuban version of Haywood's Black Belt Republic thesis.[48] In 1933, the National Union of Sugar Workers and the National Confederation of Cuban Workers, along with UNIA led massive protests of rural workers, including Cubans, Jamaicans, Haitians, and Puerto Ricans, most of whom labored in US-owned sugar and tobacco plantations.[49] Despite the black nationalist proposals which emerged from these movements, most Afro-Cubans advocated integration.[50] But that same year, Fulgencio Batista, a man of African descent from a lower-class family, led a military coup against Carlos Manuel de Céspedes y Quesada (1871–1939).[51] To face a period of social unrest which resulted in several massive strikes, the new government established a New Deal program. Even though never fully implemented, the program included the creation of a minimum wage for urban and rural workers. The new legislation also made illegal dismissal of employees without just cause.[52] Such programs associated with the lack of legal segregation were temporarily successful in appeasing Cuban black population, who in the ensuing years refrained from making more serious demands for amends for the time their ancestors lived in bondage.

In 1940, during the Second World War, Batista was officially elected the president of Cuba. His rule had a few similarities with Vargas's first government in Brazil. He ratified the Constitution of 1940, which confirmed workers' right to a minimum wage and pensions, and limited the daily workload to eight hours. Moreover, like Brazil, Cuba participated in the war along with the Allied forces. After the end of his term, Batista moved to the United States. But in 1949, during the Cold War, the former president returned to the island. Back in Cuba, in 1952, Batista led a military coup establishing a dictatorship in the country. The new dictatorial government suspended the Constitution of 1940, greatly affecting Afro-Cubans, who, despite having achieved more inclusion, were still discriminated against in various spheres of employment.[53] Batista's government was a period of widespread corruption. Evidently, he did not hesitate to use force to suppress popular demonstrations. But opposition soon emerged. On July 26, 1953, an organized group of armed men led by Fidel Castro (1926–2016) and his brother Raul Castro attacked the Moncada Barracks, in an attempt to depose Batista. The attack failed, but in the following five years, the group gathered in Sierra Maestra in the predominantly black province of Oriente from where they developed guerrilla warfare.

On December 31, 1958, the Rebel Army overthrew Batista. In the months that followed, the revolutionary government led by Fidel Castro promised to solve the racial issue. In a public speech delivered on October 22, 1959, Castro enthusiastically claimed that "With a people like this Cuba will never be slave again!"[54] In another public speech, four days later on October 26, 1959, he associated the revolution that deposed Batista with the fight against slavery:

> For the first time these exceptional circumstances arise; for the first time in the history of the Cuban nation, which four centuries ago, beginning with those Indians, persecuted, and killed by the conquerors and which continued throughout that long period of slavery in which men were bought and sold like beasts, and was concluded at this stage that cost 20,000 dead, thousands of peasant houses burned, thousands of peasants killed in the name of selfishness, greed, and large interests [. . .] the nation, convinced that it is engaged in the only struggle in which a people can engage to break free from the shackles that enslave it economically and politically.[55]

In 1959, the government issued the first Agrarian Reform Law. Until 1953, the date of the most recent census undertaken in Cuba, the island's population was 5,829,029. Of this number, 57 percent lived in urban areas, whereas 43 percent lived in rural zones.[56] The agrarian reform expropriated farms larger than approximately 1,000 acres (30 *caballerías*), even though in some industries, such as rice and sugar, it allowed the existence of properties of up to approximately 3,000 acres (100 *caballerías*). Confiscated land was redistributed to landless workers or to poor peasants who owned parcels smaller than 66 acres (2 *caballerías*).[57]

But following the failed US invasion of Bay of Pigs, the revolution took a new turn, and the government intensified the reforms. In 1963, the second Agrarian Reform Law seized all farms larger than 166 acres (5 *caballerías*). Although these measures were not intentionally conceived or presented as reparations for slavery, in his numerous speeches Castro referred to the revolution as having redeemed poor Cubans from the legacies of slavery. In 1973, Castro claimed that it was the revolution which "eradicated all forms of exploitation of man by man." According to him, the Cuban Revolution "completed that step given by Céspedes, when he freed the slaves, and that agreement of Camagüeyans, when on February 26, 1869, they decreed the abolition of slavery."[58] However, Castro forgot to mention that this early initiative abolishing slavery in Camagüey contained a provision awarding financial compensation to the slave owners. Despite the lack of democracy, and although racial inequalities and racism persisted in socialist Cuba, land reform along with other programs such as total access to free health care and education provided Afro-Cubans with symbolic and material restitutions, which were not made available to most descendants of slaves in other parts of the Americas.

In Brazil, since the 1930s, Vargas's government also introduced new legislation creating welfare programs that benefited former slaves and their descendants, especially in the urban areas, but also in the countryside.[59] By this time, there was a solid black press in states like São Paulo and numerous organizations all over the country which denounced racism and requested better work and living conditions. Despite these initiatives, historical meetings like the I Congress of the Brazilian Black, held in Rio de Janeiro from August 26 to September 4, 1950, defended a moderate integrationist program.[60] Even though these groups requested land redistribution in their agendas, by referring sometimes to the concentration of land ownership as a heritage of slavery times, they did not invoke financial and material reparations for slavery.

During the 1960s, the distribution of the Brazilian population over the country's territory contrasted with that of the United States. In Brazil, nearly 70 percent of the population resided in the rural zones, whereas in the United States 70 percent of the population lived in urban areas. In other words, it is not an exaggeration to state that Brazilian land property accrued in the hands of very few large landowners. Peasants, most of them black, remained illiterate, living and working in extremely precarious conditions. In the country's Northeast, especially, they subsisted with meager earnings and without access to decent health care, facing droughts and experiencing hunger every season. Extreme poverty propelled social unrest both in rural and urban areas, leading these men, women, and children to migrate to the cities in search of better living conditions.

Resulting from these deep social and racial inequalities, in the early 1960s, during the government of President João Goulart (1918–1976), a growing movement of peasant leagues demanding land reform emerged all over Brazil. Unlike Castro, however, Goulart intended to appease Brazilian society's inequalities through a reformist path. After taking office in 1961, he established an active dialogue with various peasant groups, many of whom were blacks who for generations had remained without access to land ownership. In November 1961, Goulart attended the I National Congress of Farmers and Agricultural workers organized by the Union of Farmers and Agricultural Workers of Brazil (ULTAB). Peasant leagues started organizing themselves through unions and federations, a movement that led to the creation of National Confederation of Workers in Agriculture (CONTAG). Although this movement failed to cite the agrarian issue as a problem inherited from the period of slavery, it contributed to the passing of the Statute of the Rural Worker.[61] In addition to regulating work contracts, this law expanded social benefits to rural workers, most of whom were Afro-Brazilians living and working in the country's Northeast. With the support of peasant groups, Goulart's government embraced a campaign to change the Constitution in order to allow confiscating unproductive land to redistribute it through an agrarian reform. Yet, during the Cold War and just five years after the Cuban Revolution, the United States perceived the implementation of these reforms as a communist threat. Goulart faced great opposition from the military and various sectors of the elites and middle class. Supported by the government of the United States, the Brazilian military initiated a plot that resulted in a coup. On April 1, 1964, the military deposed Goulart.

Brazilian black activists actively participated in the resistance against the military rule that lasted more than two decades. The new regime reinforced the ideology that the country was a racial democracy. On the one hand, the military persecuted, arrested, tortured and murdered individuals and groups who publicly denounced racism and the fallacy of racial democracy.[62] On the other hand, even among the opponents to the dictatorship, black activists could barely engage the discussion on racism and the legacies of slavery without being accused of attempting to divide the movement of resistance.[63] Ultimately, dictatorship put an end in the illusion that Brazil was a racial democracy.

"'Cause it was built off our backs"

As Brazil submerged in repressive obscurantism of a civil–military dictatorship, the Civil Rights Movement flourished in the United States. Honoring the tradition inaugurated by the movement to secure pensions for former slaves, some civil rights activists created groups that officially demanded reparations for slavery and Jim Crow from the US government. Following in the steps of previous black women who fiercely fought for reparations was Audley Eloise Moore (1898–1997), whose activism over the years won her the title of Queen Mother. Born in New Iberia, Louisiana, like previous advocates of reparations, Moore was a descendant of slaves. The mother of her father was born in slavery and like many other enslaved women, she was raped by her master. As a young woman, Moore witnessed the US South racial violence. Her mother's father and her grandmother's husband were both lynched.[64]

During the First World War, while in New Orleans, Moore and her two younger sisters supported black soldiers who were left unassisted by the Red Cross.[65] By 1919, she learned about Garvey's movement and ideas. In 1922, she met him when he came to New Orleans to create a branch of UNIA. On that occasion, two rallies were expected to take place. But the visit was marked by moments of great tension, as the police of New Orleans threatened to arrest the black nationalist leader. Thus, although the meeting planned for the first night was canceled, in the second night a crowd of thousands of supporters gathered at the Longshoreman's Hall. Among them was Moore, who attended Garvey's speech under the close surveillance of dozens of federal agents and detectives. Soon after, she joined UNIA.[66]

In 1922, along with her husband and sisters, Moore left New Orleans and moved to California, then to Chicago, and eventually arrived in New York City. Leaving behind the racially segregated South, they settled in Harlem during the effervescent period of the Harlem Renaissance. An advocate of black nationalism, Moore became a prominent activist of African American civil rights. In 1933, after UNIA's decline, she joined the CPUSA because of the party's commitment to defending civil rights and fighting segregation and racial hatred.[67] Although the party recognized her as a leader, over the years Moore became progressively interested in the connections with Africa: "I helped to Africanize, and to me that is very important, to establish our identity."[68] She eventually considered that, unlike during and just after the end of the Second World War, the party increasingly failed to address the issue of race. In 1950, she left the party and took another path: "there were certain forces within the Communist Party that was racist, definitely racist, racist to the core."[69]

Moore's Pan-Africanist interests resulted in a series of enterprises. In 1957, along with her sister Eloise, she founded the Universal Association of Ethiopian Women.[70] Gradually, her activism evolved to address the need of financial and material reparations for slavery. Invoking the comparison between slavery and genocide, an idea that already oriented the petition "We Charge Genocide" submitted to the United Nations by Patterson, Robeson, and a number of African American activists in 1952, Moore emphasized that even "the United Nations has defined our condition as mental genocide, you see, that's what we suffer. Mental genocide, oblivion."[71] This statement was linked to Marcus Garvey's ideas. Decades earlier, when he was already in exile, he stated in a famous discourse that:

> We are going to emancipate ourselves from mental slavery because whilst others might free the body none but ourselves can free the mind. Mind is your only ruler, sovereign. The man who is not able to develop and use his mind is bound to be the slave of the other man who use his mind, because man is related to man under all circumstances for good or for ill.[72]

Almost fifty years later, Garvey's slogan proposing emancipation of mental slavery spread all over the world, through the lyrics of the *Redemption Song* by Bob Marley (1945–1981), released in 1980.

Although Moore's interest in financial and material reparations for slavery were most likely inspired by Garvey's early lessons, her activism gained a new force with the approach of the one hundredth anniversary of the Emancipation Proclamation of 1863. Months before the commemoration, Moore read from an old Methodist encyclopedia, which stated "that a captive people have one hundred years to state their judicial claims against their captors or international law will consider you satisfied with your condition."[73] Thus, she realized that: "Now I have to go all over this country, honey, mobilize for a conference. I mean we cannot allow 1962 to end and we haven't stake the judicial claim."[74] Aware that Germany had paid reparations to Jews and that at that point the government of the United States had also recognized the wrongs committed against Japanese Americans and issued a formal apology, Moore and her comrades "began to find out what this reparation was, to pay back injury."[75] As they attempted to obtain federal funds to organize the commemoration activities of the Emancipation Proclamation centennial, she created the National Emancipation Proclamation Observance Committee (NEPOC). Led by Moore, the group went to the White House to address their demands to President John F. Kennedy (1917–1963), one year before his assassination, but they were unable to meet with the president.[76]

While promoting awareness regarding reparations for slavery, Moore and her fellow activists were trailblazers in questioning the existence of urban properties built with capital produced by enslaved workers:

> We'd get in automobiles and we're ride up and down the beautiful homes, honey, all those homes, saying, "This was built with slavery labor, this shall be my home." "This one was built with slave labor, this shall be my home." Up and down the avenue we'd be picking out the homes that really we were entitled to, 'cause it was built off our backs, you see.[77]

In a period when there were no museum exhibitions dedicated to presenting the history of slavery in the United States, Moore's plan to use material evidence to support her case for reparations was powerful and innovative, and certainly scared the federal authorities to whom it was conveyed. As part of the Emancipation Proclamation centennial commemorative activities and the campaign to raise awareness to the need for reparations, she wanted to publicly display various instruments used to torture the enslaved population in order to educate African American younger generations:

> I wanted a slave train to go all through the country with all the shackles the branding irons, I found branding irons out there in Seattle. A black woman, she wouldn't give them to me. Oh honey, I wanted those branding irons so bad I didn't know what to do. She got two branding irons where they used to brand them, to put their letters on our cheeks, you know. I wanted that so bad. So I wanted all of those, the yokes with the prongs around our brows to stick in our neck and all that, I wanted that to be put on a train to go throughout the country so our children could see it. I wanted a slave ship in the Mobile Bay to be resurrected. I wanted that to go on a flatcar, you know, boxcar, one of those flat boxcars. I wanted that slave ship, oh honey. I had such ideas of what we ought to be doing for our centennial. And then, I saw only then would we be in a condition to come together.[78]

The idea of a slave train carried a powerful symbolic dimension. The slave train contrasted with a previous initiative, the first Freedom Train, which toured the country between September 1947 and January 1949. Whereas the Freedom Train exhibited important historical documents to commemorate US heritage, the slave train would emphasize the most tragic chapter of the nation's history, and show that despite the achievements of the Civil Rights Movement, the legacies of slavery remained disturbingly alive. Far ahead of her time, Moore obviously did not succeed in accomplishing the project of a slave train.

Moore's claims for reparations can be better understood within the framework of Haywood's Black Belt Republic thesis. As she stated: "we decided that we're a nation and that we are entitled to reparations, and that we had no intention of having reparations given to no little clique, no little group, and do what they want with it." Yet, she insisted that the payment of financial restitutions should benefit all African Americans and their descendants. According to her proposal it would be up to each individual and group to decide what to do with the funds:

> Then if we wanted to put up some steel mills, some industry with the reparation, to benefit the whole people or some wanted to take their reparation and go to Africa [. . .] We even provided for niggers, Negroes as you call it, who want to stay and integrate with the white folks, they could do that too. They was still entitled to their reparation.[79]

In 1962, Moore became the founder and the president of the Reparations Committee for the Descendants of American Slaves (RCDAS), which was officially incorporated in Los Angeles, California.[80] This pioneer initiative, once again led by a black woman, fueled the modern movement for reparations before other groups emerged at the end of the decade. The RCDAS campaigned in several states, including New York, North Carolina, Texas, and Illinois.[81] On December 20, 1962, the committee filed a claim demanding reparations for slavery in a court of the state of California.[82] In 1963, in the name of the committee, Moore authored a detailed booklet exposing the formal demands of financial reparations as they were presented in the claim to the federal government. Furthermore, in order to validate the arguments on which the claim was based, the document also revisited the previous cases of the period after the end of the Second World War in which governments paid reparations to other victimized groups such as Jews, Japanese Americans, and American Indians:

> WE, The Committee For the Securing of Reparations For the Descendants of men and women brought from the continent of Africa, and enslaved in the United States of America for more than 244 years, and are now commonly referred as "Negroes," do now make formal request of the Government of the United States, for fair and just compensation for the loss of property rights in the labor of our foreparents, for which no payment of any kind has ever been made.[83]

The booklet justified the demands of financial restitution. It underscored that slaves provided dozens of years of unpaid work to slave owners. It also emphasized that slaveholders "unjustly enriched, thereby making possible the development of so many of the vast and numerous fortunes, which even today accounts for a very considerable portion of this nation's wealth, is now due and payable to us as victims of this loss."[84] To prove the correlation between the living and working conditions of slaves and the contemporary conditions of social exclusion of their descendants, Moore recounted the economic, social, and emotional distress that resulted from other atrocities committed during the decades that followed emancipation, including lynching, segregation, disfranchisement, raping, and police brutality.

Moore and the members of the committee defended that only reparations could provide African Americans with a chance of achieving equality, in a context where the descendants of slave owners continued to enjoy the fortunes amassed by their ancestors on the back of the slaves: "The unpaid labor of African slaves laid the foundation for the accumulation of the wealth that ultimately made the U.S.A. the richest country in the world."[85]

"And all of that slave labor that was amassed in unpaid wages"

As Moore promoted the cause of reparations, other great exponents of the Civil Rights Movement, such as Malcolm X and Martin Luther King Jr.

rhetorically addressed the problem of restitutions for slavery in their public speeches. Yet, these leaders scarcely indicated if African Americans were due symbolical, financial, or material reparations. But there were at least two exceptions. In 1963, Malcolm X was a prominent leader of the African American political and religious movement Nation of Islam (NOI), by the time led by Elijah Muhammad (1897–1975). On January 23 of that year, Malcolm X addressed the African Students Association and NAACP Campus Chapter of Michigan State University, in East Lansing, Michigan. In a speech of several minutes, titled "The Race Problem," he presented the NOI's position, opposing integration and defending separation between whites and African Americans. He sustained the idea that the slave trade and slavery were crimes committed by slave traders and slave owners against Africans and their descendants in the Americas. At the very end of his address, he eventually distinctly presented the need of financial reparations, by using arguments similar to those advanced by Queen Mother Moore:

> The greatest contribution to this country was that which was contributed by the Black man. If I take the wages, just a moment, if I take the wages of everyone here, individually it means nothing, but collectively all of the earning power or wages that you earned in one week would make me wealthy. And if I could collect it for a year, I'd be rich beyond dreams. Now, when you see this, and then you stop and consider the wages that were kept back from millions of Black people, not for one year but for 310 years, you'll see how this country got so rich so fast. And what made the economy as strong as it is today. And all that, and all of that slave labor that was amassed in unpaid wages, is due someone today. And you're not giving us anything.[86]

In similar fashion, King issued a timely evocation of financial reparations, in the essay "The Days to Come" published in his book *Why We Can't Wait*. Written in 1963, on the eve of the centennial of the Emancipation Proclamation, the book was published in July 1964, the same month that the Civil Rights Act outlawed discrimination based on race, color, religion, sex, or national origin.[87] King ably introduced the issue of restitutions by first referring to slavery times, when enslaved African Americans made provisions to buy their own freedom and the freedom of their relatives, and then by defining bondage as a "system that bartered dignity for dollars."[88] King compared the slave traders and slave owners, who sold to the slaves their own freedom, to the contemporary individuals who asked what else will the "Negro expect if he gains such rights as integrated schools, public facilities, voting rights and progress in housing? Will he, like Oliver Twist, demand more?'"[89] To King, asking these questions was like requesting "the Negro to purchase something that already belongs to him by every concept of law, justice and our Judeo-Christian heritage. Moreover, he is asking the Negro to accept half the loaf and to pay for that half by waiting willingly for the other half to be distributed in crumbs over a hard and protracted winter of justice."[90]

In other words, King made clear not only that emancipation was not synonymous with reparations, but civil rights were not any gift. He underscored that "America must seek its own ways of atoning for the injustices she has inflicted upon her Negro citizens. I do not suggest atonement for atonement's sake or because there is need for self-punishment. I suggest atonement as the moral and practical way to bring the Negro's standards up to a realistic level."[91] King insisted that symbolical reparations did not suffice and that there was need of financial and material reparations:

> The Negro today is not struggling for some abstract, vague rights, but for concrete and prompt improvement in his way of life. What will it profit him to be able to send his children to an integrated school if the family income is insufficient to buy them school clothes? What will he gain by being permitted to move to an integrated neighborhood in he cannot afford to do so because he is unemployed or has a low-paying job with no future?[92]

King also reminded his readers of past restitutions provided to specific groups and individuals in the United States, including the farmers who fought in the Revolutionary Army and other forms of compensation awarded to the veterans who fought the Second World War. And then he clearly defended the need for legislation creating financial reparatory measures for the years during which African Americans were not paid for the work they performed under slavery:

> Such compensatory treatment was approved by the majority of Americans. Certainly the Negro has been deprived. Few people consider the fact that, in addition to being enslaved for two centuries, the Negro was, during all those years, robbed of the wages of his toil. No amount of gold could provide an adequate compensation for the exploitation and humiliation of the Negro in America down through the centuries. Not all the wealth of this affluent society could meet the bill. Yet a price can be placed on unpaid wages. The ancient common law has always provided a remedy for the appropriation of the labor of one human being by another. This law should be made to apply for American Negroes. This law should be in the form of a massive program by the government of special compensatory measures which could be regarded as settlement in accordance with the accepted practice of common law. Such measures would certainly be less expensive than any computation based on two centuries of unpaid wages and accumulated interest.[93]

Although the leaders of the Civil Rights Movement never placed financial and material reparations as central elements of their political agendas, during the few years that followed the assassinations of Malcolm X and King it became clear that the legal conquest of civil rights would not end deeply rooted white supremacy, racial hatred, and racial inequalities. Many black activists understood that the battle for civil rights was not finished, and that full citizenship could not be achieved without access to financial and material resources. Based on these conclusions, at the end of the 1960s, the movement for reparations gained new strength.

"We have been slaves too long"

In the aftermath of the Civil Rights Act, new black nationalist groups continued to surface. Contrasting with the dominant approach of the Civil Rights Movement, new emerging groups made financial and material reparations dominant elements of their programs. One of these associations was the Republic of New Africa (RNA), founded on March 31, 1968, during a conference held in Detroit, Michigan, gathering two hundred black nationalists. RNA named as its president the author and civil rights leader Robert Franklin Williams (1925–1996). Williams was the head of the North Carolina's chapter of NAACP, and the author of the influential book *Negroes with Guns*. Persecuted by the FBI, like other activists of the Civil Rights Movement, he went into exile to Cuba in 1961. With Castro's support, Williams resided on the island until 1965, then moved to China. Among the other members of RNA was Richard Bullock Henry (1930–2010), alias Imari Obadele, and his brother the attorney Milton R. Henry (1919–2006), alias Gaidi Obadele, who occupied the position of first vice-president. Hajj Bahiyah Betty Shabazz (1934–1997) was the second vice-president. In the documents released by the group she is described as an activist, but mainly identified as the "wife of the father of our Revolution, Brother Malcolm."[94] Among other members of RNA's government was Audley Moore occupying the position of Minister of Health and Welfare. Other leaders included Baba Oseijeman Adefunmi (1928–2005) as Minister of Culture and Education. Adefunmi was an African American, who after being initiated to Vaudou in Haiti and to Santeria in Cuba, became a "Yoruba" priest in the United States.

According to its founders, RNA was: "a black nation, to which all black people in America who wish to, can swear allegiance. And they elected officers of the government. These officers will carry out the aims of the Declaration of Independence. They will carry out the aims of the Revolution stated in the Declaration." Through their activism, the group aimed "that black people and our new black nation become, in fact, free, independent, and successful."[95] RNA shared the ideals of self-determination, as espoused in Haywood's Black Belt Republic's thesis. Arguing that African Americans "never had legal citizenship in the United States" and that after emancipation former slaves "should have been allowed to choose what they wanted to do," the group defended the creation of a black independent state, by taking up arms if necessary.[96]

RNA embraced the cause of financial and material reparations for slavery. Its leaders demanded that the federal government award land to

African Americans for the creation of a black nation in a territory corresponding to the states of Louisiana, Mississippi, Alabama, Georgia, and South Carolina. In addition to requesting land, RNA called for the government to pay financial reparations to African Americans: "for all the labor which they stole from us during slavery and for cheating us out of a chance for a better life, by discriminating against us, after slavery." The group summoned the federal government to pay $10,000 for every black person in the United States. Although agreeing that the debt to slaves and their descendants was greater than the amount requested, the appeal indicated that the amount of $4,000 would be paid to each individual, whereas the remaining $6,000 would go to the NRA's government.[97]

Despite formulating rhetorical demands, RNA did not engage with any judicial procedures to obtain reparations from the federal government. However, exactly as happened to previous activists who demanded restitutions for slavery, federal authorities persecuted RNA members. In 1971 the group had relocated its provisional government near Jackson, Mississippi, where they planned to acquire land to launch the black independent state.[98] On August 18, 1971, heavily armed FBI officers and police agents raided RNA headquarters located at two different addresses in Jackson. Imari Obadele was arrested along with ten other RNA members.[99] Considered the first political prisoner of the United States by the Amnesty International, Obadele spent five years in prison. Although the organization still exists today, RNA's repression held back the movement, which had to spend several years fighting to liberate its prisoners.

Other movements continued giving great visibility to requests for reparations for slavery in the United States. In 1969, James Forman (1928–2005), former executive director of the Student Nonviolent Coordinating Committee and member of the Black Panther Party, along with a group of activists wrote and publicized the Black Manifesto. In the document, the group pressed for reparations from white Christian churches and Jewish synagogues "for the centuries of exploitation and oppression which they had inflicted on black people around the world."[100] It is hard to precisely determine how Forman arrived at the conclusion that churches and synagogues should pay reparations for slavery and centuries of African Americans' social and economic exclusion. In the third chapter of his autobiography, he discussed his early negative experiences in a Catholic school in Chicago.[101] Still, Forman's personal papers contained copies of documents related to the ex-slave pensions movement, suggesting that he was aware of the achievements and failures of earlier ventures in claiming reparations for slavery.[102] By certainly knowing that previous demands for reparations for slavery to the federal government were unsuccessful, the choice of targeting the churches and synagogues was rather related to the obvious wealth these institutions epitomized.

Although most of the time Forman's manifesto advocated reparations by referring to the present-day exclusion of African Americans in US society, he often conjured the slave past to defend the need for redress. Describing an idyllic image of a peaceful African continent whose peoples and resources were stolen by the Europeans, the document's arguments joined the anti-colonial discourses in vogue during the time: "We have the same rights, if you will, as the Christians had in going to Africa and raping our Motherland and bringing us away from our continent of peace and into this hostile and alien environment where we have been living in perpetual warfare since 1619."[103] The manifesto requested Christian and Jewish synagogues to pay a total of $500,000,000 in financial reparations: "This total comes to $15 per nigger. This is a low estimate for we maintain there are probably more than 30,000,000 black people in this country." Additionally, the document outlined the future use of the reparations funds, which included the creation of a Southern Land Bank, publishing companies, audiovisual networks, a research center, a black university, and an International Black Appeal to promote the creation of cooperative businesses.[104]

On April 26, 1969, Forman presented the manifesto for the first time during the National Black Economic Development Conference (NBEDC). This meeting, assembling approximately 500 participants in Detroit, Michigan, was organized by the Interreligious Foundation for Community Organization (IFCO), an ecumenical venture of several Protestant, Catholic, and Jewish organizations which funded community organization and development.[105] On May 4, 1969, Forman and other activists interrupted the Sunday service of the Riverside Church in New York City to announce the manifesto (Figures 4.1 and 4.2). Upon remembering that day in his

FIGURE 4.1 *Forman at Riverside Church*. New York City, May 4, 1969. Courtesy: Charles Bonnay/Getty Images.

FIGURE 4.2 *Forman speaks outside church.* New York City, May 4, 1969.
Courtesy: Pictorial Parade/Getty Images.

autobiography, Forman writes: "All the lies that 'Christianity' had used to enslave the poor stared me in the face."[106] Still, his use of the verb "enslave" was probably only rhetoric. As his writings suggest, Forman apparently ignored that the Catholic Church was the largest single slave owner during the period of slavery in the Americas.

The method of presenting the manifesto during the Riverside Church's Sunday service had great public impact and was widely covered by national newspapers. The following day, the *New York Times* reported the protest in detail: "About 1,500 parishioners Negro and white, looked on in shock and bewilderment yesterday as black militant took over the altar area in the nave of Riverside Church and forced the cancellation of the 11 A.M. communion service."[107] The newspaper also reported the clergymen's divided reactions: "many expressed sympathy with the militants' demands of increased efforts by the church in the field of race relations, and several endorsed the idea that American Negroes were entitled to some form of reparation for injustices from the slavery period."[108] Yet, these positions were not shared by some Jewish groups. Rabbi Meir Kahane (1932–1990), by then the national chairman of the Jewish Defense League, reacted negatively in response to the demands of reparations. According to him "the Jewish people, as such, had no hand in slavery" and "[t]heir ancestors came here long afterward." The article also reported that "[t]wo hundred league members and Kahane showed up last May 9 at Temple Emanu-El with baseball bats and iron pipes [Figure 4.3] in anticipation of a visit from Forman and his followers."[109] But eventually Forman did not come.

Whereas white churchmen criticized the form and the content of the protest, an Ad Hoc Committee of Black Churchmen issued a statement supporting the restitutions for slavery by highlighting that "by paying reparations, the churches would 'demonstrate to other American institutions the authenticity of their frequently verbalized contrition.'"[110] Moreover, leaders of the Civil Rights Movement, like Reverend Jesse Jackson, expressed their public support for the Black Manifesto. In an interview given to the magazine *Playboy* in November 1969, the interviewer asked Jackson if he agreed with Forman's "proposal that churches pay reparations to blacks." Jackson responded positively by insisting that the demands were serious and not simply symbolic. He also added that "eventually the demands will not be limited to the churches. [. . .] We've been victims of an unjust war and are due reparations from those who launched it. Business owes us reparations, first for enslaving us, then for refusing to give us work or hiring us for only the lowest paying, most grueling jobs."[111]

In a letter dated May 4, 1969, addressed to the Board of Deacons and the membership of Riverside Church, Forman explained that he met Pastor Ernest Campbell (1923–2010) on May 3, 1969 to whom he gave a copy of the Black Manifesto and read some of the stipulations addressed in the document. Despite this meeting, the pastor refused to award him time to read the manifesto on the church's premises. In this letter, Forman justified

FIGURE 4.3 *Jewish Defense League*. May 10, 1969. New York City. Courtesy: William N. Jacobellis/New York Post Archives/(c) NYP Holdings, Inc. via Getty Images.

the choice of Riverside Church by explaining that it is "in the heart of the Harlem Community, as are a few other racist institutions" and added that the "demands of Black people are Relevant to any church which is operating in or near a Black community, or anywhere in the United States for that matter."[112] He requested of the Board of Deacons a list of all church property including stock holdings, pension, retirement, and investment funds. He also demanded rent-free office space and 60 percent of the church's annual income to the NBEDC. In addition, the group asked for $500,000,000 in reparations due "to the role of the Christian and Jewish religions in exploiting Black people in this country." Moreover, he warned that the amount requested could only increase: "Due to the special power and exploitation and racist role of John D. Rockefeller (1839–1937) who endowed the Riverside Church we feel we are correct in stating that the Riverside Church must pay extra reparations to Black people, for the money of John D. Rockefeller is still exploiting people of color all around the world."[113] He gave May 11, 1969 as the deadline to fulfill the demands, and concluded by insisting on the urgency of reparations for slavery:

> Time is running out.
> We have been slaves too long.
> The Church has profited from our labor.
> The Church is racist.
> We are men and women, proud Black men and women.
> Our demands shall be met.
> Reparations or no Church.
> Victory or Death.[114]

Over the weeks that followed the proclamation of the Black Manifesto, the members of the NBEDC distributed and publicized the content of the document, by sending letters to representatives of the various churches. In a press statement sent to Cardinal Terence James Cooke (1921–1983) of the archdiocese of New York, Forman stated that religions organizations gathered approximately $5 billion in contributions and had assets of approximately $79.5 billion. Of this amount approximately $44.5 billion was held by the Roman Catholic Church. Drawing from the book *The Religion Business* by journalist Alfred Balk (1930–2010), he affirmed that the Catholic Church was probably the largest corporation in the United States, its wealth exceeding the combined assets of several US companies such as Standard Oil, AT&T, and US Steel. He also accentuated that the churches did not pay inheritance taxes, were exempted from paying corporate income taxes, and were also spared from paying property taxes. Yet, Forman's memorandum did not specify a percentage of annual donations to be given to NBEDC. According to him the amount would be determined after receiving the complete list of all assets of the Catholic Church. Finally, the memorandum concluded with a request of $200,000,000 to establish a Southern Land Bank.[115]

Similar demands were also addressed to other churches. In a memorandum sent in the name of the NBEDC fundraising's arm, the United Black Appeal, Forman requested the Episcopal Church to pay reparations in the amount of $60,000,000. Moreover, analogous to the request presented to the Catholic Church, he asked the church to provide a detailed list of its assets and to make an annual donation to the NBEDC corresponding to

60 percent of the profits accrued from such assets.[116] Forman also addressed a similar letter to the United Church of Christ in New York City, but in addition he requested $130,000,000 to develop a black university whose headquarters would be located at the historically black Tougaloo College in Jackson, Mississippi. Moreover, he also insisted on a donation of $10,000,000 to the United Black Appeal.[117]

Responses to the Black Manifesto, from the various churches, wavered. On May 19, 1969, Rev. Dr. Ben Mohr Herbster (1904–1984), President of the United Church of Christ, sent a letter to James Forman reacting to the demands for reparations for slavery. He equated the experience of enslaved men and women with that of whites who were victimized during the Civil War. Although in his later obituary, Herbster was defined as a supporter of the Civil Rights Movement, his letter to Forman reveals another facet of his views on racial relations.[118] By ridiculing different forms of black protest, Herbster aggressively opposed the idea of reparations for African Americans, by calling it blackmail:

> If the negroes are entitled to reparations for damages suffered dating back to the Civil War, then aren't the families of whites whose grandfathers, grand-uncles,—descendants—whose people fought for the North to free the slaves and in the process lost their lives, their fortunes, their futures— aren't they too entitled to reparations? Your so-called "reparations" are just a euphimistic term for black-mail. We've had it all now: Black Power, Black is Beautiful, Black Panthers, Black Militants—and now Black Mail.[119]

Other whites also reacted negatively to the Black Manifesto. In an anonymous letter addressed to Forman on July 10, 1969, a white individual from New Orleans wrote:

> Can't you see how utterly ridiculous are your efforts for reparations for so-called injustices perpetrated on blacks. You're being naïve when you labor under the delusion that blacks have been in a class by themselves where injustices and exploitation are concerned. If you know your economic history, ponder conditions prior to "child labor laws," (whites)! Consider the miners and their working and their working conditions, prior to John L. Lewis' efforts in their behalf. Consider the yellow race; especially China and her millions. Consider the red man who was in this Country long before your blacks.[120]

Equating slavery with other forms of servitude, the author of this letter employed an old argumentative strategy that consisted of minimizing the atrocities committed against African Americans and their ancestors. By associating the sufferings of African Americans with the living and working conditions of other free workers such as the Chinese, who were never enslaved in the United States, the white author positioned himself as a genuine American, in contrast with black Americans, by signing his letter as: "A true American, A white, Exploited, Now living on Social Security benefits and not making demands on anyone for so-called injustices."[121]

But among some white activists, Foreman's Black Manifesto received support. Madalyn Murray O'Hair (1919–1995), an activist for the separation between church and state and creator of the Society of Separationists, wrote a detailed letter to an unknown receiver, supporting the demands for reparations addressed to the churches and synagogues. In the letter, which accompanied a booklet, O'Hair wrote she would be happy to meet Forman and that she had "a million ideas for him." She explained that the churches owned many slums which poor individuals left to them after their death. Moreover, she also pointed out that the amount requested to the churches was too low in relation to their actual wealth.[122]

Some religious leaders who initially participated in the creation of IFCO contested Forman's initiatives and the way the organization was being used to promote the Black Manifesto. In a letter addressed to all pastors and ministers of the United Presbyterian Church, Kenneth G. Neigh (1908–1996), General Secretary of Board of National Missions, dissociated Forman's mandates from IFCO. According to him, although sponsored by IFCO, the Detroit conference was a meeting of black individuals, which since then became "the name of an autonomous vehicle to implement demands made at that meeting." By regretting that "IFCO's name has been used in news reports related to Mr. Forman's disruption tactics" the missive assured the recipients that the Board of National Missions did not "endorse either the rhetoric of the Manifesto now being publicized nor the calls for disruption. [. . .] We reflect them as being practices which will hasten the polarization of and breakdown in communications between racial groups."[123]

As they did with other groups advocating civil rights and demanding reparations for slavery, federal agents closely watched the bearers of the Black Manifesto. In the two weeks that followed the presentation of the manifesto, the FBI interviewed all individuals who participated in the Detroit conference. Moreover, the Justice Department held two special grand juries to investigate the group's activities.[124] By the summer of 1970, the NBEDC had obtained approximately $300,000 in reparations. Most of these contributions were redirected to other organizations such as the then recently created publishing venue Black Star Publications. Despite the Black Manifesto's great public visibility, the fact that the requests were made to several churches had probably the effect of dispersing the initiative. Moreover, the NBEDC neither sought, nor obtained the support from the most important African American organizations, such as the NAACP and the NOI. Finally, as its leaders distrusted official institutions, it did not engage in legal procedures or campaigns to petition the US Congress. These factors prevented the movement from getting the participation of larger numbers of African Americans who may have adhered to the idea of reparations for slavery.

New paths for reparations

The demands of restitutions for slavery gained new force and visibility with the end of the Second World War. The anti-colonial struggle in Africa and the Caribbean along with the emergence of the first demands of reparations addressed by Jews and Japanese Americans to the governments of Germany, Canada, and the United States contributed to the rise of new groups who voiced the need for reparations for the descendants of slaves.

Although the Civil Rights Movement never incorporated financial and material reparations in its agenda, during the 1960s, leaders such as Paul Robeson, Malcolm X, and Martin Luther King Jr. stressed in their speeches the relations between social and economic inequalities victimizing African Americans and the legacies of the period of slavery, by insisting on the need for redress. Still, during this period, formal demands of reparations for slavery gained influence through the work of less visible African American activists who, to a lesser or to a greater extent, were inspired by black nationalist and Pan-Africanist views. Despite formulating official demands of reparations for slavery, the programs advanced by Queen Mother Audley Moore and her RCDAS, Robert Franklin Williams and the members of RNA, and James Forman's NBEDC conveyed a pessimistic vision of the future integration of African Americans in the United States.

Even though several organized groups supported these movements, ordinary African Americans little backed the idea of reparations. This lack of support can be explained by the repressive context that marked the period of the Cold War and because of the great focus on civil rights that characterized the period after the Second World War. Despite the hindrances of the US context, no other movements defending reparations for slavery emerged during this period in other parts of the Americas. Although in revolutionary Cuba, land confiscation and agrarian reform largely benefited rural black populations, such efforts were not designed to specifically redress the legacies of slavery among the descendants of slaves. Yet, in countries like Brazil, where a military coup suffocated the project of agrarian reform, the largest population of African descent outside Nigeria would have to wait until the end of the dictatorship in 1985 to start voicing demands of financial, material, and symbolic reparations for slavery.

5

"It's Time for Us to Get Paid"

The social, political, and economic transformations that surfaced in the last decade of the twentieth century contributed to a new wave of public demands for financial and material reparations for the Atlantic slave trade and slavery. With the approach of the fiftieth anniversary of the Second World War, European governments, the Catholic Church, and other institutions gradually acknowledged their collaboration with the Nazi regime, and expressed apologies to its victims and their descendants. As the end of the Cold War favored continuous calls for reparations associated with abuses and human atrocities committed during the Second World War, the dictatorships sustained by the United States and the Soviet Union in Africa and Latin America also witnessed their last days. The fall of the Communist regimes in Eastern Europe helped to intensify and solidify the connections among the populations of African descent around the world, favoring the emergence of requests for reparations for slavery not only in the United States, but also in Brazil, Colombia, Ecuador, Caribbean countries, and West Africa.

Although initially this wave was rather characterized by demands for symbolic reparations whose focus was the creation of monuments and memorials acknowledging the central role of enslaved men and women in the construction of slave societies, a growing number of organizations and groups started emphasizing the need of financial and material reparations. This chapter shows how, for the first time since the first individual requests for reparations for slavery emerged with Belinda Sutton's petition in Massachusetts at the end of the eighteenth century, the demands for financial and material restitutions to populations of African descent gained visibility beyond the borders of the nation states. Despite the local realities that shaped power relations and the development of black organizations in the various regions of the Americas, exactly the same way that the Atlantic slave trade and slavery connected the different societies of the Atlantic world, reparations activism also acquired a transnational dimension.

The new wave of demands of reparations

The end of the Cold War greatly impacted the fight for reparations for slavery and the slave trade in the Americas, Europe, and Africa. In Brazil, the military dictatorship that took control of the country between 1964 and 1985, along with the pervasive influence of the ideology of racial democracy, hindered the ability of black organizations to effectively fight against racism and, in turn, for civil rights. This context also prevented the emergence of calls for financial and material reparations as occurred in the United States during the same period. By the end of the 1970s, when the military regime started a process of political opening up, the Brazilian black movement, especially through the newly created Movimento Negro Unificado (Black Unified Movement), continued centering its activities on publicly denouncing racism. In addition to addressing the federal, state, and municipal governments with a broad range of civil rights demands, black activists called for the implementation of affirmative action, which in the Brazilian context was presented as a reparatory measure, even though only symbolic. Other groups conveyed calls for reparations through a series of demands of cultural recognition. But from time to time, requests for material and symbolic reparations for slavery reemerged in the public debate.

The end of military rule expanded the scope of action of Brazilian black organizations. In 1986, the country elected new representatives for the Brazilian National Congress. Between February 1987 and September 1988, members of the Federal Senate and the Chamber of Deputies composed a National Constituent Assembly in charge of writing the new Brazilian Constitution. On this occasion, Afro-Brazilian activists formed the Black National Convention for the Constituent Assembly with the goal of submitting demands for inclusion in the new constitution. During a meeting held in Brasília in 1986, 185 delegates, representing dozens of organizations of the black movement, produced a document with proposals to the Constituent Assembly. The report covered several areas related to work conditions, healthcare, women, police violence, culture, international relations, and the agrarian issue, most of which did not specifically address questions related to the populations of African descent. But some proposals included symbolic reparations for slavery. Among them was making November 13, the date of the death of Zumbi, the leader *quilombo* of Palmares, a national holiday to celebrate a Black Consciousness Day. Black organizations also proposed the inclusion of African and Afro-Brazilian history in school and university curricula. Two other proposals were also crucial. First, the criminalization of racism. Second, and most important, the award of land titles to the remnant black communities (*quilombos*), whether in urban or rural areas, which was the sole claim that could be understood as material reparations for slavery.[1] In 1987, as the centennial of the abolition of slavery approached, Afro-Brazilian civil rights groups stressed that since 1888, the black population continued "to face the same situation it suffered before the Princess Isabel's gesture, and nothing changed in the nation's face."[2]   _? What did that look like?

The new Brazilian Constitution of 1988 criminalized racism. One year later, Law no. 7.716 established sentences for the offenders. Moreover, the work of various Afro-Brazilian organizations and Constituent deputies, such as Carlos Alberto Caó (Democratic Labor Party), Paulo Renato Paim (Workers' Party), Edmílson Valentim (Communist Party of Brazil), and Benedita da Silva (Workers' Party) made possible the approval of Article 68 of the Act of the Transitional Provisions of the new Constitution.[3] The Article determined that "to the remnants of *quilombo* communities who are occupying their lands it is recognized to be definitive ownership, and the state shall grant them the respective titles."[4] In that same year Law no. 7.668 of August 22, 1988 created the Palmares Cultural Foundation. This new institution was mandated with preserving and promoting Afro-Brazilian heritage, and the responsibility of identifying and delimitating the territories as well as conferring legal land titles to the *quilombo* communities. One hundred years after the abolition of slavery in Brazil, this new legislation opened a first breach to measures that, if they materialized, could be interpreted as material reparations for slavery. But as in other former slave societies there were many obstacles to affording restitutions to the communities and individuals identified as descendants of slaves.

On November 9, 1989, several days of popular protest led to the fall of the Berlin Wall. In that same year, Poland started a democratic transition and in 1991 the Soviet Union formally collapsed. The Iron Curtain's disintegration made Holocaust extermination camps, located in Poland, such as Auschwitz and Treblinka, much more visible and accessible to Western audiences. The end of the Cold War also contributed to political change in West African and Latin American countries, where the end of dictatorial regimes allowed the debates associated with the Atlantic slave trade to emerge. Likewise in Europe, the approach of the fiftieth anniversary of the end of the Second World War inspired the development of various proposals calling for symbolic reparations to the victims of the Holocaust through the creation of monuments, memorials, and museums. On April 12, 1990, Lothar de Maizière, the newly democratically elected East German Prime Minister, recognized East Germany's "joint responsibility on behalf of the people for the humiliation, expulsion and murder of Jewish women, men, and children [...] We feel sad and ashamed and acknowledge this burden of German history."[5]

The wave of apologies and demands for financial and symbolic reparations also found a fertile ground in West Africa. On June 28, 1992, during a meeting of the Organization of African Unity (today's African Union) held in Abuja, Nigeria, a collective of political leaders, intellectuals, artists, and public personalities, named the Group of Eminent Persons (GEP), signed a manifesto supporting reparations to the African continent for the centuries of slavery and Atlantic slave trade.[6] The demands for reparations, also discussed in a conference held in the following year in Nigeria, did not include any cash amount, but rather consisted of capital transfer, debt cancellation, and other demands such as increased African representation in the United Nations Security Council.[7]

Although not always calling for financial reparations for the Atlantic slave trade, African leaders utilized their public speeches to establish relations between the bloodshed provoked by the Atlantic slave trade, which took from the continent its young population, and contemporary Africa's economic and social problems. In one public address, in 1992, President of Republic of Benin, Nicéphore Soglo, emphasized that the African continent was "impoverished, emptied of its substance, its valuable men who were gone to other lands, now wealthy." But, although Africans paid these rich nations with "their sweat, their blood, and their labor," they do not have access to the fruits of the wealth they produced.[8] In 1993, during the 29th Assembly of Heads of State and Governments of the Organization of African Unity held in Cairo, Egypt, President Soglo again invoked the Atlantic slave trade to his audience, pointing to how colonization took from Africa its "most valuable arms and a great part of its most important natural resources."[9] Yet, despite insisting on the responsibility of European countries for the Atlantic slave trade and colonization that provoked Africa's underdevelopment, his speech did not clearly address the issue of financial reparations. Although the African Union made further attempts to revive the debates about reparations, most West African nations such as Ghana, Republic of Benin, and Senegal concentrated their efforts rather in ventures such as the Slave Route Project, an initiative aimed at memorializing the Atlantic slave trade and developing cultural tourism, which could be conceived as symbolic reparations.

Meanwhile in Europe and the United States, additional legislation established the terms for restitution of stolen art objects during the Second World War.[10] In 1995, French President Jacques Chirac also publicly recognized the French state's collaboration with the Nazi regime.[11] Likewise in the United States, also in 1995, the US Foreign Claims Settlement Commission launched the Holocaust Survivors Claims Program, endeavoring to obtain financial reparations from the German government for the US nationals who were victims of "loss of liberty or damage to body or health" as a consequence of the German Nazi Regime.[12] After receiving victims' claims for two years and certifying the decisions regarding these claims, the United States and Germany settled an agreement that resulted in the payment of approximately $18.5 billion to the US Department of the Treasury to be distributed to the eligible survivors.[13] Until the end of 2016, the Conference on Jewish Material Claims Against Germany has received more than $60 billion from the German government for the damages inflicted on Jews during the Nazi regime. It also acquired additional financial reparations from German and Austrian industries, the government of Austria, and from funds created by banks in Germany, Switzerland, and Hungary and insurance companies. Three years later, in March 1998, Pope John Paul II apologized for the Catholic Church's anti-Semitism and for its silence during the Holocaust.[14]

In Europe and in the United States, this wave of apologies was also accompanied by symbolic reparations, through the creation of a growing number of monuments, memorials, and museums commemorating the victims of the Holocaust. This new trend favored the emergence of similar initiatives regarding slavery and the Atlantic slave trade. Despite the lack of success in gaining financial and material reparations for slavery and the Atlantic slave trade, in Europe, Africa, and the Americas, activists identifying themselves as descendants of slaves also fought to obtain symbolic reparations by calling for the construction of monuments, memorials, and museums to honor enslaved men and women. In countries such as in Senegal, Ghana, Republic of Benin, Brazil, Cuba, Colombia, Venezuela, Jamaica, and the United States, local communities and governments transformed newly built monuments and heritage sites associated with slavery and the slave trade into sites to attract local, national, and international tourists.

But despite the clear focus on apologies and symbolic reparations, demands for material restitutions remained alive in Latin America, through requests for land ownership rights for black communities. In addition to Brazil, other South American countries produced legislation recognizing the distinctive aspects of their populations of African descent and awarding black groups land ownership rights. In 1991, Colombia enacted a new Constitution, which established that in subsequent years the federal government would form a commission to produce a study aimed at endorsing a special law recognizing the right to land ownership of black communities occupying uncultivated land in rural areas adjoining the rivers of the Pacific Basin. According to the new Constitution, the future law would create mechanisms to protect the cultural identity and rights of these black groups as well as promote their economic and social development.[15]

The Constitution of Columbia gave rise to further developments. Two years after its enactment Colombia sanctioned Law 70 of August 27, 1993 that recognized the right of collective land ownership of Afro-Colombian populations. The law defined various terms such as the name of the rivers composing the Pacific Basin, riverine rural areas, uncultivated lands, black communities, collective occupation, and traditional practices of production, in order to frame demands for recognition of black territories and the consequent awarding of land titles to these communities.[16] Still, the law excluded a great majority of the populations of African descent who lived in urban areas such as Bogota, Cartagena, Cali, Barranquilla, and Medellín y Pereira.[17] As scholars point out, both the Constitution of 1991 and this new law can hardly be referred to as reparations, but rather as a form of empowerment to Colombian black rural populations.[18]

Other South American nations took similar paths to those of Brazil and Colombia by passing legislation criminalizing racism and creating measures to implement land redistribution. Since 1979, the penal code of Ecuador incorporated a chapter titled "Offences against constitutional guarantees and racial equality," in which racial discrimination is criminalized with prison sentences. Two decades later, the Constitution of Ecuador of 1998 declared it a multiethnic and multicultural country. It also prohibited any kind of discrimination regarding place of birth and ethnic origin. Moreover, it granted to the black and Afro-Ecuadorian populations the same general rights bestowed to the indigenous populations, including the ownership of collective and ancestral lands.[19]

At least on paper, the new Ecuadorian Constitution opened the way for the creation of autonomous black territories, an idea that perhaps could invoke black nationalist projects which developed in the United States during the twentieth century. On May 10, 2006, the National Congress enacted the Law of Collective Rights of Black and Afro-Ecuadorian peoples.[20] Drawing from the Constitution of 1998, this law established specific elements regarding the collective rights of black Ecuadorians, including questions related to cultural identity, education, healthcare, natural resources, and land ownership. The law also mandated the creation of an autonomous National Council of Afro-Ecuadorian Development (CONDAE) consisting of elected representatives. The goals of CONDAE include "proposing policies of social inclusion and reparation for Afro-Ecuadorians."[21] As in other countries of Latin America, Ecuador conceived the issue of reparations by addressing the problem of land redistribution to black communities and by proposing measures to fight racial inequalities.

The enacting of this legislation continued reverberating in the following years. In 2006, Rafael Correa was elected President of Ecuador. After taking office on January 13, 2007, he carried out the proposal already advanced during his campaign, that of calling a referendum to consult the population regarding the creation of a new Constituent Assembly to provide the country with a new constitution, which among others would integrate the concerns of indigenous and black populations.[22] After a referendum, a Constituent Assembly was elected in September 2007. One year later, the new Constitution of Ecuador of 2008 was approved in a referendum giving the president of the country more powers to effect social reforms.

The new Ecuadorian Constitution of 2008 expanded the rights awarded to black and indigenous populations, especially regarding land ownership rights: "the ancestral, indigenous, Afro-Ecuadorians and Montubio [mestizo indigenous of the coastal areas] peoples may constitute territorial districts for the preservation of their culture. The law shall regulate their composition. Communes with collective ownership of land, as an ancestral form of territorial organization, are recognized."[23] Despite the new legislation, Afro-Ecuadorians, which represent 7.2 percent of a population of 14,483,499 people, had to continue fighting for land ownership. Yet, as in Colombia and

Brazil, the Constitution of 2008 represented a first step toward material reparations for slavery in Ecuador.[24]

Combining litigation and massive demonstrations

Whereas some Latin American countries started addressing the issue of land ownership for their rural black populations, African American and Afro-Brazilian activists also called for reparations for slavery by using litigation and massive demonstrations as combined strategies. In the United States, black activists continued the one-century tradition of fighting for financial reparations. In 1978, Dorothy Benton Lewis (1918–2012) and Irving B. Davis (1937–1982) created the Black Reparations Commission, with the goal of promoting connections among the movements defending reparations for slavery across the countries with populations of African descent.[25] In 1982, the African People's Socialist Party created the African National Reparations Organization (ANRO). Led by Omali Yeshitela (born Joseph Waller), the group organized the First World Tribunal on Reparations for African People in Brooklyn, New York City, which concluded that the United States owed $4.1 trillion for the crime of genocide against African Americans and the unpaid labor provided by them and their descendants during the period of slavery.[26]

The 1980s announced itself as a promising decade for the fight for reparations for slavery in the United States. On September 17, 1987, the Civil Liberties Act that granted reparations to Japanese Americans passed the House. On April 20, 1988, it passed the Senate, and was eventually signed by President Reagan on August 10, 1988. Within this new context, after the government of the United States awarded reparations to a group of victimized individuals during wartime, the movement demanding financial and material reparations for slavery gained new strength. Drawing from past experiences, on September 26, 1987, a group of African American activists launched National Coalition of Blacks for Reparations (N'COBRA) in America. Among the founders of the new organization were two RNA members, the brothers Imari Obadele and Adjoa Aiyetoro.[27] Another crucial founder of the new organization was Dorothy Benton Lewis. Like Audley Moore, three decades later, she was awarded the title of Queen Mother Nana Yaa Asantewaa Ohema, whose name paid homage to the homonymous queen of the Ashanti empire who fought British colonization.[28] Since its creation N'COBRA has been the only organization of its time whose mission is exclusively dedicated to fight for reparations for slavery.

Gathering African Americans who identify themselves as descendants of enslaved men and women of African descent, N'COBRA's general mission is to obtain material, financial, and symbolic reparations from governments and corporations. The organization is composed of individual members, but it also includes several chapters spread across the United States, as well as in Ghana and England. Despite its national character, N'COBRA actively participated in the activities of several initiatives to promote reparations in the international arena. As part of its mission, the coalition initiates legislation, publishes newsletters, and sponsors meetings.[29]

This new rich dynamic was fruitful. In January 1989, during the agitated context of the end of the Cold War that culminated with the election of George H. Bush as President of the United States, African American Congressman John Conyers from Michigan introduced the Bill titled "Commission to Study Reparation Proposals for African Americans Act" (H.R.40) in the House of Representatives, which since then has been resubmitted every congressional session. The name of the Bill invoked the concept of "forty acres and a mule," derived from the Sherman's Special Field Orders, no. 15 and the Freedmen's Bureau Act, that became the symbol of the unfulfilled promise of redistributing land as material reparations for slavery. The Bill listed several goals, such as: to acknowledge slavery's injustice and inhumanity; to create a commission to study slavery and its legacies of racial and economic discrimination against freedpeople and their descendants; and to make "recommendations to Congress on appropriate remedies to redress the harm inflicted on living African Americans."[30] Yet, unlike previous initiatives, this Bill did not directly address any demands of financial reparations. Instead, it was rather aimed at introducing the discussion in order to establish facts allowing for identification of those who should provide reparations and those who should receive them.

During the 1990s, N'COBRA expanded its structure by creating various committees, including the Legal Strategies Commission aimed at developing legislative efforts, especially by providing support to promote H.R.40.[31] In the following years, along with other groups, N'COBRA led several projects to disseminate the cause of reparations for slavery, including an annual convention. In June 1992, the organization held its annual conference in Charleston, South Carolina. Efia Nwangaza, an attorney of South Carolina, who supported the conference's organization emphasized that with "each generation, the quality of consciousness [. . .] increases."[32]

The efforts continued in the following year. From June 11 to June 13, 1993, during Bill Clinton's first term as President of the United States, N'COBRA held its annual convention in Baton Rouge, Louisiana. At that point the organization attracted new members, including civil rights and Black Power activist, Muhammad Ahmad. In the letter and flyer advertising the convention, which were sent to him and to other members of the association, Johnita Obadele (former wife of RNA's founder, Imari Obadele) situated N'COBRA in a long-term historical perspective. She presented the organization as a continuation of the movement led by Callie House and Isaiah H. Dickerson in the late nineteenth century which she referred to as the "Ex-Slaves Bounty and Reparations Society."[33] The goal of N'COBRA convention was to ask the following questions: "*How Can We Win Reparations? Who Should get Reparations? How Should Reparations Be Used?*"[34]

In 1994, N'COBRA held another annual convention in Detroit, Michigan. Although visible in the public sphere, by the time the organization gathered nearly 5,000 adherents, a much smaller number of members than gathered by the National Ex-Slave Mutual Relief, Bounty and Pension Association eight decades earlier.[35] Hundreds of individuals, such as NOI ministers, academics, and activists attended the meeting. Among its distinguished participants was ninety-five-year-old Queen Mother Audley Moore, who called the audience to carry on fighting for reparations: "Keep on. Keep on. We've got to win."[36] The various participants discussed different kinds of restitution for slavery, including cash, tax exemptions, and land, whereas others referred to the creation of a scholarship fund and also formal apologies. Yet, many attendees underscored the focus on demands for financial reparations, and not symbolic reparations. Zainabu Sipiowe, an elementary school teacher from Washington, DC, who attended the conference insisted: "We are owed reparations. We have built this country. [. . .] Everyone else seems to be getting partial due or their due. And the African is being completely thrown under the rug, again, and again and again." Likewise, the Chicago activist Jahahara Harry Armstrong also stated: "It's time. It's time for us to get paid [. . .] People don't know their self-worth." Sammi Muhammad, a Minister of the NOI in Detroit, clearly affirmed: "We're here to get paid. Money, that's what we want."[37]

The conclusions on the need to the fight for reparations were not only a matter of debate. Activists along with attorneys took concrete actions. In 1995, two groups of African American plaintiffs, collectively identified as Cato, filed a lawsuit against the United States in the US District Court for the Northern District of California. The litigants demanded reparations "for damages due to the enslavement of African Americans and subsequent discrimination against them, for an acknowledgement of discrimination, and for an apology." In addition, the plaintiffs sought: "compensation of $100,000,000 for forced, ancestral indoctrination into a foreign society; kidnapping of ancestors from Africa; forced labor; breakup of families; removal of traditional values; deprivations of freedom; and imposition of oppression, intimidation, miseducation and lack of information about various aspects of their indigenous character."[38] Moreover, they requested that "the court order an acknowledgment of the injustice of slavery in the United States and in the 13 American colonies between 1619 and 1865, as well as of the existence of discrimination against freed slaves and their descendants from the end of the Civil War to the present" and also "an apology from the United States."[39]

Although Judge Saundra Brown Armstrong declared that "[d]iscrimination and bigotry of any type is intolerable, and the enslavement of Africans by this Country is inexcusable," she also determined that the court was "unable to identify any legally cognizable basis upon which plaintiff's claims may proceed against the United States."[40] As in 1915, when the Ex-Slave Mutual, Relief, Benevolent, and Aid Association filed a class-action lawsuit against the Secretary of the United States Department of the Treasury McAdoo, the judge ruled that the complaint presented no basis "upon which the United States might have consented to suit."[41] In other words, as legal scholars have confirmed, because the government of the United States must agree to be prosecuted, a successful outcome for these lawsuits is "nearly impossible."[42]

Starting in the 1990s, Brazilian black organizations led protests and introduced Bills in the National Congress calling for financial reparations from the Brazilian federal government. In 1993, black students and activists, members of the Group of Black Consciousness in the University of São Paulo, created the Movement for Afro-Descendant Reparations (MPR). Launched in São Paulo, the venture was led by then graduate student Fernando Costa da Conceição, today an Associate Professor in the Department of Communication of the Federal University of Bahia. That same year, the group wrote an official document establishing the principles of reparations for slavery in Brazil, which was presented in the First National Seminar of Black University Students, held at the Federal University of Bahia.

Following these initiatives, on November 19, 1993 the MPR officially commenced its activities with a debate held at the University of São Paulo Law School, on the eve of the celebration of the anniversary of Zumbi of Palmares, which by the time was gradually replacing the celebration of the abolition of slavery on May 13. After the debate, twelve members of the group went to the Bela Vista restaurant in the distinguished hotel Maksoud Plaza, where they had an expensive meal with drinks. When a bill of about US$700 was brought to the table, they stood up, showed their t-shirts with the slogan Reparations Now (Reparações Já), and then left the restaurant without paying the bill. Following the demonstration, the hotel sued the group, who eventually paid the bill in court to avoid being sentenced as swindlers.[43]

In December 1994, the MPR submitted a declaratory judgment action to the federal court of the state of São Paulo, in which they requested that the Brazilian state pay financial reparations to the descendants of slaves. The document had an important political and symbolical dimension, as in addition to being signed by twelve activists, it also included the signature of a former enslaved woman, Maria do Carmo Jerônimo (1871–2000) who was still alive at the time. Born just few months before the passing of the Free Womb Law, Jerônimo was considered the oldest person alive in Brazil and the world.[44] The declaration requested the court recognize that the 70 million Afro-Brazilians had the right to receive financial restitutions from the Brazilian state for 350 years of slavery. The MPR argued that the Brazilian government was guilty of omission, because despite the abolition of slavery in 1888, Afro-Brazilians never got social and economic emancipation, having remained prisoners of prejudice. It is important to highlight that when referring to financial reparations, the various documents produced by the MPR do not use the terms "black" or "Afro-Brazilian," but rather the category "descendant of enslaved African," a group to which they claimed to belong.[45] Yet, the statements by Fernando Costa da Conceição, the leader of the movement, underscored that defining the categories "black" and "descendant of slave" was not a simple task. In his own words: "We want this indemnification to any descendant of African who was enslaved, independently of the skin color."[46] Ten years prior to the approval of the Law Taubira in France, Conceição was also a pioneer in highlighting that "the enslavement of black Africans was a crime against humanity."[47]

Despite MPR's strong arguments, the various organizations of the Brazilian black movement never aligned themselves behind the idea of financial reparations. For example, at the time, according to Ronaldo Siqueira, President of the Afro-Brazilian Institute, reparation could be a "throwback in life," even though he also recognized that "when someone is drowning, any help is welcome."[48] The story received great visibility from the media for about two years, and even made the news in the most popular Brazilian television show, *Fantástico*, broadcast every Sunday evening by Globo television.[49] However, despite giving the news, the newspaper *Folha de São Paulo* emphasized that the amount of the financial reparations, calculated as US$102,000 to each Afro-Brazilian could represent US$6,100,000,000 a sum forty-four times the total value of Brazil's external debt.[50] The declaration requesting financial reparations was eventually not successful.

On January 21, 1995, the MPR had its first national meeting in Rio de Janeiro. On this occasion the convention discussed a campaign to gather one million signatures to petition for a Bill requesting reparations for slavery (Figure 5.1). Although strong in Rio de Janeiro, other local meetings were also held in other Brazilian states. Despite its national scope, the movement was not isolated. Although not formally in contact with US organizations such as N'COBRA, Afro-Brazilian militants were especially aware of the requests for reparations for the slave trade and colonization formulated by African nations during that time.[51] Conceição explained that the basis of their movement requesting financial reparations relied on Pan-Africanist ideas, according to which Europe and the West were responsible for the misery of African countries: "Nigeria and Angola are requesting pardon of their external debt and resources to projects of reconstruction and development." In addition, he stressed, as comparison, that the "state of Israel is the result of reparations to Jews by Germany."[52]

On November 20, 1995, the MPR participated in the great march commemorating the three-hundredth anniversary of Zumbi's death held in Brasília. At that event the group delivered a draft Bill on reparations, with

FIGURE 5.1 Cover of *Jornal das reparações*, a newspaper of the Movement for Reparations Now (Brazil). São Paulo, October, 1994.

more than 10,000 signatures, to then federal deputy Paim. But over the following years the idea of financial reparations for slavery again lost strength and public visibility. The main leaders of the Brazilian black movement never endorsed the financial compensation claims. Indeed, during the two terms (1995–2002) of President Fernando Henrique Cardoso, it was clear that black activists focused on other forms of reparation, by increasingly centering on the distribution of lands to the remnants of *quilombos* and affirmative action in federal universities. Drawing from these new efforts, in 1998 federal deputy Paim proposed to the National Congress the Racial Equality Statute. In its original version, this statute included claims for symbolic reparations as well as affirmative action in several spheres, especially the establishment of quotas for admission of Afro-Brazilians in public universities.[53]

During this same period, African American activists organized one memorable rally, which included demands for reparations for slavery. In 1994, Minister Louis Farrakhan (born Louis Eugene Wolcott), the NOI's leader, called black men to join the Million Man March, a massive demonstration to be held later that year in the National Mall in Washington, DC. A day dedicated to protesting the social, economic, and racial issues

faced by the black population in the United States, the march was also a call
to fight the image of black men as "clowns and buffoons and criminals."[54]
Held on October 16, 1995, the Million Man March was accompanied
by another protest titled The Day of Absence, which was conceived as a
Holy Day of atonement, reconciliation, and responsibility. Both activities
resulted from combined efforts of several black committees and organizations
spread all over the country, which comprised not only the NOI, but also
other groups such as the RNA and the National Black United Front.[55]
Although requests for financial and material reparations for slavery were
not central elements of the agendas of the two initiatives, their mission
statement called for the continuous need to focus on: "the ongoing struggle
for reparations in the fullest sense that is to say: public recognition of
the Holocaust of African Enslavement and appropriate compensation by
the government; and support for the Conyers Reparations Bill on the
Holocaust."[56]

Several prominent male and female speakers addressed the crowd during
the rally, including Betty Shabazz, Maya Angelou (1928–2014), Dorothy I.
Height (1912–2010), Tynnetta Muhammad (1941–2015), and Rosa Parks
(1913–2005). The demonstration was also the last public appearance of
longtime activist Queen Mother Audley Moore (Figure 5.2). In her speech,

FIGURE 5.2 Million Man March, Washington, DC, October, 16, 1995. In the
picture: Rosa Parks (far left), Dr. Delois Blakely (Queen Mother of Harlem), Queen
Mother Audley Moore (seated), Elaine Steele (right). Courtesy: Library of Congress
Prints and Photographs Division, Washington, DC, United States.

she was among the few who insisted on the need of reparations. By exaggerating the estimated number of Africans who perished in the slave trade, she compared it to the Holocaust: "My sons, I ask that you remember: reparations, reparations, reparations! Over four hundred million plus Africans died in the Middle Passage. The greatest Holocaust is the African Holocaust. My sons, you must fight for your human rights and your dignity!"[57]

An immense success, the march largely surpassed the March on Washington of August 27, 1963 in number of participants.[58] Although not a central element in his very long address, Farrakhan quickly invoked the issue of reparations:

> Now, look brother, sisters. Some people don't mind confessing. Some people don't mind making some slight repentance. But, when it comes to doing something about the evil that we've done we fall short.
>   But, atonement means satisfaction or reparation for a wrong or injury. It means to make amends. It means penance, expiation, compensation and recompense made or done for an injury or wrong.[59]

In their coverage of the event, mainstream newspapers such as the *New York Times* and the *Washington Post* emphasized the demonstration's success. African American newspapers highlighted how the protest uplifted black men and women around the country.[60] Yet, none of the newspapers gave any attention to the demands for reparations, which had a marginal role in the overall demonstration. Even though activists and attorneys continued filing lawsuits demanding restitutions for slavery, street demonstrations did not seem to share the same enthusiasm.

At the turn of the twentieth-first century, reparations continued to gain attention. In 2000, Randall Robinson, a lawyer, activist, and founder of TransAfrica Forum, published a popular book titled *The Debt: What America Owes to Blacks*, which reached thousands of readers, and again brought the issue of reparations to the public sphere.[61] In that same year, Robinson called a meeting with activists, scholars, and politicians, in Washington, DC, to discuss the issue of black reparations, in which Congressman Conyers gave a keynote address.[62] As the call for reparations acquired greater public visibility, opposed voices also surfaced. In an article published in the news website *Salon*, conservative activist and writer David Horowitz outlined ten reasons to oppose the proposal of reparations for slavery. Among his several arguments was that the demands of reparations place African Americans in a position of victimhood and send a "damaging message."[63] Horowitz's article did not gain much public attention. Yet, in March 2001, he attempted to spread the controversy by paying for the publication of advertisements, featuring his ten reasons for opposing reparations, in various university student newspapers across the United States.[64] The ads generated protests on several campuses, including Brown University and Princeton University, institutions which in the next decade acknowledged having benefited from slavery and the Atlantic slave trade.[65]

Reparations in a global era

In the early twenty-first century, despite dissenting voices variously supporting and opposing reparations, the debates seeking to define different forms of redress for slavery and the slave trade reached international institutions. In 2001, the International Law Commission of the United Nations adopted the document *Responsibility of States for Internationally Wrongful Acts*.[66] Its Article 31, stated that "the responsible State is under an obligation to make full reparation for the injury caused by the international wrongful act." Moreover, the article opened the path to moral and symbolic reparations by defining injury as "any damage, whether material or moral."[67] In addition, Article 33 of the same document established three forms of reparations. The first is restitution, which consists of reestablishing the situation in place before the wrongful act was committed, if this is reasonably possible. The second form is compensation to the state and its nationals, including legal or natural persons. Finally, the third form of reparation is satisfaction. Although satisfaction can accompany restitution and financial compensation, it can also be given when neither restitution, nor compensation are possible. Forms of satisfaction can include acknowledgment of the wrongdoing, expression of regret, and formal apologies. As part of this context where the United Nations paid greater attention to legal dimensions of past wrongs, several other international requests for redress emerged.

France pioneered the recognition of slavery and the slave trade as historical wrongs. On May 21, 2001, France enacted Law 2001–434 (Law Taubira). Its first article declared that the French Republic recognized slavery and the transatlantic slave trade as crimes against humanity.[68] Other articles referred to the promotion of academic research and the implementation of measures to include the history of slavery in school curricula. It also created a national committee for the memory of slavery. Yet, the final version of the law excluded all references to the possible further study of the issue of reparations for slavery.[69]

Also in 2001, the United Nations called the World Conference Against Racism, Racial Discrimination, Xenophobia, and Related Intolerance, which was held from August 31 to September 2001, in Durban, South Africa. In the United States, Brazil, and in other countries of Latin America and Africa, numerous organizations, such as N'COBRA, participated in preparatory meetings for the conference, in which they discussed reparations for slavery as an important element to be addressed during the international meeting. But because of disagreements regarding the draft declaration document, in which initially Zionism was referred to as racism, both Israel and the United States withdrew from the conference. Articles 13, 14, and 15 of Durban's final declaration acknowledged slavery and the Atlantic slave trade as crimes against humanity. It also insisted that these two crimes, along with colonialism, apartheid, and genocide shaped the development of racism, racial discrimination, xenophobia, and related intolerance. Moreover, Article 29 also condemned the persistent practice of slavery in various parts of the world.[70] Although not referring to it directly, the conference contributed to the debates on reparations not only in Africa, but also in the Americas and Europe.

The participation of the Brazilian delegation in the Durban conference was a turning point for the organization of its black movement, whose agenda gained unprecedented attention during the two terms (2003–2010) of President Luiz Inácio Lula da Silva, a member of the Workers' Party. In his first term, Lula implemented major changes regarding the legislation on symbolical reparations for slavery and affirmative action for the countries populations of African descent. While the Racial Equality Statute remained stuck in the National Congress for more than a decade, facing opposition from various sectors of Brazilian elites, Law no. 10.639 of January 9, 2003, was sanctioned. The new legislation, modifying Law no. 9.394 of December 1996, dealt with national education, and made mandatory the inclusion of Afro-Brazilian history and culture in the curricula of primary schools and high schools. The law also established November 20 as national Black Consciousness Day, even though by that time the date had already become an official holiday in dozens of Brazilian cities. Moreover, in that same year the National Congress transformed provisional measure number 111 of March 21, 2003 into Law no. 10.678 of May 23, 2003, establishing the creation of Secretariat for Policies to Promote Racial Equality (SEPPIR).[71] This new institution, which remained in existence for more than a decade, formulated, coordinated, and articulated public policies to promote racial equality in Brazil.

Also in 2003, the Brazilian federal government took an important step to execute Article 68 of the Constitution of 1988 regarding the remnants of *quilombos*. The presidential Decree no. 4.887 of November 20, 2003 mandated the "classification of remnants of *quilombo* communities to be attested following the principle of self-definition by the community itself." It established that *quilombos* would be understood as "ethnic-racial groups, according to self-assignment criteria, carrying their own historical trajectory and specific territorial relations, with assumed black ancestry related to resistance to historical oppression."[72] As a result, the decree expanded the historical definition of *quilombos* (as runaway settlements) to include various communities of poor black peasants who since the period that followed the abolition of slavery were historically excluded from access to land ownership.[73] Despite these important achievements, the rule of the Workers Party also contributed to institutionalizing the black movement. Therefore, several Afro-Brazilian activists started occupying official positions in the government. Perhaps satisfied and probably optimistic about the new civil rights gains, black militants gradually neglected the idea of financial reparations. This context confirms the general trend observed in other parts of the Americas such as the United States, where demands for financial reparations tended to decline in periods civil rights were apparently secured.

Meanwhile in the United States, African American lawyers, supported by various black organizations, started several other litigations directed at obtaining financial reparations for slavery not only from the federal government, but also from municipal and state governments as well as US corporations.[74] In March 2002, Edward Fagan filed a class-action suit in a Brooklyn federal court in the name of Deadria Farmer-Paellmann, an African American activist, lawyer, and founder of the Reparations Study group, and all other persons in a similar situation. Like previous militants of the reparations' cause, Farmer-Paellmann is a descendant of slaves as her great-grandfather Abel Hines (1846–1921) was enslaved in South Carolina.[75] The lawsuit requested a formal apology and financial reparations from three US companies that profited from slavery: FleetBoston Financial Corporation which succeeded the Providence Bank, founded by Rhode Island slave trader John Brown (1736–1803); the CSX Corporation; and Aetna Insurance Company, which held an insurance policy in the name of her enslaved great-grandfather.[76] As happened with Forman's Black Manifesto, opponents to reparations qualified Farmer-Paellmann's lawsuit as blackmail. After a court hearing in 2003, the case was dismissed in 2004. Among others, the judge argued that the defendants were not slave owners and that the plaintiffs could not prove to be descendants of slaves.[77] Later refilings were also dismissed. But in 2006, the US Court of Appeals for the Seventh Circuit allowed the plaintiffs to pursue consumer protection claims exposing the companies cited in the lawsuit for deceiving their customers about their involvement in slavery. According to some legal scholars these claims might be the most promising venues for future calls for reparations.[78]

Activists and lawmakers continued targeting corporations who benefited from slavery with demands for reparations. On June 19, 2002, Councilman Charles Barron introduced the Queen Mother Moore Reparations Bill in the City Council of New York. Like other lawsuits presented during the same period, the Bill was "designed to study what role the municipal government played in promoting, profiting or protecting the enslavement of Africans in the city of New York."[79] The Bill also stipulated the creation of a commission to investigate which private corporations benefited from slavery and whether the government of New York City collaborated with these enterprises. Several black politicians and activists, including Congressman Conyers, Conrad Worrill, the chairman of the Black United Front, Viola Plummer of the December 12th Movement, and Reverend Herbert Daughtry, founder of the National Black United Front, supported the proposed law.[80] Similar to the lawsuit proposed by Farmer-Paellmann, this Bill was not an isolated proposition as since the previous decade, with the recovery of the African Burial Ground in Manhattan, scholars and black social actors were debating New York City's slave past in the public sphere.[81] Although politicians, lawyers, and activists were not successful in passing these Bills or winning these lawsuits, they continued introducing legislation and filing new claims in the following years.[82]

Along with litigation efforts and proposed legislation demanding reparations from insurance companies, banks, railroads, and the federal government, during the first years of the new millennium, public demonstrations requesting redress for slavery continued to emerge in the United States. Seven years after the Million Man March, several black organizations called a massive protest demanding reparations for slavery (Figure 5.3) on August 17, 2002, the day of Marcus Garvey's 115th birthday. Featuring banners stating "40 Acres and a Mule" (Figure 5.4), the Millions for Reparations Rally gathered approximately 58,000 participants in the National Mall in Washington, DC. Among its organizers were Conrad Worrill and Viola Plummer. Speakers included Reverend Herbert Daughtry, Dorothy Benton Lewis, John Conyers, and NOI's leader, Louis Farrakhan. According to Plummer "Washington is an appropriate location for the rally because it is an example of a city built through the labor of slaves." Confirming the idea that reparations should be paid to the descendants of slaves, Worrill asserted that the "United States government owes black people [...] and many of the corporations that are multimillion, multibillion-dollar

FIGURE 5.3 Slave Reparations Focus on NYC Protest, New York City, United States, August 9, 2002. In the picture, Lindi Bobb, six years old, attends a slavery reparations protest outside New York Life Insurance Company offices, featuring posters calling for the Washington, DC rally of August 17, 2002. Courtesy: Mario Tama/Getty Images.

FIGURE 5.4 Millions for Reparations Rally, Washington, DC, United States, August 17, 2002. In the picture (right) Andrea Levy from Queens, New York City, NY. Courtesy: Manny Ceneta/Getty Images.

corporations, they actually received the basis of their wealth from the enslavement and labor of black people."[83]

A new transnational era for the demands of reparations

The second decade of the twenty-first century marked a new moment in the movement calling for reparations for slavery. In Brazil, despite the favorable context for the development of affirmative action, in 2010, Waldemar Annunciação Borges de Medeiros, president of the Association Eduardo Banks, submitted an unexpected and curious proposal to the Commission of Participative Legislation of the Brazilian National Congress. Based in Rio de Janeiro, the nonprofit organization created in 2006 is named after its founder, Eduardo Banks, a far-right-wing journalist. The proposal requested the change of the Golden Law that abolished slavery in 1888, in order to establish "the right to compensate the slave owners, their descendants or successors."[84] Without discussion, the federal deputy and commission's president, Paulo Roberto Pimenta of the Workers' Party, rejected it by arguing that "slavery was an immense error [. . .] and recognizing the right to compensation would be a step back in the current legislation and an attack on human dignity."[85] Although in that context such a proposal had no chance to make its way through the National Congress, its very existence revealed that the memory of the attempts made by Brazilian former slave owners to obtain indemnities remained alive.

Every other year, the issue of financial reparations to the descendants of slaves makes a return to the Brazilian public scene, but without much success. In 2012, Claudete Alves, a black militant and teacher from São Paulo, presented a public civil action to the Public Prosecutor's Office against the Brazilian state requesting compensation for the damages caused to all descendants of enslaved Africans living in Brazil and residing in the city of São Paulo.[86] An experienced activist and a member of the Workers' Party, Alves was elected councilwoman of the city of São Paulo in 2003, a position she occupied until 2006. In this capacity, she co-authored the Bill that gave origin to Law no. 13.707 of January 7, 2004, which made November 20, National Day of Black Consciousness, a municipal observed holiday in the city of São Paulo.[87] According to Alves's lawyers, each slave descendant should receive R$2,000,000 (approximately US$610,000). In response to the request, the Secretary of SEPPIR and a longtime Afro-Brazilian activist, Matilde Ribeiro, stated that the measures already approved during Lula's government were more efficient as reparation instruments. She underscored that for the Brazilian government financial reparations were out of consideration.

In 2012, after almost two decades of debates, President Dilma Rousseff sanctioned Law no. 12.771. The law mandated all federal higher education institutions to establish admission quotas until 2016 based on attendance at public high school, family income, or being indigenous, black, or brown. Also in 2012, the eleven judges of the Brazilian Supreme Court unanimously upheld the constitutionality of both class and race-based quotas. Following the solution for the controversial issue of affirmative action in Brazilian federal universities, in 2013, the government presented to the National Congress a new Bill instituting quotas of 20 percent for Afro-Brazilians in the federal public service. The Bill did not face much opposition. After passing in the National Congress, on June 9, 2014, President Rousseff sanctioned Law no. 12.990. At this point the resistance against affirmative action was much less visible than in the previous twenty years, when the first debates about quotas in public universities had started.

Meanwhile, the requests for financial reparations for slavery made the news again in 2012, when the Commission of Human Rights and Participative Legislation examined Bill no. 3 of 2008, authored by the Institute All Aboard: A Call for Full Citizenship. The Bill suggested the creation of a Commission of Compensation to the Descendants of Enslaved Black Africans in Brazil, which would determine the amount of financial reparations to the descendants of slaves. But unlike the formulation presented by the MPR in the 1990s, the proposed Bill indicated that pecuniary reparations should be awarded to the individuals declaring themselves "descendants of enslaved blacks," and "presenting phenotype or traits or documents proving this descent."[88] Without massive support from Brazilian black organizations, which preferred obtaining gains by negotiating directly with the government of the Workers' Party, the Senate commission rejected the Bill in July 2013. According to the report by the then Brazilian Senator Eduardo Lopes (Brazilian Republican Party), it was impossible to estimate its impact and its financial consequences on the public budget, the federal debt, and the fiscal policy.[89]

Despite the symbolic reparations implemented in Brazil since 2002, more than in other former slave societies such as the United States, the scars of slavery are still visible in the various spheres of Brazilian society. The country maintains a difficult relation with its slave past and by consequence with the various dimensions of its rich African heritage that derived from this tragic period.[90] Social indicators confirm that Brazil's population of African descent have remained racially discriminated and socially marginalized.[91] If over the last fifteen years symbolic reparations in the form of initiatives to memorialize slavery in the country's public space were gradually developed, during this same period the debates on financial reparations for slavery were not as visible as they were in the United States. Brazil continues to be one of the most unequal nations in the world. Although composing the majority of the population, Afro-Brazilians continue to be socially and economically excluded.

In 2014, as Brazil hosted the FIFA World Cup, the international media devoted a lot of attention to the country, especially to its population of African descent. An article published in two parts in the *Huffington Post*, and shared hundreds of times on Facebook and Twitter, defined the movement of Brazilian *quilombo* communities as the largest program of reparations for slavery in the world.[92] Yet, in Latin American countries like Brazil, there is an enormous distance between the enactment of legislation and its application. Despite the sensationalist title of *Huffington Post*'s article and the presidential Decree no. 4.887 of 2003, the SEPPIR estimated that only 12,428 of a total of 214,000 *quilombola* families were living in territories owning legal land titles in 2014. In fact, from 1995 and 2015, the federal government provided the legal ownership titles to only 164 *quilombo* territories, in which more than 230 *quilombo* communities are settled. Meanwhile, there are 1,533 territories awaiting their titles. Even if the Palmares Foundation certified approximately 2,849 *quilombos* (which can receive federal financial support) in 2015, most of these communities are still waiting on National Institute of Colonization and Agrarian Reform (INCRA) to obtain the titles that will give them full ownership of their lands.[93] Given this situation, it is very difficult to make the claim that Brazil has the largest program of reparations for slavery in the world.[94] In reality, although Brazilian government authorities, academics, and many members of black organizations have employed the term reparations to designate a variety of measures associated with civil rights and cultural recognition, material reparations through land ownership remain an unachieved project in Brazil.

Not by chance, in November 2014, the Order of Attorneys of Brazil (OAB) launched the National Truth Commission of Black Slavery in Brazil. With branches in several states, the working group follows the model of the commission that recently investigated the crimes perpetrated during the civil–military dictatorship of 1964–1985. Comparable to what is proposed in Bill H.R.40 authored by Congressman Conyers in the United States, the committee is examining the period of slavery in Brazil with the goal of reinforcing the importance of affirmative action as an instrument of reparations for slavery. In a first preliminary report, the commission's branch in Rio de Janeiro stated that for more than three centuries Brazil, Portugal, and the Catholic Church were the main responsible agents for Brazilian slavery and the violation of human rights of Africans and their descendants. It also specified that the next step is to establish forms of reparations.[95] Although not referring to material and financial reparations, the report's conclusion suggests that affirmative action and other symbolic measures implemented over past years were unsatisfactory.

Similar appeals demanding symbolic and financial reparations surfaced in the United Kingdom and the former British colonies in the Caribbean, with the approach of the bicentennial of the British abolition of the slave trade in 2007.[96] At that occasion, Prime Minister Tony Blair expressed his sorrow for the involvement of Britain in the Atlantic slave trade in the pages of the *New Nation*, the most important Afro-Caribbean newspaper published in Britain. Yet, probably fearing formal requests of reparations, the British government failed to issue an official apology.[97] But in the former British colonies the issue of reparations remained central during one of the numerous activities held during the commemorations. In March 2007, Prime Minister of Barbados Owen Arthur gave a speech in which he addressed the issue of reparations.[98] Owen stressed that he knew that "reparation, at least for the victims of the transatlantic and their descendants, has been a controversial issue." Yet to him, reparations was a question "not of retribution, but of morality. We need to bring equity to the emancipation process, and closure to the criminal activity that was racial chattel slavery."[99] Owen advocated that reparations "should be upheld, advocated and promoted through the establishment of a fund to facilitate material compensation to countries which were victimized, and by pursuit of national and international policies to confront and eradicate the legacies of slavery."[100]

In France, the echoes of the demands for reparations for slavery and the Atlantic slave trade were also heard. After the passing of the Law Taubira in 2001 recognizing slavery and the slave trade as crimes against humanity, the French the government along with the administration of several French cities and black associations developed a series of plans to memorialize and commemorate slavery. These projects entailed a national day to commemorate the memories of the slave trade, slavery, and their abolitions, the creation of a committee for the memory of slavery, and the unveiling of monuments and memorials in various French cities such as Paris, Nantes, and Bordeaux, along with the organization of museum exhibitions. Yet, to social actors who identify themselves as descendants of slaves, these memorial devices (a form of symbolic reparations) did not seem to suffice. Soon the debates regarding the huge indemnities paid by Haiti to have its independence recognized by France reemerged in the public debate as well. One year before the coup d'état that removed him from power, Haitian President Jean-Bertrand Aristide gave a speech in which he called on France to pay back the financial compensations disbursed by the Caribbean country in order to obtain recognition for its independence.

Years later, the echoes of Aristide's words continued getting public attention. Especially after the earthquake of January 2010, two open letters signed by several public figures supporting the debt's reimbursement were made public in French newspapers.[101] In May 2012, the Representative Council of Black Associations (CRAN), the International Movement for Reparations (MIR), and the Collective Daughters and Sons of Deported Africans (COFFAD) launched a campaign for reparations in France.[102] Moreover, some months later the CRAN released an appeal signed by activists, politicians, and intellectuals, published in the French newspaper *Le Monde*, demanding a national debate about reparations associated with slavery.[103] Despite these calls for discussion of the issue of reparations in France, and in particular to give back to Haiti the amount paid for the recognition of its independence, the French state remains rather engaged in promoting symbolic reparations, especially through projects focusing on the memorialization of slavery.

In 2013, CARICOM, an organization that gathers fifteen Caribbean nations and dependencies to promote integration, decided that each country member would create a commission for reparations.[104] Weeks later, CARICOM created a Reparations Commission chaired by Sir Hilary Beckles. Like the early advocates of reparations, Beckles identifies himself as a descendant of slaves. His great-great grandparents were enslaved on the Cleland sugar plantation in Saint Andrew, Barbados, owned by the ancestors of the British actor, Benedict Cumberbatch, who after the British abolition of slavery obtained nearly £6,000 in compensation for the loss of their human property.[105]

On March 11, 2014, the caucus gathering all presidents of CARICOM member states adopted a plan consisting of ten demands of symbolic and financial reparations for slavery, the Atlantic slave trade, and the genocide of indigenous populations. Addressed to Denmark, France, Portugal, the Netherlands, the United Kingdom, and Sweden, CARICOM's ten-point reparations plan includes a formal apology. The plan also refers to "support repatriation for those desiring resettlement in Africa," even though no specific African nations are mentioned. Moreover, the only point of the program that clearly refers to financial reparations is "the reduction of domestic debt and cancellation of international debt." Most other measures of the plan are demands of symbolic reparations, such as the "support for cultural institutions such as museums and research centers that expose the colonialists' crime against humanity and affirm Caribbean people's humanity" as well as school programs connecting Caribbean blacks to their African heritage.[106]

Despite these gaps, all over the world, the media gave great attention to the release of CARICOM ten-point reparations plan. The most important US and European newspapers such as the *New York Times*, *The Guardian*, *O Público*, and *El País* published recurring articles about CARICOM's demands and how various European countries responded to them. In the days that followed the announcement of the ten-point plan, other nations in the Americas also publicly backed the call for reparations. For example, on March 25, 2014, during a session of the United Nations General Assembly in New York commemorating the International Day of Remembrance for the Victims of Slavery and the Transatlantic Slave Trade, diplomat Daylenis Moreno Guerra declared Cuban support to the requests for apologies and the "consequent compensations demanded by the state members of the Caribbean Community (CARICOM) as reparations for the genocide of Natives and the enslavement of Africans."[107]

In the United States, various African American organizations also endorsed CARICOM's ten-point plan, in what revealed itself as an occasion to reinvigorate the movement for reparations. On April 19, 2014, the Institute of the Black World, an organization created in 2001 to promote cooperation among grassroots, activists and action-oriented groups, held the forum "Revitalizing the Reparations Movement Program," at Chicago State University, in Chicago, Illinois. Invited as the meeting's keynote speaker, Beckles defended CARICOM's ten-point plan to a large audience, which included several distinguished guests such as Farrakhan and Conyers, as well as other advocates of reparations such as Ron Daniels, president of the Institute of the Black World, and JoAnn Watson, then co-chair of N'COBRA. All these activists enthusiastically supported the emerging demands of reparations from Caribbean countries.

In April 2015, CARICOM Reparations Commission and the National African American Reparations Commission organized a National and International Reparations Summit in New York City, gathering delegates from commissions on reparations from Martinique, US Virgin Islands, Canada, United Kingdom, and several other countries. Among the several deliberations, the meeting reached the compromise of consolidating and expanding the global movement for reparations. It also agreed on CARICOM's support to the National African-American Reparations Commission. The demands for reparations for slavery gained attention not only from black organizations but also from predominantly white elite universities in the United States and Britain, where Hilary Beckles has been a constant guest speaker.

Whereas black organizations in the United States and other countries in the Americas applauded CARICOM demands for reparations, the governments of European countries to which the claims were addressed received these calls with silence and indifference. Of course, this irresponsiveness is not new. Eight years after the bicentennial of the abolition of the British slave trade, when Tony Blair expressed his sorrow for the role of Britain in the Atlantic slave trade, British Prime Minister David Cameron, also a descendant of slave owners, responded sharply to the CARICOM ten-point reparations plan. During a state visit to Jamaica, in September 2015, he acknowledged slavery "was abhorrent in all its forms," but insisted that Britain and Jamaica should "move on from this painful legacy and continue to build for the future."[108] Cameron did not reveal what the promising projects for the future of Britain and Jamaica were, but during his visit to the Caribbean country, he announced financial aid packages for the development of infrastructure projects and the construction of a new Jamaican prison. Almost two centuries after the British abolition of slavery, the unfortunate association between bondage and prison was not as fortuitous as it appeared. Since the nineteenth century, former slave societies envisioned the prison system as a solution for the future of freed populations. Moreover, as discussed in Chapter 4, during the twentieth century, activists who advocated reparations for slavery were often persecuted and sent to prison. From a historical point of view, Cameron's regrettable response to CARICOM's demands of reparations was hardly surprising.

Despite the lack of success in gaining financial and material reparations for slavery and the Atlantic slave trade, in Europe, Africa, and the Americas, social actors identifying themselves as descendants of slaves also have been more successful in obtaining symbolic reparations through the construction of monuments, memorials, and museums to honor enslaved men and women. In countries such as in Senegal, Ghana, Republic of Benin, Brazil, Cuba, Colombia, Venezuela, Jamaica, and the United States, local communities and governments transformed newly built monuments and heritage sites associated with slavery and the slave trade into sites to attract local, national, and international tourists. Over the last two decades, the recovery of slave wharfs and slave cemeteries, in Brazil and the United States, have contributed to the official recognition of the importance of slavery in the urban and rural landscapes of these countries. In the United States, especially after Obama's election as president in 2008, the debates about the central place of slavery in building the country's wealth became increasingly visible in the public sphere. Heritage sites such as the old homes of the US founding fathers George Washington, Thomas Jefferson, and James Madison, which in the past barely referred to slavery, are now engaged in acknowledging the role of enslaved men and women. In former European, West African, and West Central African slave ports such as Nantes, Bordeaux, Liverpool, Cacheu, Ouidah, Badagry, Gorée Island, and Luanda, black associations and individuals also succeeded in approving the construction of memorials honoring the victims of the Atlantic slave trade and the preservation of heritage sites associated with the slave trade. Likewise, monuments honoring slaves and black social actors who fought against slavery, such as Frederick Douglass, Denmark Vesey, Zumbi of Palmares, Sojourner Truth, José Leonardo Chirino, Benkos Bioho, and many others were unveiled across the Americas. Engaged in a fight for symbolic reparations, black militants, sometimes supported by scholars who provide their expertise to the study of the newly uncovered sites, propelled the governments of various countries which were deeply involved in the Atlantic slave trade and slavery to officially recognize these atrocities as central elements of their national histories. But as symbolic reparations were accomplished in many instances, obtaining material and financial reparations remains an unachieved project.

A continuous battle

Unlike the previous decades, the end of the Cold War smashed the barriers that prevented the emergence of a dialogue among the populations of African descent in different former slave societies. If until the 1980s, the United States dominated the landscape of reparations activism, the last two decades of the twentieth century marked a shift in this paradigm. Yet, the debates on reparations were shaped in different ways depending on the constitution of local black movements and how particular societies conceived the idea of race. In Latin America, black activists and groups continued privileging symbolic reparations. Except for the demands for land ownership to black populations, the demands of civil rights and the fight against racism and affirmative action continued to prevail. But despite this context, a few requests for financial reparations evolved in Brazil. Moreover, black militants in Brazil, Colombia, and Ecuador succeeded in obtaining the approval of new legislation on land redistribution to communities of African descent, even though to this day many of these groups remain fighting for the titles that will give them definitive ownership rights over these lands.

At the turn of the twenty-first century, international reparation activism expanded through new avenues. In the United States, several organizations combined efforts to organize massive demonstrations by at the same time supporting litigation and the introduction of legislation in the National Congress. African nations, and more recently Caribbean countries, engaged in multinational initiatives demanding various forms of reparations for slavery and the Atlantic slave trade. Although most of these calls still privilege apologies and symbolic restitutions, they also include debt cancellation as financial reparations. Regardless of any current concrete outcomes resulting from these recent demands, the internationalization of this new activism has favored the growing visibility of demands of reparations in Europe, Africa, and the Americas.

Epilogue

Unfinished Struggle

The history of demands of reparations for slavery and the Atlantic slave trade remains unfinished. In the last two decades, international organizations such as the United Nations and individual countries such as France have recognized these atrocities as crimes against humanity. Heads of state of the United States, United Kingdom, and Brazil, as well as religious leaders such as Pope John Paul II expressed their sorrow for the participation of their countries and of the Catholic Church in the development of slavery and the slave trade. Numerous nations in Africa, Europe, and the Americas continue developing countless initiatives such as monuments, memorials, and museums to honor the victims of these atrocities. In this context, where the past of slavery continues to live on in the present, requests for financial and material redress remain in progress. Their history is still being written.

As I revised this book three important developments occurred, signifying that the demands for reparations for slavery and the Atlantic slave trade are gaining additional national and international attention from individuals who identify themselves as descendants of slaves, from social movements, and from public institutions. In August 2016, the Movement for Black Lives, a coalition of fifty black organizations from all over the United States, including Black Lives Matter, developed a platform to fight the problem of growing police violence against black men, women, and children. This program includes six sets of policies intended to end criminalization, incarceration, and killing of black people; create investments in education, health, and safety for black populations; provide economic justice to black communities; control laws, institutions, and policies that impact black communities; and implement Black Power and black self-determination. In addition, one set of policies focuses on reparations for past and continuing harms. The coalition states that "government, responsible corporations and other institutions that have profited off of the harm they have inflicted on Black people—from colonialism to slavery through food and housing redlining, mass incarceration, and surveillance—must repair the harm done."

Among the five elements emphasized, the coalition demands "legislation at the federal and state level that requires the United States to acknowledge the lasting impacts of slavery" and requests a plan to address these problems. In particular, it demands the "immediate passage of H.R.40, the 'Commission to Study Reparation Proposals for African-Americans Act' or subsequent versions which call for reparations remedies."[1]

The major US news outlets covered the Movement for Black Lives' support of reparations.[2] For the first time in decades demands for reparations for slavery became part of the program of black organizations whose social base are youth groups, including a large number of black young women as well. On August 1, 2016, the anniversary of the date of the abolition of slavery in the British Caribbean, Black Lives Matter organized an encampment at City Hall Park in New York City, renaming it Abolition Square. The protest intended to denounce the Broken Windows policing that promotes police violence against blacks by criminalizing minor offenses in urban areas. At that occasion, young activist Nelini Stamp expressed to the online magazine *Salon* her enthusiasm about the inclusion of reparations in the demands made by the coalition. Stating that slavery and Jim Crow are the original sins of the United States, Stamp affirmed that "We are in the middle of a breakthrough on reparations."[3] Yet, the demands of reparations for slavery on the platform of the Movement for Black Lives raised criticism. Political commentator and academic John McWhorter criticized the platform for being "unsuitably woke to the past." According to him, a number of initiatives such as Affirmative Action were reparations, even though they were not financial or material reparations.[4]

Other public debates regarding symbolic reparations recently surfaced as well. In 2015, a wave of demonstrations, in great part associated with the activities of Black Lives Matter, emerged in universities all over the United States. In addition to protest racism and racial exclusion, students of color also demanded the removal of markers associated with slavery which are still displayed on several buildings on university campuses. These demands were associated with previous and ongoing debates concerning the connections between white elite universities and slavery. As a result, several universities created study groups and produced reports examining the ties of these institutions with slavery.[5]

Georgetown University, a Jesuit institution of higher education in Washington, DC was among these universities. But unlike other institutions, Georgetown's relation to slavery carries particular features. Members of the Society of Jesus, an order of the Roman Catholic Church, the Jesuits were the largest slave owners in the Americas. As in other parts of the continent, the Jesuits also owned plantations and slaves in the United States.[6] In 1838, for several reasons but especially with the aim of paying a major debt contracted by Georgetown University, the Jesuits sold 272 enslaved men, women, and children to cotton and sugar plantations in Louisiana. The sale generated approximately $3.3 million in today's currency. As further research identified numerous descendants of the slaves sold by the Jesuits to save the university, the President of Georgetown University, John J. DeGioia called the formation of a Working Group on Slavery, Memory, and Reconciliation to examine in detail the ties of the university with slavery.[7] Among the recommendations made by Georgetown's Working Group was the suggestion "that the University offer a formal, public apology for its historical relationship with slavery." Although stating that an "apology is a precondition for reconciliation" the document omits any reference to reparations to the descendants of the slaves sold in 1838.[8]

Major newspapers around the world reported in several languages the main results revealed in the Working Group's report announced by Georgetown's President DeGioia on September 1, 2016. The formal apology is among the measures to be taken by Georgetown's administration to come into terms with its slave past. Additional measures include the creation of an institute to study slavery and the construction of a memorial to honor the slaves sold in 1838. Additional measures, include renaming two university buildings after an African American educator and an African American enslaved man. Moreover, the university's president decided to offer preferential admission to all descendants of slaves who worked for Georgetown.[9] Despite the media's positive reaction to the announced measures, it became clear that none of these initiatives included financial and material reparations to the descendants of slaves. One week after the DeGioia's announcement, the GU272 Foundation, a group consisting of various descendants of the slaves sold in 1838, emphasized that the announced measures did not meaningfully contribute to the elaboration of the Working Group's recommendations. According to Karran Harper-Royal, one member of the group, the descendants of slaves sold in Louisiana were disadvantaged in comparison to white children.[10] Consequently, they proposed that Georgetown University helps to raise $1 billion to create a foundation to support the education of the descendants of those sold in 1838.[11] To this day, Georgetown University had neither issued the promised formal apology, nor responded to the creation of the proposed foundation.

Also on September 26, 2016, the UN Working Group of Experts on People of African Descent, which reports to the Higher Commissioner on Human Rights, presented the report of its mission to the United States, during the meeting of the UN Human Rights Council. The conclusions advanced by the committee composed of Ricardo A. Sunga III (Chairperson, Philippines), Mireille Fanon-Mendes-France (France), Sabelo Gumedze (South Africa), Michal Balcerzak (Poland), and Ahmed Reid (Jamaica) underscored the living legacies of slavery and racial segregation in the United States. Similar to the policies proposed by the Movement for Black Lives, in its conclusions, the Working Group report expressed several concerns. In particular, it stated that "the legacy of colonial history, enslavement, racial subordination and segregation, racial terrorism and racial inequality in the United States remains a serious challenge, as there has been no real commitment to reparations and to truth and reconciliation for people of African descent."[12] In its recommendations, the report advises the erection of "monuments, memorials, and markers" to "facilitate the public dialogue." It also stresses the need to acknowledge the "transatlantic trade in Africans, enslavement, colonization and colonialism," as crimes against humanity, and address past and present atrocities with reparatory justice.[13] Moreover, the Working Group encouraged the United States Congress to pass H.R.40 and to "consider applying analogous elements contained in the Caribbean Community's Ten-Point Action Plan on Reparations."[14] As expected, the US government had not responded to these recommendations.

As the debates about reparations for slavery remain alive in the international arena, many questions wait to be answered. Throughout its various chapters, this book has surveyed the long history of collective and individual demands for reparations for slavery and the Atlantic slave trade. I showed that since the period of slavery, white and black abolitionists, including slaves themselves, discussed how to redress the injustices of slavery. Yet, governments, slave owners, and several abolitionists did not defend reparations for slavery, but were, rather, concerned about how to compensate for the financial losses that emancipation would impose on slave owners. In most former slave societies, former masters and planters obtained financial compensation after the end of slavery.

In my study of the history of demands for reparations for slavery a persistent trend seems to be revealed. In periods when social actors have pushed for the demands of civil rights and citizenship, the requests for resources in the form of financial and material reparations for past injustice have been neglected. However, during phases of civil rights decline, the demands for financial and material redress tended to increase.

After the abolition of slavery, despite the existence of many regional and national nuances, the governments of former slave societies such as the United States, Brazil, Jamaica, Cuba, and Colombia did not award freedpeople with material and financial reparations for the period they lived in bondage. In all these societies, former slaves continued fighting for access to decent living and working conditions. Depending on the country, ex-slaves were more or less successful in gaining landownership and citizenship. In Latin America and the Caribbean, regions where legal segregation was absent and the ideologies of racial democracy and *mestizaje* contributed to mask the persistence of racism and racial inequalities, descendants of former slaves waited until the second half of the twentieth century to collectively fight for reparations for slavery. In the United States, however, the rise of legal segregation, racial violence, and suppression of voting rights led to the first wave of demands for reparations during the 1890s, when thousands of former slaves joined a movement demanding pensions to ex-slaves.

Since the nineteenth century the most important movements demanding reparations were led by activists who identified themselves as descendants of slaves, a term that establishes a clear connection between past and present injustice. In the United States, and later in Cuba and Brazil, black women played a leading role in voicing demands for financial and material reparations for slavery. During the nineteenth century and until the 1920s, black women were deprived of voting rights: more than men, they were socially and economically excluded. With less access to education, even in an old age they were those running the households. To most former enslaved women, whereas expectations of future social mobility were unrealistic, pensions and land were seen as provisions that could supply them with autonomy.

Yet, both in the past as in the present, many African Americans opposed the idea of fighting for financial and material reparations, because these demands for resources would place them again in a position of victimhood. Whites also opposed reparations for a variety of reasons, but especially because it would mean losing their own resources. Despite these hindrances, until the early twentieth century, the movement for pensions led by Callie House and Isaiah Dickerson gathered an estimated 600,000 members. The importance of the National Ex-Slave Mutual Relief, Bounty and Pension Association of the United States of America can be illustrated by how federal authorities fiercely persecuted its leaders until they succeeded in dismantling the movement. Still, in the 1930s, elder former slaves remembered the movement, and its tradition is still invoked by activists in the movement for reparations. Its legacy is still honored by present-day reparations activists.

During the first five decades of the twentieth century, demands for reparations in their most varied forms continued to be invoked in the discourses of activists such as Marcus Garvey and Paul Robeson. Likewise, financial and material reparations were not central elements in the Civil Rights Movement. But during the 1960s, and especially after the passing of the Civil Rights Act and the backlash provoked by the assassination of Malcolm X and Martin Luther King Jr., a second wave of reparations activism resurfaced in the United States, through the work of Queen Mother Audley Moore, James Forman, and the various RNA members.

The end of the Cold War opened the third wave in the fight for reparations for slavery. Unlike the previous ones, however, this new phase was marked by the internationalization of the demands of redress for slavery. Although the United States continued occupying a leading role through the work of organizations such as the NOI and N'COBRA who worked on litigation cases, introduction of Bills, and the organization of massive demonstrations, the struggle of reparations gained new international players in Africa, Europe, Latin America, and the Caribbean. However, even though governments, organizations, and black groups largely endorsed public apologies and various forms of symbolic reparations, especially the construction of monuments and memorials, providing financial and material reparations remains a controversial issue. Despite their long history and in the face of having been victims of fierce persecution, to this day movements requesting financial and material reparations for slavery and the Atlantic slave trade remain marginalized ventures in the agenda of organized black groups around the world.

In 2014 new calls for reparations, addressed to several European countries by CARICOM, and later by the Movement for Black Lives and the United Nations to the United States, may suggest the rise of a new powerful wave of reparations activism. Still, many questions remain unsolved. To organizations and activists, which kinds of reparations are due (symbolic, financial, or material, or all of them) remain unclear. Even in the recent CARICOM ten-point program symbolic reparations predominate. Moreover, there is no consensus on who should give reparations and who should obtain them. These questions are particularly difficult when discussing the issue of reparations in African societies which participated in the Atlantic slave trade. In many African countries, descendants of rulers and other members of the elites who benefited from the commerce on human beings continue to occupy positions of political and economic power. Should these leaders be the ones to control the reception of possible financial restitutions? The same question should also be asked regarding countries such as Haiti and Jamaica, which along with other Caribbean countries addressed demands for redress to European nations. Will financial reparations be employed to improve the living conditions of the largest part of the population or will they again be stolen by the ruling elites? Although I raise these questions in these final pages, it is up to activists and organizations advocating reparations to answer them. Meanwhile, I hope this book helps to shed some light on the difficult history of slavery and the Atlantic slave trade and the transnational struggle to obtain justice for these past atrocities.

ABBREVIATIONS

AGN	Archivo General de la Nación, Mexico City, Mexico
ANH	Archivo Nacional Histórico, Santiago de Chile, Chile
BNRJ	Biblioteca Nacional do Rio de Janeiro, Rio de Janeiro, Brazil
CHS	Connecticut Historical Society, Hartford, CT, United States
FCRB	Fundação Casa de Rui Barbosa, Rio de Janeiro, Brazil
FWPWPA	Federal Writers' Project of the Works Progress Administration
GCLAU	Gale Cengage Learning, Archives Unbound, online
HUA	Harvard University Archives, Harvard University, Cambridge, MA, United States
IHGB	Instituto Histórico e Geográfrico Brasileiro, Rio de Janeiro, RJ, Brazil
LCMSS	Library of Congress, Manuscript Division, Washington, DC, United States
MSRC	Moorland-Spingarn Research Center, Howard University, Washington, DC, United States
NARA	National Archives, Washington, DC, United States
NYSA	New York State Archives, New York, NY
SLHWA	Schlesinger Library on the History of Women in America, Harvard University, Boston, MA, United States
TNA	The National Archives, London, United Kingdom
WLHCL	Widener Library, Collection Development Department, Harvard College Library, Harvard University, Cambridge, MA, United States

ABBREVIATIONS

NOTES

Introduction: Reparations in the Past and Present

1   For detailed estimates, see the *Trans-Atlantic Slave Trade Database: Voyages*, Emory University, http://www.slavevoyages.org.

2   See Ana Lucia Araujo, *Shadows of the Slave Past: Memory, Heritage, and Slavery* (New York: Routledge, 2014).

3   Alfred L. Brophy, *Reparations: Pro & Con* (New York: Oxford University Press, 2006), 11.

4   Mary Frances Berry, *My Face Is Black Is True: Callie House and the Struggle for Ex-Slave Reparations* (New York: Alfred A. Knopf, 2005).

5   Ta-Nehisi Coates, "The Case for Reparations," *The Atlantic*, June 2014, 51–68 and "Are Reparations Due to African Americans," *New York Times*, June 8, 2014, http://www.nytimes.com/roomfordebate/2014/06/08/are-reparations-due-to-african-americans.

Chapter 1: "Greatest Riches in All America Have Arisen From Our Blood and Tears"

1   See Orlando Patterson, *Slavery and Social Death: A Comparative Study* (Cambridge, MA: Harvard University Press, 1982), 26.

2   John K. Thornton, *A Cultural History of the Atlantic World, 1250–1820* (New York: Cambridge University Press, 2012), 183.

3   Toby Green, *The Rise of the Trans-Atlantic Slave Trade in Western Africa, 1300–1589* (New York: Cambridge University Press, 2012), 100.

4   Linda M. Heywood, "Slavery and Its Transformation in the Kingdom of Kongo: 1491–1800," *Journal of African History* 50 (2009): 6–7.

5   Joseph C. Miller, *Way of Death: Merchant Capitalism and the Angolan Slave Trade, 1740–1830* (Madison: University of Wisconsin Press, 1988), 42–43.

6   Miller, *Way of Death*, 105.

7   John K. Thornton, *Africa and Africans in the Making of the Atlantic World, 1400–1800* (New York: Cambridge University Press, 1998), 99.

8   Heywood, "Slavery and Its Transformation," 5.

9 Walter Hawthorne, *From Africa to Brazil: Culture, Identity, and an Atlantic Slave Trade, 1600–1830* (New York: Cambridge University Press, 2010), 64.

10 Heywood, "Slavery and Its Transformation," 6, 8.

11 Robin Law, *Ouidah: The Social History of a West African Slaving Port (1727–1892)* (Athens, OH: Ohio University Press, 2004), 149. See A. Le Hérissé, *L'Ancien Royaume du Dahomey: Mœurs, Religion, Histoire* (Paris: Emile Larose, 1911), 56.

12 Mariana P. Candido, *An African Slaving Port and the Atlantic World: Benguela and Its Hinterland* (New York: Cambridge University Press, 2013), 9.

13 Randy J. Sparks, *Where the Negroes Are Masters: An African Port in the Era of the Slave Trade* (Cambridge, MA: Harvard University Press, 2014), 19.

14 Candido, *An African Slaving Port,* 149.

15 On Portugal's migration policies, see Vitorino Magalhães Godinho, "L'émigration portugaise (XVe–XXe Siècles): une constante structural et les réponses aux changements du monde," *Revista de história econômica e social* 1 (1978): 5–32. On white indentured servants in Virginia, see David Brion Davis, *Inhuman Bondage: The Rise and Fall of Slavery in the New World* (New York: Oxford University Press, 2006), 127, 132–133.

16 See Stuart Schwartz, *Sugar Plantations in the Formation of Brazilian Society: Bahia, 1550–1835* (New York: Cambridge University Press, 1985), 51–72 and Laird W. Bergad, *The Comparative Histories of Slavery in Brazil, Cuba, and the United States* (New York: Cambridge University Press, 2007), 13.

17 See Annemarie Jordan, "Image of Empire: Slaves in the Lisbon Household and Court of Catherine of Austria," in *Black Africans in Renaissance Europe*, ed. Tom F. Earle and Kate J. P. Lowe (Cambridge: Cambridge University Press, 2010), 160. On the costumes worn by the Knights of the Order of Santiago, see Terence Wise and Richard Scollins, *The Knights of Christ: Religious/Military Orders of Knighthood 1118–1565* (London: Osprey, 1984), 36.

18 Herbert S. Klein and Ben Vinson III, *African Slavery in Latin America and the Caribbean* (New York: Oxford University Press, 2007), 29.

19 Bergad, *The Comparative Histories of Slavery,* 23.

20 Ira Berlin, *Many Thousands Gone: The First Two Centuries of Slavery in North America* (Cambridge, MA: Belknap Press of Harvard University Press, 1998), 8.

21 Klein and Vinson, *African Slavery,* 30–31.

22 Klein and Vinson, *African Slavery,* 42.

23 See Herbert S. Klein, *The Atlantic Slave Trade* (New York: Cambridge University Press, 2010), 97.

24 See Miller, *Way of Death*; Pierre Verger, *Flux et reflux de la traite des nègres entre le Golfe de Bénin et Bahia de Todos os Santos, du XVIIe au XIXe siècle* (Paris: Mouton, 1968); Luiz Felipe de Alencastro, *O trato dos viventes: formação do Brasil no Atlântico Sul* (São Paulo: Companhia das Letras, 2000); Roquinaldo Ferreira, *Cross-Cultural Exchange in the Atlantic World: Angola and Brazil During the Era of the Slave Trade* (New York: Cambridge

University Press, 2012); and Candido, *An African Slaving Port and the Atlantic World.*

25 Luiz Felipe de Alencastro, "Continental Drift: The Independence of Brazil (1822), Portugal and Africa," in *From Slave Trade to Empire: Europe and the Colonisation of Black Africa, 1780s–1880s*, ed. Olivier Pétré-Grenouilleau (London: Routledge, 2004), 103, 108 n8.

26 See Charles R. Boxer, *Salvador de Sá and the Struggle for Brazil and Angola, 1602–1654* (Oxford: Clarendon Press, 1957); Alencastro, *O trato dos viventes*; and Filipa Ribeiro da Silva, *Dutch and the Portuguese in Western Africa: Empires, Merchants and the Atlantic System 1580–1674* (Leiden: Brill, 2011).

27 See the *Trans-Atlantic Slave Trade Database.*

28 Klein and Vinson, *African Slavery,* 43–44.

29 James Lockhart, and Stuart Schwartz, *Early Latin America: A History of Colonial Spanish America and Brazil* (New York: Cambridge University Press, 1999), 249.

30 Klein and Vinson, *African Slavery,* 51.

31 Philip D. Morgan, *Slave Counterpoint: Black Culture in the Eighteenth-Century Chesapeake and Lowcountry* (Chapel Hill: University of North Carolina Press, 1998), 8–9.

32 See the *Trans-Atlantic Slave Trade Database.*

33 Heywood, "Slavery and Its Transformation," 14–15.

34 The territories of the Kingdom of Dahomey and the Mahi Kingdom are part of the area of present-day Republic of Benin, whereas former kingdoms of Onim (Porto-Novo) and Ketu are also current cities of Republic of Benin. The Kingdom of Oyo and the Kingdom of Badagry are part of present-day Nigeria. On Tegbesu's embassy, see Pierre Verger, *Fluxo e refluxo do tráfico de escravos entre o Golfo do Benin e a Bahia de Todos os Santos* (Salvador: Corrupio, 1987), 279–287 and Silvia Hunold Lara, *Fragmentos Setecentistas: Escravidão, cultura e poder na América portuguesa* (São Paulo: Companhia das Letras, 2007), 194.

35 Tegbesu, whose original name was Avissou, was the youngest son of King Agaja, who reigned in Dahomey from 1716 to 1740. Tegbesu ruled Dahomey from 1740 to 1774. See Edna G. Bay, *Wives of the Leopard: Gender, Politics, and Culture in the Kingdom of Dahomey* (Charlottesville: University of Virginia Press, 1998), 82.

36 The description of the Dahomean embassy is based on José Freire de Montarroyos Mascarenhas, *Relaçam da Embayxada, que o poderoso Rey de Angome Kiayy Chiri Broncom, Senhor dos dilatadissimos Sertões de Guiné mandou ao Illustrissimo e Excellentissimo Senhor D. Luiz Peregrino de Ataide, Conde de Atouguia, Senhor das Villas de Atouguia, Peniche, Cernache, Monforte, Vilhaens, Lomba, e Paço da Ilha Dezerta, Cõmendador das Cõmendas de Santa Maria de Adaufe, e Villa velha de Rodam, na Ordem de Christo, do Conselho de Sua Magestade, Governador, e Capitão General, que foy do Reyno de Algarve & actualmente Vice-Rey do Estado do Brasil: pedindo a amizade, e aliança do muito alto; e poderoso Senhor Rey de Portugal Nosso Senhor/escrita por J. F. M. M. Lisboa: Na Officina de Francisco da Silva, anno de 1751.*

37 Mascarenhas, *Relaçam da Embayxada*, 7.

38 Mascarenhas, *Relaçam da Embayxada*, 11.

39 Verger, *Fluxo e refluxo*, 285.

40 Verger, *Fluxo e refluxo*, 308, n13. This voyage, this vessel and this captain are absent from *The Trans-Atlantic Slave Trade Database*.

41 As the dates of birth of Dahomean kings are not precisely known, I preferred here to use the period of their reigns.

42 Law, *Ouidah*, 156.

43 BNRJ, "Ofício do Rei de Dahomey a D. Fernando José de Portugal enviando um branco chamado Luís Caetano e dois embaixadores para serem enviados a El-Rei e falando sobre a ida de navios a seu prêto. Abome, 20 de março de 1795," II–34, 2, 10, Document (Doc.) 551, folio (fl.) 1, March 20, 1795.

44 BNRJ, Ofício do Rei de Dahomey, II–34, 2, 10, Doc. 551, fl. 1, March 20, 1795.

45 Verger, *Fluxo e refluxo*, 287.

46 See Robin Law, *The Slave Coast of West Africa, 1550–1750: The Impact of the Atlantic Slave Trade on an African Society* (Oxford: Clarendon Press, 1991), 202–204, and David Northrup, *Africa's Discovery of Europe, 1450–1850* (New York: Oxford University Press, 2002), 81.

47 Robert Norris, "A Journey to the Court of Bossa Ahadee, King of Dahomey, in the Year of 1772," in Archibald Dalzel, *The History of Dahomy: An Inland Kingdom of Africa* (London: Elibron Classics, 2005 [1793]), 119.

48 Dalzel, *The History of Dahomy*, 31; Norris, "A Journey to the Court of Bossa Ahadee," 112.

49 Norris, "A Journey to the Court of Bossa Ahadee," 107, 132.

50 Norris, "A Journey to the Court of Bossa Ahadee," 138.

51 Norris, "A Journey to the Court of Bossa Ahadee," 119; Northrup, *Africa's Discovery of Europe*, 87.

52 Pires published an account of the years spent in Dahomey. See Vicente Ferreira Pires, *Viagem de África em o Reino de Dahomé escrita pelo Padre Vicente Ferreira Pires no ano de 1800 e até o presente inédita* (São Paulo: Companhia Editora Nacional, 1957), 7. On the mission see Júnia Ferreira Furtado, "The Eighteenth-Century Luso-Brazilian Journey to Dahomey: West Africa Through a Scientific Lens," *Atlantic Studies: Global Currents* 11, no. 2 (2014): 256–276.

53 I. A. Akinjogbin, *Dahomey and Its Neighbours* (Cambridge: Cambridge University Press, 1967), 185.

54 Akinjogbin, *Dahomey and Its Neighbours*, 186; Bay, *Wives of the Leopard*, 155; Verger, *Fluxo et refluxo*, 276, 72.

55 See Robin Law, "The Politics of Commercial Transition: Factional Conflict in Dahomey in the Context of the Ending of the Atlantic Slave Trade," *Journal of African History* 38 (1997): 213–233.

56 Akinjogbin, *Dahomey and Its Neighbours*, 186; Bay, *Wives of the Leopard*, 162. Na Agontimé, one of the several wives of King Agonglo and putative mother of Prince Gakpe, who would later become King Gezo (r. 1818–1858), was probably among these opponents and became the most well-known victim of Adandozan. See Ana Lucia Araujo, "History, Memory and Imagination: Na Agontimé, a Dahomean Queen in Brazil," in *Beyond Tradition: African Women and Cultural Spaces*, ed. Toyin Falola and Sati U. Fwatshak (Trenton, NJ: Africa World Press, 2011), 45–68.

57 Olaudah Equiano and Vincent Carretta, *The Interesting Narrative and Other Writings* (New York: Penguin, 2003), 46–47.

58 Quobna Ottobah Cugoano and Vincent Carretta, *Thoughts and Sentiments on the Evil of Slavery* (New York: Penguin, 1999), 13.

59 See Philip D. Curtin, *Africa Remembered: Narratives by West Africans From the Era of the Slave Trade* (Prospect Heights, IL: Waveland Press, 1997). On the narratives of enslavement, see Ana Lucia Araujo, *Shadows of the Slave Past: Memory, Heritage, and Slavery* (New York: Routledge, 2014), Chapter 1.

60 James H. Sweet, *Domingos Álvares, African Healing, and the Intellectual History of the Atlantic World* (Chapel Hill: University of North Carolina Press, 2013), 26–27.

61 Venture Smith, *A Narrative of the Life and Adventures of Venture Smith, A Native of Africa: but Resident about Sixty Years in the United States of America. Related by Himself* (New London, CT: Holt, 1798), 6.

62 In 1821, the Brazilian captaincies were transformed into provinces.

63 Paul E. Lovejoy and Robin Law, *The Biography of Mahommah Gardo Baquaqua: His Passage from Slavery to Freedom in African and America* (Princeton: Markus Wiener Publishers, 2003), 121.

64 Ana Lucia Araujo, "Images, Artefacts and Myths: Reconstructing the Connections Between Brazil and the Kingdom of Dahomey," in *Living History: Encountering the Memory of the Heirs of Slavery*, ed. Ana Lucia Araujo (Newcastle upon Tyne: Cambridge Scholars Publishing, 2009), 180–202.

65 Akinjogbin, *Dahomey and Its Neighbours*, 187–188; Ana Lucia Araujo, "Dahomey, Portugal, and Bahia: King Adandozan and the Atlantic Slave Trade," *Slavery & Abolition* 3, no. 1 (2012): 1–19.

66 IHGB, Lata 137, Pasta 62, Doc. 1, fl. 3, 3v, n.d. This letter is not dated, but was probably written in 1804 and sent with the embassy of 1805.

67 IHGB, Lata 137, Pasta 62, Doc. 1, fl. 6, n.d.

68 IHGB, Lata 137, Pasta 62, Doc. 1, fl. 6v, 7, n.d.

69 BNRJ, II-24, 5, 4, Doc. 124, fl. 3, November 20, 1804.

70 Among these travelogues, see Dalzel, *The History of Dahomy*, and Frederick E. Forbes, *Dahomey and the Dahomans: Being the Journals of Two Missions to the King of Dahomey, and Residence at His Capital* (London: Longman, Brown, Green, and Longmans, 1851).

71 IHGB, Lata 137, Pasta 62, Doc. 2, fl. 1, October 9, 1810.

72 IHGB, Lata 137, Pasta 62, Doc. 2, fl. 3, October 9, 1810.

73 IHGB, Lata 137, Pasta 62, Doc. 2, fl. 4, October 9, 1810.

74 IHGB, Lata 137, Pasta 62, Doc. 2, fl. 5, October 9, 1810.

75 Klein and Vinson, *African Slavery,* 54.

76 Thomas C. Holt, *The Problem of Freedom: Race, Labor, and Politics in Jamaica and Britain, 1832–1938* (Baltimore: Johns Hopkins University Press, 1992), 87.

77 Vincent Brown, *The Reaper's Garden: Death and Power in the World of Atlantic Slavery* (Cambridge, MA: Harvard University Press, 2008), 15.

78 Klein and Vinson, *African Slavery,* 55.

79 Laurent Dubois, *Avengers of the New World: The Story of the Haitian Revolution* (Cambridge, MA: Belknap Press of Harvard University Press, 2004), 19.

80 Carolyn E. Fick, *The Making of Haiti: The Saint Domingue Revolution From Below* (Knoxville: University of Tennessee Press, 1990), 278 n14. Dubois, *Avengers of the New World,* 30.

81 Dubois, *Avengers of the New World,* 21.

82 Berlin, *Many Thousands Gone,* 7–8.

83 On this transformation see Allan Kulikoff, *Tobacco and Slaves: The Development of Southern Cultures in the Chesapeake, 1680–1800* (Chapel Hill: University of North Carolina Press, 1986).

84 See Peter H. Wood, *Black Majority: Negroes in Colonial South Carolina from 1670 Through the Stono Rebellion* (New York: Knopf, 1974).

85 Leslie A. Schwalm, *A Hard Fight for We: Women's Transition From Slavery to Freedom in South Carolina* (Urbana: University of Illinois Press, 1997), 19.

86 Sven Beckert, *Empire of Cotton: A Global History* (New York: Alfred A. Knopf, 2014), 103.

87 Edward E. Baptist, *The Half Has Never Been Told: Slavery and the Making of American Capitalism* (New York: Basic Books, 2014), 153.

88 Bergad, *The Comparative Histories of Slavery,* 7.

89 On the impacts of the Saint-Domingue Revolution in Brazil, see João José Reis and Flávio dos Santos Gomes, "Repercussions of the Haitian Revolution in Brazil, 1791–1850," in *The World of the Haitian Revolution,* ed. David Patrick Geggus and Norman Fiering (Bloomington: Indiana University Press, 2009), 284–313. On Cuba, see Ada Ferrer, *Freedom's Mirror: Cuba and Haiti in the Age of Revolution* (New York: Cambridge University Press, 2014).

90 Ferrer, *Freedom's Mirror,* 12–13.

91 On British Caribbean absentee slave owners, see Nicholas Draper, *The Price of Emancipation: Slave-Ownership, Compensation and British Society at the End of Slavery* (Cambridge: Cambridge University Press, 2010), 17–74. See also Holt, *The Problem of Freedom,* 89, and Brown, *The Reaper's Garden,* 21–22. On slave owners' absenteeism in the French Caribbean, see Antoine Gisler, *L'esclavage aux Antilles françaises (XIIe–XIXe siècle)* (Paris: Karthala, 1981), 87–88.

92 See Maria Helena Machado, *O plano e o pânico: os movimentos sociais na década da abolição* (São Paulo: Editora da Universidade de São Paulo, 1994),

21. See also Rafael de Bivar Marquese, *Administração e escravidão: idéias sobre a gestão da agricultura escravista brasileira* (São Paulo: Editora Hucitec, 1999), 73.

93 On Jamaica, see Stanley L. Engerman and B; W. Higman, "The Demographic Structure of the Caribbean Slave Societies in the Eighteenth and Nineteenth Centuries," in *General History of the Caribbean. vol. 3: The Slave Societies of the Caribbean*, ed. Franklin Knight (London: UNESCO Publications, Macmillan Education, 1997), 74. On Brazil, see Schwartz, *Sugar Plantations*, 94; 149.

94 "Return of the Whole Number of Persons within Several Districts of the United States, According to 'An Act Providing for the Enumeration of the Inhabitants of the United States,' Passed March the First, One Thousand Seven Hundred and Ninety-One" (Philadelphia: Childs And Swaine, 1793), 4.

95 See George Reid Andrews, *Afro-Latin America, 1800–2000* (New York: Oxford University Press, 2004), 41; Christopher Schmidt-Nowara, *Slavery, Freedom, and Abolition in Latin America and the Atlantic World* (Albuquerque: University of New Mexico Press, 2011), 4.

96 Davis, *Inhuman Bondage*, 125.

97 Herbert S. Klein and Francisco Vida Luna, *Slavery in Brazil* (New York: Cambridge University Press, 2010), 45.

98 See Eduardo França Paiva, *Escravidão e universo cultural na colônia: Minas Gerais, 1716–1789* (Belo Horizonte: Editora da Universidade de Minas Gerais, 2006).

99 See Mieko Nishida, *Slavery and Identity: Ethnicity, Gender, and Race in Salvador, Brazil, 1808–1888* (Bloomington: Indiana University Press, 2003), 20.

100 On New York, see Graham Russell Hodges, *Root and Branch: African Americans in New York and East Jersey, 1613–1863* (Chapel Hill: University of North Carolina Press, 1999), and Leslie Harris, *In the Shadow of Slavery: African Americans in New York City, 1626–1863* (Chicago: University of Chicago Press, 2003). On Baltimore, see T. Stephen Whitman, *The Price of Freedom: Slavery and Manumission in Baltimore and Early National Maryland* (Lexington: University Press of Kentucky, 1997), Mariana L. R. Dantas, *Black Townsmen: Urban Slavery and Freedom in the Eighteenth-Century Americas* (New York: Palgrave Macmillan, 2008), and Seth Rockman, *Scraping by: Wage Labor, Slavery, and Survival in Early Baltimore* (Baltimore: Johns Hopkins University Press, 2009). On Charleston, see Cynthia M. Kennedy, *Braided Relations, Entwined Lives: The Women of Charleston's Urban Slave Society* (Bloomington, IN: Indiana University Press, 2005), and Amrita Chakrabarti Myers, *Forging Freedom: Black Women and the Pursuit of Liberty in Antebellum Charleston* (Chapel Hill: University of North Carolina Press, 2011). On Richmond, see Midori Takagi, *Rearing Wolves to Our Own Destruction: Slavery in Richmond, Virginia, 1782–1865* (Charlottesville: University Press of Virginia, 1999), and James M. Campbell, *Slavery on Trial: Race, Class, and Criminal Justice in Antebellum Richmond, Virginia* (Gainesville: University Press of Florida, 2007). On New Orleans see Walter Johnson, *Soul by Soul: Life Inside the Antebellum Slave Market*

(Cambridge, MA: Harvard University Press, 1999), and Judith Kelleher Schafer, *Becoming Free, Remaining Free: Manumission and Enslavement in New Orleans, 1846–1862* (Baton Rouge: Louisiana State University, 2003).

101 Davis, *Inhuman Bondage*, 125.

102 Klein and Vinson, *African Slavery*, 41.

103 Ann Twinam, *Purchasing Whiteness: Pardos, Mulattos, and the Quest for Social Mobility in the Spanish Indies* (Stanford: Stanford University Press, 2015), 208.

104 Russell Lohse, *Africans Into Creoles: Slavery, Ethnicity, and Identity in Colonial Costa Rica* (Albuquerque: University of New Mexico Press, 2014), 119.

105 On slaves' dressing in Lima, Peru, see Tamara J. Walker, "'He Outfitted His Family in Notable Decency': Slavery, Honour and Dress in Eighteenth-Century Lima, Peru," *Slavery & Abolition* 30, no. 3 (2009): 383–402; on Chile and Mexico City, see Rebecca Earle, "'Two Pairs of Pink Satin Shoes!!': Clothing, Race and Identity in the Americas, 17th–19th Centuries," *History Workshop Journal* 52 (2001): 175–195; on Salvador and Rio de Janeiro, see Sylvia Hunold Lara, "The Signs of Color: Women's Dress and Racial Relations in Salvador and Rio de Janeiro, ca. 1750–1815," *Colonial Latin American Review* 6, no. 2 (1997): 205–224.

106 See Ana Lucia Araujo, *Brazil Through French Eyes: A Nineteenth-Century Artist in the Tropics* (Albuquerque: University of New Mexico Press), Chapter 3.

107 See Frank Tannenbaum, *Slave and Citizen, The Negro in the Americas* (New York: A. A. Knopf, 1946), 53.

108 Keila Grinberg, "Freedom Suits and Civil Law in Brazil and the United States," *Slavery & Abolition* 22, no. 3 (2001): 66–82.

109 Alejandro de la Fuente and Ariela Gross, "Comparative Studies of Law, Slavery, and Race in the Americas," *Annual Review of Law and Social Science* 6 (2010): 469–485.

110 See Silvia Hunold Lara, ed. *Ordenações filipinas, Livro V* (São Paulo: Companhia das Letras, 1999). The *Ordenações filipinas* replaced the *Ordenações manoelinas*. After 1603, the code was complemented by uncodified laws (*leis extravagantes*).

111 Lara, *Ordenações Filipinas*, 158.

112 See Timothy Joel Coates, "Exiles and Orphans: Forced and State-Sponsored Colonizers in the Portuguese Empire, 1550–1720" (Ph.D. diss. University of Minnesota, 1993), 36–37. See also Timothy Joel Coates, *Convicts and Orphans: Forced and State-Sponsored Colonizers in the Portuguese Empire, 1550–1755* (Stanford: Stanford University Press, 2001), 224–225.

113 See Robert I. Burns and Samuel Parsons Scott, *Las Siete Partidas*, vol. 4 (Philadelphia: University of Pittsburg Press, 2000), Title XXI, LAW II, 977.

114 Burns and Scott, *Las Siete Partidas*, vol. 4, Title V, LAW III, 902. See also Andrews, *Afro-Latin America*, 31.

115 Andrews, *Afro-Latin America*, 42.

116 On self-purchase, see Berlin, *Many Thousands Gone*, 36–38. See William Waller Hening, ed. *The Statutes at Large Being a Collection of All the Laws of Virginia from the First Session of the Legislature in the Year 1619* (New York: R. & W. & G. Bartow, 1823), vol. 3, 86. On Virginia, see also Berlin, *Many Thousands Gone*, 124; and Anthony S. Parent, *Foul Means: The Formation of a Slave Society in Virginia, 1660–1740* (Chapel Hill: University of North Carolina Press, 2003), 120.

117 See David J. McCord, ed. *The Statutes at Large of South Carolina, containing the acts relating to Charleston, Courts, Slaves, and Rivers*, vol. 7, "Acts relating to Slaves," 1735 (Columbia, SC: A. S. Johnson, 1840), 396.

118 "An Act to Authorize the Manumission of Slaves," May 1782 of Commonwealth, in William Waller Hening, ed. *The Statutes at Large; Being a Collection of All the Laws of Virginia from the First Session of the Legislature, in the Year 1619* (Richmond: J. & G. Cochran, 1821), vol. 11, 39.

119 Bergad, *The Comparative Histories of Slavery*, 196–197.

120 James H. Sweet, "Manumission in Rio de Janeiro, 1749–54: An African Perspective," *Slavery & Abolition* 24, no. 1 (2003): 63.

121 See the case of Maria in Ana Lucia Araujo, "Black Purgatory: Enslaved Women's Resistance in Nineteenth-Century Rio Grande do Sul, Brazil," *Slavery & Abolition* 36, no. 4 (2015): 568–585; and the famous case of Margaret Garner in Nikki M. Taylor, *Driven Towards Madness: The Fugitive Slave Margaret Garner and Tragedy on the Ohio* (Athens: Ohio University Press, 2016).

122 Several monographs explore cases of former slaves who became slave owners in Brazil. In Bahia, see João José Reis, *Slave Rebellion in Brazil: The Muslim Uprising of 1835 in Bahia* (Baltimore: Johns Hopkins University Press, 1993); João José Reis, *Domingos Sodré: Um sacerdote africano. Escravidão, liberdade e candomblé na Bahia do século XIX* (São Paulo: Companhia das Letras, 2008); and João José Reis, Flávio dos Santos Gomes, and Marcus J. M. de Carvalho, *O alufá Rufino: tráfico, escravidão e liberdade no Atlântico negro (c. 1822–c. 1853)* (São Paulo: Companhia das Letras, 2010). On former slaves who owned slaves in Minas Gerais, see Kathleen J. Higgins, *Licentious Liberty in a Brazilian Gold-Mining Region: Slavery, Gender and Social Control in Eighteenth-Century Sabará, Minas Gerais* (University Park, PA: Penn State University Press, 1999); in Rio de Janeiro, see Mary C. Karasch, *Slave Life in Rio de Janeiro, 1808–1850* (Princeton: Princeton University Press, 1987); and Luiz Carlos Soares, *O "povo de Cam" na capital do Brasil: A escravidão urbana no Rio de Janeiro do século XIX* (Rio de Janeiro: 7Letras, 2007).

123 On slaves who owned slaves, see Kátia de Queirós Mattoso, *Être Esclave au Brésil, XVIe–XIXe siècles* (Paris: Hachette, 1979), 150–151; and João José Reis, "De escravo a rico liberto: A trajetória do africano Manoel Joaquim Ricardo na Bahia oitocentista," *Revista de História*, no. 174 (2016): 15–68.

124 Nishida, *Slavery and Identity*, 19.

125 Klein and Luna, *Slavery in Brazil*, 143.

126 Brown, *The Reaper's Garden*, 56.

127 See Testimony of Dr. Harrison, February 12, 1791 cited in Brown, *The Reaper's Garden*, 188. See also Bergad, *The Comparative Histories of Slavery*, 102. For a comparison of mortality rates in Bahia and Jamaica plantations see Schwartz, *Sugar Plantations*, 373.

128 See Dubois, *Avengers of the New World*, 40.

129 Brown, *The Reaper's Garden*, 256.

130 Bernard Moitt, *Women and Slavery in the French Antilles, 1635–1848* (Bloomington: Indiana University Press, 2001), 52. See also Dubois, *Avengers of the New World*, 45.

131 Schwartz, *Sugar Plantations*, 143.

132 Richard S. Dunn, *A Tale of Two Plantations: Slave Life and Labor in Jamaica and Virginia* (Cambridge, MA: Harvard University Press, 2014), 165.

133 Mary Prince, *The History of Mary Prince* (New York: Penguin, 2000), 14.

134 Sojourner Truth, *Narrative of Sojourner Truth* (New York: Barnes and Noble Classics, 2005), 31–32.

135 Harriet Jacobs, *Incidents in the Life of a Slave Girl* (New York: Barnes and Noble Classics, 2005), 34.

136 Jacobs, *Incidents in the Life of a Slave Girl*, 47–48.

137 Araujo, "Black Purgatory," 579.

138 On Celia see Annette Gordon-Reed, "Celia's Case (1857)" in *Race on Trial: Law and Justice in American History*, ed. Annette Gordon-Reed (New York: Oxford University Press, 2002), 48–60.

139 This case was extensively explored by historian Keila Grinberg. See Keila Grinberg, *Liberata: a lei da ambiguidade. As ações de liberdade da Corte de Apelação do Rio de Janeiro no século XIX* (Rio de Janeiro: Relume Dumará, 1994). A summary of the case in English is available in Sue Peabody and Keila Grinberg, *Slavery, Freedom, and the Law in the Atlantic World: A Brief History with Documents* (Boston, MA: Bedford/St. Martins, 2007), 141–144.

140 On the need of taking the lived experiences of enslaved Africans into account, see Barbara Solow, "The Transatlantic Slave Trade: A New Census," *William and Mary Quarterly, New Perspectives on the Transatlantic Slave Trade* 58, no. 1 (2001): 11.

141 See Walter Rodney, "Slavery and Other Forms of Social Possession on the Upper Guinea Coast in the Context of the Atlantic Slave Trade," *Journal of African History* 7, no. 4 (1966): 431–443; and Walter Rodney, *How Europe Underdeveloped Africa* (Washington, DC: Howard University Press, 1982).

142 Works minimizing the impact of the Atlantic slave trade in depopulating the African continent include John Donnelly Fage, "Slavery and the Slave Trade in the Context of West African History," *Journal of African History* 10, no. 3 (1969): 393–404; John Donnelly Fage, "The Effect of the Export Slave Trade on African Populations," in *The Population Factor in African Studies*, ed. Richard Rathbone and Rowland Percy Moss (London: University of London Press, 1975), 15–23; John K. Thornton, "The Slave Trade in Eighteenth Century

Angola: Effects on Demographic Structures," *Revue canadienne des études africaines/Canadian Journal of African Studies* 14, no. 3 (1981): 417–427; David Eltis, *Economic Growth and the Ending of the Transatlantic Slave Trade* (New York: Oxford University Press, 1987); and David Eltis and Lawrence C. Jennings, "Trade Between Western Africa and the Atlantic World in the Pre-Colonial Era," *American Historical Review* 43, no. 4 (1988): 936–959.

143 See C. C. Wrigley, "Historicism in Africa: Slavery and State Formation," *African Affairs* 70, no. 279 (1971): 115; Joseph E. Inikori, "The Slave Trade and the Atlantic Economies, 1451–1870," in *The African Slave Trade from the Fifteenth to the Nineteenth Century: Reports and Papers of the Meeting of Experts Organized by UNESCO at Port-au-Prince Haiti, 31 January to 4 February 1978,* UNESCO (Paris: UNESCO, 1979), 56–87; Joseph E. Inikori, "Under-Population in Nineteenth-Century West Africa: The Role of the Export Slave Trade," *African Historical Demography* 11 (1981): 283–313; Patrick Manning, "The Enslavement of Africans: A Demographic Model," *Revue canadienne des études africaines/Canadian Journal of African Studies* 15, no. 3 (1981): 499–526. See also Patrick Manning and William S. Griffiths, "Divining the Unprovable: Simulating the Demography of African Slavery," *Journal of Interdisciplinary History* 19, no. 2 (1988): 177–201; Paul E. Lovejoy, "The Impact of the Atlantic Slave Trade on Africa: A Review of the Literature," *The Journal of African History* 30, no. 3 (1989): 365–394; and Patrick Manning, "The Slave Trade: The Formal Demography of a Global System," *Social Science History* 14, no. 2 (1990): 255–279. On the debates among these historians, see Ana Lucia Araujo, *Public Memory of Slavery: Victims and Perpetrators in the South Atlantic* (Amherst: Cambria Press, 2010), 19–48, and Candido, *An African Slaving Port,* 143–144.

144 Araujo, *Public Memory of Slavery,* 30.

145 Fage, "Slavery and the Slave Trade in the Context of West African History."

146 The estimates cover the period between 1448 and 1867. This timeframe is justified as in 1448 Portugal and its Atlantic islands imported approximately 1,000 Africans. Also, the last slave ship arrived in Cuba in 1867. See James Walvin, *Atlas of Slavery* (Harlow: Pearson, Longman, 2006), 31.

147 Philip D. Curtin, *The Atlantic Slave Trade: A Census* (Madison: University of Wisconsin Press, 1969), 268.

148 For a discussion on early estimates, see Paul E. Lovejoy, "The Volume of the Atlantic Slave Trade: A Synthesis," *Journal of African History* 23 (1982): 496. On Curtin's criticism see Joseph E. Inikori, "Measuring the Atlantic Slave Trade: An Assessment of Curtin and Anstey," *Journal of African History* 17, no. 2 (1976): 197–223, and Joseph E. Inikori, "The Origin of the Diaspora: The Slave From Africa," *Tarikh* 5, no. 4 (1978): 1–19. For other estimates, see James A. Rawley, *The Transatlantic Slave Trade: A History* (New York: W. W. Norton & Co., 1981), 428, Jean Mettas, *Répertoire des expéditions négrières françaises au XVIIIe siècle,* ed. Serge Daget and Michèle Daget, 2 vols. (Paris, Société Française d'Outre-Mer, 1978), Charles Becker, "Note sur les chiffres de la traite atlantique française au XVIIIe siècle," *Cahiers d'études africaines* 26,

no. 24 (1986): 633–679, David Richardson, "Slave Exports From West
and West-Central Africa, 1700–1810: New Estimates of Volume and
Distribution," *Journal of African History* 30, no. 1 (1989): 1–22, Eltis,
Economic Growth and the Ending of the Transatlantic Slave Trade, 241–254,
and José C. Curto, "A Quantitative Reassessment of the Legal Portuguese
Slave Trade From Luanda, Angola, 1710–1830," *African Economic History*
20 (1992): 16–25.

149 Here I refer to the conference *Transatlantic Slaving and the African Diaspora:
     Using the W. E. B Du Bois Institute Dataset of Slaving Voyages*, Williamsburg,
     Virginia, September 11–13, 1998.

150 The W. E. B. database was an initiative led by David Eltis and Barbara Solow,
     in collaboration with Stephen D. Behrendt and David Richardson. Later it
     was made available on a CD-ROM, see David Eltis, Stephen D. Behrendt,
     David Richardson, and Herbert S. Klein, eds., *The Trans-Atlantic Slave Trade
     Database on CD-ROM* (Cambridge: Cambridge University Press, 1999). *The
     Trans-Atlantic Slave Trade Database: Voyages* was made available online in
     2007.

151 Attempts to include the voices of enslaved Africans in the historiography of
     slavery are rather recent. See Anne C. Bailey, *African Voices of the Atlantic
     Slave Trade, Beyond the Silence and the Shame* (Boston: MA, Beacon Press,
     2005), Stephanie E. Smallwood, *Saltwater Slavery, A Middle Passage from
     Africa to American Diaspora* (Cambridge, MA, Harvard University Press,
     2007), Marcus Rediker, *The Slave Ship, A Human History* (New York: Viking,
     2007), and Alice Bellagamba, Sandra E. Greene, and Martin A. Klein, eds.,
     African Voices on Slavery and the Slave Trade (New York: Cambridge
     University Press, 2013). See also the digital project African Origins, http://
     www.african-origins.org/.

152 See the two reviews of Smallwood, *Saltwater Slavery*: Stephen D. Behrendt,
     Review of *Saltwater Slavery: A Middle Passage from Africa to American
     Diaspora* by Stephanie E. Smallwood (Cambridge, MA: Harvard University
     Press, 2007), *New West Indian Guide/Nieuwe West-Indische Gids* 83, no. 3/4
     (2009): 300–302, and Paul E. Lovejoy, Review of *Saltwater Slavery: A Middle
     Passage from Africa to American Diaspora* by Stephanie E. Smallwood
     (Cambridge, MA: Harvard University Press, 2007), *Labor* 6, no. 4 (2008):
     138–140.

153 See Curtin, *The Atlantic Slave Trade*, xvii.

154 Joseph C. Miller, "A Marginal Institution on the Margin of the Atlantic
     System: The Portuguese Southern Atlantic Slave Trade in the Eighteenth
     Century," in *Slavery and the Rise of the Atlantic System*, ed. Barbara L. Solow
     (New York: Cambridge University Press, 1991), 122, 139; Eric Williams,
     Capitalism and Slavery (Chapel Hill: University of North Carolina Press,
     1941), 169.

155 David Walker, *Walker's Appeal in Four Articles Together With a Preamble to
     the Colored Citizens of the World, but in Particular and Very Expressly to
     Those of the United States of America, Written in Boston, in the State of
     Massachusetts, September 28th, 1820* (Boston, MA: Printed for the Author,
     1829), 64.

Chapter 2: "And What Should We Wait of These Brutish Spirits?"

1   Alain Gilbert, *Black Patriots and Loyalists: Fighting for Emancipation in the War for Independence* (Chicago: University of Chicago Press, 2012), 91.

2   Manisha Sinha, *The Slave's Cause: A History of Abolition* (New Haven: Yale University Press, 2016), 49–52. Sierra Leone officially became a British colony in 1807.

3   Sinha, *The Slave's Cause*, 77.

4   Joanne Pope-Melish, *Disowning Slavery: Gradual Emancipation and "Race" in New England, 1780–1860* (Ithaca: Cornell University Press, 1998), 59. Ira Berlin, *The Long Emancipation: The Demise of Slavery in the United States* (Cambridge, MA: Harvard University Press, 2015), 63. Christopher Leslie Brown, *Moral Capital: Foundations of British Abolitionism* (Chapel Hill: University of North Carolina Press, 2006), 105–106.

5   Robin Blackburn, *The American Crucible: Slavery, Emancipation, and Human Rights* (London: Verso, 2011), 166.

6   David Menschel, "Abolition Without Deliverance: The Law of Connecticut Slavery 1784–1848," *Yale Law Journal* 111, no. 1 (2001): 183–222.

7   See Leslie Harris, *In the Shadow of Slavery: African Americans in New York City, 1626–1863* (Chicago: University of Chicago Press, 2003), 56.

8   See Blackburn, *The American Crucible*, 161.

9   See Sinha, *The Slave's Cause*, 76.

10 The Avalon Project: Documents in Law, History, and Diplomacy. Yale Law School, Lillian Goldman Law Library, "Constitution of Vermont, July 8, 1777," http://avalon.law.yale.edu/18th_century/vt01.asp.

11 See Harvey Amani Whitfield, *The Problem of Slavery in Early Vermont, 1777–1810: Essays and Primary Sources* (Barre, VT: Vermont Historical Society, 2014), 16, 19.

12 Vermont State Archives and Records Administration, Middlesex, VT, "An Account of Leonard Spaulding [Commissioner of Sequestration], Regarding Tory Estate of Timothy Lovel and a Bill for Sale for Pomp Brake," 37, 26; Manuscript Vermont State Papers, 1777–1861 (series SE–188). SE1880–0037, as reproduced in Whitfield, *The Problem of Slavery in Early Vermont*, 63.

13 The Avalon Project: Documents in Law, History, and Diplomacy, Yale Law School, Lillian Goldman Law Library, "Pennsylvania: An Act for the Gradual Abolition of Slavery, 1780," http://avalon.law.yale.edu/18th_century/pennst01.asp.

14 In 1788 a new amendment added restrictions regarding the transportation of pregnant enslaved women and separation of families.

15 Sinha, *The Slave's Cause*, 41–44; and Roy E. Finkenbine, "Belinda's Petition: Reparations for Slavery in Revolutionary Massachusetts," *The William and Mary Quarterly* 64, no. 1 (2007): 100.

16 Pope-Melish, *Disowning Slavery*, 56.

17 WLHCL, "Petition of Belinda an African, to the Honourable Senate and House of Representatives in General Court Assembled, February 14, 1783," Digital Archive of Massachusetts Anti-Slavery and Anti-Segregation Petitions, Massachusetts Archives, Boston, MA, v. 239–Revolution Resolves, 1783, SCI/ series 45X, 239, fl. 12.

18 The Royall House & Slave Quarters, located in Medford, MA, is a National Historic Landmark and its open to public visitation, http://www.royallhouse. org/.

19 *Vital Records of Medford, Massachusetts, to the Year 1850* (Boston, MA: New England Historic Genealogical Society, 1907), 173.

20 HUA, "Will of Isaac Royall, Jr., May 26, 1778," Harvard University Corporation, Records of gifts and donations, 1643–1955, UAI 15.400, Box 4, vol. 1, HOLLIS 1708738. See *Royall House & Slave Quarters*, "Belinda Sutton and her Petitions." http://www.royallhouse.org/slavery/belinda-sutton- and-her-petitions/.

21 For the section of the will bequeathing land to Harvard University, see Charles Warren, *History of the Harvard Law School and of Early Legal Conditions in America* (New York, Lewis Publishing Company, 1908), vol. 1, 281–282.

22 WLHCL, "Petition of Belinda an African, to the Honourable Senate and House of Representatives in General Court Assembled, February 14, 1783," Digital Archive of Massachusetts Anti-Slavery and Anti-Segregation Petitions, Massachusetts Archives, Boston, MA, v. 239–Revolution Resolves, 1783, SCI/ series 45X, 239, ff. 2–13.

23 WLHCL, "Petition of Belinda an African, to the Honourable Senate and House of Representatives in General Court Assembled, February 19, 1783," Digital Archive of Massachusetts Anti-Slavery and Anti-Segregation Petitions, Massachusetts Archives, Boston, MA, v. 239–Revolution Resolves, 1783, SCI/ series 45X, 239, fl. 14v. See also Finkenbine, "Belinda's Petition," 102.

24 Finkenbine, "Belinda's Petition," 95.

25 Finkenbine, "Belinda's Petition," 102–103.

26 Sinha, *The Slave's Cause*, 66.

27 WLHCL, "Belinda Royall," Digital Archive of Massachusetts Anti-Slavery and Anti-Segregation Petitions, Massachusetts Archives, Boston, MA, House Unpassed Legislation 1785, Docket 1707, SC1/series 230.

28 WLHCL, "Resolve in the Memorial of Belinda an African, granted, November 23, 1787," Digital Archive of Massachusetts Anti-Slavery and Anti-Segregation Petitions, Massachusetts Archives, Boston, MA, Passed Resolves, Resolves 1787, c. 142, SCI/series 228, petition 1.

29 WLHCL, "Petition of Belinda Sutton," Digital Archive of Massachusetts Anti-Slavery and Anti-Segregation Petitions, Massachusetts Archives, Boston, MA, Council; Council Files March 13, 1788, GC3/series 378.

30 WLHCL, "Petition of Belinda Royall for a continuation of the bounty of I. Royall," Digital Archive of Massachusetts Anti-Slavery and Anti-Segregation Petitions, Massachusetts Archives, Boston, MA, Senate Unpassed Legislation 1795, Docket 2007, SC1/series 231, February 25, 1795, fl. 1.

31 Finkenbine, "Belinda's Petition," 104.

32 Rhode Island, General Assembly, "An Act Authorizing the Manumission of Negroes, Mallattoes, & Others, and for the Gradual Abolition of Slavery," 1784, in Virtual Exhibits, Item #71, http://sos.ri.gov/virtualarchives/items/show/71.

33 Title CL. Slaves, Chap. I, "An Act Concerning Indian, Mulatto, and Negro Servants and Slaves," *Acts and Laws Passed by the General Assembly of the State of Connecticut, The Public Laws of the State of Connecticut* (Hartford, CT: Hudson and Goodwin, 1808), Book 1, 625. See also, Menschel, "Abolition Without Deliverance," 187–188.

34 NYSA, Department of State, Bureau of Miscellaneous Records, Enrolled Acts of the State Legislature, 1788–2005, Series 130367-8, Laws of 1799, Chapter 62, "An Act for the Gradual Abolition of Slavery," March 29, 1799, 1–2. See also Ira Berlin, *Many Thousands Gone: The First Two Centuries of Slavery in North America* (Cambridge, MA: Belknap Press of Harvard University Press, 1998), 234; Daniel Nathaniel Gellman, *Emancipating New York: The Politics of Slavery and Freedom, 1777–1827* (Baton Rouge: Louisiana State University Press, 2008), 153; Harris, *In the Shadow of Slavery*, 11.

35 Maurice Jackson, *Let This Voice Be Heard: Anthony Benezet, Father of Atlantic Abolitionism* (Philadelphia: University of Pennsylvania Press, 2009), 211–213.

36 CHS, Miscellaneous Manuscripts, Levi Hart, "Thoughts on the Subject of Freeing the Negro Slaves in the Colony of Connecticut, humbly offered to the Consideration of all friends to liberty and justice," c. 1775 (typescript by Doris E. Cook, manuscript cataloguer), 1–9. Joanne Pope-Melish examined it in detail in *Disowning Slavery*, 57–64. Quakers from New Jersey also agreed with the principle of compensating the masters, see James J. Gigantino II, *The Ragged Road to Abolition: Slavery and Freedom in New Jersey, 1775–1865* (Philadelphia: University of Pennsylvania Press, 2015), 23. On the contrary, in the 1820s and 1830s, black abolitionists rejected payment to slaveholders. See Eric Foner, *The Fiery Trial: Abraham Lincoln and American Slavery* (New York: W. W. Norton, 2011), 19. In Brazil, the gradualist view is visible in the abolitionist newspapers, see "Questões sociais modernas: Abolicionismo e esclavagismo," *O Abolicionista* (April 1, 1881), 4.

37 Sinha, *The Slave's Cause*, 67.

38 Foner, *The Fiery Trial*, 15; Menschel, "Abolition Without Deliverance," 183–184.

39 Sinha, *The Slave's Cause*, 574–575.

40 Martin R. Delany, William Webb, Augustus R. Green, Edward Butler, H. S. Douglass, A. Dudley, Conaway Barbour, W. M. J. Fuller, W. M. Lambert, J. Theodore Holly, T. A. White, and John Warren, "Political Destiny of the Colored Race on the American Continent: To the Colored Inhabitants of the United States," *Proceedings of the National Emigration Convention of Colored People Held at Cleveland, Ohio, on Thursday, Friday, and Saturday, the 24th, 25th, and 26th August 1954* (Pittsburgh: A. A. Anderson, 1854), 68.

41 See the case *Negro Peter v. Steel* in Alfred L. Brophy, *Reparations Pro & Con* (New York: Oxford University Press, 2006), 20.

42 Calvin Schermerhorn, *The Business of Slavery and the Rise of American Capitalism, 1815–1860* (New Haven: Yale University Press, 2015), 170.

43 See Solomon Northup, *Twelve Years a Slave: Narrative of Solomon Northup, A Citizen of New-York, Kidnapped in Washington City in 1841, and Rescued in 1853, From a Cotton Plantation Near the Red River, in Louisiana* (Auburn, NY: Derby and Miller, 1854), and Steve McQueen, dir., *12 Years a Slave*, 2013.

44 See *Frederick Douglass' Paper*, March 17, 1854 and April 28, 1854. On the movement provide reparations to Northup, see Roy Finkenbine, "'Who Will Pay for Their Sufferings?': New York Abolitionists and the Campaign to Compensate Solomon Northup," *New York History* 95, no. 4 (2014): 640.

45 NARA, Records of the House of Representatives (RG 233), Committee of the Judiciary, N.A 44 for LC Box 152, "New York: A Petition of the Citizens of Niagara County, State of New York in relation to Solomon Northup," February 20, 1854, 2.

46 NARA, Records of the House of Representatives (RG 233), Committee of the Judiciary, N.A 44 for LC Box 152, "New York: Petition of the Citizens of Pekin, Niagara County, State of New York in relation to Solomon Northup," June 10, 1854, 2.

47 Henry C. Wright, "Solomon Northup," *The Liberator*, March 23 (1855), 47.

48 Finkenbine, "'Who Will Pay for Their Sufferings?'," 645.

49 According to other sources consulted by Gerald Horne, Lytle was born in Charleston, South Carolina and sold into slavery when he was still a child. See Gerald Horne, *Race to Revolution: The US and Cuba During Slavery and Jim Crow* (New York: Monthly Review Press, 2014), 277n4.

50 Dale T. Graden, *Disease, Resistance, and Lies: The Demise of the Transatlantic Slave Trade to Brazil, and Cuba* (Baton Rouge: Louisiana University Press, 2014), 174–176.

51 Laurent Dubois, *Avengers of the New World: The Story of the Haitian Revolution* (Cambridge, MA: Belknap Press of Harvard University Press, 2004), 68.

52 Dubois, *Avengers of the New World*, 72.

53 Carolyn E. Fick, *The Making of Haiti: The Saint Domingue Revolution From Below* (Knoxville: University of Tennessee Press, 1990), 25.

54 Dubois, *Avengers of the New World*, 77.

55 C. L. R. James, *The Black Jacobins: Toussaint L'Ouverture and the San Domingo Revolution* (New York: Vintage Books, 1963), 89.

56 Dubois, *Avengers of the New World*, 126.

57 Dubois, *Avengers of the New World*, 216.

58 TNA, "Haitian Declaration of Independence," January 1, 1804, fl. 7v.

59 David Walker, *Walker's Appeal in Four Articles Together With a Preamble to the Colored Citizens of the World, but in Particular and Very Expressly to Those of the United States of America, Written in Boston, in the State of*

Massachusetts, September 28th, 1820 (Boston, MA: Printed for the Author, 1829), 21.

60 Itazienne Eugène, "La normalisation des relations franco-haïtiennes (1825–1838)," *Outre-mers* 90, no. 340–341 (2003): 141.

61 See Gigantino, *The Ragged Road to Abolition*, 67–69.

62 Gigantino, *The Ragged Road to Abolition*, 117.

63 "An Act for the Gradual Abolition of Slavery," February 15, 1804, Acts 28th, General Assembly, 2n sitting, ch. CIII, 251–254.

64 Christopher Schmidt-Nowara, *Slavery, Freedom, and Abolition in Latin America and the Atlantic World* (Albuquerque: University of New Mexico Press, 2011), 90–91.

65 Sidney Chalhoub, *A força da escravidão: Ilegalidade e costume no Brasil oitocentista* (São Paulo: Companhia das Letras, 2012), 36. Ana Lucia Araujo, *Brazil Through French Eyes: A Nineteenth-Century Artist in the Tropics* (Albuquerque: University of New Mexico Press), 38–39.

66 Seymour Drescher, *Abolition: A History of Slavery and Antislavery* (New York: Cambridge University Press, 2009), 212.

67 Drescher, *Abolition*, 268.

68 Nicholas Draper, *The Price of Emancipation: Slave-Ownership, Compensation and British Society at the End of Slavery* (Cambridge: Cambridge University Press, 2010), 37.

69 Augustus Hardin Beaumont, *Compensation to Slave Owners Fairly Considered in an Appeal to the Common Sense of the People of England* (London: Effingham Wilson, 1826), 23.

70 Draper, *The Price of Emancipation*, 79; 81.

71 Draper, *The Price of Emancipation*, 85.

72 Draper, *The Price of Emancipation*, 93–94.

73 House of Commons, "Mr. Stanley on the resolutions," Tuesday, May 14, 1833, *Debates in Parliament, Session 1833 on the Resolutions and Bill for the Abolition of Slavery in the British Colonies* (London: Printed by Maurice & Co. 1834), 79.

74 On Antigua's exception, see Natasha Lightfoot, *Troubling Freedom: Antigua and the Aftermath of British Emancipation* (Durham, NC: Duke University Press, 2015).

75 Great Britain, *An Act for the Abolition of Slavery Throughout the British Colonies; for Promoting the Industry of the Manumitted Slaves; and for Compensating the Persons Hitherto Entitled to the Services of Such Slaves, 28 August 1833* (Edinburgh: Sir D. Huntler Blair and M. T. Bruce, 1833), 3 and 4 Gulielmi IV, cap. LXXIII.

76 Thomas C. Holt, *The Problem of Freedom: Race, Labor, and Politics in Jamaica and Britain, 1832–1938* (Baltimore: Johns Hopkins University Press, 1992), 57.

77 Draper, *The Price of Emancipation*, 139. See also Nicholas Draper, "Possessing People: Absentee Slave-Owners Within British Society," in Catherine Hall,

Nicholas Draper, Keith McClelland, Katie Donington, and Rachel Lang, *Legacies of British Slave-Ownership: Colonial Slavery and the Formation of Victorian Britain* (Cambridge: Cambridge University Press, 2014), 37. On the project *Legacies of British Slave Ownership*, see https://www.ucl.ac.uk/lbs/.

78 Richard S. Dunn, *A Tale of Two Plantations: Slave Life and Labor in Jamaica and Virginia* (Cambridge, MA: Harvard University Press, 2014), 381–382.

79 Gigantino, *The Ragged Road to Abolition*, 214–215. Consequently, the apprentices only obtained free status, when slavery was eventually abolished in the United States in 1865.

80 Foner, *The Fiery Trial*, 25.

81 Manisha Sinha, *The Counterrevolution of Slavery: Politics and Ideology of Antebellum South Carolina* (Chapel Hill: University of North Carolina Press, 2000), 229.

82 "Declaration of the Immediate Causes which Induce and Justify the Secession of South Carolina from the Federal Union," December 24, 1860, *The Avalon Project: Documents in Law, History, and Diplomacy*, Yale Law School, Lillian Goldman Law Library, http://avalon.law.yale.edu/19th_century/csa_scarsec.asp.

83 "First Inaugural Address of Abraham Lincoln," The Avalon Project: Documents in Law, History, and Diplomacy. Yale Law School, Lillian Goldman Law Library, March 4, 1861, http://avalon.law.yale.edu/19th_century/lincoln1.asp.

84 Foner, *The Fiery Trial*, 242.

85 Foner, *The Fiery Trial*, 168.

86 Foner, *The Fiery Trial*, 206–207.

87 Foner, *The Fiery Trial*, 208. Eric Foner, *Reconstruction: America's Unfinished Revolution, 1863–1877* (New York: Harper Collins, 2014), 3.

88 See Kate Masur, *An Example for All the Land: Emancipation and the Struggle Over Equality in Washington, D.C.* (Chapel Hill: University of North Carolina Press, 2010), 19–22.

89 Masur, *An Example for All the Land*, 23–24.

90 Foner, *The Fiery Trial*, 182.

91 Berlin, *The Long Emancipation*, 15.

92 Foner, *Reconstruction*, 7.

93 Alice L. Baumgartner, "Rethinking Abolition in Mexico," paper presented in the Gilder Lehrman Center International Conference, October 30–31, 2015.

94 There are no clear estimates and historians do not agree on the estimated number of slaves in Mexico in 1810. Jaime Olveda Legaspi, "La abolición de la esclavitud en México, 1810–1917," *Signos Históricos*, no. 29 (2013): 11, estimates 9,000 and 10,000 slaves. According to Herbert S. Klein and Ben Vinson III, *African Slavery in Latin America and the Caribbean* (New York: Oxford University Press, 2007), 31, in the last decade of the eighteenth century, there were approximately 6,000 slaves in Mexico. According to Vincent, there were nearly 15,000 slaves in Mexico in 1810. See Theodore G. Vincent, "The Contributions of Mexico's First Black Indian President, Vicente Guerrero," *The Journal of Negro History* 86, no. 2 (2001), 150.

95 George Reid Andrews, *Afro-Latin America, 1800–2000* (New York: Oxford University Press, 2004), 87.

96 John Tutino, *From Insurrection to Revolution in Mexico: Social Bases of Agrarian Violence, 1750–1940* (Princeton: Princeton University Press, 1986), 134–136.

97 On Hidalgo's possible visions on slavery, see Carlos Herrejón Peredo, "La abolición de la esclavitud en Miguel Hidalgo," *Letras Históricas*, no. 5 (2011–2012): 39–52.

98 Legaspi, "La abolición de la esclavitud en México," 13.

99 AGN, Operaciones de Guerra, "Bando de D. José Maria Ansorena aboliendo la esclavitud, el pago de tributo y otras gabelas," Valladolid, October 18, 1810, vol. 4, exp. 4, fl. 87. The document is transcribed in Juan E. Hernandez y Dávalos, ed. *Colección de documentos para la historia de la guerra de independencia de Mexico de 1808 a 1821* (Mexico: Biblioteca de "El Sistema Postal de la República Mexicana," José María Sandoval, Impresor, 1878), vol. II, 169–170. It is reproduced in María Elisa Velázquez and Gabriela Iturralde Nieto, *Afrodescendientes en México: Una historia de silencio y discriminación* (Mexico: Consejo Nacional para Prevenir la Discriminación and Instituto Nacional de Antropología e Hisoria, 2012), 87. It is also transcribed as "Mundum del bando de Miguel Hidalgo aboliendo la esclavitud, Valladolid, 18 octubre de 1810," *Boletín del Archivo General de la Nación* 6, no. 17 (2007): 143–145.

100 "Bando del Sr. Hidalgo declarando la libertad de los esclavos dentro del término de diez días, abolición del tributo, y otras providencias," Guadalajara, December 6, 1810, document number 152, in Dávalos, *Colección de documentos*, volume II, 256.

101 Legaspi, "La abolición de la esclavitud en México," 15–16.

102 Legaspi, "La abolición de la esclavitud en México," 18–19.

103 An overview of the articles regarding slavery is available on Legaspi, "La abolición de la esclavitud en México," 22–26.

104 Alice Baumgartner extensively discusses how property loss was a great concern among slave owners in Mexico, see Baumgartner, "Rethinking Abolition in Mexico."

105 "Abolición de la esclavitud," September 15, 1829, "Decretos Expedidos por el Gobierno en Virtud de las Facultades Extraordinarias," in *Coleccion de Leyes y Decretos del Congreso General de los Estados-Unidos Mejicanos, en los años de 1829 y 1830* (Mexico: Imprenta de Galvan, 1831), 149–150.

106 Vincent, "The Contributions of Mexico's First Black Indian President," 148. On Guerrero, see also Theodore G. Vincent, *The Legacy of Vicente Guerrero: Mexico's First Black Indian President* (Gainesville: University Press of Florida, 2001).

107 Decretos Expedidos por el Gobierno en Virtud de las Facultades Extraordinarias, "Abolición de la esclavitud," September 15, 1829, 150.

108 Baumgartner, "Rethinking Abolition in Mexico."

109 On Uruguay and Argentina, see Alex Borucki, *From Shipmates to Soldiers: Emerging Black Identities in the Río de La Plata* (Albuquerque: University of New Mexico Press, 2015), 50–51.

110 Andrews, *Afro-Latin America*, 64. George Reid Andrews, *Blackness in the White Nation: A History of Afro-Uruguay* (Chapel Hill: University of North Carolina Press, 2010), 32. See also Borucki, *From Shipmates to Soldiers*, 17.

111 By then, present-day Argentina was part of United Provinces of the Río de La Plata.

112 On Chile, see Guillermo Feliú Cruz, *La abolición de la esclavitud en Chile* (Santiago de Chile: Editorial Universitaria, 1973), 39–40. On Argentina, see George Reid Andrews, *Los afroargentinos de Buenos Aires* (Buenos Aires, Ediciones de la Flor, 1989), 59.

113 Andrews, *Afro-Latin America, 1800–2000*, 64.

114 ANH, Fondo Ministerio del Interior, Decree of July 28, 1823, vol. 32, fl. 268–268v.

115 "Constitución Politica del Estado de Chile, Promulgada en 29 de Diciembre de 1823," (Santiago de Chile, Imprenta Nacional, 1823), Titulo 1, Articulo 8, 6.

116 Borucki, *From Shipmates to Soldiers*, 136.

117 On the French abolition see Lawrence C. Jennings, *French Anti-Slavery: The Movement for the Abolition of Slavery in France, 1802–1848* (Cambridge: Cambridge University Press, 2000). Article 8 of the Law of April 27, 1848, also determined that French citizens living abroad were not allowed to own, purchase, or sell slaves, nor to participate in the slave trade. French citizens who were slave owners abroad were given three years to free their slaves, and failing to follow these determinations would lead to the loss of French citizenship. See Lawrence C. Jennings, "L'abolition de l'esclavage par la IIe République et ses effets en Louisiane (1848–1858)," *Revue française d'histoire d'outre-mer* 56, no. 205 (1969): 377.

118 Jason McGraw, *The Work of Recognition: Caribbean Colombia and the Postemancipation Struggle for Citizenship* (Chapel Hill: University of North Carolina Press, 2014), 282–289. Andrews, *Afro-Latin America, 1800–2000*, 57. Slavery continued to exist in the province of Buenos Aires until 1861. This province was an independent country from the Confederacy of Argentina from 1853 to 1861.

119 José Bonifacio d'Andrada e Silva, "Representação à Assembléia Geral Constituinte e Legislativa do Império do Brasil sobre a escravatura," (Paris: Firmin Didot, 1825), 9.

120 Silva, "Representação à Assembleia Geral Constituinte," 21.

121 "Convenção entre o Senhor D. Pedro I Imperador do Brasil, e Jorge IV Rei da Grã-Bretanha, com o fim de pôr termo ao commercio de escravatura da Costa d'Africa, assignada no Rio de Janeiro em 23 de Novembro de 1826, e ratificada por parte do Brasil no mesmo dia, e anno, e pela da Grã-Bretanha a 28 de Fevereiro de 1827," *Colleção das Leis do Império do Brasil de 1826* (Rio de Janeiro: Typographia Nacional, 1880), 389–393.

122 Emília Viotti da Costa, *A Abolição* (São Paulo: Editora da Universidade Estadual de São Paulo, 2008), 27.

123 "Lei de 7 de Novembro de 1831," *Colleção das Leis do Império do Brazil de 1831* (Rio de Janeiro: Typographia Nacional, 1875), vol. 1, part I, 182. In April 1831, following a political crisis, Dom Pedro I abdicated the Brazilian throne in favor of his son Pedro (1825–1891), and returned to Portugal. As Dom Pedro II was too young to rule the country, a regency was formed to rule the Brazilian empire until the new emperor attained majority age.

124 "Lei de 7 de Novembro de 1831."

125 On Brazil, see Beatriz Gallotti Mamigonian, "To Be a Liberated African in Brazil: Labour and Citizenship in the Nineteenth Century" (Ph.D. dissertation, University of Waterloo, 2002). On liberated Africans in the British Caribbean, see Rosanne Marion Adderley, *New Negroes From Africa: Slave Trade Abolition and Free African Settlement in the Nineteenth-Century Caribbean* (Bloomington: Indiana University Press, 2006).

126 Leslie Bethell, *The Abolition of the Brazilian Slave Trade: Britain, Brazil and the Slave Trade Question: 1807–1869* (New York: Cambridge University Press, 1970), 380. See also Beatriz G. Mamigonian, "A Harsh and Gloomy Fate: Liberated Africans in the Service of the Brazilian State, 1830s–1860s," in *Extending the Diaspora: New Histories of Black People*, ed. Dawne Y. Curry, Eric D. Duke, and Marshanda A. Smith (Urbana: University of Illinois Press, 2009), 24.

127 On these cases see Keila Grinberg, "Slavery, Manumission and the Law in Nineteenth-Century Brazil: Reflections on the Law of 1831 and the 'Principle of Liberty' on the Southern Frontier of the Brazilian Empire," *European Review of History/Revue européenne d'histoire* 16, no. 3 (2009): 401–411, and Karl Monsma and Valéria Dorneles Fernandes, "Fragile Liberty: The Enslavement of Free People in the Borderlands of Brazil and Uruguay, 1846–1866," *Luso-Brazilian Review* 50, no. 1 (2013): 7–25.

128 See Christopher Schmidt-Nowara, *Empire and Antislavery: Spain, Cuba, and Puerto Rico, 1833–1874* (Pittsburgh: Pittsburgh University Press 1999), 27, and Schmidt-Nowara, *Slavery, Freedom, and Abolition*, 135.

129 Laird W. Bergad, Fe Iglesias García, and María del Carmen Barcia, *The Cuban Slave Market, 1790–1880* (New York: Cambridge University Press, 1995), 59.

130 See the *Trans-Atlantic Slave Trade Database*. However, in both cases these numbers exclude the slaves introduced in the two colonies via the inter-Caribbean slave trade. Slave imports from Africa to Puerto Rico had stopped by 1842. On the slave imports to Puerto Rico, see Luis A. Figueroa, *Sugar, Slavery, and Freedom in Nineteenth-Century Puerto Rico* (Chapel Hill: University of North Carolina Press, 2005), 72.

131 After the final prohibition in 1850, until 1866, approximately 7,318 enslaved Africans were introduced in Brazil. See the *Trans-Atlantic Slave Trade Database*.

132 See Ana Lucia Araujo, "Transnational Memory of Slave Merchants: Making the Perpetrators Visible in the Public Space," in *Politics of Memory: Making Slavery Visible in the Public Space*, ed. Ana Lucia Araujo (New York: Routledge, 2012), 15–34; and Graden, *Disease, Resistance, and Lies*, 38.

133 Bethell, *The Abolition of the Brazilian Slave Trade*, 69, 340.

134 See "Escândalos," *Radical Paulistano*, September 30, 1869, 2. Although Luiz
     Gama authored another article in the same page, the article cited is not signed
     by him. Yet, according to Ligia Fonseca Ferreira, *Com a palavra, Luiz Gama:
     poemas, artigos, cartas máximas* (São Paulo: Imprensa Oficial, 2011), 117, it
     is very possible that this article as well as all other articles on slavery
     published in this newspaper were authored by Gama.

135 Elciene Azevedo, *Orfeu de carapinha: a trajetória de Luiz Gama na imperial
     cidade de São Paulo* (Campinas: Editora da Universidade de Campinas, 1999),
     35–38; Ferreira, *Com a palavra, Luiz Gama*, 200.

136 *Relatório do Ministério da Justiça (1868) apresentado à Assembléia Geral
     Legislativa pelo Ministro e Secretário de Estado José Martiniano de Alencar*
     (Rio de Janeiro: Typographia Progresso, 1869), 134–135, quoted by Beatriz
     Gallotti Mamigonian, "Conflicts Over the Meanings of Freedom: The
     Liberated Africans' Struggle for Final Emancipation in Brazil, 1840s–1860s,"
     in *Paths to Freedom: Manumission in the Atlantic World*, ed. Rosemary
     Brana-Shute and Randy J. Sparks (Columbia, SC: University of South
     Carolina Press, 2009), 257n3. See also Beatriz Gallotti Mamigonian, "O
     direito de ser africano livre: Os escravos e as interpretações da lei de 1831," in
     Direitos e justiças no Brasil, ed. Silvia Hunold Lara and Joseli Maria Nunes
     Mendonça (Campinas: Editora da Universidade Estadual de Campinas, 2007),
     131.

137 Ulrike Schmieder, "Martinique and Cuba Grande: Commonalities and
     Differences During the Periods of Slavery, Abolition, and Post-Emancipation,"
     Review (Fernand Braudel Center) XXXVI, no. 1 (2013): 92–93.

138 Schmidt-Nowara, *Empire and Antislavery*, 102.

139 Rebecca J. Scott, *Slave Emancipation in Cuba: The Transition to Free Labor,
     1860–1899* (Pittsburgh: University of Pittsburgh Press, 2000), 39.

140 Camillia Cowling, *Conceiving Freedom: Women of Color, Gender, and the
     Abolition of Slavery in Havana and Rio de Janeiro* (Chapel Hill: University of
     North Carolina Press, 2013), 39.

141 Ada Ferrer, *Insurgent Cuba: Race, Nation, and Revolution, 1868–1898*
     (Chapel Hill: University of North Carolina Press, 1999), 27.

142 Schmidt-Nowara, *Empire and Antislavery*, 127.

143 Scott, *Slave Emancipation in Cuba*, 53–55.

144 Scott, *Slave Emancipation in Cuba*, 23.

145 Ley de Cuatro de Julio de 1870 Sobre Abolición de la Esclavitud y
     Reglamento para su ejecución en las islas de Cuba y Puerto Rico (Habana:
     Imprenta del Gobierno y Capitania general por S. M, 1872), 3.

146 Ley de Cuatro de Julio de 1870, 3–4.

147 Scott, *Slave Emancipation in Cuba*, 73.

148 Hendrik Kraay, "Arming Slaves in Brazil from the Seventeenth Century to the
     Nineteenth Century," in *Arming Slaves: From Classical Times to the Modern
     Age*, ed. Christopher Leslie Brown and Philip D. Morgan (New Haven: Yale
     University Press, 2006), 168.

149 For example, in 1777, during the American Revolutionary War, a bill permitted slave owners to free healthy slaves and allowed them to obtain a financial compensation. See Pope-Melish, *Disowning Slavery*, 67. Kraay, "Arming Slaves in Brazil from the Seventeenth Century to the Nineteenth Century," 168.

150 Angela Alonso, *Flores, votos e balas: o movimento abolicionista brasileiro (1868–1888)* (São Paulo: Companhia das Letras, 2015), 109.

151 On the public debates see Beatriz Gallotti Mamigonian, "O Estado nacional e a instabilidade da propriedade escrava: a Lei de 1831 e a matrícula dos escravos de 1872," *Almanack*, no. 2 (2011): 28–29.

152 "Illegitimidade da propriedade constituida sobre o escravo. Natureza da mesma. Abolição da escravidão; em que termos," Discurso pronunciado na sessão magna do Instituto dos Advogados Brasileiros em 7 de Setembro de 1863 pelo seu president Dr. A. M. Perdigão Malheiro (Rio de Janeiro: Typographia de Quirino e Irmão, 1863).

153 Agostinho Marques Perdigão Malheiro, *Escravidão no Brasil: Ensaio Histórico-Jurídico-Social* (Rio de Janeiro: Typographia Nacional, 1866), vol. 1, 179–180.

154 Malheiro, *Escravidão no Brasil*, vol. 3, 144–146.

155 Agostinho Marques Perdigão Malheiro, *Discurso proferido na sessão da câmara temporária de 12 de julho de 1871 sobre a proposta do governo para reforma do estado servil* (Rio de Janeiro: Typ. Imp. E Const. de J. Villeneuve & C., 1871), 40.

156 Luis Alvares dos Santos, *A emancipação: Ligeiras e decisivas considerações sobre o total acabamento da escravidão sem o menor prejuízo dos proprietários* (Bahia: Typographia do Correio da Bahia, 1871), 7.

157 See *Elemento servil Parecer e projecto de lei apresentado á Camara dos srs. deputados na sessão de 16 de agosto de 1870 pela Commissão especial nomeada pela mesma Camara em 24 de maio de 1870* (Rio de Janeiro: Typographia nacional, 1870).

158 These estimates are based on the Census of 1872, which established the Brazilian population at 9,930.478. See *Recenseamento do Brazil em 1872* (Rio de Janeiro: Typ. G. Leuzinger, 1874), vol. 1, 7.

159 Christiane Laidler, "A Lei do Ventre Livre: Interesses e disputas em torno do projeto de abolição gradual," *Escritos* 5, no. 5 (2011): 173.

160 Biblioteca Digital do Senado Federal, Lei no. 2040 de 28 de setembro de 1871 [Lei do Ventre Livre], manuscript document.

161 Robert Conrad, *Abolitionism: The Brazilian Antislavery Struggle* (Urbana: University of Illinois Press, 1977), 55.

162 Alonso, *Flores, votos e balas*, 78, 80. During this period, Brazilian currency was the *mil-réis* (1$000), and a *conto* was the equivalent of 1,000 *mil-réis*.

163 See Kim D. Butler, *Freedoms Given, Freedoms Won: Afro-Brazilians in Post-Abolition São Paulo and Salvador* (New Brunswick: Rutgers University Press, 2000), 28.

164 Lei no. 2040 de 28 de setembro de 1871, fl. 7.

165 Mamigonian, "O Estado nacional," 33–34, 37.

166 On the demonstrations see Schmidt-Nowara, *Empire and Antislavery*, 151.

167 Schmidt-Nowara, *Empire and Antislavery*, 153; Luis A. Figueroa, *Sugar, Slavery, and Freedom in Nineteenth-Century Puerto Rico* (Chapel Hill: University of North Carolina Press, 2005), 126.

168 Scott, *Slave Emancipation in Cuba*, 128.

169 Cowling, *Conceiving Freedom*, 58.

170 On the limitations of the *patronato* system for *patrocinados* and *patronos* see Scott, *Slave Emancipation in Cuba*, 141–171, 172–197.

171 Scott, *Slave Emancipation in Cuba*, 137.

172 Scott, *Slave Emancipation in Cuba*, 140.

173 Robert Conrad, *The Destruction of Brazilian Slavery, 1850–1888* (Los Angeles: University of California Press, 1972), 157.

174 André Rebouças, *Á Democracia Rural Brazileira* (Rio de Janeiro, 1875).

175 See Maria Helena Machado, *O plano e o pânico: os movimentos sociais na década da abolição* (São Paulo: Editora da Universidade de São Paulo, 1994), 52.

176 Henrique Pedro Carlos de Beaurepaire-Rohan, *O futuro da grande lavoura e da grande propriedade do Brazil* (Rio de Janeiro: Nacional, 1878), 10–16, cited in Celia Maria Marinho de Azevedo, *Onda negra, medo branco: o negro no imaginário das elites, século XIX* (São Paulo: Annablume, 2004), 43–44.

177 "Manifesto da Sociedade Brasileira Contra a Escravidão" (Rio de Janeiro, Typographia de G. Leuzinger & Filhos, 1880), 16. The manifesto has no author, but according to André Rebouças's journal it was authored by Joaquim Nabuco, see André Rebouças, Ignacio José Verissimo, and Anna Flora Verissimo, *Diário e notas autobiográficas* (Rio de Janeiro: José Olympio, 1938), 291.

178 On November 20, 1880, the Sociedade Brasileira Contra a Escravidão offered a banquet "to honor the minister of the United States, Mr. Henry W. Hilliard as a way to thank him for a letter of support in which he discusses the abolition of slavery in the United States." *O Abolicionista: Orgão da Sociedade Brasileira Contra a Escravidão*, November 1, 1880, 6; "Avisos," *Jornal do Commercio*, November 20, 1880, 2. Hilliard's departure from Brazil was decried by the black abolitionist Luiz Gama, who did not seem to be bothered by the fact that Hilliard was a former Confederate. On Hilliard in Brazil, see Conrad, *The Destruction of Brazilian Slavery*, 142; Celia Maria Marinho de Azevedo, *Abolicionismo: Estados Unidos e Brasil, uma história comparada, século XIX* (São Paulo: Annablume, 2003), 196–198; Alonso, *Flores, votos e balas*, 164–166.

179 On the relations between Nabuco and the British abolitionists, see Leslie Bethell and José Murilo de Carvalho, eds. *Joaquim Nabuco, British Abolitionists and the End of Slavery in Brazil: Correspondence 1880–1905* (London: Institute for the Study of the Americas, University of London, School of Advanced Study, 2009).

180 "A Nossa Missão," *O Abolicionista*, November 1, 1880, 1.

181 "Sociedade Brasileira Contra a Escravidão," *O Abolicionista: Orgão da Sociedade Brasileira Contra a Escravidão*, November 1, 1880, 2. The Treaty of Ghent of 1814 stated that the slave trade violated the principles of humanity and justice. Also, the Final Act of the Congress of Vienna of 1815 stated the end of the slave trade by declaring that it violated the principles of humanity and justice. See Francisco Forrest Martin, *The Constitution as Treaty: The International Legal Constructionist Approach to the US Constitution* (New York: Cambridge University Press, 2007), 101 and "Act, No. XV, Declaration of the Powers on the Abolition of the Slave Trade, of the 8th February 1815," in *The Parliamentary Debates from the Year 1803 to the Present Time* (London: T. C. Hansard, 1816), vol. XXXII, 200.

182 Luiz Gama, "Arrematação de escravos," *O Abolicionista: Orgão da Sociedade Brasileira Contra a Escravidão*, December 1, 1880, 6. In 1881, other notices denounced the continuity of these public auctions, see "Praça de Africanos," *O Abolicionista,* June 1, 1881, 8; "Ainda o leilão de escravos," *O Abolicionista,* December 1, 1881, 7; "Africanos que são homens livres," *O Abolicionista*, September 28, 1881, 8. On the public auctions of Africans who arrived after 1831 and were kept enslaved see Chalhoub, *A força da escravidão*, 201.

183 See Grinberg, "Slavery, Manumission and the Law in Nineteenth-Century Brazil," and Monsma and Fernandes, "Fragile Liberty."

184 Luiz Gama, "Questão Jurídica," *O Abolicionista*, April 1, 1881, 5–8; May 1, 1881, 12; July 1, 1881, 5–6.

185 Chalhoub, *A força da escravidão*.

186 Confederação Abolicionista, "Abolição immediata e sem indemnisação," Pamphleto no. 1 (Rio de Janeiro: Typ. Central, de Evaristo R. da Costa, 1883), 4. On the emancipation funds and the abolitionist movement, see Celso Castilho and Camillia Cowling, "Funding Freedom, Popularizing Politics: Abolitionism and Local Emancipation Funds in 1880s Brazil," *Luso-Brazilian Review* 47, no. 1 (2010), 91–92.

187 Confederação Abolicionista, "Abolição immediata e sem indemnisação," 5.

188 Confederação Abolicionista, "Abolição immediata e sem indemnisação," 10.

189 Confederação Abolicionista, "Abolição immediata e sem indemnisação," 14.

190 See Rebouças, *Á Democracia Rural Brazileira*, and Alonso, *Flores, votos e balas*, 244.

191 Miguel Lemos, *O Pozitivismo e a Escravidão Moderna Trechos extrahidos das obras de Augusto Comte, seguidos de documentos positiviztas relativos a questão da escravatura no Brasil e precedidos de uma introdução por Miguel Lemos Presidente Perpetuo da Sociedade Pozitivista do Rio de Janeiro* (Rio de Janeiro: Sede da Sociedade Pozitivista, 1884), cover page.

192 Lemos, *O Pozitivismo*, 36.

193 Regarding the issue of land, the manifesto states: "Adstrição ao solo do ex-trabalhador escravo, sob a direção dos seus respectivos chefes actuaes." Lemos, *O Pozitivismo*, 37.

194 Alonso, *Flores, votos e balas*, 251; 253.

195   Wlamyra Albuquerque, *O jogo da dissimulação: Abolição e cidadania negra no Brasil* (São Paulo: Companhia das Letras, 2009), 112.

196   Alonso, *Flores, votos e balas*, 258–259; 262. Yet it was a conditional dissolution, because the Chamber of Deputies still had to vote on the budget. Consequently, despite being dissolved the Chamber of Deputies continued working.

197   Alonso, *Flores, votos e balas*, 270.

198   Alonso, Flores, votos e balas, 282.

199   Luiz Carlos Soares, *O "povo de Cam" na capital do Brasil: A escravidão urbana no Rio de Janeiro do século XIX* (Rio de Janeiro: 7Letras, 2007), 299. Cowling, *Conceiving Freedom*, 42.

200   Joseli Maria Nunes Mendonça, *Entre a mão e os anéis: a lei dos sexagenários e os caminhos da abolição no Brasil* (Campinas: Editora da Universidade Estadual de Campinas, 1999), 221.

201   Flávio dos Santos Gomes, "Slavery, Black Peasants and Post-Emancipation Society in Brazil (Nineteenth-Century Rio de Janeiro)," *Social Identities* 10, no. 6 (2004): 742.

202   Machado, *O plano e o pânico*, 76, 82.

203   Celso T. Castilho, *Slave Emancipation and Transformations in Brazilian Political Citizenship* (Pittsburgh: University of Pittsburgh Press, 2016), 88.

204   See Albuquerque, *O jogo da dissimulação*, 105.

205   Costa, *A Abolição*, 10. According to the census of 1890, Brazil had a population of about 14,333,915 individuals. See Directoria Geral de Estatística, *Synopse do recenseamento de 31 de dezembro de 1890* (Rio de Janeiro: Officina da estatística, Imprimerie du Bureau de Statistique, 1898), 5.

206   See Albuquerque, *O jogo da dissimulação*, 96.

Chapter 3: "We Helped to Pay This Cost"

1   Julia Gaffield, *Haitian Connections: Recognition After the Revolution in the Atlantic World* (Chapel Hill: University of North Carolina Press, 2015), 49.

2   C. K. Webster, *The Congress of Vienna, 1814–1815* (London: Oxford University Press, 1918), 42; François Blancpain, "Note sur les 'dettes' de l'esclavage: le cas de l'indemnité payée par Haïti (1825–1883)," *Outre-mers* 90, no. 340–341 (2003): 243.

3   Julia Gaffield explains that despite the lack of official recognition, Britain and other European nations as well as the United States and several colonies in the Caribbean kept close commercial and political relations with Haiti. See Gaffield, *Haitian Connections*.

4   Laurent Dubois, *Haiti: The Aftershocks of History* (New York: Metropolitan Books, 2012), 71.

5   See the letter "Thomas Clarkson to King Henry, September 7, 1819," in *Henry Christophe and Thomas Clarkson: A Correspondence*, ed. Leslie Griggs, and Clifford H. Prator (New York: Greenwood Press, 1968), 71–72.

6 Constitution of Hayti (1805), English translation, *New York Evening Post*, July 15, 1805, 2.

7 Letter "The Duke of Limonade to Thomas Clarkson, November 20, 1819" in *Henry Christophe and Thomas Clarkson*, 176. I was not able to find the dates of birth and death of the Duke of Limonade.

8 Blancpain, "Note sur les 'dettes' de l'esclavage," 243.

9 Itazienne Eugène, "La normalisation des relations franco-haïtiennes (1825–1838)." *Outre-mers* 90, no. 340–341 (2003): 140; Dubois, *Haiti: The Aftershocks of History*, 98.

10 J. B. Duvergier, *Collection complète des lois, décrets, ordonnances, réglements et avis du Conseil d'État (de 1788 à 1824 inclusivement, par ordre chronologique)* (Paris: Directeur de l'Administration, 1840), vol. 4, 67.

11 "L'ordonnance de Charles X du 17 avril 1825," *Outre-mers* 90, nos. 340–341 (2003): 249.

12 See Frédérique Beauvois, "Monnayer l'incalculable? L'indemnité de Saint-Domingue, entre approximations et bricolage," *Revue historique*, no. 655 (2010): 613–614; Anne Ulentin, "Garantir leur avenir: Les gens de couleur libres de Saint-Domingue et l'indemnité de l'indépendance de 1825," *Bulletin de la Société d'Histoire de la Guadeloupe*, no. 173 (2016): 70.

13 "Proclamation du président Boyer acceptant l'ordonnance française," in Thomas Madiou, *Histoire d'Haïti*, vol. 6 (Port-au-Prince, Haiti: Éditions Henri Deschamps, 1988), 468–469.

14 Beauvois, "Monnayer l'incalculable?," 616.

15 Ulentin, "Garantir leur avenir," 70.

16 Beauvois, "Monnayer l'incalculable?," 616.

17 The names of 7,900 planters and 1,500 owners of other properties are listed in the six volumes of *État détaillé des liquidations opérées par la Commission chargée de répartir l'indemnité attribuée aux anciens colons de Saint-Domingue, en exécution de la loi du 30 avril 1826* (Paris, 1828–1834). Regarding the requests for indemnities, a volume containing information about the second session of the commission is available in the Archives nationales d'outre-mer in Aix-en-Provence, see Beauvois, "Monnayer l'incalculable?" 612.

18 Beauvois, "Monnayer l'incalculable?" 613.

19 Beauvois, "Monnayer l'incalculable?" 633; Ulentin, "Garantir leur avenir," 77–78.

20 Alex Dupuy, *Haiti in the World Economy: Class, Race, and Underdevelopment Since 1700* (Boulder, CO: Westview Press, 1989), 126.

21 The two treaties are reproduced in Thomas Madiou, *Histoire d'Haïti*, vol. 7 (Port-au-Prince, Haiti: Éditions Henri Deschamps, 1988), 215.

22 Robert J. Reinstein, "Is the President's Recognition Power Exclusive?" *Temple Law Review* 86, no. 1 (2013): 32.

23 Blancpain, "Note sur les 'dettes' de l'esclavage": 244.

24 Charles Forsdick, "Haiti and France: Settling the Debts of the Past," in *Politics and Power in Haiti*, ed. Kate Quinn and Paul Sutton (New York: Palgrave Macmillan 2013), 147–148.

25 Dupuy, *Haiti in the World Economy*, 52.

26 Natasha Lightfoot, *Troubling Freedom: Antigua and the Aftermath of British Emancipation* (Durham, NC: Duke University Press, 2015), 84–85.

27 Diana Paton, *No Bound but the Law: Punishment, Race, and Gender in Jamaican State* (Durham, NC: Duke University Press, 2004), 146.

28 On indentured workers in the British Caribbean after 1834, see Monica Schuler, *Alas, Alas, Kongo: A Social History of Indentured African Immigration into Jamaica, 1841–1865* (Baltimore: Johns Hopkins University Press, 1980); Walton Look Lai, *Indentured Labor, Caribbean Sugar: Chinese and Indian Migrants to the British West Indies, 1838–1918* (Baltimore: Johns Hopkins University Press, 1993); Madhavi Kale, *Fragments of Empire: Capital, Slavery, and Indian Indentured Labor in the British Caribbean* (Philadelphia: University of Pennsylvania Press, 1998); and Rosanne Marion Adderley, *New Negroes From Africa: Slave Trade Abolition and Free African Settlement in the Nineteenth-Century Caribbean* (Bloomington: Indiana University Press, 2006).

29 Thomas C. Holt, *The Problem of Freedom: Race, Labor, and Politics in Jamaica and Britain, 1832–1938* (Baltimore: Johns Hopkins University Press, 1992), 127, 134–136; Colin A. Palmer, *Freedom's Children: The 1938 Labor Rebellion and the Birth of Modern Jamaica* (Chapel Hill: University of North Carolina Press, 2014), 87–88.

30 Holt, *The Problem of Freedom*, 215–216.

31 Holt, *The Problem of Freedom*, 299–300.

32 Holt, *The Problem of Freedom*, 338, 350.

33 Holt, *The Problem of Freedom*, 144–146; Palmer, *Freedom's Children*, 93.

34 "Décret relatif à l'abolition de l'esclavage dans les colonies et possessions françaises du 27 avril 1848," *Bulletin des Lois de la République Française, Xe Série, Premier Semestre de 1848 (2e partie), contenant les lois, décrets et arrêtes d'intérêt public et général publiés depuis le 24 février jusqu'au 30 juin* (Paris: Imprimerie Nationale, 1848), tome premier, 321. See also Christine Chivallon, *L'esclavage, du souvenir à la mémoire: Contribution à une anthropologie de la Caraïbe* (Paris: Karthala, 2012), 65.

35 Masters were also indemnified in other French colonies. In 1848, Reunion Island had 60,651 slaves and masters obtained 33.88 francs per slave. In Sénégal, there 9,800 slaves and masters were paid 10.75 francs per slave. Finally, Nossi-Bé and Sainte-Marie had 3,300 slaves and masters were awarded 3.3 francs per slave. See Laurent Sermet, *Une anthropologie juridique des droits de l'homme* (Paris: Éditions des archives contemporaines, 2009), 142.

36 Total amounts per slave were: Martinique, 405 francs; Guadeloupe, 447 francs; French Guiana, 594.8 francs; Senegal, 215.2 francs; and Nossi-Bé and Saint-Marie, 66.6 francs. See Sermet, *Une anthropologie*, 142.

37 Ulrike Schmieder, "Martinique and Cuba Grande: Commonalities and Differences During the Periods of Slavery, Abolition, and Post-Emancipation." *Review* XXXVI, no. 1 (2013): 95.

38 See Chivallon, *L'esclavage, du souvenir à la mémoire*, 205–206; 211. Schmieder, "Martinique and Cuba Grande," 97.

39 See Céline Flory, *De l'esclavage à la liberté forcée: histoire des travailleurs africains engagés dans la Caraïbe française au XIXe siècle* (Paris: Karthala, 2015), 19, and Céline Flory, "New Africans in the Post-Slavery French West Indies and Guiana: Close Encounters? (1857–1889)," in *Paths of the Atlantic Slave Trade: Interactions, Identities, and Images*, ed. Ana Lucia Araujo (Amherst: Cambria Press, 2011), 109–130.

40 Flory, *De l'esclavage*, 21.

41 Leslie Schwalm, *A Hard Fight for We: Women's Transition From Slavery to Freedom in South Carolina* (Urbana: University of Illinois Press, 1997), 167–168.

42 The amendment was ratified by the states on December 6, 1865.

43 "Letter from a Freedman to his Old Master," *New-York Daily Tribune*, August 22, 1865, 7. On the letter see Leon F. Litwack, *Been in the Storm So Long: The Aftermath of Slavery* (New York: Knopf, 1979), 333–334; and Alfred L. Brophy, *Reparations: Pro & Con* (New York: Oxford University Press, 2006), 21–22.

44 Mary Frances Berry, *My Face Is Black Is True: Callie House and the Struggle for Ex-Slave Reparations* (New York: Alfred A. Knopf, 2005), 24.

45 Cornell University Law School, Legal Information Institute, U.S. Constitution, 15th Amendment, Section 1, https://www.law.cornell.edu/constitution/amendmentxv.

46 Wendell Philips, for example, defended the idea that the federal government should lend money to former slaves in order to allow them to purchase land. See Roy E. Finkenbine, "Wendell Philipps and the 'The Negro's Claim': A Neglected Reparations Document," *Massachusetts Historical Review* 7 (2005): 114.

47 Jeffrey R. Kerr-Ritchie, "Forty Acres, or An Act of Bad Faith," in *Redress for Historical Injustices in the United States: On Reparations for Slavery, Jim Crow, and Their Legacies*, edited by Michael T. Martin and Marilyn Yaquinto (Durham, NC: Duke University Press, 2007), 225–226.

48 United States, *Statutes at Large, Treaties, and Proclamations of the United States of America, from December 1863 to December 1865*, vol. 13 (Boston, MA: Little, Brown, and Company, 1866), 508.

49 See Rebecca J. Scott, *Degrees of Freedom: Louisiana and Cuba After Slavery* (Cambridge, MA: Belknap Press of Harvard University Press, 2005), 38, and Brophy, *Reparations Pro & Con*, 26–27.

50 Eric Foner, *Reconstruction: America's Unfinished Revolution, 1863–1877* (New York: Harper Collins, 2014), 246; Scott, *Degrees of Freedom*, 38.

51 Scott, *Degrees of Freedom*, 39.

52 Sojourner Truth, *Narrative of Sojourner Truth* (New York: Barnes and Noble Classics, 2005), 143–144.

53 Truth, *Narrative of Sojourner Truth*, 145. See also, Carol Faulkner, *Women's Radical Reconstruction* (Philadelphia: University of Pennsylvania Press, 2004), 112–113.

54 Berry, *My Face Is Black Is True*, 31.

55 Nell Irvin Painter, *Exodusters: Black Migration to Kansas After Reconstruction* (New York: Knopf, 1976), 126–127.

56 Martha Biondi, "The Rise of the Reparations Movement," in *Redress for Historical Injustices in the United States: On Reparations for Slavery, Jim Crow, and Their Legacies*, ed. Michael T. Martin and Marilyn Yaquinto (Durham, NC: Duke University Press, 2007), 257.

57 Bishop Henry McNeal Turner, "Justice or Emigration Should Be Our Watchword," in *Integration vs. Separatism: The Colonial Period to 1945*, ed. Marcus D. Pohlmann, African American Political Thought, Volume 5 (New York: Routledge, 2003), 92–93.

58 Turner, "Justice or Emigration Should Be Our Watchword," 99.

59 Focusing on Callie House, a leader of the National Ex-Slave Mutual Relief, Bounty and Pension Association, historian Mary Frances Berry was the first to write a book-length study on the movement, see Berry, *My Face Is Black Is True*. Previous works include Walter L. Fleming, *Ex-Slaves Pension Frauds* (Baton Rouge: Ortlier's Printing House, 1910) who clearly portrayed the early requests for reparations by African American organizations as fraudulent. More recent works include Mary Frances Berry, "Reparations for Freedmen, 1890–1916: Fraudulent Practices or Justice Deferred," *Journal of Negro History* 57, no. 3 (1972): 219–230; Walter Hill, "The Ex-Slave Pension Movement: Some Historical and Genealogical Notes," *Negro History Bulletin* 59, no. 4 (1996): 7–11; James M. Davidson, "Encountering the Ex-Slave Reparations Movement from the Grave: The National Industrial Council and National Industrial Council and National Liberty Party, 1901–1907," *Journal of African American History* 97, no. 1–2 (2012): 13–38, and Miranda Booker Perry, "The Prospect of Justice: African-American Redress and the Ex-Slave Pension Movement, 1865–1937" (Ph.D. dissertation, Howard University, 2012).

60 "A Bill for an Act to Provide Pensions for Freedmen Released From Involuntary Servitude, and to Afford Aid and Assistance for Certain Persons Released, that They May Be Maintained in Old Age," prepared by W. R. Vaughan of Omaha, and introduced by Hon. W. J. Connell, M.C. from the First Nebraska District, by request, June 24, 1890. Senate Bill 1176, 56th Congress, 1st Session, and House Bill 11404, 57th Congress, 1st Session. The text of the Bill is reproduced in Walter R. Vaughan, *Vaughan's "Freedmen's Pension Bill: Being an Appeal in Behalf of Men Released from Slavery, A Plea for American Freedmen and a Rational Proposition to Grant Pensions to Persons of Color Emancipated From Slavery"* (Chicago, 1891), 39–40.

61 Fleming, *Ex-Slaves Pension Frauds*, 4.

62 Vaughan, *Vaughan's "Freedmen's Pension Bill,"* 32.

63 Vaughan, Vaughan's "Freedmen's Pension Bill," 82. Relations between the US federal government and American Indian nations were ruled by a series of treaties established between 1778 and 1871. Although the US Constitution, in its Article 1, and Section 8, recognized American Indians groups are part of the nation, Native Americans' territorial rights continued to be questioned, which led American Indian groups to fight for land rights in court during the nineteenth century, reason why probably Vaughan refer to Native Americans as rebellious and ungrateful.

64 Vaughan, Vaughan's "Freedmen's Pension Bill," 119.

65 Letter from Benjamin O. Jones to W. J. Connell, June 27, 1890, reproduced in Vaughan, Vaughan's "Freedmen's Pension Bill," 43–44.

66 Letter from S. P. Havis to W. R. Vaughan, Esq., July 12, 1890, reproduced in Vaughan, Vaughan's "Freedmen's Pension Bill," 44–45.

67 Handwritten letter from Frederick Douglass to W. R. Vaughan, July 25, 1891 reproduced in Vaughan, Vaughan's "Freedmen's Pension Bill," 183–184. The full letter is also transcribed in Perry, "The Prospect of Justice," 58.

68 Davidson, "Encountering the Ex-Slave Reparations Movement from the Grave," 17.

69 The image of Vaughan as mentally ill is supported by Fleming, Ex-Slaves Pension Frauds, 8. On Vaughan's intent to use the pensions to develop the economy of the South, see Berry, My Face Is Black Is True, 37. Perry also makes a similar argument, see Perry, "The Prospect of Justice," 65. Yet, both Berry and Perry recognize the strong arguments brought by Vaughan in his defense of pensions for ex-slaves. For Vaughan's own justifications for a law providing pensions to freedpeople see Vaughan, Vaughan's "Freedmen's Pension Bill," 59.

70 Vaughan, Vaughan's "Freedmen's Pension Bill," 126–127.

71 Vaughan, Vaughan's "Freedmen's Pension Bill," 134.

72 Berry, My Face Is Black Is True, 143–144.

73 Vaughan, Vaughan's "Freedmen's Pension Bill," 127.

74 Berry, My Face Is Black Is True, 144.

75 Perry, "The Prospect of Justice," 54.

76 Perry, "The Prospect of Justice," 64.

77 Perry, "The Prospect of Justice," 66.

78 Robin D. G. Kelley, Freedom Dreams: The Black Radical Imagination (Boston, MA: Beacon Press, 2002), 117.

79 Among these organizations were the Ex-Slave Petitioners' Assembly; the Western Division Association; the Great National Ex-Slave Congressional Legislative and Pension Association, National Ex-Slave Union Congressional and Legislative Association of the United States and the Ex-Slave Department Industrial Association of America.

80 NARA, RG 28, Records of the Post Office Department, Entry 50, "Fraud Order Case Files," Box 13, Row 9, Comp 12, Shelf 5, Case file 1321, Ex-Slave Mutual Relief, Bounty and Pension of the United States, "Constitution and By

Laws governing the National, State, and Local Associations of the National Ex-Slave Mutual Relief, Bounty and Pension Association of the United States of America, Senate Bill 1176, introduced December 11, 1899" (Nashville, TN: The National Industrial Advocate, 1900), 5.

81 NARA, RG 28, Entry 50, "Fraud Order Case Files," Box 13, Row 9, Comp 12, Shelf 5, Case file 1321, Ex-Slave Mutual Relief, Bounty and Pension of the United States, "Constitution and By Laws," 2.

82 The estimated number of 600,000 was claimed by the association's president Reverend D. D. McNairy. See NARA, RG 28, Box 13, Row 9, Comp 12, Shelf 5, Case file 1321, "Constitution and By Laws," 22. See also Berry, *My Face Is Black Is True*, 82; 253–254n2.

83 Perry, "The Prospect of Justice," 126.

84 NARA, RG 15, Records of the Department of Veterans Affairs, National Archives Microfilm Publication M2110, single roll, Correspondence and Reports Pertaining to Ex-Slave Pension Movement, 1892–1916, Letter from Anderson Dillon to President William McKinley, November 15, 1899, 309–311.

85 NARA, RG 15, M2110, Letter by L. J. Taylor, Department of the Interior, Bureau of Pensions, Nashville, TN, May 30, 1897, 6.

86 NARA, RG 15, M2110, Letter from Theo Hardwick, Special Examiner, to Commissioner of Pensions, Washington, DC, January 22, 1898, 180.

87 NARA, RG 15, M2110, Letter from J. L. Walton, December 2, 1897, 82.

88 NARA, RG 15, M2110, Letter from Reverend T. Parker, President, and Miss Mary Parker, Secretary to H. Clay Evans, Commissioner of Pensions, August 29, 1899, 288.

89 NARA, RG 28, Entry 50, "Fraud Order Case Files," Box 13, Row 9, Comp 12, Shelf 5, Case file 1321, Letter from Isaiah H. Dickerson to J. Barrett, Assistant Attorney General for the Department of Post Office, September 20, 1899, 2.

90 NARA, RG 28, Entry 50, "Fraud Order Case Files," Box 13, Row 9, Comp 12, Shelf 5, Case file 1321, Letter from Callie House to J. Barrett, Assistant Attorney General for the Department of Post Office, September 29, 1899, 1.

91 NARA, RG 28, Entry 50, "Fraud Order Case Files," Box 13, Row 9, Comp 12, Shelf 5, Case file 1321, Letter from Callie House to J. Barrett, Assistant Attorney General for the Department of Post Office, September 29, 1899, 2–3.

92 See for example Boyrereau Brinch and Benjamin Franklin Prentiss, *The Blind African Slave, or Memoirs of Boyrereau Brinch, Nick-Named Jeffrey Brace: Containing an Account of the Kingdom of Bow-Woo, in the Interior of Africa; with the Climate and Natural Productions, Laws, and Customs Peculiar to That Place* (St. Albans, VT: Harry Whitney 1810), 9. See also Frederick Douglass, *Oration, Delivered in Corinthian Hall, Rochester, by Frederick Douglass, July 5th, 1852* (Rochester, NY: Lee, Mann & Co., 1852).

93 NARA, RG 15, M2110, Letter from Callie House to H. Clay Evans, December 13, 1900, 370.

94 In one letter addressed to the Post Master, Dickerson complained that his personal mail was being retained, including letters from his children. NARA, RG 28, Entry 50, "Fraud Order Case Files," Box 13, Row 9, Comp 12, Shelf 5, Case file 1321, Letter from Isaiah H. Dickerson to Post Master, typed, November 9, 1899, 1.

95 NARA, RG 28, Entry 50, "Fraud Order Case Files," Box 13, Row 9, Comp 12, Shelf 5, Case file 1321, Introductory: The National Ex-Slave Mutual, Relief, Benevolent, and Aid, Association of the U.S.A., typed memo, November 14, 1899. According to a letter by J. E. Purdy, Pastor of Tabernacle Baptist Church in Nashville, he suggested the change in a meeting of the association's board held on November 14, 1899. See NARA, RG 28, Entry 50, "Fraud Order Case Files," Box 13, Row 9, Comp 12, Shelf 5, Case file 1321, Letter from J. E. Purdy to Maj. A. N. Mills P.M., November 14, 1899, 1–2.

96 NARA, RG 28, Entry 50, "Fraud Order Case Files," Box 13, Row 9, Comp 12, Shelf 5, Case file 1321, Letter from Callie House to Harrison J. Barrett, December 18, 1899, 1–2.

97 NARA, RG 28, Entry 50, "Fraud Order Case Files," Box 13, Row 9, Comp 12, Shelf 5, Case file 1321, Letter from Callie House to Harrison J. Barrett, April 5, 1900, 2–3.

98 See Berry, *My Face Is Black Is True*, 176–178, and Perry, "The Prospect of Justice," 151.

99 Berry, *My Face Is Black Is True* 179–180.

100 Berry, *My Face Is Black Is True*, 180.

101 NARA, RG 15, M2110, Letter from Laurense Dudley to Commissioner of Pensions, April 24, 1917, 756.

102 NARA, RG 15, M2110, Letter from Commissioner of Pensions to Laurense Dudley, April 27, 1917, 758.

103 Berry, *My Face Is Black Is True*, 184.

104 Berry, *My Face Is Black Is True*, 190–191.

105 Berry, *My Face Is Black Is True*, 254n2.

106 "Contracts Are Let for Approaches to Lincoln Memorial," *The Washington Times*, September 22, 1916, 5.

107 On the construction of monuments commemorating Lincoln in Washington, DC, see Ana Lucia Araujo, *Shadows of the Slave Past: Memory, Heritage, and Slavery* (New York: Routledge, 2014), 155–160.

108 "Ex-Slaves to Hold Meeting in Capital," *The Washington Times*, September 22, 1916, 5.

109 Drew was the president of the organization, which was incorporated in 1915. See *Thirteenth Annual Report of the State Corporation Commission of Virginia for the Year Ending December 31, 1915, General Report* (Richmond, VA: Davis Bottom, Superintendent Public Printing, 1916), 276.

110 "A Grand Baptist Rally," *The Colored American: A National Negro Newspaper* X, no. 34, March 5, 1904, 1.

111 "Negroes Plan Memorial to Booker Washington," *Richmond Times Dispatch*, November 16, 1915, 3.

112 "Protests 'Birth of Nation'," *The Washington Herald*, April 16, 1916, 4. See D. W. Griffith, *The Birth of a Nation*, United States, 1915.

113 "5,000 Free Dinners for Aged Ex-Slaves," *The Washington Herald*, October 9, 1916, 7.

114 C. Elliott Freeman, Jr., "Dr. Simon Drew Found Guilty of Mail Fraud," *Afro-American*, October 25, 1930, 5; "New York Minister Sentenced in U.S. Mail Fraud," *The New Amsterdam News*, November 19, 1930, 1; "Rev. S. P. W. Drew Dies Suddenly in Washington, DC," *The Pittsburgh Courier*, December 22, 1934, A10.

115 Aline Helg, *Our Rightful Share: The Afro-Cuban Struggle for Equality, 1886–1912* (Chapel Hill: University of North Carolina Press, 1995), 25–27; Alejandro de la Fuente, *A Nation for All: Race, Inequality and Politics in Twentieth Century Cuba* (Chapel Hill: University of North Carolina Press, 2001), 260.

116 Rebecca J. Scott, "Fault Lines, Color Lines, and Party Lines: Race, Labor, and Collective Action in Louisiana and Cuba, 1862–1912," in *Beyond Slavery: Explorations of Race, Labor, and Citizenship in Postemancipation Societies*, Frederick Cooper, Thomas C. Holt, and Rebecca J. Scott (Chapel Hill: University of North Carolina Press, 2000), 87.

117 Rebecca J. Scott, *Slave Emancipation in Cuba: The Transition to Free Labor, 1860–1899* (Pittsburgh: University of Pittsburgh Press, 2000), 228.

118 Scott, *Degrees of Freedom*, 215.

119 Scott, *Degrees of Freedom*, 218. See also Rebecca J. Scott and Michael Zeuske, "Le 'droit d'avoir des droits': Les revendications des ex-esclaves à Cuba (1872–1909)," *Annales: Histoire, Sciences Sociales* 59, no. 3 (2004): 521–545.

120 "Notarial Volumes of Felipa Silva y Gil, May 22, 1906," transcribed and translated by Rebecca Scott and Daniel Nemser in *Slavery, Freedom, and the Law in the Atlantic World: A Brief History with Documents*, ed. Sue Peabody and Keila Grinberg (Boston, MA: Bedford/St. Martin's, 2007), 168–169.

121 "Julián Cabrera y Cao, In the Case of *Andreas Quesada v. Heirs of Manuel Blanco*, Cienfuegos, April 1907," transcribed and translated by Rebecca Scott and Daniel Nemser in *Slavery, Freedom, and the Law*, 169.

122 "Julián Cabrera y Cao, In the Case of *Andreas Quesada v. Heirs of Manuel Blanco*, Cienfuegos, April 1907," 170.

123 Scott, *Degrees of Freedom*, 219.

124 "Notarial Volumes of Felipa Silva y Gil, May 22, 1906," 169, 175.

125 "Emilio Menéndez, In the Case of *Andreas Quesada v. Heirs of Manuel Blanco*, Cienfuegos, April 1907," transcribed and translated by Rebecca Scott and Daniel Nemser in *Slavery, Freedom, and the Law*, 172.

126 "Judge Antonio J. Varona, Ruling, April 12, 1907," transcribed and translated by Rebecca Scott and Daniel Nemser in *Slavery, Freedom, and the Law*, 174–175.

127 After emancipation, former slaves did not have a particular legal status imposed on them. Moreover, legal documents stopped identifying freedpeople by their color, as it was done previously. Yet when the color was indicated it was usually intended to emphasize the legal condition of slave or former slave. On this issue, see Hebe Maria Mattos de Castro, *Das cores do silêncio: os significados da liberdade no sudeste escravista, Brasil século XIX* (Rio de Janeiro: Arquivo Nacional, 1995), 107–109.

128 See Castro, *Das cores do silêncio*, 311, 315, 323.

129 Petrônio Domingues, *A nova abolição* (São Paulo: Selo Negro Edições, 2008), 48–50.

130 Flávio dos Santos Gomes, "Slavery, Black Peasants and Post-Emancipation Society in Brazil (Nineteenth-Century Rio de Janeiro)," *Social Identities* 10, no. 6 (2004): 748.

131 See Castro, *Das cores do silêncio*, 361–362, and Walter Fraga, "Migrações, itinerários e esperança de mobilidade social no Recôncavo baiano após a Abolição," in *Política, instituições e personagens da Bahia (1850–1930)*, ed. Jefferson Bacelar and Cláudio Pereira (Salvador: Editora da Universidade Federal da Bahia, 2013), 53.

132 FCRB, CR 1566/2, "Carta da comissão de libertos de Paty de Alferes a Rui Barbosa," April 19, 1889, ff. 1–2. Wlamyra Albuquerque, *O jogo da dissimulação: Abolição e cidadania negra no Brasil* (São Paulo: Companhia das Letras, 2009), 185–186, and Flávio dos Santos Gomes commented on this letter in a newspaper article: "De ex-libertos a quase cidadãos: Surgimento de periódicos e associações apontam para uma atuação efetiva de movimentos negros na vida política do Brasil desde o fim da escravidão," *Folha de São Paulo*, November 23, 2003, Caderno Mais, 14–15.

133 FCRB, CR 1566/2, "Carta da comissão de libertos de Paty de Alferes a Rui Barbosa," April 19, 1889, fl. 1.

134 FCRB, CR 1566/2, "Carta da comissão de libertos de Paty de Alferes a Rui Barbosa," April 19, 1889, fl. 2.

135 Albuquerque, *O jogo da dissimulação*, 187–188.

136 See Wlamyra Albuquerque, "'A vala comum da "raça emancipada': abolição e racialização no Brasil, breve comentário," *História Social*, no. 19 (2010): 97; 102.

137 Albuquerque, *O jogo da dissimulação*, 121. See also Américo Jacobina Lacombe, Eduardo Barbosa Silva, and Francisco de Assis, *Rui Barbosa e a queima dos arquivos* (Rio de Janeiro: Fundação Casa de Rui Barbosa, 1988), 51.

138 *Diário Oficial*, Rio de Janeiro, November 12, 1890, p. 5.216, col. 2.

139 "Decisão sem número de 14 de dezembro de 1890," in Rui Barbosa, *Obras completas de Rui Barbosa*, vol. XVII, tome 2, 1890: Atos legislativos. Decisões ministeriais e circulares (Rio de Janeiro: Fundação Casa de Rui Barbosa, 1943), 338–340. See also Clóvis Moura, *Dicionário da Escravidão Negra no Brasil* (São Paulo: Editora da Universidade de São Paulo, 2004), 332.

140 On the issue of which documents were actually burned, see Robert W. Slenes, "O que Rui Barbosa não queimou: novas fontes para o estudo da escravidão no século XIX," *Estudos Econômicos* 13, no. 1 (1983): 117–149. To understand Barbosa's motivations, see Lacombe et al., *Rui Barbosa e a queima dos arquivos*; and Ana Lucia Araujo, *Public Memory of Slavery of Slavery: Victims and Perpetrators in the South Atlantic* (Amherst: Cambria Press, 2010), 37–38.

141 Kim D. Butler, *Freedoms Given, Freedoms Won: Afro-Brazilians in Post-Abolition São Paulo and Salvador* (New Brunswick: Rutgers University Press, 2000), 28.

142 Araujo, *Shadows of the Slave Past*, chapter 5.

143 See Araujo, *Shadows of the Slave Past*, 148–149. Among the studies emphasizing the role of Isabel in the late abolitionist movement see Robert Daibert Jr., *Isabel a "redentora" dos escravos: uma história da princesa entre olhares negros e brancos, 1846–1988* (Florianópolis: Editora da Universidade Federal de Santa Catarina, 2004) and Eduardo Silva, *As camélias do Leblon e a abolição da escravatura: Uma investigação de história cultural* (São Paulo: Companhia das Letras, 2003). See also Eduardo Silva, "Black Abolitionists in the Quilombo of Leblon, Rio de Janeiro: Symbols, Organizers, and Revolutionaries," in *The Multilayered Legacy of Africans in Latin America and the Caribbean*, ed. Darién J. Davis (Lanham, MD: Rowman & Littlefield, 2007), 109–122.

144 Historian Maria de Fátima Moraes Argon, recovered the letter, pertaining to a private collection. The letter was reproduced in a Brazilian history monthly magazine in May 2006, month of the anniversary of the Brazilian abolition, and gained great attention from the media. See Priscilla Leal, "O lado rebelde da princesa Isabel," *Nossa História* 3, no. 31, May

145 On the debates in the Chamber of Deputies in 1879, see Michele de Leão, "A participação de Rui Barbosa na reforma eleitoral que excluiu os analfabetos do direito de voto no Brasil," (MA thesis, Universidade Federal do Rio Grande do Sul, 2013), 82–107.

146 Alceu Ravanello Ferraro, "Educação, classe, gênero e voto no Brasil imperial: Lei Saraiva—1881," *Educar em Revista*, no. 50 (2013): 186.

147 Rui Barbosa, *Obras completas de Rui Barbosa*, vol. VI, 1879, tome 1: Discursos parlamentares, Câmara dos Deputados (Rio de Janeiro: Ministério da Educação e Saúde, 1943), 247. See also Maria Cristina Gomes Machado, *Rui Barbosa: pensamento e ação: uma análise do projeto modernizador para a sociedade brasileira com base na questão educacional* (Rio de Janeiro: Fundação Casa de Rui Barbosa, 2002), 64.

148 According to the Census of 1872. See Alceu Ravanello Ferraro and Michele de Leão, "Lei Saraiva (1881): Dos argumentos invocados pelos liberais para a exclusão dos analfabetos do direito de voto," *Educação Unisinos* 16, no. 3 (2012): 241–250.

149 Barbosa, *Obras completas de Rui Barbosa*, vol. VI, 1879, tome 1, 258.

150 Ferraro and Leão, "Lei Saraiva (1881)," 247.

151 Gisele Silva Araújo, "Tradição liberal, positivismo e pedagogia: A síntese derrotada de Rui Barbosa," *Perspectivas* 37 (2010): 122. Yet, despite these hindrances, in the years that followed the decree a growing number of low-status workers appear listed in some districts of the city of São Paulo. See also Ana Flávia Magalhães Pinto, "Fortes laços em linhas rotas: Literatos negros, racismo e cidadania na segunda metade do século XIX," Ph.D. dissertation (Campinas: Universidade Estadual de Campinas, 2014), 252.

152 Pinto, "Fortes laços em linhas rotas," 258–259.

153 Scott, *Degrees of Freedom*, 148.

154 See Sección Segunda, "Derecho de Sufragio," Article 38 of the "Constitución de la República de Cuba (1901)," in *Las Constituciones de Cuba Republicana*, ed. Beatriz Bernal (Miami, FL: Instituto y Biblioteca de la Libertad 2003), 80.

155 Scott, *Degrees of Freedom*, 214.

156 Fuente, *A Nation for All*, 55.

157 Carolina Vianna Dantas, "Monteiro Lopes (1867–1910), um 'líder da raça negra,' na capital da República," *Afro-Ásia* 41 (2010): 172.

158 Petrônio Domingues, "Vai ficar tudo preto: Monteiro Lopes e a cor na política," *Novos Estudos* 95 (2013): 68; Dantas, "Monteiro Lopes (1867–1910)," 183.

159 Domingues, "Vai ficar tudo preto," 76 and Dantas, "Monteiro Lopes (1867–1910)," 170–175.

160 Joseli Maria Nunes Mendonça, *Entre a mão e os anéis: A lei dos sexagenários e os caminhos da abolição no Brasil* (Campinas: Editora da Universidade de Campinas, 1999), 74.

161 Schmieder, "Martinique and Cuba Grande," 89.

162 Butler, *Freedoms Given, Freedoms Won*, 138.

163 Butler, *Freedoms Given, Freedoms Won*, 103.

164 "Estatutos da Frente Negra Brasileira," *Diário Oficial do Estado de São Paulo*, November 4, 1931, 12.

165 Butler, *Freedoms Given, Freedoms Won*, 120.

166 Elisa Larkin Nascimento, "O movimento social afro-brasileiro no século XX: Um esboço sucinto," in *Cultura em movimento: Matrizes africanas e ativismo negro no Brasil*, ed. Elisa Larkin Nascimento (São Paulo: Selo Negro, 2008) 99.

167 Vargas governed Brazil from 1930 to 1945 and again later from 1951 to 1954. The first term was divided into three different phases, the provisional phase (1930–1934), the constitutional phase (1934–1937), and the dictatorial period of the New State (1937–1945).

168 Araujo, *Shadows of the Slave Past*, 162.

169 Ana Lugão Rios and Hebe Mattos, *Memórias do cativeiro: Família, trabalho e cidadania no pós-abolição* (Rio de Janeiro: Civilização Brasileira, 2005), 56.

Chapter 4: "What Else Will the Negro Expect?"

1   See "Speech by Marcus Garvey," Liberty Hall, January 1, 1922 in *The Marcus Garvey and Universal Negro Improvement Association Papers*, vol. IV, ed. Robert A. Hill (Berkeley: University of California Press, 1983), 323.

2   *The Marcus Garvey and Universal Negro Improvement Association Papers*, vol. I, ed. Robert A. Hill (Berkeley: University of California Press, 1983), 13; Colin Grant, *Negro With a Hat: The Rise and Fall of Marcus* Garvey (New York: Oxford University Press, 2008), 8.

3   See the Treaty of Versailles, Part VIII. Reparation, section 1, General Provisions, Article 231. According to the treaty's Article 232, the amount to be paid by Germany would be determined by a Reparation Commission, see *The Avalon Project: Documents in Law, History, and Diplomacy*, http://avalon.law. yale.edu/imt/partviii.asp. On the postwar debates, see Richard M. Buxbaum, "A Legal History of International Reparations," *Berkeley Journal of International Law* 23, no. 2 (2005): 319–320.

4   Adam Ewing, *The Age of Garvey: How a Jamaican Activist Created a Mass Movement and Changed Global Black Politics* (Princeton: Princeton University Press, 2014), 118.

5   Marcus Garvey, "The Sign by Which We Conquer," Liberty Hall, New York, September 16, 1923 in *The Marcus Garvey and Universal Negro Improvement Association Papers*, vol. V, ed. Robert A. Hill (Berkeley: University of California Press, 1986), 461.

6   W. E. B. Du Bois, "Opinion," *The Crisis* 28, no. 1 (May 1924), 8. *The Crisis* is the NAACP (National Association for the Advancement of Colored People) magazine.

7   FWPWPA for the State of Arkansas, *Slave Narratives: A Folk History of Slavery in the United States From Interviews with Former Slaves* (Washington, DC: Library of Congress, 1941), vol. I, Arkansas Narratives, part 1, 13.

8   Amsy O. Alexander, resident of Little Rock, Arkansas, 74 years old, interviewed by Samuel S. Taylor, and Diana Alexander, resident of Brinkley, Arkansas, 74 years old, interviewed by Miss Irene Robertson, in FWPWPA for the State of Arkansas, *Slave Narratives*, vol. I, Arkansas Narratives, part 1, 25; 28.

9   Aunt Mittie Freeman, age 86, North Little Rock, Arkansas, interviewed by Beulah Sherwood Hagg in FWPWPA for the State of Arkansas, *Slave Narratives*, vol. II, Arkansas Narratives, part 2, 348.

10 FWPWPA for the State of Arkansas, *Slave Narratives*, vol. I, Arkansas Narratives, part 1, 170.

11 FWPWPA for the State of Texas, *Slave Narratives*, vol. XVI, Texas Narratives, part 2, 204.

12 FWPWPA for the State of Arkansas, *Slave Narratives*, vol. III, Arkansas Narratives, part 2, 19.

13 FWPWPA for the State of Arkansas, *Slave Narratives*, vol. II, Arkansas Narratives, part 2, 11.

14 FWPWPA for the State of Florida, *Slave Narratives*, vol. III, Florida Narratives, 38.

15 Ibid.

16 This was the case of Diana Alexander, a resident of Brinkley, Arkansas, 74 years old, interviewed by Miss Irene Robertson, see FWPWPA for the State of Arkansas, *Slave Narratives*, vol. I, Arkansas Narratives, part 1, 28.

17 FWPWPA for the State of Arkansas, *Slave Narratives*, vol. II, Arkansas Narratives, part 2, 65.

18 FWPWPA for the State of South Carolina, *Slave Narratives*, vol. XIV, South Carolina Narratives, part 1, 300.

19 FWPWPA for the State of Arkansas, *Slave Narratives*, vol. I, Arkansas Narratives, part 1, 170–171.

20 FWPWPA for the State of Arkansas, *Slave Narratives*, vol. II, Arkansas Narratives, part 6, 323.

21 "Case Concerning the Factory of Chorzów (Claim for Indemnity), (Jurisdiction)," *Publications of the Permanent Court of International Justice*, Series A, No. 9, July 26, 1927, 1–34.

22 Buxbaum, "A Legal History of International Reparations," 337.

23 See The Conference on Jewish Material Claims Against Germany, http://www.claimscon.org/.

24 NARA, RG 11, The General Records of the United States Government, Book and Printed Materials Collection, Franklin D. Roosevelt Executive Orders, Executive Order 9066.

25 Approximately 10,000 German Americans and German nationals, as well as 3,000 Italian Americans and Italian nationals were also confined in US internment camps spread around the country.

26 The Executive Order 9102 issued on March 18, 1942 created the War Relocation Authority.

27 Public Law No. 80–886, July 2, 1948, in *United States Statutes at Large Containing Laws and Concurrent Resolutions Enacted During the Second Session of the Eightieth Congress of the United States of America, 1948*, Volume 62 (Washington, DC: Government Printing Office, 1948), Chapter 814, 1231.

28 *United States vs. Sioux Nation of Indians*, 448 U.S. 371 (1980).

29 Public Law No. 100–383, August 10, 1988, https://www.congress.gov/bill/100th-congress/house-bill/00442.

30 John Torpey, *Making Whole What Has Been Smashed: On Reparations Politics* (Cambridge, MA: Harvard University Press, 2006), 81.

31 MSRC, Manuscript Division, Paul and Eslanda Robeson, Series A: Writings, BOX 19, Folder "Writings by, 1950's," Paul Robeson, "My Background," autobiographical typescript.

32 Harry Haywood and Gwendolyn Midlo Hall, *A Black Communist in the Freedom Struggle: The Life of Harry Haywood* (Minneapolis: University of Minnesota Press, 2012), 112.

33 Rhonda Y. Williams, *Concrete Demands: The Search for Black Power in the 20th Century* (New York: Routledge, 2015), 34. See also, John A. Gronbeck-Tedesco, *Cuba, the United States, and Cultures of the Transnational Left, 1930–1975* (New York: Cambridge University Press, 2015), 118.

34 MSRC, Manuscript Division, Paul and Eslanda Robeson, Series A: Writings, BOX 19, "Writings by Paul Robeson, folder 1950's," Paul Robeson, "Racial Responsibility," in *Pioneering for a Civilized World: Report of the New York Herald Tribune Twelfth Forum on Current Problems at the Waldorf-Astoria, New York City, November 16 and 17, 1943* (New York: New York Herald Tribune, 1943), 44.

35 MSRC, Manuscript Division, Paul and Eslanda Robeson, Series A: Writings, BOX 19, "Writings by Paul Robeson, folder 1950's," Paul Robeson, *Forge: Negro-Labor Unity for Peace and Jobs* (New York: Harlem Trade Union Council, 1950), 4. Italics in the original.

36 MSRC, Manuscript Division, Paul and Eslanda Robeson, Series A: Writings, BOX 19, "Writings by Paul Robeson," folder "1950's," Trade Union Convention speech, 4–5.

37 MSRC, Manuscript Division, Paul and Eslanda Robeson, Series A: Writings, BOX 19, "Writings by Paul Robeson," folder "1950's notes," "International Struggle for Freedom," 1950, 1.

38 Civil Rights Congress, *We Charge Genocide: The Historic Petition to the United Nations for Relief From a Crime of the United States Government Against the Negro People* (New York: Civil Rights Congress, 1951).

39 MSRC, Manuscript Division, Paul and Eslanda Robeson, Series A: Writings, BOX 19, "Writings by 1950," Paul Robeson, "Genocide Stalks the U.S.A." *New World Review*, February 1952, 26.

40 United Nations General Assembly, December 9, 1948, Resolution 260 (III), Prevention and Punishment of the Crime of Genocide, Article II, 174, http://www.un-documents.net/a3r260.htm.

41 MSRC, Manuscript Division, Paul and Eslanda Robeson, Series A: Writings, BOX 19, Folder "Writings by Paul Robeson," folder "1952," Paul Robeson, "Genocide Stalks the U.S.A." *New World Review*, February 1952, 28.

42 MSRC, Manuscript Division, Paul and Eslanda Robeson, Series A: Writings, BOX 19, "Writings by 1950," folder "1952," Paul Robeson, "Article for Jewish Life," draft typescript, 1. This article was published as "Bonds of Brotherhood," *Jewish Life*, November 1954.

43 On August 24, 1954, President Dwight Eisenhower (1890–1969) signed the Communist Control Act (68 Stat. 775, 50 U.S.C. 841–844) outlawing the CPUSA. The Act also criminalized membership in the party.

44 "Paul Robeson Receives Stalin Peace Prize," *New World Review*, October 1953, 18.

45 Alejandro de la Fuente, *A Nation for All: Race, Inequality and Politics in Twentieth Century Cuba* (Chapel Hill: University of North Carolina Press, 2001), 76–77.

46 Joanna Swanger, *Rebel Lands of Cuba: The Campesino Struggles of Oriente and Escambray, 1934–1974* (Lanham, MD: Lexington Books, 2015), 90.

47 Oriente was one of the six provinces of Cuba until 1976. It comprised the present-day provinces of Las Tunas, Granma, Holguín, Santiago de Cuba, and Guantánamo.

48 Gronbeck-Tedesco, *Cuba*, 121.

49 Caribbean workers were among the 300,000 foreign workers who came to Cuba during the First World War's sugar boom. See Gronbeck-Tedesco, *Cuba*, 121.

50 Swanger, *Rebel Lands of Cuba*, 100.

51 On racist depictions of Batista, see Lillian Guerra, *Visions of Power in Cuba: Revolution, Redemption, and Resistance, 1959–1971* (Chapel Hill: University of North Carolina Press, 2012), 52–53.

52 Harold Sims, "Cuba," in *Latin America Between the Second World War and the Cold War: Crisis and Containment, 1944–1948*, ed. Leslie Bethell and Ian Roxborough (Cambridge: Cambridge University Press, 1992), 219.

53 Fuente, *A Nation for All*, 260.

54 "Discurso pronunciado por El Comandante Fidel Castro Ruz, Primer Ministro del Gobierno Revolucionario, en el campamento "Agramonte," en Camagüey, el 21 de octubre de 1959," in *Discursos e intervenciones del Comandante en Jefe Fidel Castro Ruz, Presidente del Consejo de Estado de la República de Cuba*, http://www.cuba.cu/gobierno/discursos/1959/esp/f211059e.html.

55 "Discurso pronunciado por El Comandante Fidel Castro Ruz, Primer Ministro del Gobierno Revolucionario ante el pueblo congregado en el Palacio Presidencial para reafirmar su apoyo al gobierno revolucionario y como protesta contra la cobarde agresión perpetrada contra el pacifico pueblo de la Habana por aviones procedentes de territorio extranjero, el 26 de octubre de 1959," in *Discursos e intervenciones del Comandante en Jefe Fidel Castro Ruz*, http://www.cuba.cu/gobierno/discursos/1959/esp/f261059e.html.

56 Oficina Nacional de Estadísticas, *Los censos de población y viviendas en Cuba, 1907–1953* Anexo VII, Tablas seleccionadas, Censo de 1953 (La Habana, 2007), 352.

57 Guerra, *Visions of Power in Cuba*, 60.

58 Discurso pronunciado por Fidel Castro Ruz, Presidente de la República de Cuba, efectuado en la velada solemne por el centenario de la caida en combate del Mayor General Ignacio Agramonte Loynaz, Camaguey, el 11 de mayo de 1973, "Año del XX Aniversario," in *Discursos e intervenciones del Comandante en Jefe Fidel Castro Ruz*, http://www.cuba.cu/gobierno/discursos/1973/esp/f110573e.html.

59 See Clifford Andrew Welch, "Vargas and the Reorganization of Rural Life in Brazil (1930–1945)," *Revista brasileira de história* 36, no. 71 (2016): 1–25.

60 Elisa Larkin Nascimento, "O movimento social afro-brasileiro no século XX: Um esboço sucinto." In *Cultura em movimento: Matrizes africanas e ativismo*

negro no Brasil, edited by Elisa Larkin Nascimento (São Paulo: Selo Negro, 2008), 139–140.

61 Law no. 4.214 of March 2, 1963. The law was revoked by Law no. 5.889 of 1973.

62 See Karin Sant'Anna Kössling, "As lutas anti-racistas de afro-descendentes sob vigilância do DEOPS/SP (1964–1983)," (MA thesis, Universidade de São Paulo, 2007); Paulina Alberto, *Terms of Inclusion: Black Intellectuals in Twentieth-Century Brazil* (Chapel Hill: University of North Carolina Press, 2011), 269–270.

63 Alberto, *Terms of Inclusion*, 266.

64 SLHWA, Black Women Oral History Project, Interviews, 1976–1981, Interview with Audley (Queen Mother) Moore, OH–31, 4.

65 SLHWA, Black Women Oral History Project, Interviews, 1976–1981, Interview with Audley (Queen Mother) Moore, OH–31, 2.

66 SLHWA, Black Women Oral History Project, Interview with Audley (Queen Mother) Moore, June 6 and 8, 1978, OH–31, 9; Grant, *Negro with a Hat*, 356.

67 SLHWA, Black Women Oral History Project, Interview with Audley (Queen Mother) Moore, June 6 and 8, 1978, OH–31, 16–17.

68 SLHWA, Black Women Oral History Project, Interview with Audley (Queen Mother) Moore, June 6 and 8, 1978, OH–31, 17. See also, Ashley Farmer, "Reframing African American Women's Grassroots Organizing: Audley Moore and the Universal Association of Ethiopian Women, 1957–1963," *The Journal of African American History* 101, no. 1–2 (2016): 73.

69 SLHWA, Black Women Oral History Project, Interview with Audley (Queen Mother) Moore, June 6 and 8, 1978, OH–31, 8.

70 Farmer, "Reframing African American Women's Grassroots Organizing," 77.

71 SLHWA, Black Women Oral History Project, Interview with Audley (Queen Mother) Moore, June 6 and 8, 1978, OH–31, 25.

72 Marcus Garvey, "The Work that Has Been Done," speech given at Menelik Hall, Sydney, Nova Scotia, Canada, October 1, 1937, in *The Marcus Garvey and Universal Negro Improvement Association Papers*, vol. VII, ed. Robert A. Hill (Berkeley: University of California Press, 1990), 791.

73 SLHWA, Black Women Oral History Project, Interview with Audley (Queen Mother) Moore, June 6 and 8, 1978, OH-31, 39.

74 SLHWA, Black Women Oral History Project, Interview with Audley (Queen Mother) Moore, June 6 and 8, 1978, OH-31, 39.

75 In her interview Moore stated that "the United States government had paid the Japanese reparations." Yet reparations were paid only in the 1980s. Harvard University, Schlesinger Library on the History of Women in America, Black Women Oral History Project, Interview with Audley (Queen Mother) Moore, June 6 and 8, 1978, OH-31, 40.

76 SLHWA, Black Women Oral History Project, Interview with Audley (Queen Mother) Moore, June 6 and 8, 1978, OH-31, 45.

77 SLHWA, Black Women Oral History Project, Interview with Audley (Queen Mother) Moore, June 6 and 8, 1978, OH-31, 41.

78 SLHWA, Black Women Oral History Project, Interview with Audley (Queen Mother) Moore, June 6 and 8, 1978, OH-31, 46.

79 Ibid.

80 Audley M. Moore, *Why Reparations? Reparations is the Battle Cry for the Economic, and Social Freedom of More than 25 Million Descendants of American Slaves* (n.p, 1963), 4.

81 Farmer, "Reframing African American Women's Grassroots Organizing," 87. Alondra Nelson, *The Social Life of DNA: Race, Reparations, and Reconciliation After the Genome* (Boston, MA: Beacon Press, 2016), 116. Other historians state that the committee was created in 1955, among them see Williams, *Concrete Demands*, 65.

82 Audley M. Moore, *Why Reparations?*, 7; Williams, *Concrete Demands*, 87; Farmer, "Reframing African American Women's Grassroots Organizing," 88.

83 Audley M. Moore, *Why Reparations?*, 2.

84 Ibid.

85 Audley M. Moore, *Why Reparations?*, 5.

86 Malcolm X, "The Race Problem," African Students Association and NAACP Campus Chapter, Michigan State University, East Lansing, Michigan, January 23, 1963. The various extracts of the audio file of this speech are available in *The Autobiography of Malcolm X*, as part of the Malcolm X Project by Columbia Center for New Media Teaching and Learning and the Center for Contemporary Black History, http://ccnmtl.columbia.edu/projects/mmt/mxp/speeches/index.html.

87 Public Law 88–352, 78 Stat. 241, July 2, 1964.

88 Martin Luther King Jr., *Why We Can't Wait* (Boston, MA: Beacon Press, 2010), 150.

89 King, *Why We Can't Wait*, 151.

90 Ibid.

91 King, *Why We Can't Wait*, 160.

92 King, *Why We Can't Wait*, 161.

93 King, *Why We Can't Wait*, 163.

94 MSRC, Manuscript Division, Civil Rights Vertical Files, Series A, Box 159–11, Folder 13 "Republic of New Africa," "Now We Have a Nation: The Republic of New Africa" (Detroit: The Republic of New Africa, n. d.), 14.

95 MSRC, Manuscript Division, Civil Rights Vertical Files, Series A, Box 159–11, Folder 13 "Republic of New Africa," "Now We Have a Nation: The Republic of New Africa" (Detroit: The Republic of New Africa, n. d.), 2.

96 MSRC, Manuscript Division, Civil Rights Vertical Files, Series A, Box 159–11, Folder 13 "Republic of New Africa," "Now We Have a Nation: The Republic of New Africa" (Detroit: The Republic of New Africa, n. d.), 3, 12.

97   Tougaloo College, 96.04, Republic of New Africa, Box 1, folder 4, record 40, The Republic of New Africa Short Official Basic Documents, "What is the Republic of New Africa," leaflet, New Orleans, Louisiana, unknown date. Retrieved at Brown-Tougaloo Cooperation Exchange, http://cds.library. brown.edu/projects/FreedomNow/do_search_single.php?searchid=40.

98   Paul Karolczyk, "Subjugated Territory: The New Afrikan Independence Movement and the Space of Black Power" (Ph.D. dissertation, Louisiana State University, 2014), 224.

99   Karolczyk, "Subjugated Territory," 247.

100 James Forman, *The Making of Black Revolutionaries* (Seattle: University of Washington Press, 1997), 545.

101 Forman, *The Making of Black Revolutionaries*, 23–24.

102 LCMSS, James Forman Papers, Subject File, 1848–2005, James Forman, Box 82, folder 7. Among others the folder contains a copy of a certificate of membership of the National Ex-Slave Mutual Relief, Bounty and Pension Association of the United States of America.

103 LCMSS, James Forman Papers, Subject File, 1848–2005, James Forman, Box 62, folder 6 "'Black Manifesto' address and printed copies," "The Black Manifesto and the Response of the Reformed Church in America," 6–7.

104 LCMSS, James Forman Papers, Subject File, 1848–2005, James Forman, Box 62, folder 6 "'Black Manifesto' address and printed copies," "The Black Manifesto and the Response of the Reformed Church in America," 8–10.

105 Arnold Schuchter, *Reparations: The Black Manifesto and Its Challenges to White America* (Philadelphia: Lippincott Company, 1970), 2.

106 Forman, *The Making of Black Revolutionaries*, 547.

107 Emanuel Perlmutter, "'Reparations' Are Asked—Lindsay is Shocked," *New York Times* (May 5, 1969), 1.

108 Eduard B. Fiske, "Churchmen Critical of Forman's Militant Tactics," *New York Times* (May 6, 1969), 1.

109 Henry Lee, "Jewish Group Hits Forman's Cash Demands," *New York Post* (May 10, 1969) 2.

110 Fiske, "Churchmen Critical of Forman's Militant Tactics," 36.

111 "Playboy Interview: Jesse Jackson: A Candid Conversation with the Fiery Heir Apparent to Martin Luther King," *Playboy* 16, no. 11 (November 1969): 5.

112 LCMSS, James Forman Papers, Subject File, 1848–2005, James Forman, Box 61, folder 11 "'Black Manifesto' Correspondence," March–June 1969, "The Black Manifesto and specific demands upon Riverside Church," Memorandum from James Forman to the Board of Deacons and the members of Riverside Church, May 4, 1969, 1.

113 LCMSS, James Forman Papers, Subject File, 1848–2005, James Forman, Box 61, folder 11 "'Black Manifesto' Correspondence," March–June 1969, "The Black Manifesto and specific demands upon Riverside Church," Memorandum from James Forman to the Board of Deacons and the members of Riverside Church, May 4, 1969, 2.

114 LCMSS, James Forman Papers, Subject File, 1848–2005, James Forman, Box 61, folder 11 "'Black Manifesto' Correspondence," March–June 1969, "The Black Manifesto and specific demands upon Riverside Church," Memorandum from James Forman to the Board of Deacons and the members of Riverside Church, May 4, 1969, 2.

115 LCMSS, James Forman Papers, Subject File, 1848–2005, James Forman, Box 61, folder 11 "'Black Manifesto' Correspondence," March–June 1969, "Re: Black Manifesto," Memorandum from James Forman to Cardinal Cooke, May 9, 1969, 1.

116 LCMSS, James Forman Papers, Subject File, 1848–2005, James Forman, Box 61, folder 11 "'Black Manifesto' Correspondence," March–June 1969, Memorandum from James Forman to Dr. Ben Herbster, President of the United Church of Christ and Dr. Howard E. Spragg, Executive Vice President of the Board of Homeland Ministries of the United Church of Christ, May 1969, 1.

117 LCMSS, James Forman Papers, Subject File, 1848–2005, James Forman, Box 61, folder 11 "'Black Manifesto' Correspondence," March–June 1969, June, Memorandum from James Forman to Most Rev. John E. Hines, May 13, 1969, 2.

118 "Dr. Ben M. Herbster; United Church Leader," Obituaries, *New York Times*, December 23, 1984.

119 LCMSS, James Forman Papers, Subject File, 1848–2005, James Forman, Box 61, folder 11 "'Black Manifesto' Correspondence," March–June 1969, Memorandum from Dr. Ben Herbster, President of the United Church of Christ to James Forman, Student Nonviolent Coordinating Committee c/o Interreligious Foundation for Community Organization, Inc, May 19, 1969, 1.

120 LCMSS, James Forman Papers, Subject File, 1848–2005, James Forman, Box 61, folder 11 "'Black Manifesto' Correspondence," March–June 1969, Anonymous letter to James Forman, July 10, 1969, 1.

121 Ibid.

122 LCMSS, James Forman Papers, Subject File, 1848–2005, James Forman, Box 61, folder 11 "'Black Manifesto' Correspondence," Letter by Madalyn Murray O'Hair addressed to "Mae," July 13, 1969, 1–2.

123 LCMSS, James Forman Papers, Subject File, 1848–2005, James Forman, Box 61, folder 11 "'Black Manifesto' Correspondence," March–June 1969, Letter from Kenneth Neigh, General Secretary of the Board of National Missions to all pastors and ministers of the United Presbyterian Church," May 7, 1969, 2.

124 Forman, *The Making of Black Revolutionaries*, 545.

Chapter 5: "It's Time for Us to Get Paid"

1   See Convenção Nacional do Negro pela Constituinte, 20 e 27 de Agosto de 1986, typed document, and "Movimento Negro faz propostas à Constituinte," *Folha de São Paulo*, November 8 (1986): 10.

2   Alexandre Ribondi, "De como a Princesa Isabel não fez nada pelos negros," *Correio Braziliense,* May 13 (1987): 23.

3   "Terras de quilombos vão ser desapropriadas," *Estado de São Paulo*, December 13 (1987): 6.

4   Constituição da República Federativa do Brasil de 1988: Texto consticional promulgado em 5 de outubro de 1988, com as alterações adotadas pelas Emendas Constitucionais nos. 1/1992 a 68/2011, pelo Decreto Legislativo no. 186/2008 e pelas Emandas Constitucionais de Revisão nos. 1 a 6/1994 (Brasília: Câmara dos Deputados, Edições da Câmara, 2012), Título X, Ato das Disposições Constitucionais Transitórias, Artigo 88, 155.

5   Ferdinand Protzman, "Upheaval in the East: The East Germans Issue an Apology for Nazis' Crimes," *New York Times*, April 13, 1990, A7.

6   The group of eminent persons included: M. K. O. Abiola (1937–1998), Jacob F. Ade Ajayi (1929–2014), Josef Ki-Zerbo (1922–2006), Miriam Makeba (1932–2008), Ali Mazrui (1933–2014), Aristide Maria Pereira (1923–2011), Alex Quaison-Sackey (1924–1992), Dudley J. Thompson (1800–1874), Samir Amin, Ron Dellums, Gracha Machel, and Amadou-Makhtar M'Bow. Rhoda E. Howard-Hassmann, "Reparations to Africa and the Group of Eminent Persons," *Cahiers d'Études Africaines* 44, no. 1–2 (2004): 84.

7   Rhoda E. Howard-Hassmann and Anthony P. Lombardo, *Reparations to Africa* (Philadelphia: University of Pennsylvania Press, 2008), 27.

8   "Visite du Pape au Bénin: un pèlerin de la paix," *La Nation*, February 5, 1993, 5.

9   Nicéphore Soglo, "Nous devons reprendre confiance en nous-mêmes et nous mettre au travail. Discours de son excellence Monsieur Nicéphore D. Soglo à l'ouverture des travaux de la 29e conférence des chefs d'État et de gouvernement de l'OUA," *La Nation*, July 9, 1993, 4.

10 On the debates on restitutions, see Thérèse O'Donnell, "The Restitution of Holocaust Looted Art and Transitional Justice: The Perfect Storm or the Raft of the Medusa," *The European Journal of International Law* 22, no. 1 (2011): 49–80.

11 See "Discours de Jacques Chirac sur la responsabilité de Vichy dans la déportation, 1995," http://fresques.ina.fr/jalons/fiche-media/InaEdu01248/discours-de-jacques-chirac-sur-la-responsabilite-de-vichy-dans-la-deportation–1995.html.

12 Article 1, "Claims: Agreement Between the United States of America and Germany," signed at Bonn, September 19, 1995 with Exchange of Notes *and* Supplementary Agreement Effected by Exchanges of Notes Signed at Bonn, January 25, 1999, Treaties and other International Acts Series 13019, 2.

13 Foreign Claims Settlement Commission of the United States, "2011 Annual Report," (Washington, DC: US Department of Justice, 2011), 44–46.

14 For the full text, see Commission for Religious Relations with the Jews, "We Remember: A Reflection on the Shoah," March 16, 1998, http://www.vatican.va/roman_curia/pontifical_councils/chrstuni/documents/rc_pc_chrstuni_doc_16031998_shoah_en.html.

15 Constitución Política de Colombia de 1991, Actualizada con los Actos
    Legislativos hasta 2010 (Bogotá: Imprenta Nacional de Colombia, 2010),
    Disposiciones transitorias, Capítulo 8, artículo 55, 212–213.

16 "Ley 70 de 1993: Por la cual se desarrolla el artículo transitorio 55 de la
    Constitución Política." *Diario Oficial*, no. 4.013, August 31, 1993.

17 Claudia Mosquera Rosero-Labbé, Luiz Claudio Barcelos, and Andrés Gabriel
    Arévalo Robles, "Contribuciones a los debates sobre las Memorias de la
    Esclavitud y las Afro-reparaciones en Colombia desde el campo de los estudios
    afrocolombianos, afrolatinoamericanos, afrobrasileros, afroestadunidenses y
    afrocaribeños," in *Afro-reparaciones: Memorias de la Esclavitud y Justicia
    Reparativa para negros, afrocolombianos y raizales*, ed. Claudia Mosquera
    Rosero-Labbé and Luiz Claudio Barcelos (Bogotá: Universidad Nacional de
    Colombia, Observatorio del Caribe Colombiano, 2017), 19.

18 Oscar Almario García, "Reparaciones contemporáneas: de la Memoria de la
    Esclavitud al cuestionamiento de la exclusión social y el racismo," *Afro-
    reparaciones: Memorias de la Esclavitud y Justicia Reparativa para negros,
    afrocolombianos y raizales*, ed. Claudia Mosquera Rosero-Labbé and Luiz
    Claudio Barcelos (Bogotá: Universidad Nacional de Colombia, Observatorio
    del Caribe Colombiano, 2017), 188.

19 Constitución Política de la República del Ecuador de 1998, http://pdba.
    georgetown.edu/Constitutions/Ecuador/ecuador98.html.

20 "Ley no. 2006–46: Ley de los Derechos Colectivos de los Pueblos Negros o
    Afroecuátorianos," *Registro Oficial* no. 275, Quito, May 22, 2006.

21 Ibid.

22 Marc Becker, "Correa, Indigenous Movements, and the Writing of a New
    Constitution in Ecuador," *Latin American Perspectives* 38, no. 176 (2011): 48.

23 Constitución de la Republica de Ecuador, *Registro Oficial*, no. 449, Quito,
    October 20, 2008, Section 9, Chapter 4, Article 60, 17.

24 Instituto Nacional de Estadística y Censos, Resultados del Censo 2010, http://
    www.ecuadorencifras.gob.ec/resultados/

25 Adjoa Aiyetoro and Adrienne D. Davis. "Historic and Modern Social
    Movements for Reparations: The National Coalition for Reparations in
    America (N'COBRA) and its Antecedents," *Texas Wesleyan Law Review* 16,
    June 18 (2010): 729.

26 Charles P. Henry, *Long Overdue: The Politics of Racial Reparations* (New
    York: New York University Press, 2007), 108.

27 Martha Biondi, "The Rise of the Reparations Movement," in *Redress for
    Historical Injustices in the United States: On Reparations for Slavery, Jim
    Crow, and Their Legacies*, ed. Michael T. Martin and Marilyn Yaquinto
    (Durham, NC: Duke University Press, 2007), 257.

28 Lewis was enthroned Queen Mother on June 24, 2006, in Indianapolis, IN.

29 National Coalition of Blacks for Reparations in America, http://www.
    ncobraonline.org.

30 Statement by Representative John Conyers (D-MI), "The Impact of Slavery on
    African Americans Today, April 5, 2005," Jyotsna Sreenivasan, *Poverty and the*

Government in America: A Historical Encyclopedia (Santa Barbara, CA: ABC CLIO, 2009), 536.

31 Aiyetoro and Davis, "Historic and Modern Social Movements for Reparations," 734.

32 Bruce Smith, "Group Seeks Reparations for American Slavery," *The Philadelphia Tribune Life*, June 23, 1992, 3-C.

33 Yet, the name of the organization did not contain the term "reparations," and was rather called National Ex-Slave Mutual Relief, Bounty and Pension Association of the United States of America. Only in 1962, the term "reparations" was included in the title of an African American organization, when Audley Moore founded the Reparations Committee for the Descendants of American Slaves (RCDAS). GCLAU, Personal Papers Collection of Muhammad Ahmad, Programs National Coalition of Black for Reparations in America, Convention 1993, "The Annual National Convention Committee, The National Coalition of Blacks for Reparations in America, N'COBRA," letter by Johnita Obadele, April 27, 1993.

34 Ibid.

35 Lena Williams, "Blacks Press the Case for Reparations for Slavery," *New York Times*, July 21, 1994, B10.

36 "Black Group Backs Fight for Slavery Reparations," *The Register-Guard*, July 24, 1994, 3A.

37 Ibid.

38 *Cato vs. United States*, 70 F. 3d 1103 (9th Cir. 1995).

39 The initial group consisted of Jewel Cato, Joyce Cato, Howard Cato, and Edward Cato. It was joined with the Johnson case, which included Leerma Patterson, Charles Patterson, and Bobbie Trice Johnson. Eventually as Cato was the only individual who signed the complaint and the *in forma pauperis* declaration in No. 94–17102, and Johnson was the only plaintiff in her action, the district court dismissed the plaintiffs. See *Cato vs. United States*.

40 Ibid.

41 Ibid.

42 Yanessa L. Barnard, "Better Late than Never: A Takings Clause Solution to Reparations," *Washington and Lee Journal of Civil Rights and Social Justice* 12, no. 1 (2005): 122.

43 "Proposto pagamento em juízo do consumo realizado no hotel; Intenção do Maksoud é condenar negros como estelionatários," *Jornal das reparações*, no. 2, October 1994, 2. In her recent book, anthropologist Francine Saillant mentions Conceição as a student who led a demonstration in São Paulo, but fails to explain that this demonstration was not fortuitous but part of an organized movement. See Francine Saillant, *Le mouvement noir au Brésil (2000–2010): Réparations, droits et citoyenneté* (Québec: Presses de l'Université Laval, 2014), 129, 142.

44 Monica Prado, "Negros querem indenização por escravidão," *Correio Braziliense* (December 25, 1994): 19.

45 Tânia Regina dos Santos Silva, "Ação pede indenização para os negros do país," *Estado de São Paulo*, December 14, 1994, 6; "Negros," *Jornal do Brasil*, December 14, 1994.

46 Prado, "Negros querem indenização por escravidão," 19.

47 Ibid.

48 Ibid.

49 "Negros querem lei de reparação," *Folha de São Paulo*, January 21, 1995.

50 Cláudia Trevisan, "Movimento pede US$6,1 tri para indenizar descendente de escravo," *Folha de São Paulo*, May 13, 1994, 4.

51 I explored this issue in my book, Ana Lucia Araujo, *Public Memory of Slavery of Slavery: Victims and Perpetrators in the South Atlantic* (Amherst: Cambria Press, 2010), 49–90.

52 Prado, "Negros querem indenizaçãoo por escravidão," 19.

53 Araujo, *Public Memory of Slavery*, 230.

54 "Farrakhan, Chavis Call for 1995 Million Man March on Washington," *New Pittsburgh Courier*, December 31, 1994, 1.

55 Coalition of Black Power organizations created by the end of the 1960s, with numerous chapters spread all over the United States.

56 Maulana Karenga, "The Million Man March/Day of Absence Mission Statement," *The Black Scholar* 25, no. 4 (1995): 10.

57 Queen Mother Audley Moore was on the stage, even though her speech which I partly transcribed here was read by Dr. Delois Blakely (Queen Mother of Harlem) (see Figure 5.2). See "Speech of Maya Angelou and guest speakers at Million Man March on Washington," October 16, 1995, https://www.youtube.com/watch?v=SeLfvkaobos.

58 The numbers were controversial. The National Park Service estimated it at 400,000 whereas the march's organizers refer to 1,500,000 to 2,000,000 participants. See Eric L. Clark, "Brothers in Arms: The Million Man March," *The Crisis*, November, December, 1995, 10.

59 "Minister Louis Farrakhan Challenges Black Men: Remarks During the Million Man March, October 16, 1995," in *Voices of the African American Experience*, ed. Lionel C. Bascom (Westport, CT: Greenwood Press, 2009), vol. 1, 624.

60 Connie Cass, "Million Man March: Black Men Still 'Energized' by the Spirit of the March," *Philadelphia Tribune*, October 24, 1995, 8-C.

61 Randall Robinson, *The Debt: What America Owes to Blacks* (New York: Dutton, 2000). Robinson founded TransAfrica Forum in 1977. The organization's activities consist of lobbying the US government regarding issues concerning countries in Africa and the Caribbean as well as issues related to the African diaspora.

62 John Torpey, "Legalism and Its Discontents: The Case of Reparations for Black Americans," in *The Limits of the Law*, ed. Austin Sarat, Lawrence Douglas, Martha Merrill Umphrey (Stanford: Stanford University Press, 2005), 85–86,

Alondra Nelson, *The Social Life of DNA: Race, Reparations, and Reconciliation After the Genome* (Boston, MA: Beacon Press, 2016), 120.

63 David Horowitz, "The Latest Civil Rights Disaster: Ten Reasons Why Reparations for Blacks is a Bad Idea for Blacks," May 30, 2000, http://www.salon.com/2000/05/30/reparations/.

64 Kendall Wilson, "Anti-Reparations Ad Sparks Protests," *Philadelphia Tribune*, April 3, 2001, 3A, and Richard Lewis, "Newspaper Slavery Ad Sparks Backlash at University," *Los Angeles Sentinel*, March 22, 2001, B6.

65 See Brown University, *Slavery and Justice* (Providence, RI: Brown University, 2007); and Deborah Yaffe, "Class Begins to Paint Picture of Princeton's Ties to Slavery," *Princeton Alumni Weekly*, May 15, 2013, 20–21.

66 United Nations General Assembly, *Draft Articles on Responsibility of States for Internationally Wrongful Acts with Commentaries* (New York: United Nations, 2001), 31.

67 United Nations, "Responsibility of States for Internationally Wrongful Acts," Annex to General Assembly resolution 56/83 of 12 December 2001, 2005, 7. Moral damages include "pain and suffering, loss of loved ones and affronts to honour, dignity or prestige," see Anthony Aust, *Handbook of International Law* (New York: Cambridge University Press, 2010), 386.

68 "Loi 2001–434 du 21 mai 2001 tendant à la reconnaissance de la traite et de l'esclavage en tant que crime contre l'humanité," *Journal Officiel*, no. 19, May 23, 2001, 8175.

69 Charles Forsdick, "Compensating for the Past: Debating Reparations for Slavery in Contemporary France," *Contemporary French and Francophone Studies* 19, no. 4 (2015): 423.

70 United Nations, *World Conference Against Racism, Racial Discrimination, Xenophobia and Related Intolerance: Durban, South Africa, 31 August–7 September 2001* (New York: United Nations Department of Public Information, 2001).

71 During her second term as president of Brazil, on October 2, 2015, President Dilma Rousseff extinguished SEPPIR, which, along with other secretariats, became a single Ministry of Women, Racial Equality, and Human Rights.

72 Decree no. 4.887 of November 20, 2003, http://www.planalto.gov.br/ccivil_03/decreto/2003/d4887.htm.

73 See Hebe Mattos, "'Remanescentes das comunidades dos quilombos': Memória do cativeiro e políticas de reparação no Brasil," *Revista USP*, no. 68 (2005–2006): 108.

74 Only in 2002, approximately nine lawsuits demanding reparations for slavery from corporations were filed in various US federal courts.

75 Nelson, *The Social Life of* DNA, 121.

76 *Farmer-Paellmann vs. FleetBoston et al.*, 02cv1862, United States District Court for the Eastern District of New York, March 26, 2002. Later Farmer-Paellmann filed suit in California, see *Hurdle vs. FleetBoston*, CGC–02–412,388 (Supreme Court, San Francisco, CA, 2003), Nelson, *The Social Life of*

DNA, 125, and Alfred L. Brophy, *Reparations: Pro & Con* (New York: Oxford University Press. 2006), 4, 215n7.

77 Nelson, *The Social Life of DNA*, 128–129, and Salamishah Tillet, *Sites of Slavery: Citizenship and Racial Democracy in the Post-Civil Rights Imagination* (Durham, NC: Duke University Press, 2012), 146–147.

78 Tara Kolar Ramchandani, "Judicial Recognition of the Harms of Slavery: Consumer Fraud as an Alternative to Reparations Litigation," *Harvard Civil Rights-Civil Liberties Review* 42, no. 2 (2007): 541–556.

79 Ron Daniels, "Queen Mother Moore Reparations Bill Introduced," *New Pittsburgh Courier*, July 15–20, 2002, 5.

80 Daniels, "Queen Mother Moore Reparations Bill Introduced," 5.

81 See Araujo, *Shadows of the Slave Past*, 93–97.

82 Among these lawsuits are: *Obadele vs. United States*, 52 Fed. Cl 432 (2002), *Abdullah vs. United States*, 2003 US Dist. LEXIS 5129 (2003) (N. D. Connecticut).

83 "Rally on the National Mall to Seek Slavery Reparations," *Reading Eagle*, August 13, 2002, A 9.

84 Isabel Braga, "Na Câmara, uma proposta para mudar a Lei Áurea," *O Globo*, April 29, 2010, 3.

85 Ibid.

86 In the lawsuit they are referred by the acronym Descendants of Black Africans Enslaved in Brazil (DNAEB).

87 Alves authored a book defending the idea of financial reparations. See Claudete Alves, *Negros: o Brasil nos deve milhões! 120 anos de uma abolição inacabada* (São Paulo: Scortecci Editora, 2008).

88 Senate Bill, no. 432 of 2012, 1–2, https://www25.senado.leg.br/web/atividade/materias/-/materia/109355.

89 "Comissão rejeita indenização a descendentes de escravos," *Jornal do Senado*, July 17, 2013, 4.

90 For an overview of this issue, see Ana Lucia Araujo, ed. *African Heritage and Memories of Slavery in Brazil and the South Atlantic World* (Amherst: Cambria Press, 2015).

91 In comparison to whites, Afro-Brazilians receive lower salaries, and have less access to education and healthcare. There are numerous official studies conducted by Instituto de Pesquisa Econômica Aplicada (IPEA), including Tatiana Dias Silva and Fernanda Lira Goes, ed. *Igualdade racial no Brasil: Reflexões no Ano Internacional dos Afrodescendentes* (Rio de Janeiro: Instituto de Pesquisa Econômica Aplicada, 2013).

92 See Roque Planas, "Brazil's 'Quilombo' Movement May Be the World's Largest Slavery Reparations Program," July 10, 2014, http://www.huffingtonpost.com/2014/07/10/brazil-quilombos_n_5572236.html; and Roque Planas, "Afro-Brazilians Demand Slavery Reparations Because 'Poverty Has a Color'," August 26, 2014, http://www.huffingtonpost.com/2014/08/26/quilombos-brazil_n_5692077.html.

93   See Palmares Cultural Foundation, "Quadro Geral de Comunidades
     Remanescentes de Quilombos," http://www.palmares.gov.br/wp-content/
     uploads/2016/06/QUADRO-RESUMO.pdf.

94   See Commissão Pró-Índio de São Paulo, http://www.cpisp.org.br/terras/ and
     "Terras quilombolas: governo Dilma titula apenas nove terras, todas
     parcialmente." http://amazonia.org.br/2014/11/terras-quilombolas--governo-
     dilma-titula-apenas-nove-terras-todas-parcialmente/.

95   Commissão estadual da verdade da escravidão negra no Brasil, Ordem dos
     Advogados do Brasil, Rio de Janeiro, "Relatório parcial da Comissão
     estadual da verdade da escravidão negra no Brasil, OAB, RJ," Rio de Janeiro,
     2015, 311.

96   Hilary McD. Beckles, *Britain's Black Debt* (Kingston, Jamaica: University of
     West Indies Press, 2013), 223.

97   Ana Lucia Araujo, *Public Memory of Slavery: Victims and Perpetrators in the
     South Atlantic* (Amherst: Cambria Press, 2010), 67–68.

98   Beckles, *Britain's Black Debt*, 224.

99   Caribbean Community Secretariat, Government of Barbados, "Address by the
     Rt. Hon. Owen Arthur Prime Minister of Barbados in Commemoration of the
     200th Anniversary of the Abolition of the Trans-Atlantic Slave Trade," Holy
     Trinity Church, Hull, England, March 25, 2007, 14, see http://archive.
     caricom.org/jsp/speeches/slavery_abolition_arthur.pdf.

100 Caribbean Community Secretariat, Government of Barbados, "Address by the
     Rt. Hon. Owen Arthur," 15.

101 Forsdick, "Compensating for the Past," 425.

102 Louis-George Tin, *Esclavage et réparations: comment faire face aux crimes de
     l'histoire* (Paris: Stock, 2013), 10.

103 "Appel pour un débat national sur les réparations liées à l'esclavage," *Le
     Monde*, October 12, 2012, http://www.lemonde.fr/idees/article/2012/10/12/
     appel-pour-un-debat-national-sur-les-reparations-liees-a-l-esclavage_1774364_
     3232.html?xtmc=appel_pour_un_debat_national&xtcr=3.

104 These nations are Antigua and Barbuda, Bahamas, Barbados, Belize,
     Dominica, Grenada, Guyana, Haiti, Jamaica, Montserrat, Saint Kitts and
     Nevis, Saint Lucia, Saint Vincent and the Grenadines, Suriname, and Trinidad
     and Tobago.

105 See Ed Pilkington, "Caribbean Nations Prepare Demand For Slavery
     Reparations," March 9, 2014, https://www.theguardian.com/world/2014/
     mar/09/caribbean-nations-demand-slavery-reparations. Benedict
     Cumberbatch's ancestor is Abraham Parry Cumberbatch (1784–1840). For
     more information on him, see *Legacies of British Slave-Ownership*, https://
     www.ucl.ac.uk/lbs/person/view/2146630501.

106 The ten-point CARICOM plan of reparations was reproduced in
     "Ten-Point Program for Reparations for African Americans in the United
     States," *The Black Scholar* 44, no. 3 (2014): 68. See also, "CARICOM
     Nations Unanimously Approve 10 Point Plan for Slavery Reparations,"
     Leigh Day, March 2014, https://www.leighday.co.uk/News/2014/

March–2014/CARICOM-nations-unanimously-approve–10-point-
plan.

107 "Cuba apoya en ONU reclamo caribeño de compensación por esclavitud,"
    Granma: Órgano Oficial del Comité Central del Partido Comunista de Cuba,
    March 26, 2014, 1.

108 "David Cameron Rules Out Slavery Reparation During Jamaica Visit," *BBC
    News*, September 30, 2015, http://www.bbc.com/news/uk–34401412.

Epilogue: Unfinished Struggle

1   The Movement for Black Lives, *A Vision for Black Lives: Policy Demands for
    Black Power, Freedom & Justice*, https://policy.m4bl.org/reparations/.

2   Yamiche Alcindor, "Black Lives Matter Coalition Makes Demands as
    Campaign Heats Up," *New York Times*, August 1, 2016, http://www.nytimes.
    com/2016/08/02/us/politics/black-lives-matter-campaign.html.

3   Ben Norton, "Black Lives Matter Activists Launch Abolition Square
    Encampment, Demanding Reparations, End to Broken Windows Policing,"
    Salon, August 5, 2016, http://www.salon.com/2016/08/05/black-lives-matter-
    activists-launch-abolition-square-encampment-demanding-reparations-end-to-
    broken-windows-policing/.

4   John McWhorter, "Black Lives Matter is 'Woke' to Old Problems—But Still
    Sleeping on Solutions," *New York Times*, August 9, 2016, https://www.
    washingtonpost.com/posteverything/wp/2016/08/09/black-lives-matter-and-
    the-limits-of-being-woke/?utm_term=.f81668960eae.

5   In 2015, an organization titled "Universities Studying Slavery" (USS) was
    created. The organization gathers Brown University, Emory University,
    Georgetown University, University of North Carolina, University of
    Mississippi, Hollins University, Clemson University, University of South
    Carolina, the College of William and Mary, University of Virginia, and
    other universities in the state of Virginia, several of which created special
    commissions to study their ties with slavery and produced reports resulting
    from these investigations. Other universities such as Harvard University,
    Princeton University, Yale University, Columbia University, and University of
    Maryland also recognized their ties with slavery.

6   See Thomas Richard Murphy, "'Negroes of Ours': Jesuit Slaveholding in
    Maryland, 1717–1838" (Ph.D. dissertation, University of Connecticut, 1998).

7   "Report of the Working Group on Slavery, Memory, and Reconciliation to the
    President of Georgetown University, Washington, DC," Summer 2016, xi.

8   "Report of the Working Group on Slavery, Memory, and Reconciliation," 28.

9   See Rachel L. Swarns, "Georgetown University Plans Steps to Atone for Slave
    Past," *New York Times*, September 1, 2016, http://www.nytimes.
    com/2016/09/02/us/slaves-georgetown-university.html?_r=0.

10 Terry L. Jones, "Georgetown Slave Descendants Ask University for Help
    Raising $1 Billion For Foundation," *The Advocate*, September 10, 2016,

http://www.theadvocate.com/baton_rouge/news/communities/westside/
article_814c2770–76aa–11e6-a126-db8d1b99098e.html.

11 Susan Svrluga, "Descendants of Slaves Sold to Benefit Georgetown Call for a
$1 Billion Foundation for Reconciliation," *Washington Post*, September 9,
2016, https://www.washingtonpost.com/news/grade-point/wp/2016/09/08/
descendants-of-slaves-sold-by-georgetown-call-for-a–1-billion-foundation-for-
reconciliation/.

12 United Nations General Assembly, *Report of the Working Group of Experts on
People of African Descent on Its Mission to the United States of America*,
August 18, 2016, Article 68, 16.

13 *Report of the Working Group of Experts on People of African Descent on Its
Mission to the United States of America*, Article 91, 19.

14 *Report of the Working Group of Experts on People of African Descent on Its
Mission to the United States of America*, Article 94, 20.

BIBLIOGRAPHY

Archives and libraries consulted

Archives Nationales, Porto-Novo, Republic of Benin
Archivo General de la Nación, Mexico City, Mexico
Archivo Nacional Histórico, Santiago de Chile, Chile
Arquivo do Estado do Rio Grande do Sul, Porto Alegre, RS, Brazil
Beinecke Rare Book & Manuscript Library, Yale University, New Haven, CT,
    United States
Biblioteca Digital do Senado Federal, Brasília, DF, Brazil
Biblioteca Nacional do Rio de Janeiro, Rio de Janeiro, RJ, Brazil
Bibliothèque Nationale de France, Paris, France
Connecticut Historical Society, Hartford, CT, United States
Fundação Casa de Rui Barbosa, Rio de Janeiro, RJ, Brazil
Gale Cengage Learning, Archives Unbound, online
Harvard University Archives, Harvard University, Cambridge, MA, United States
Instituto Histórico e Geográfico Brasileiro, Rio de Janeiro, RJ, Brazil
Library of Congress, Manuscript Division, Washington, DC, United States
Moorland-Spingarn Research Center, Howard University, Washington, DC, United
    States
The National Archives, London, United Kingdom
National Archives, Washington, DC, United States
New York Public Library, New York, NY, United States
New York State Archives, New York, NY, United States
Schlesinger Library on the History of Women in America, Harvard University,
    Boston, MA, United States
Widener Library, Collection Development Department, Harvard College Library,
    Harvard University, Cambridge, MA, United States

Periodical publications cited

Afro-American (United States)
The Advocate (United States)
The Atlantic (United States)
The Colored American: A National Negro Newspaper (United States)
Correio Braziliense (Brazil)
The Crisis (United States)

Granma: Órgano Oficial del Comité Central del Partido Comunista de Cuba (Cuba)
Diário Oficial (Brazil)
Diario Oficial (Colombia)
Diário Oficial do Estado de São Paulo (Brazil)
Estado de São Paulo (Brazil)
Folha de São Paulo (Brazil)
Frederick Douglass' Paper (United States)
The Guardian (United Kingdom)
Jornal das reparações (Brazil)
Jornal do Brasil (Brazil)
Jornal do Povo (Brazil)
Jornal do Senado (Brazil)
Journal Officiel (France)
La Nation (Republic of Benin)
Le Monde (France)
Leigh Day (United Kingdom)
The Liberator (United States)
Los Angeles Sentinel (United States)
The New Amsterdam News (United States)
New Pittsburgh Courier (United States)
New-York Daily Tribune (United States)
New World Review (United States)
New York Evening Post (United States)
New York Times (United States)
Nossa História (Brazil)
O Abolicionista: Orgão da Sociedade Brasileira Contra a Escravidão (Brazil)
O Globo (Brazil)
Philadelphia Tribune (United States)
The Philadelphia Tribune Life (United States)
The Pittsburgh Courier (United States)
Playboy (United States)
Princeton Alumni Weekly (United States)
Radical Paulistano (Brazil)
Reading Eagle (United States)
The Register-Guard (United States)
Registro Oficial (Ecuador)
Richmond Times Dispatch (United States)
The Washington Herald (United States)
The Washington Times (United States)
The Washington Post (United States)
Zero Hora (Brazil)

Printed primary sources

Abdullah vs. United States, 2003 US Dist. LEXIS 5129 (2003) (N. D. Connecticut).
"An Act for the Gradual Abolition of Slavery," February 15, 1804, Acts 28th,
    General Assembly, 2n sitting, ch. CIII, 251–254.

Acts and Laws Passed by the General Assembly of the State of Connecticut, The Public Laws of the State of Connecticut. Hartford: Hudson and Goodwin, 1808.

Barbosa, Rui. *Obras completas de Rui Barbosa*, vol. VI, tome 1, 1879: Discursos parlamentares, Câmara dos Deputados. Rio de Janeiro: Ministério da Educação e Saúde, 1943.

Barbosa, Rui. *Obras completas de Rui Barbosa*, vol. XVII, tome 2, 1890: Atos legislativos. Decisões ministeriais e circulares. Rio de Janeiro: Fundação Casa de Rui Barbosa, 1943.

Beaumont, Augustus Hardin. *Compensation to Slave Owners Fairly Considered in an Appeal to the Common Sense of the People of England.* London: Effingham Wilson, 1826.

Brinch, Boyrereau and Benjamin Franklin Prentiss. *The Blind African Slave, or Memoirs of Boyrereau Brinch, Nick-Named Jeffrey Brace: Containing an Account of the Kingdom of Bow-Woo, in the Interior of Africa; with the Climate and Natural Productions, Laws, and Customs Peculiar to That Place.* St. Albans: Harry Whitney 1810.

Brown University. *Slavery and Justice.* Providence, RI: Brown University, 2007.

"Case Concerning the Factory of Chorzów (Claim for Indemnity), (Jurisdiction)." Publications of the Permanent Court of International Justice, Series A, No. 9, July 26, 1927, 1–34.

Cato vs. United States, 70 F. 3d 1103 (9th Cir. 1995).

Civil Rights Congress. *We Charge Genocide: The Historic Petition to the United Nations for Relief From a Crime of the United States Government Against the Negro People.* New York: Civil Rights Congress, 1951.

Coleccion de Leyes y Decretos del Congreso General de los Estados-Unidos Mejicanos, en los años de 1829 y 1830. Mexico: Imprenta de Galvan, 1831.

Colleção das Leis do Império do Brasil de 1826. Rio de Janeiro: Typographia Nacional, 1880.

Colleção das Leis do Império do Brazil de 1831. Vol. 1, part I. Rio de Janeiro: Typographia Nacional, 1875.

Commissão estadual da verdade da escravidão negra no Brasil, Ordem dos Advogados do Brasil, Rio de Janeiro. "Relatório parcial da Comissão estadual da verdade da escravidão negra no Brasil, OAB, RJ," Rio de Janeiro, 2015.

Confedereção Abolicionista. "Abolição immediata e sem indemnisação." Pamphleto no. 1. Rio de Janeiro: Typ. Central, de Evaristo R. da Costa, 1883.

Constitución de la República de Ecuador, *Registro Oficial*, no. 449, Quito, October 20, 2008.

Constitución Política de Colombia de 1991, Actualizada con los Actos Legislativos hasta 2010. Bogotá: Imprenta Nacional de Colombia, 2010.

Constitución Politica del Estado de Chile, Promulgada en 29 de Diciembre de 1823. Santiago de Chile, Imprenta Nacional, 1823.

Constituição da República Federativa do Brasil de 1988: Texto consticional promulgado em 5 de outubro de 1988, com as alterações adotadas pelas Emendas Constitucionais nos. 1/1992 a 68/2011, pelo Decreto Legislativo no. 186/2008 e pelas Emandas Constitucionais de Revisão nos. 1 a 6/1994. Brasília: Câmara dos Deputados, Edições da Câmara, 2012.

Cugoano, Quobna Ottobah and Vincent Carretta. *Thoughts and Sentiments on the Evil of Slavery.* New York: Penguin, 1999.

Dalzel, Archibald. *The History of Dahomy: An Inland Kingdom of Africa*. London: Elibron Classics, 2005 [1793].

Dávalos, Juan E. Hernandez y, ed. *Colección de documentos para la historia de la guerra de independencia de Mexico de 1808 a 1821*, vol. II. México: Biblioteca de "El Sistema Postal de la República Mexicana," José María Sandoval, Impresor, 1878.

Debret, Jean-Baptiste. *Voyage pittoresque et historique au Brésil ou séjour d'un artiste français au Brésil depuis 1816 jusqu'en 1831 inclusivement*. Paris: Firmin Didot Frères, 1834–1839.

"Décret relatif à l'abolition de l'esclavage dans les colonies et possessions françaises du 27 avril 1848." *Bulletin des Lois de la République Française, Xe Série, Premier Semestre de 1848 (2e partie), contenant les lois, décrets et arrêtes d'intérêt public et général publiés depuis le 24 février jusqu'au 30 juin*. Paris: Imprimerie Nationale, 1848.

Directoria Geral de Estatística. *Synopse do recenseamento de 31 de dezembro de 1890*. Rio de Janeiro: Officina da estatística, Imprimerie du Bureau de Statistique, 1898.

Douglass, Frederick. *Oration, Delivered in Corinthian Hall, Rochester, by Frederick Douglass, July 5th, 1852*. Rochester: Lee, Mann & Co., 1852.

Duvergier, J. B. *Collection complète des lois, décrets, ordonnances, réglemens et avis du Conseil d'État (de 1788 à 1824 inclusivement, par ordre chronologique)*, vol 4. Paris: Directeur de l'Administration, 1840.

Elemento servil Parecer e projecto de lei apresentados á Camara dos srs. deputados na sessão de 16 de agosto de 1870 pela Commissão especial nomeada pela mesma Camara em 24 de maio de 1870. Rio de Janeiro: Typographia nacional, 1870.

Equiano, Olaudah and Vincent Carretta. *The Interesting Narrative and Other Writings*. New York: Penguin, 2003.

État détaillé des liquidations opérées par la Commission chargée de répartir l'indemnité attribuée aux anciens colons de Saint-Domingue, en exécution de la loi du 30 avril 1826. 6 volumes. Paris, 1828–1834.

Farmer-Paellmann vs. FleetBoston et al., 02cv1862, United States District Court for the Eastern District of New York, March 26, 2002.

Federal Writers' Project of the Works Progress Administration for the State of Arkansas. *Slave Narratives: A Folk History of Slavery in the United States with Interviews with Former Slaves*. Volume I, Arkansas Narratives, part 1. Washington, DC: Library of Congress, 1941.

Federal Writers' Project of the Works Progress Administration for the State of Arkansas. *Slave Narratives: A Folk History of Slavery in the United States with Interviews with Former Slaves*. Volume II, Arkansas Narratives, part 2. Washington, DC: Library of Congress, 1941.

Federal Writers' Project of the Works Progress Administration for the State of Arkansas. *Slave Narratives: A Folk History of Slavery in the United States with Interviews with Former Slaves*. Volume II, Arkansas Narratives, part 6. Washington, DC: Library of Congress, 1941.

Federal Writers' Project of the Works Progress Administration for the State of Texas. *Slave Narratives: A Folk History of Slavery in the United States with Interviews with Former Slaves*. Volume XVI, Texas Narratives, part 2. Washington, DC: Library of Congress, 1941.

Federal Writers' Project of the Works Progress Administration for the State of Florida. *Slave Narratives: A Folk History of Slavery in the United States with Interviews with Former Slaves.* Volume III, Florida Narratives. Washington, DC: Library of Congress, 1941.

Federal Writers' Project of the Works Progress Administration for the State of South Carolina. *Slave Narratives: A Folk History of Slavery in the United States with Interviews with Former Slaves.* Volume XIV, South Carolina Narratives, part 1. Washington, DC: Library of Congress, 1941.

Forbes, Frederick E. *Dahomey and the Dahomans: Being the Journals of Two Missions to the King of Dahomey, and Residence at His Capital.* London: Longman, Brown, Green, and Longmans, 1851.

Foreign Claims Settlement Commission of the United States. "2011 Annual Report." Washington, DC: US Department of Justice, 2011.

Great Britain. *An Act for the Abolition of Slavery throughout the British Colonies; for Promoting the Industry of the Manumitted Slaves; and for Compensating the Persons Hitherto Entitled to the Services of Such Slaves, 28 August 1833.* Edinburgh: Sir D. Hunter Blair and M. T. Bruce, 1833.

Great Britain. *Debates in Parliament, Session 1833 on the Resolutions and Bill for the Abolition of Slavery in the British Colonies.* London: Printed by Maurice & Co., 1834.

Hening, William Waller, ed. *The Statutes at Large Being a Collection of All the Laws of Virginia from the First Session of the Legislature in the Year 1619, volume 3.* New York: R. & W. & G. Bartow, 1823.

Hening, William Waller, ed. *The Statutes at Large; Being a Collection of All the Laws of Virginia from the First Session of the Legislature, in the Year 1619, volume 11.* Richmond: J. & G. Cochran, 1821.

Hill, Robert A. ed. *The Marcus Garvey and Universal Negro Improvement Association Papers.* Volume I. Berkeley: University of California Press, 1983.

Hill, Robert A. ed. *The Marcus Garvey and Universal Negro Improvement Association Papers.* Volume VII. Berkeley: University of California Press, 1990.

Hill, Robert A. ed. *The Marcus Garvey and Universal Negro Improvement Association Papers.* Volume V. Berkeley: University of California Press, 1986.

Hill, Robert A. ed. *The Marcus Garvey and Universal Negro Improvement Association Papers.* Volume IV. Berkeley: University of California Press, 1983.

Hurdle vs. FleetBoston, CGC-02-412, 388. Supreme Court, San Francisco, CA, 2003.

Jacobs, Harriet. *Incidents in the Life of a Slave Girl.* New York: Barnes and Noble Classics, 2005.

King, Martin Luther, Jr. *Why We Can't Wait.* Boston, MA: Beacon Press, 2010.

"L'ordonnance de Charles X du 17 avril 1825." *Outre-mers* 90, nos. 340–341 (2003): 249.

"Ley 70 de 1993: Por la cual se desarrolla el artículo transitorio 55 de la Constitución Política." *Diario Oficial,* no. 4.013, August 31, 1993.

"Ley de Cuatro de Julio de 1870 Sobre Abolición de la Esclavitud y Reglamento para su ejeucución en las islas de Cuba y Puerto Rico." Habana: Imprenta del Gobierno y Capitania general por S. M, 1872.

"Ley no. 2006–46: Ley de los Derechos Colectivos de los Pueblos Negros o Afroecuátorianos." *Registro Oficial* no. 275, Quito, May 22, 2006.

Lemos, Miguel. *O Pozitivismo e a Escravidão Moderna Trechos extrahidos das obras de Augusto Comte, seguidos de documentos positiviztas relativos a questão da escravatura no Brasil e precedidos de uma introdução por Miguel Lemos Prezidente Perpetuo da Sociedade Pozitivista do Rio de Janeiro.* Rio de Janeiro: Sede da Sociedade Pozitivista, 1884.

Lovejoy, Paul E. and Robin Law. *The Biography of Mahommah Gardo Baquaqua: His Passage from Slavery to Freedom in African and America.* Princeton: Markus Wiener Publishers, 2003.

Madiou, Thomas. *Histoire d'Haïti*, vol. 6. Port-au-Prince: Éditions Henri Deschamps, 1988.

Madiou, Thomas. *Histoire d'Haïti*, vol. 7. Port-au-Prince: Éditions Henri Deschamps, 1988.

"Malheiro, A. M. Perdigão. Illegitimidade da propriedade constituida sobre o escravo. Natureza da mesma. Abolição da escravidão; em que termos," Discurso pronunciado na sessão magna do Instituto dos Advogados Brasileiros em 7 de Setembro de 1863 pelo seu president Dr. A. M. Perdigão Malheiro. Rio de Janeiro: Typographia de Quirino e Irmão, 1863.

Malheiro, A. M. Perdigão. *Discurso proferido na sessão da câmara temporária de 12 de julho de 1871 sobre a proposta do governo para reforma do estado servil.* Rio de Janeiro: Typ. Imp. E Const. de J. Villeneuve & C., 1871.

Malheiro, Agostinho Marques Perdigão. *Escravidão no Brasil: Ensaio Histórico-Jurídico-Social.* 3 vols. Rio de Janeiro: Typographia Nacional, 1866.

"Manifesto da Sociedade Brasileira Contra a Escravidão." Rio de Janeiro, Typographia de G. Leuzinger & Filhos, 1880.

Mascarenhas, José Freire de Montarroyos. *Relaçam da Embayxada, que o poderoso Rey de Angome Kiayy Chiri Broncom, Senhor dos dilatadissimos Sertões de Guiné mandou ao Illustrissimo e Excellentissimo Senhor D. Luiz Peregrino de Ataide, Conde de Atouguia, Senhor das Villas de Atouguia, Peniche, Cernache, Monforte, Vilhaens, Lomba, e Paço da Ilha Dezerta, Cõmendador das Cõmendas de Santa Maria de Adaufe, e Villa velha de Rodam, na Ordem de Christo, do Conselho de Sua Magestade, Governador, e Capitão General, que foy do Reyno de Algarve & actualmente Vice-Rey do Estado do Brasil: pedindo a amizade, e aliança do muito alto; e poderoso Senhor Rey de Portugal Nosso Senhor/escrita por J. F. M. M.* Lisboa: Na Officina de Francisco da Silva, anno de 1751.

McCord, David J. ed. *The Statutes at Large of South Carolina, Containing the Acts Relating to Charleston, Courts, Slaves, and Rivers,* vol. 7. Columbia, SC: A. S. Johnson, 1840.

Moore, Audley M. *Why Reparations? Reparations is the Battle Cry for the Economic, and Social Freedom of More than 25 Million Descendants of American Slaves.* N.p., 1963.

"Mundum del bando de Miguel Hidalgo aboliendo la esclavitud, Valladoid, 18 octubre de 1810," *Boletín del Archivo General de la Nación* 6, no. 17 (2007): 143–145.

Norris, Robert. "A Journey to the Court of Bossa Ahadee, King of Dahomey, in the Year of 1772." In Archibald Dalzel, *The History of Dahomy: An Inland Kingdom of Africa.* London: Elibron Classics, 2005 [1793].

Northup, Solomon. *Twelve Years a Slave: Narrative of Solomon Northup, A Citizen of New-York, Kidnapped in Washington City in 1841, and Rescued in 1853,*

From a Cotton Plantation Near the Red River, in Louisiana. Auburn, NY: Derby and Miller, 1854.

Obadele vs. United States, 52 Fed. Cl 432 (2002).

Oficina Nacional de Estadísticas. *Los censos de población y viviendas en Cuba, 1907–1953,* Anexo VII, Tablas seleccionadas, Censo de 1953. La Habana, 2007.

Peabody, Sue and Keila Grinberg. *Slavery, Freedom, and the Law in the Atlantic World: A Brief History with Documents.* Boston, MA: Bedford/St. Martins, 2007.

Pires, Vicente Ferreira. *Viagem de África em o Reino de Dahomé escrita pelo Padre Vicente Ferreira Pires no ano de 1800 e até o presente inédita.* São Paulo, Companhia Editora Nacional, 1957.

Prince, Mary. *The History of Mary Prince.* New York: Penguin, 2000.

Proceedings of the National Emigration Convention of Colored People Held at Cleveland, Ohio, on Thursday, Friday, and Saturday, the 24th, 25th, and 26th August 1854. Pittsburgh: A. A. Anderson, 1854.

Recenseamento do Brazil em 1872. Vol. 1. Rio de Janeiro: Typ. G. Leuzinger, 1874.

"Report of the Working Group on Slavery, Memory, and Reconciliation to the President of Georgetown University." Washington, DC, Summer 2016.

"Return of the Whole Number of Persons within Several Districts of the United States, According to 'An Act Providing for the Enumeration of the Inhabitants of the United States,' Passed March the First, One Thousand Seven Hundred and Ninety-One." Philadelphia: Childs And Swaine, 1793.

Santos, Luis Alvares dos. *A emancipação: Ligeiras e decisivas considerações sobre o total acabamento da escravidão sem o menor prejuízo dos proprietários.* Bahia: Typographia do Correio da Bahia, 1871.

Silva, José Bonifacio d'Andrada e. "Representação à Assembléia Geral Constituinte e Legislativa do Império do Brasil sobre a escravatura." Paris: Firmin Didot, 1825.

Smith, Venture. *A Narrative of the Life and Adventures of Venture Smith, A Native of Africa: but Resident about Sixty Years in the United States of America. Related by Himself.* New London, CT: Holt, 1798.

"Ten-Point Program for Reparations for African Americans in the United States." *The Black Scholar* 44, no. 3 (2014): 68–70.

The Parliamentary Debates from the Year 1803 to the Present Time. Vol. XXXII. London: T. C. Hansard, 1816.

Thirteenth Annual Report of the State Corporation Commission of Virginia for the Year Ending December 31, 1915, General Report. Richmond: Davis Bottom, Superintendent Public Printing, 1916.

Truth, Sojourner. *Narrative of Sojourner Truth.* New York: Barnes and Noble Classics, 2005.

Turner, Henry McNeal. "Justice or Emigration Should Be Our Watchword," in *Integration vs. Separatism: The Colonial Period to 1945,* edited by Marcus D. Pohlmann, African American Political Thought, vol. 5, 91–100. New York: Routledge, 2003.

United Nations General Assembly. *Draft Articles on Responsibility of States for Internationally Wrongful Acts with Commentaries.* New York: United Nations, 2001.

United Nations General Assembly. *Report of the Working Group of Experts on People of African Descent on Its Mission to the United States of America.* New York: United Nations, August, 18, 2016.

United Nations. "Responsibility of States for Internationally Wrongful Acts."
    Annex to General Assembly resolution 56/83 of 12 December 2001, 2005.
United States. *Statutes at Large Containing Laws and Concurrent Resolutions
    Enacted During the Second Session of the Eightieth Congress of the United
    States of America, 1948*. vol. 62. Washington, DC: Government Printing Office,
    1948.
United States. *Statutes at Large, Treaties, and Proclamations of the United States of
    America, from December 1863 to December 1865*. vol. 13. Boston, MA: Little,
    Brown, and Company, 1866.
United Nations. *World Conference Against Racism, Racial Discrimination,
    Xenophobia and Related Intolerance: Durban, South Africa, 31 August–7
    September 2001*. New York: United Nations Department of Public Information,
    2001.
Vaughan, Walter R. *Vaughan's "Freedmen's Pension Bill: Being an Appeal in Behalf
    of Men Released from Slavery, A Plea for American Freedmen and a Rational
    Proposition to Grant Pensions to Persons of Color Emancipated From Slavery."*
    Chicago, 1891.
Vital Records of Medford, Massachusetts, to the Year 1850. Boston, MA: New
    England Historic Genealogical Society, 1907.
Walker, David. *Walker's Appeal in Four Articles Together With a Preamble to the
    Colored Citizens of the World, but in Particular and Very Expressly to Those of
    the United States of America, Written in Boston, in the State of Massachusetts,
    September 28th, 1820*. Boston, MA: Printed for the Author, 1829.

Printed secondary sources

Adderley, Rosanne Marion. *New Negroes From Africa: Slave Trade Abolition and
    Free African Settlement in the Nineteenth-Century Caribbean*. Bloomington:
    Indiana University Press, 2006.
Aiyetoro, Adjoa and Adrienne D. Davis. "Historic and Modern Social Movements
    for Reparations: The National Coalition for Reparations in America
    (N'COBRA) and its Antecedents." *Texas Wesleyan Law Review* 16, June 18
    (2010): 687–766.
Akinjogbin, I. A. *Dahomey and Its Neighbours*. Cambridge: Cambridge University
    Press, 1967.
Alberto, Paulina. *Terms of Inclusion: Black Intellectuals in Twentieth-Century
    Brazil*. Chapel Hill: University of North Carolina Press, 2011.
Albuquerque, Wlamyra. "'A vala comum da "raça emancipada': abolição e
    racialização no Brasil, breve comentário." *História Social*, no. 19 (2010):
    91–108.
Albuquerque, Wlamyra. *O jogo da dissimulação: Abolição e cidadania negra no
    Brasil*. São Paulo: Companhia das Letras, 2009.
Alencastro, Luiz Felipe de. "Continental Drift: The Independence of Brazil (1822),
    Portugal and Africa." In *From Slave Trade to Empire: Europe and the
    Colonisation of Black Africa, 1789s–1880s*, edited by Olivier Pétré-
    Grenouilleau, 98–109. London: Routledge, 2004.
Alencastro, Luiz Felipe de. *O trato dos viventes: formação do Brasil no Atlântico
    Sul*. São Paulo: Companhia das Letras, 2000.

Alonso, Angela. *Flores, votos e balas: o movimento abolicionista brasileiro (1868–1888)*. São Paulo: Companhia das Letras, 2015.

Alves, Claudete. *Negros: o Brasil nos deve milhões!: 120 anos de uma abolição inacabada*. São Paulo: Scortecci Editora, 2008.

Andrews, George Reid. *Afro-Latin America, 1800–2000*. New York: Oxford University Press, 2004.

Andrews, George Reid. *Blackness in the White Nation: A History of Afro-Uruguay*. Chapel Hill: University of North Carolina Press, 2010.

Andrews, George Reid. *Los afroargentinos de Buenos Aires*. Buenos Aires, Ediciones de la Flor, 1989.

Araujo, Ana Lucia, ed. *African Heritage and Memories of Slavery in Brazil and the South Atlantic World*. Amherst: Cambria Press, 2015.

Araujo, Ana Lucia. "Black Purgatory: Enslaved Women's Resistance in Nineteenth-Century Rio Grande do Sul, Brazil." *Slavery & Abolition* 36, no. 4 (2015): 568–585.

Araujo, Ana Lucia. *Brazil Through French Eyes: A Nineteenth-Century Artist in the Tropics*. Albuquerque: University of New Mexico Press, 2015.

Araujo, Ana Lucia. "Dahomey, Portugal, and Bahia: King Adandozan and the Atlantic Slave Trade." *Slavery & Abolition* 3, no. 1 (2012): 1–19.

Araujo, Ana Lucia. "History, Memory and Imagination: Na Agontimé, a Dahomean Queen in Brazil." In *Beyond Tradition: African Women and Cultural Spaces*, edited by Toyin Falola and Sati U. Fwatshak, 45–68. Trenton, NJ: Africa World Press, 2011.

Araujo, Ana Lucia. "Images, Artefacts and Myths: Reconstructing the Connections Between Brazil and the Kingdom of Dahomey." In *Living History: Encountering the Memory of the Heirs of Slavery*, edited by Ana Lucia Araujo, 180–202. Newcastle upon Tyne: Cambridge Scholars Publishing, 2009.

Araujo, Ana Lucia. *Public Memory of Slavery: Victims and Perpetrators in the South Atlantic*. Amherst: Cambria Press, 2010.

Araujo, Ana Lucia. *Shadows of the Slave Past: Memory, Heritage, and Slavery*. New York: Routledge, 2014.

Araujo, Ana Lucia. "Transnational Memory of Slave Merchants: Making the Perpetrators Visible in the Public Space." In *Politics of Memory: Making Slavery Visible in the Public Space*, edited by Ana Lucia Araujo, 15–34. New York: Routledge, 2012.

Araújo, Gisele Silva. "Tradição liberal, positivismo e pedagogia: A síntese derrotada de Rui Barbosa." *Perspectivas* 37 (2010): 113–144.

Aust, Anthony. *Handbook of International Law*. New York: Cambridge University Press, 2010.

Azevedo, Celia Maria Marinho de. *Abolicionismo: Estados Unidos e Brasil, uma história comparada, século XIX*. São Paulo: Annablume, 2003.

Azevedo, Celia Maria Marinho de. *Onda negra, medo branco: o negro no imaginário das elites, século XIX*. São Paulo: Annablume, 2004.

Azevedo, Elciene. *Orfeu de carapinha: a trajetória de Luiz Gama na imperial cidade de São Paulo*. Campinas: Editora da Universidade de Campinas, 1999.

Bailey, Anne C. *African Voices of the Atlantic Slave Trade: Beyond the Silence and the Shame*. Boston, MA: Beacon Press, 2005.

Baptist, Edward E. *The Half Has Never Been Told: Slavery and the Making of American Capitalism*. New York: Basic Books, 2014.

Barnard, Yanessa L. "Better Late than Never: A Takings Clause Solution to Reparations." In *Washington and Lee Journal of Civil Rights and Social Justice* 12, no. 1 (2005): 109–151.

Bascom, Lionel C., ed. *Voices of the African American Experience.* Westport: Greenwood Press, 2009, Vol. 1.

Baumgartner, Alice L. "Rethinking Abolition in Mexico." Paper presented in the Gilder Lehrman Center International Conference, October 30–31, 2015.

Bay, Edna G. *Wives of the Leopard: Gender, Politics, and Culture in the Kingdom of Dahomey.* Charlottesville: University of Virginia Press, 1998.

Beauvois, Frédérique. "Monnayer l'incalculable? L'indemnité de Saint-Domingue, entre approximations et bricolage." *Revue historique,* no. 655 (2010): 609–636.

Becker, Charles. "Note sur les chiffres de la traite atlantique française au XVIIIe siècle." *Cahiers d'études africaines* 26, no. 24 (1986): 633–679.

Becker, Marc. "Correa, Indigenous Movements, and the Writing of a New Constitution in Ecuador." *Latin American Perspectives* 38, no. 176 (2011): 47–62.

Beckert, Sven. *Empire of Cotton: A Global History.* New York: Alfred A. Knopf, 2014.

Beckles, Hilary McD. *Britain's Black Debt.* Kingston, Jamaica: University of West Indies Press, 2013.

Behrendt, Stephen D. Review of *Saltwater Slavery: A Middle Passage from Africa to American Diaspora* by Stephanie E. Smallwood. Cambridge, MA: Harvard University Press, 2008. *New West Indian Guide/Nieuwe West-Indische Gids* 83, no. 3/4 (2009): 300–302.

Bellagamba, Alice, Sandra E. Greene, and Martin A. Klein, eds. *African Voices on Slavery and the Slave Trade.* New York: Cambridge University Press, 2013.

Bergad, Laird W. *The Comparative Histories of Slavery in Brazil, Cuba, and the United States.* New York: Cambridge University Press, 2007.

Bergad, Laird W., Fe Iglesias García, and María del Carmen Barcia. *The Cuban Slave Market, 1790–1880.* New York: Cambridge University Press, 1995.

Berlin, Ira. *The Long Emancipation: The Demise of Slavery in the United States.* Cambridge, MA: Harvard University Press, 2015.

Berlin, Ira. *Many Thousands Gone: The First Two Centuries of Slavery in North America.* Cambridge, MA: Belknap Press of Harvard University Press, 1998.

Bernal, Beatriz, ed. *Las Constituciones de Cuba Republicana.* Miami, FL: Instituto y Biblioteca de la Libertad, 2003.

Berry, Mary Frances. "Reparations for Freedmen, 1890–1916: Fraudulent Practices or Justice Deferred." *Journal of Negro History* 57, no. 3 (1972): 219–230.

Berry, Mary Frances. *My Face Is Black Is True: Callie House and the Struggle for Ex-Slave Reparations.* New York: Alfred A. Knopf, 2005.

Bethell, Leslie. *The Abolition of the Brazilian Slave Trade: Britain, Brazil and the Slave Trade Question: 1807–1869.* New York: Cambridge University Press, 1970.

Bethell, Leslie and José Murilo de Carvalho, eds. *Joaquim Nabuco, British Abolitionists and the End of Slavery in Brazil: Correspondence 1880–1905.* London: Institute for the Study of the Americas, University of London, School of Advanced Study, 2009.

Biondi, Martha. "The Rise of the Reparations Movement." In *Redress for Historical Injustices in the United States: On Reparations for Slavery, Jim Crow, and Their Legacies*, edited by Michael T. Martin and Marilyn Yaquinto, 255–269. Durham, NC: Duke University Press, 2007.

Blackburn, Robin. *The American Crucible: Slavery, Emancipation, and Human Rights*. London: Verso, 2011.

Blancpain, François. "Note sur les 'dettes' de l'esclavage: le cas de l'indemnité payée par Haïti (1825–1883)." *Outre-mers* 90, no. 340–341 (2003): 241–245.

Borucki, Alex. *From Shipmates to Soldiers: Emerging Black Identities in the Río de La Plata*. Albuquerque: University of New Mexico Press, 2015.

Boxer, Charles R. *Salvador de Sá and the Struggle for Brazil and Angola, 1602–1654*. Oxford: Clarendon Press, 1957.

Brophy, Alfred L. *Reparations Pro & Con*. New York: Oxford University Press, 2006.

Brown, Christopher Leslie. *Moral Capital: Foundations of British Abolitionism*. Chapel Hill: University of North Carolina Press, 2006.

Brown, Vincent. *The Reaper's Garden: Death and Power in the World of Atlantic Slavery*. Cambridge, MA: Harvard University Press, 2008.

Burns, Robert I. and Samuel Parsons Scott. *Las Siete Partidas*, vol. 4. Philadelphia: University of Pittsburg Press, 2000.

Butler, Kim D. *Freedoms Given, Freedoms Won: Afro-Brazilians in Post-Abolition São Paulo and Salvador*. New Brunswick: Rutgers University Press, 2000.

Buxbaum, Richard M. "A Legal History of International Reparations." *Berkeley Journal of International Law* 23, no. 2 (2005): 314–346.

Campbell, James M. *Slavery on Trial: Race, Class, and Criminal Justice in Antebellum Richmond, Virginia*. Gainesville: University Press of Florida, 2007.

Candido, Mariana P. *An African Slaving Port and the Atlantic World: Benguela and Its Hinterland*. New York: Cambridge University Press, 2013.

Castilho, Celso T. *Slave Emancipation and Transformations in Brazilian Political Citizenship*. Pittsburgh: University of Pittsburgh Press, 2016.

Castilho, Celso and Camillia Cowling. "Funding Freedom, Popularizing Politics: Abolitionism and Local Emancipation Funds in 1880s Brazil." *Luso-Brazilian Review* 47, no. 1 (2010): 89–120.

Castro, Hebe Maria Mattos de. *Das cores do silêncio: os significados da liberdade no sudeste escravista Brasil século XIX*. Rio de Janeiro: Arquivo Nacional, 1995.

Chalhoub, Sidney. *A força da escravidão: Ilegalidade e costume no Brasil oitocentista*. São Paulo: Companhia das Letras, 2012.

Chivallon, Christine. *L'esclavage, du souvenir à la mémoire: Contribution à une anthropologie de la Caraïbe*. Paris: Karthala, 2012.

Coates, Timothy Joel. *Convicts and Orphans: Forced and State-Sponsored Colonizers in the Portuguese Empire, 1550–1755*. Stanford: Stanford University Press, 2001.

Coates, Timothy Joel. "Exiles and Orphans: Forced and State-Sponsored Colonizers in the Portuguese Empire, 1550–1720." Ph.D. dissertation University of Minnesota, 1993.

Conrad, Robert. *Abolitionism: The Brazilian Antislavery Struggle*. Urbana: University of Illinois Press, 1977.

Conrad, Robert. *The Destruction of Brazilian Slavery, 1850–1888*. Los Angeles: University of California Press, 1972.

Costa, Emília Viotti da. *A Abolição*. São Paulo: Editora da Universidade Estadual de São Paulo, 2008.

Cowling, Camillia. *Conceiving Freedom: Women of Color, Gender, and the Abolition of Slavery in Havana and Rio de Janeiro*. Chapel Hill: University of North Carolina Press, 2013.

Cruz, Guillermo Feliú. *La abolición de la esclavitud en Chile*. Santiago de Chile: Editorial Universitaria, 1973.

Curtin, Philip D. *Africa Remembered: Narratives by West Africans From the Era of the Slave Trade*. Prospect Heights: Waveland Press, 1997.

Curtin, Philip D. *The Atlantic Slave Trade: A Census*. Madison: University of Wisconsin Press, 1969.

Curto, José C. "A Quantitative Reassessment of the Legal Portuguese Slave Trade From Luanda, Angola, 1710–1830." *African Economic History* 20 (1992): 16–25.

Daibert, Robert, Jr. *Isabel a "redentora" dos escravos: uma história da princesa entre olhares negros e brancos, 1846–1988*. Florianópolis: Editora da Universidade Federal de Santa Catarina, 2004.

Dantas, Carolina Vianna. "Monteiro Lopes (1867–1910), um 'líder da raça negra,' na capital da República." *Afro-Ásia* 41 (2010): 167–209.

Dantas, Mariana L. R. *Black Townsmen: Urban Slavery and Freedom in the Eighteenth-Century Americas*. New York: Palgrave Macmillan, 2008.

Davidson, James M. "Encountering the Ex-Slave Reparations Movement from the Grave: The National Industrial Council and National Industrial Council and National Liberty Party, 1901–1907." *Journal of African American History* 97, no. 1–2 (2012): 13–38.

Davis, David Brion. *Inhuman Bondage: The Rise and Fall of Slavery in the New World*. New York: Oxford University Press, 2006.

Domingues, Petrônio. "Vai ficar tudo preto: Monteiro Lopes e a cor na política." *Novos Estudos* 95 (2013): 59–95.

Domingues, Petrônio. *A nova abolição*. São Paulo: Selo Negro Edições, 2008.

Draper, Nicholas. "Possessing People: Absentee Slave-Owners Within British Society." In Catherine Hall, Nicholas Draper, Keith McClelland, Katie Donington, and Rachel Lang, *Legacies of British Slave-Ownership: Colonial Slavery and the Formation of Victorian Britain*, 34–77. Cambridge: Cambridge University Press, 2014.

Draper, Nicholas. *The Price of Emancipation: Slave-Ownership, Compensation and British Society at the End of Slavery*. Cambridge: Cambridge University Press, 2010.

Drescher, Seymour. *Abolition: A History of Slavery and Antislavery*. New York: Cambridge University Press, 2009.

Dubois, Laurent. *Avengers of the New World: The Story of the Haitian Revolution*. Cambridge, MA: Belknap Press of Harvard University Press, 2004.

Dubois, Laurent. *Haiti: The Aftershocks of History*. New York: Metropolitan Books, 2012.

Dunn, Richard S. *A Tale of Two Plantations: Slave Life and Labor in Jamaica and Virginia*. Cambridge, MA: Harvard University Press, 2014.

Eltis, David. *Economic Growth and the Ending of the Transatlantic Slave Trade*. New York: Oxford University Press, 1987.

Eltis, David and Lawrence C. Jennings. "Trade Between Western Africa and the Atlantic World in the Pre-Colonial Era." *American Historical Review* 43, no. 4 (1988): 936–959.

Engerman, Stanley L. and B. W. Higman, "The Demographic Structure of the Caribbean Slave Societies in the Eighteenth and Nineteenth Centuries." In *General History of the Caribbean*. Vol. 3: *The Slave Societies of the Caribbean*, edited by Franklin Knight, 45–104. London: UNESCO Publications, Macmillan Education, 1997.

Eugène, Itazienne. "La normalisation des relations franco-haïtiennes (1825–1838)." *Outremers* 90, no. 340–341 (2003): 139–154.

Ewing, Adam. *The Age of Garvey: How a Jamaican Activist Created a Mass Movement and Changed Global Black Politics*. Princeton: Princeton University Press, 2014.

Fage, John Donnelly. "The Effect of the Export Slave Trade on African Populations." In *The Population Factor in African Studies*, edited by Richard Rathbone and Rowland Percy Moss, 15–23. London: University of London Press, 1975.

Fage, John Donnelly. "Slavery and the Slave Trade in the Context of West African History." *Journal of African History* 10, no. 3 (1969): 393–404.

Farmer, Ashley. "Reframing African American Women's Grassroots Organizing: Audley Moore and the Universal Association of Ethiopian Women, 1957–1963." *The Journal of African American History* 101, no. 1–2 (2016): 69–96.

Faulkner, Carol. *Women's Radical Reconstruction*. Philadelphia: University of Pennsylvania Press, 2004.

Ferraro, Alceu Ravanello. "Educação, classe, gênero e voto no Brasil imperial: Lei Saraiva—1881." *Educar em Revista*, no. 50 (2013): 181–206.

Ferraro. Alceu Ravanello and Michele de Leão. "Lei Saraiva (1881): Dos argumentos invocados pelos liberais para a exclusão dos analfabetos do direito de voto." *Educação Unisinos* 16, no. 3 (2012): 241–250.

Ferreira, Ligia Fonseca. *Com a palavra, Luiz Gama: poemas, artigos, cartas máximas*. São Paulo: Imprensa Oficial, 2011.

Ferreira, Roquinaldo. *Cross-Cultural Exchange in the Atlantic World: Angola and Brazil During the Era of the Slave Trade*. New York: Cambridge University Press, 2012.

Ferrer, Ada. *Freedom's Mirror: Cuba and Haiti in the Age of Revolution*. New York: Cambridge University Press, 2014.

Ferrer, Ada. *Insurgent Cuba: Race, Nation, and Revolution, 1868–1898*. Chapel Hill: University of North Carolina Press, 1999.

Fick, Carolyn E. *The Making of Haiti: The Saint Domingue Revolution From Below*. Knoxville: University of Tennessee Press, 1990.

Figueroa, Luis A. *Sugar, Slavery, and Freedom in Nineteenth-Century Puerto Rico*. Chapel Hill: University of North Carolina Press, 2005.

Finkenbine, Roy E. "Belinda's Petition: Reparations for Slavery in Revolutionary Massachusetts." *The William and Mary Quarterly* 64, no. 1 (2007): 95–104.

Finkenbine, Roy E. "Wendell Phillips and the 'The Negro's Claim': A Neglected Reparations Document." *Massachusetts Historical Review* 7 (2005): 105–119.

Finkenbine, Roy. "'Who Will Pay for Their Sufferings?': New York Abolitionists and the Campaign to Compensate Solomon Northup." *New York History* 95, no. 4 (2014): 637–646.

Fleming, Walter L. *Ex-Slaves Pension Frauds*. Baton Rouge: Ortlier's Printing House, 1910.

Flory, Céline. *De l'esclavage à la liberté forcée: histoire des travailleurs africains engagés dans la Caraïbe française au XIXe siècle*. Paris: Karthala, 2015.

Flory, Céline. "New Africans in the Post-Slavery French West Indies and Guiana: Close Encounters? (1857–1889)." In *Paths of the Atlantic Slave Trade: Interactions, Identities, and Images*, edited by Ana Lucia Araujo: 109–130. Amherst: Cambria Press, 2011.

Foner, Eric. *The Fiery Trial: Abraham Lincoln and American Slavery*. New York: W. W. Norton, 2011.

Foner, Eric. *Reconstruction: America's Unfinished Revolution, 1863–1877*. New York: Harper Collins, 2014.

Forman, James. *The Making of Black Revolutionaries*. Seattle: University of Washington Press, 1997.

Forsdick, Charles. "Compensating for the Past: Debating Reparations for Slavery in Contemporary France." *Contemporary French and Francophone Studies* 19, no. 4 (2015): 420–429.

Forsdick, Charles. "Haiti and France: Settling the Debts of the Past." In *Politics and Power in Haiti*, edited by Kate Quinn and Paul Sutton, 141–160. New York: Palgrave Macmillan 2013.

Fraga, Walter. "Migrações, itinerários e esperança de mobilidade social no Recôncavo baiano após a Abolição." In *Política, instituições e personagens da Bahia (1850–1930)*, edited by Jefferson Bacelar and Cláudio Pereira, 43–71. Salvador: Editora da Universidade Federal da Bahia, 2013.

Fuente, Alejandro de la. *A Nation for All: Race, Inequality and Politics in Twentieth Century Cuba*. Chapel Hill: University of North Carolina Press, 2001.

Fuente, Alejandro de la and Ariela Gross. "Comparative Studies of Law, Slavery, and Race in the Americas." *Annual Review of Law and Social Science* 6 (2010): 469–485.

Furtado, Júnia Ferreira. "The Eighteenth-Century Luso-Brazilian Journey to Dahomey: West Africa Through a Scientific Lens." *Atlantic Studies: Global Currents* 11, no. 2 (2014): 256–276.

Gaffield, Julia. *Haitian Connections: Recognition After the Revolution in the Atlantic World*. Chapel Hill: University of North Carolina Press, 2015.

García, Oscar Almario. "Reparaciones contemporáneas: de la Memoria de la Esclavitud al cuestionamiento de la exclusión social y el racismo." In *Afro-reparaciones: Memorias de la Esclavitud y Justicia Reparativa para negros, afrocolombianos y raizales*, edited by Claudia Mosquera Rosero-Labbé, and Luiz Claudio Barcelos, 183–212. Bogotá: Universidad Nacional de Colombia, Observatorio del Caribe Colombiano, 2017.

Gellman, Daniel Nathaniel. *Emancipating New York: The Politics of Slavery and Freedom, 1777–1827*. Baton Rouge: Louisiana State University Press, 2008.

Gigantino II, James J. *The Ragged Road to Abolition: Slavery and Freedom in New Jersey, 1775–1865*. Philadelphia: University of Pennsylvania Press, 2015.

Gilbert, Alain. *Black Patriots and Loyalists: Fighting for Emancipation in the War for Independence*. Chicago: University of Chicago Press, 2012.

Gisler, Antoine. *L'esclavage aux Antilles françaises (XIIe–XIXe siècle)*. Paris: Karthala, 1981.

Godinho, Vitorino Magalhães. "L'émigration portugaise (XVe–XXe Siècles): une constante structural et les réponses aux changements du monde." *Revista de história econômica e social* 1 (1978): 5–32.

Gomes, Flávio dos Santos. "Slavery, Black Peasants and Post-Emancipation Society in Brazil (Nineteenth-Century Rio de Janeiro)." *Social Identities* 10, no. 6 (2004): 735–755.

Gordon-Reed, Annette. "Celia's Case (1857)." In *Race on Trial: Law and Justice in American History*, edited by Annette Gordon-Reed, 48–60. New York: Oxford University Press, 2002.

Graden, Dale T. *Disease, Resistance, and Lies: The Demise of the Transatlantic Slave Trade to Brazil, and Cuba*. Baton Rouge: Louisiana University Press, 2014.

Grant, Colin. *Negro With a Hat: The Rise and Fall of Marcus Garvey*. New York: Oxford University Press, 2008.

Green, Toby. *The Rise of the Trans-Atlantic Slave Trade in Western Africa, 1300–1589*. New York: Cambridge University Press, 2012.

Griggs, Leslie and Clifford H. Prator, eds. *Henry Christophe and Thomas Clarkson: A Correspondence*. New York: Greenwood Press, 1968.

Grinberg, Keila. "Freedom Suits and Civil Law in Brazil and the United States." *Slavery & Abolition* 22, no. 3 (2001): 66–82.

Grinberg, Keila. *Liberata: a lei da ambiguidade. As ações de liberdade da Corte de Apelação do Rio de Janeiro no século XIX*. Rio de Janeiro: Relume Dumará, 1994.

Grinberg, Keila. "Slavery, Manumission and the Law in Nineteenth-Century Brazil: Reflections on the Law of 1831 and the 'Principle of Liberty' on the Southern Frontier of the Brazilian Empire." *European Review of History/Revue européenne d'histoire* 16, no. 3 (2009): 401–411.

Gronbeck-Tedesco, John A. *Cuba, the United States, and Cultures of the Transnational Left, 1930–1975*. New York: Cambridge University Press, 2015.

Guerra, Lillian. *Visions of Power in Cuba: Revolution, Redemption, and Resistance, 1959–1971*. Chapel Hill: University of North Carolina Press, 2012.

Harris, Leslie. *In the Shadow of Slavery: African Americans in New York City, 1626–1863*. Chicago: University of Chicago Press, 2003.

Hawthorne, Walter. *From Africa to Brazil: Culture, Identity, and an Atlantic Slave Trade, 1600–1830*. New York: Cambridge University Press, 2010.

Haywood, Harry and Gwendolyn Midlo Hall. *A Black Communist in the Freedom Struggle: The Life of Harry Haywood*. Minneapolis: University of Minnesota Press, 2012.

Helg, Aline. *Our Rightful Share: The Afro-Cuban Struggle for Equality, 1886–1912*. Chapel Hill: University of North Carolina Press, 1995.

Henry, Charles P. *Long Overdue: The Politics of Racial Reparation*. New York: New York University Press, 2007.

Heywood, Linda M. "Slavery and Its Transformation in the Kingdom of Kongo: 1491–1800." *Journal of African History* 50 (2009): 1–22.

Higgins, Kathleen J. *Licentious Liberty in a Brazilian Gold-Mining Region: Slavery, Gender and Social Control in Eighteenth-Century Sabará, Minas Gerais*. University Park: Penn State University Press, 1999.

Hill, Walter. "The Ex-Slave Pension Movement: Some Historical and Genealogical Notes." *Negro History Bulletin* 59, no. 4 (1996): 7–11.

Hodges, Graham Russell. *Root and Branch: African Americans in New York and East Jersey, 1613–1863*. Chapel Hill: University of North Carolina Press, 1999.

Holt, Thomas C. *The Problem of Freedom: Race, Labor, and Politics in Jamaica and Britain, 1832–1938*. Baltimore: Johns Hopkins University Press, 1992.

Horne, Gerald. *Race to Revolution: The US and Cuba During Slavery and Jim Crow*. New York: Monthly Review Press, 2014.

Howard-Hassmann, Rhoda E. "Reparations to Africa and the Group of Eminent Persons." *Cahiers d'Études Africaines* 44, no. 1–2 (2004): 81–97.

Howard-Hassmann Rhoda E. and Anthony P. Lombardo. *Reparations to Africa*. Philadelphia: University of Pennsylvania Press, 2008.

Inikori, Joseph E. "Measuring the Atlantic Slave Trade: An Assessment of Curtin and Anstey." *Journal of African History* 17, no. 2 (1976): 197–223.

Inikori, Joseph E. "The Origin of the Diaspora: The Slave From Africa." *Tarikh* 5, no. 4 (1978): 1–19.

Inikori, Joseph E. "The Slave Trade and the Atlantic Economies, 1451–1870." In *The African Slave Trade from the Fifteenth to the Nineteenth Century: Reports and Papers of the Meeting of Experts Organized by UNESCO at Port-au-Prince Haiti, 31 January to 4 February 1978*, UNESCO, 56–87. Paris: UNESCO, 1979.

Inikori, Joseph E. "Under-Population in Nineteenth-Century West Africa: The Role of the Export Slave Trade." *African Historical Demography* 11 (1981): 283–313.

Jackson, Maurice. *Let This Voice Be Heard: Anthony Benezet, Father of Atlantic Abolitionism*. Philadelphia. University of Pennsylvania Press, 2009.

James, C. L. R. *The Black Jacobins: Toussaint L'Ouverture and the San Domingo Revolution*. New York: Vintage Books, 1963.

Jennings, Lawrence C. *French Anti-Slavery: The Movement for the Abolition of Slavery in France, 1802–1848*. Cambridge: Cambridge University Press, 2000.

Jennings, Lawrence C. "L'abolition de l'esclavage par la IIe République et ses effets en Louisiane (1848–1858)." *Revue française d'histoire d'outre-mer* 56, no. 205 (1969): 375–397.

Johnson, Walter. *Soul by Soul: Life Inside the Antebellum Slave Market*. Cambridge, MA: Harvard University Press, 1999.

Jordan, Annemarie. "Image of Empire: Slaves in the Lisbon Household and Court of Catherine of Austria." In *Black Africans in Renaissance Europe*, edited by Tom F. Earle and Kate J. P. Lowe, 155–180. Cambridge: Cambridge University Press, 2010.

Kale, Madhavi. *Fragments of Empire: Capital, Slavery, and Indian Indentured Labor in the British Caribbean*. Philadelphia: University of Pennsylvania Press, 1998.

Karasch, Mary C. *Slave Life in Rio de Janeiro, 1808–1850*. Princeton: Princeton University Press, 1987.

Karenga, Maulana. "The Million Man March/Day of Absence Mission Statement." *The Black Scholar* 25, no. 4 (1995): 2–11.

Karolczyk, Paul. "Subjugated Territory: The New Afrikan Independence Movement and the Space of Black Power." Ph.D. dissertation, Louisiana State University, 2014).

Kelley, Robin D. G. *Freedom Dreams: The Black Radical Imagination*. Boston: Beacon Press, 2002.

Kennedy, Cynthia M. *Braided Relations, Entwined Lives: The Women of Charleston's Urban Slave Society*. Bloomington: Indiana University Press, 2005.

Kerr-Ritchie, Jeffrey R. "Forty Acres, or An Act of Bad Faith." In *Redress for Historical Injustices in the United States: On Reparations for Slavery, Jim Crow, and Their Legacies*, edited by Michael T. Martin and Marilyn Yaquinto, 222–237. Durham, NC: Duke University Press, 2007.

Klein, Herbert S. *The Atlantic Slave Trade*. New York: Cambridge University Press, 2010.

Klein, Herbert S. and Francisco Vida Luna. *Slavery in Brazil*. New York: Cambridge University Press, 2010.

Klein, Herbert S. and Ben Vinson III. *African Slavery in Latin America and the Caribbean*. New York: Oxford University Press, 2007.

Kraay, Hendrik. "Arming Slaves in Brazil From the Seventeenth Century to the Nineteenth Century." In *Arming Slaves: From Classical Times to the Modern Age*, edited by Christopher Leslie Brown and Philip D. Morgan, 146–179. New Haven: Yale University Press, 2006.

Kulikoff, Allan. *Tobacco and Slaves: The Development of Southern Cultures in the Chesapeake, 1680–1800*. Chapel Hill: University of North Carolina Press, 1986.

Kössling, Karin Sant'Anna. "As lutas anti-racistas de afro-descendentes sob vigilância do DEOPS/SP (1964–1983)." MA thesis, Universidade de São Paulo, 2007.

Lacombe, Américo Jacobina, Eduardo Barbosa Silva, and Francisco de Assis. *Rui Barbosa e a queima dos arquivos*. Rio de Janeiro: Fundação Casa de Rui Barbosa, 1988.

Lai, Walton Look. *Indentured Labor, Caribbean Sugar: Chinese and Indian Migrants to the British West Indies, 1838–1918*. Baltimore: Johns Hopkins University Press, 1993.

Laidler, Christiane. "A Lei do Ventre Livre: Interesses e disputas em torno do projeto de abolição gradual." *Escritos* 5, no. 5 (2011): 169–205.

Lara, Silvia Hunold. *Fragmentos Setecentistas: Escravidão, cultura e poder na América portuguesa*. São Paulo: Companhia das Letras, 2007.

Lara, Silvia Hunold ed. *Ordenações filipinas, Livro V*. São Paulo: Companhia das Letras, 1999.

Lara, Sylvia Hunold. "The Signs of Color: Women's Dress and Racial Relations in Salvador and Rio de Janeiro, ca. 1750–1815." *Colonial Latin American Review* 6, no. 2 (1997): 205–224.

Law, Robin. *Ouidah: The Social History of a West African Slaving Port (1727–1892)*. Athens: Ohio University Press, 2004.

Law, Robin. "The Politics of Commercial Transition: Factional Conflict in Dahomey in the Context of the Ending of the Atlantic Slave Trade." *Journal of African History* 38 (1997): 213–233.

Law, Robin. *The Slave Coast of West Africa, 1550–1750: The Impact of the Atlantic Slave Trade on an African Society*. Oxford: Clarendon Press, 1991.

Le Hérissé, A. *L'Ancien Royaume du Dahomey: Mœurs, Religion, Histoire*. Paris: Emile Larose, 1911.

Leão, Michele de. "A participação de Rui Barbosa na reforma eleitoral que excluiu os analfabetos do direito de voto no Brasil." MA thesis, Universidade Federal do Rio Grande do Sul, 2013.

Legaspi, Jaime Olveda. "La abolición de la esclavitud en México, 1810–1917." *Signos Históricos*, no. 29 (2013): 8–34.

Lightfoot, Natasha. *Troubling Freedom: Antigua and the Aftermath of British Emancipation*. Durham, NC: Duke University Press, 2015.

Litwack, Leon F. *Been in the Storm So Long: The Aftermath of Slavery*. New York: Knopf, 1979.

Lockhart, James and Stuart Schwartz. *Early Latin America: A History of Colonial Spanish America and Brazil*. New York: Cambridge University Press, 1999.

Lohse, Russell. *Africans Into Creoles: Slavery, Ethnicity, and Identity in Colonial Costa Rica*. Albuquerque: University of New Mexico Press, 2014.

Lovejoy, Paul E. "The Impact of the Atlantic Slave Trade on Africa: A Review of the Literature." *The Journal of African History* 30, no. 3 (1989): 365–394.

Lovejoy, Paul E. "Review of *Saltwater Slavery: A Middle Passage from Africa to American Diaspora* by Stephanie E. Smallwood. Cambridge, MA: Harvard University Press, 2007." *Labor* 6, no. 4 (2008): 138–140.

Lovejoy, Paul E. "The Volume of the Atlantic Slave Trade: A Synthesis." *Journal of African History* 23 (1982): 473–501.

Machado, Maria Cristina Gomes. *Rui Barbosa: pensamento e ação: uma análise do projeto modernizador para a sociedade brasileira com base na questão educacional*. Rio de Janeiro: Fundação Casa de Rui Barbosa, 2002.

Machado, Maria Helena. *O plano e o pânico: os movimentos sociais na década da abolição*. São Paulo: Editora da Universidade de São Paulo, 1994.

Mamigonian, Beatriz G. "A Harsh and Gloomy Fate: Liberated Africans in the Service of the Brazilian State, 1830s–1860s." In *Extending the Diaspora: New Histories of Black People*, edited by Dawne Y. Curry, Eric D. Duke, and Marshanda A. Smith, 24–45. Urbana: University of Illinois Press, 2009.

Mamigonian, Beatriz Gallotti. "Conflicts Over the Meanings of Freedom: The Liberated Africans' Struggle for Final Emancipation in Brazil, 1840s–1860s," in *Paths to Freedom: Manumission in the Atlantic World* edited by Rosemary Brana-Shute and Randy J. Sparks, 235–263. Columbia, SC: University of South Carolina Press, 2009.

Mamigonian, Beatriz Gallotti. "O direito de ser africano livre: Os escravos e as interpretações da lei de 1831." In *Direitos e justiças no Brasil*, edited by Silvia Hunold Lara and Joseli Maria Nunes Mendonça. Campinas: Editora da Universidade Estadual de Campinas, 2007.

Mamigonian, Beatriz Gallotti. "O Estado nacional e a instabilidade da propriedade escrava: a Lei de 1831 e a matrícula dos escravos de 1872." *Almanack*, no. 2 (2011): 20–37.

Mamigonian, Beatriz Gallotti. *To Be a Liberated African in Brazil: Labour and Citizenship in the Nineteenth Century*. Ph.D. dissertation, University of Waterloo, 2002.

Manning, Patrick. "The Enslavement of Africans: A Demographic Model." *Revue Canadienne des Études Africaines/Canadian Journal of African Studies* 15, no. 3 (1981): 499–526.

Manning, Patrick. "The Slave Trade: The Formal Demography of a Global System." *Social Science History* 14, no. 2 (1990): 255–279.

Manning, Patrick and William S. Griffiths. "Divining the Unprovable: Simulating the Demography of African Slavery." *Journal of Interdisciplinary History* 19, no. 2 (1988): 177–201.

Marquese, Rafael de Bivar. *Administração e escravidão: idéias sobre a gestão da agricultura escravista brasileira*. São Paulo: Editora Hucitec, 1999.

Martin, Francisco Forrest. *The Constitution as Treaty: The International Legal Constructionist Approach to the US Constitution*. New York: Cambridge University Press, 2007.

Masur, Kate. *An Example for All the Land: Emancipation and the Struggle Over Equality in Washington, D.C.* Chapel Hill: University of North Carolina Press, 2010.

Mattos, Hebe. "'Remanescentes das comunidades dos quilombos': Memória do cativeiro e políticas de reparação no Brasil." *Revista USP*, no. 68 (2005–2006): 104–111.

Mattoso, Kátia de Queirós. *Être Esclave au Brésil, XVIe–XIXe siècles*. Paris: Hachette, 1979.

McGraw, Jason. *The Work of Recognition: Caribbean Colombia and the Postemancipation Struggle for Citizenship*. Chapel Hill: University of North Carolina Press, 2014.

Mendonça, Joseli Maria Nunes. *Entre a mão e os anéis: a lei dos sexagenários e os caminhos da abolição no Brasil*. Campinas: Editora da Universidade Estadual de Campinas, 1999.

Menschel, David. "Abolition Without Deliverance: The Law of Connecticut Slavery 1784–1848." *Yale Law Journal* 111, no. 1 (2001): 183–222.

Mettas, Jean. *Répertoire des expéditions négrières françaises au XVIIIe siècle*, edited by Serge Daget and Michèle Daget, 2 vols. Paris, Société Française d'Outre-Mer, 1978.

Miller, Joseph C. "A Marginal Institution on the Margin of the Atlantic System: The Portuguese Southern Atlantic Slave Trade in the Eighteenth Century." In *Slavery and the Rise of the Atlantic System*, edited by Barbara L. Solow, 120–150. New York: Cambridge University Press, 1991.

Miller, Joseph C. *Way of Death: Merchant Capitalism and the Angolan Slave Trade, 1740–1830*. Madison: University of Wisconsin Press, 1988.

Moitt, Bernard. *Women and Slavery in the French Antilles, 1635–1848*. Bloomington: Indiana University Press, 2001.

Monsma, Karl and Valéria Dorneles Fernandes. "Fragile Liberty: The Enslavement of Free People in the Borderlands of Brazil and Uruguay, 1846–1866." *Luso-Brazilian Review* 50, no. 1 (2013): 7–25.

Morgan, Philip D. *Slave Counterpoint: Black Culture in the Eighteenth-Century Chesapeake and Lowcountry*. Chapel Hill: University of North Carolina Press, 1998.

Moura, Clóvis. *Dicionário da Escravidão Negra no Brasil*. São Paulo: Editora da Universidade de São Paulo, 2004.

Murphy, Thomas Richard. "'Negroes of Ours': Jesuit Slaveholding in Maryland, 1717–1838." Ph.D. dissertation, University of Connecticut, 1998.

Mustakeem, Sowande M. *Slavery at Sea: Terror, Sex, and Sickness in the Middle Passage*. Urbana: University of Illinois Press, 2016.

Myers, Amrita Chakrabarti. *Forging Freedom: Black Women and the Pursuit of Liberty in Antebellum Charleston*. Chapel Hill: University of North Carolina Press, 2011.

Nascimento, Elisa Larkin. "O movimento social afro-brasileiro no século XX: Um esboço sucinto." In *Cultura em movimento: Matrizes africanas e ativismo negro no Brasil*, edited by Elisa Larkin Nascimento, 93–178. São Paulo: Selo Negro, 2008.

Nelson, Alondra. *The Social Life of DNA: Race, Reparations, and Reconciliation After the Genome.* Boston, MA: Beacon Press, 2016.

Nishida, Mieko. *Slavery and Identity: Ethnicity, Gender, and Race in Salvador, Brazil, 1808–1888.* Bloomington: Indiana University Press, 2003.

Northrup, David. *Africa's Discovery of Europe, 1450–1850.* New York: Oxford University Press, 2002.

O'Donnell, Thérèse. "The Restitution of Holocaust Looted Art and Transitional Justice: The Perfect Storm or the Raft of the Medusa." *The European Journal of International Law* 22, no. 1 (2011): 49–80.

Painter, Nell Irvin. *Exodusters: Black Migration to Kansas After Reconstruction.* New York: Knopf, 1976.

Paiva, Eduardo França. *Escravidão e universo cultural na colônia: Minas Gerais, 1716–1789.* Belo Horizonte: Editora da Universidade de Minas Gerais, 2006.

Palmer, Colin A. *Freedom's Children: The 1938 Labor Rebellion and the Birth of Modern Jamaica.* Chapel Hill: University of North Carolina Press, 2014.

Parent, Anthony S. *Foul Means: The Formation of a Slave Society in Virginia, 1660–1740.* Chapel Hill: University of North Carolina Press, 2003.

Paton, Diana. *No Bound but the Law: Punishment, Race, and Gender in Jamaican State.* Durham, NC: Duke University Press, 2004.

Patterson, Orlando. *Slavery and Social Death: A Comparative Study.* Cambridge, MA: Harvard University Press, 1982.

Peredo, Carlos Herrejón. "La abolición de la esclavitud en Miguel Hidalgo." *Letras Históricas*, no. 5 (2011–2012): 39–52.

Perry, Miranda Booker. "The Prospect of Justice: African-American Redress and the Ex-Slave Pension Movement, 1865–1937." Ph.D. dissertation, Howard University, 2012.

Pinto, Ana Flávia Magalhães. "Fortes laços em linhas rotas: Literatos negros, racismo e cidadania na segunda metade do século XIX." Ph.D. dissertation, Campinas: Universidade Estadual de Campinas, 2014.

Pope-Melish, Joanne. *Disowning Slavery: Gradual Emancipation and "Race" in New England, 1780–1860.* Ithaca: Cornell University Press, 1998.

Ramchandani, Tara Kolar. "Judicial Recognition of the Harms of Slavery: Consumer Fraud as an Alternative to Reparations Litigation." Harvard Civil Rights-Civil Liberties Review 42, no. 2 (2007): 541–556.

Rawley, James A. *The Transatlantic Slave Trade: A History.* New York: W. W. Norton & Co, 1981.

Rebouças, André. *Á Democracia Rural Brazileira.* Rio de Janeiro, 1875.

Rebouças, André, Ignacio Jose Verissimo, and Anna Flora Verissimo. *Diário e notas autobiograficas.* Rio de Janeiro: José Olympio, 1938.

Rediker, Marcus. *The Slave Ship: A Human History.* New York: Viking, 2007.

Reinstein, Robert J. "Is the President's Recognition Power Exclusive?" *Temple Law Review* 86, no. 1 (2013): 1–60.

Reis, João José. "De escravo a rico liberto: A trajetória do africano Manoel Joaquim Ricardo na Bahia oitocentista." *Revista de História*, no. 174 (2016): 15–68.

Reis, João José. *Domingos Sodré: Um sacerdote africano. Escravidão, liberdade e candomblé na Bahia do século XIX.* São Paulo: Companhia das Letras, 2008.

Reis, João José. *Slave Rebellion in Brazil: The Muslim Uprising of 1835 in Bahia.* Baltimore: Johns Hopkins University Press, 1993.

Reis, João José and Flávio dos Santos Gomes. "Repercussions of the Haitian
    Revolution in Brazil, 1791–1850." In *The World of the Haitian Revolution*,
    edited by David Patrick Geggus and Norman Fiering, 284–313. Bloomington:
    Indiana University Press, 2009.
Reis, João José, Flávio dos Santos Gomes, and Marcus J. M. de Carvalho. *O alufá
    Rufino: tráfico, escravidão e liberdade no Atlântico negro (c. 1822–c. 1853).* São
    Paulo: Companhia das Letras, 2010.
Richardson, David. "Slave Exports From West and West-Central Africa,
    1700–1810: New Estimates of Volume and Distribution." *Journal of African
    History* 30, no. 1 (1989): 1–22.
Rios, Ana Lugão and Hebe Mattos. *Memórias do Cativeiro: Família, trabalho e
    cidadania no pós-abolição.* Rio de Janeiro: Civilização Brasileira, 2005.
Robinson, Randall. *The Debt: What America Owes to Blacks.* New York: Dutton,
    2000.
Rockman, Seth. *Scraping by: Wage Labor, Slavery, and Survival in Early Baltimore.*
    Baltimore: Johns Hopkins University Press, 2009.
Rodney, Walter. *How Europe Underdeveloped Africa.* Washington, DC: Howard
    University Press, 1982.
Rodney, Walter. "Slavery and Other Forms of Social Possession on the Upper
    Guinea Coast in the Context of the Atlantic Slave Trade." *Journal of African
    History* 7, no. 4 (1966): 431–443.
Rosero-Labbé, Claudia Mosquera, Luiz Claudio Barcelos, and Andrés Gabriel
    Arévalo Robles. "Contribuciones a los debates sobre las Memorias de la
    Esclavitud y las Afro-reparaciones en Colombia desde el campo de los estudios
    afrocolombianos, afrolatinoamericanos, afrobrasileros, afroestadunidenses
    y afrocaribeños." In *Afro-reparaciones: Memorias de la Esclavitud y
    Justicia Reparativa para negros, afrocolombianos y raizales*, edited by
    Claudia Mosquera Rosero-Labbé and Luiz Claudio Barcelos, 13–69. Bogotá:
    Universidad Nacional de Colombia, Observatorio del Caribe Colombiano,
    2007.
Saillant, Francine. *Le mouvement noir au Brésil (2000–2010): Réparations, droits
    et citoyenneté.* Québec: Presses de l'Université Laval, 2014.
Schafer, Judith Kelleher. *Becoming Free, Remaining Free: Manumission and
    Enslavement in New Orleans, 1846–1862.* Baton Rouge: Louisiana State
    University, 2003.
Schermerhorn, Calvin. *The Business of Slavery and the Rise of American
    Capitalism, 1815–1860.* New Haven: Yale University Press, 2015.
Schmidt-Nowara, Christopher. *Empire and Antislavery: Spain, Cuba, and Puerto
    Rico, 1833–1874.* Pittsburgh: Pittsburgh University Press, 1999.
Schmidt-Nowara, Christopher. *Slavery, Freedom, and Abolition in Latin America
    and the Atlantic World.* Albuquerque: University of New Mexico Press,
    2011.
Schmieder, Ulrike. "Martinique and Cuba Grande: Commonalities and Differences
    During the Periods of Slavery, Abolition, and Post-Emancipation." *Review
    (Fernand Braudel Center)* XXXVI, no. 1 (2013): 83–112.
Schuchter, Arnold. *Reparations: The Black Manifesto and Its Challenges to White
    America.* Philadelphia: Lippincott Company, 1970.
Schuler, Monica. *Alas, Alas, Kongo: A Social History of Indentured African Immigration
    into Jamaica, 1841–1865.* Baltimore: Johns Hopkins University Press, 1980.

Schwalm, Leslie A. *A Hard Fight for We: Women's Transition From Slavery to Freedom in South Carolina.* Urbana: University of Illinois Press, 1997.

Schwartz, Stuart. *Sugar Plantations in the Formation of Brazilian Society: Bahia, 1550–1835.* New York: Cambridge University Press, 1985.

Scott, Rebecca J. *Degrees of Freedom: Louisiana and Cuba After Slavery.* Cambridge, MA: Belknap Press of Harvard University Press, 2005.

Scott, Rebecca J. "Fault Lines, Color Lines, and Party Lines: Race, Labor, and Collective Action in Louisiana and Cuba, 1862–1912." In *Beyond Slavery: Explorations of Race, Labor, and Citizenship in Postemancipation Societies,* edited by Frederick Cooper, Thomas C. Holt, and Rebecca J. Scott, 61–106. Chapel Hill: University of North Carolina Press, 2000.

Scott, Rebecca J. *Slave Emancipation in Cuba: The Transition to Free Labor, 1860–1899.* Pittsburgh: University of Pittsburgh Press, 2000.

Scott, Rebecca J. and Michael Zeuske. "Le 'droit d'avoir des droits': Les revendications des ex-esclaves à Cuba (1872–1909)." *Annales: Histoire, Sciences Sociales 59,* no. 3 (2004): 521–545.

Sermet, Laurent. *Une anthropologie juridique des droits de l'homme.* Paris: Éditions des archives contemporaines, 2009.

Silva, Eduardo. *As camélias do Leblon e a abolição da escravatura: Uma investigação de história cultural.* São Paulo: Companhia das Letras, 2003.

Silva, Eduardo. "Black Abolitionists in the Quilombo of Leblon, Rio de Janeiro: Symbols, Organizers, and Revolutionaries." In *The Multilayered Legacy of Africans in Latin America and the Caribbean,* edited by Darién J. Davis, 109–122. Lanham: Rowman & Littlefield, 2007.

Silva, Filipa Ribeiro da. *Dutch and the Portuguese in Western Africa: Empires, Merchants and the Atlantic System 1580–1674.* Leiden: Brill, 2011.

Silva, Tatiana Dias and Fernanda Lira Goes, eds. *Igualdade racial no Brasil: Reflexões no Ano Internacional dos Afrodescendentes.* Rio de Janeiro: Instituto de Pesquisa Econômica Aplicada, 2013.

Sims, Harold. "Cuba." In *Latin America Between the Second World War and the Cold War: Crisis and Containment, 1944–1948,* edited by Leslie Bethell and Ian Roxborough, 217–242. Cambridge: Cambridge University Press, 1992.

Sinha, Manisha. *The Counterrevolution of Slavery: Politics and Ideology of Antebellum South Carolina.* Chapel Hill: University of North Carolina Press, 2000.

Sinha, Manisha. *The Slave's Cause: A History of Abolition.* New Haven: Yale University Press, 2016.

Slenes, Robert W. "O que Rui Barbosa não queimou: novas fontes para o estudo da escravidão no século XIX." *Estudos econômicos 13,* no. 1 (1983): 117–149.

Smallwood, Stephanie E. *Saltwater Slavery: A Middle Passage from Africa to American Diaspora.* Cambridge, MA: Harvard University Press, 2007.

Soares, Luiz Carlos. *O "povo de Cam" na capital do Brasil: A escravidão urbana no Rio de Janeiro do século XIX.* Rio de Janeiro: 7Letras, 2007.

Solow, Barbara. "The Transatlantic Slave Trade: A New Census." *William and Mary Quarterly, New Perspectives on the Transatlantic Slave Trade 58,* no. 1 (2001): 9–16.

Sparks, Randy J. *Where the Negroes Are Masters: An African Port in the Era of the Slave Trade.* Cambridge, MA: Harvard University Press, 2014.

Sreenivasan, Jyotsna. *Poverty and the Government in America: A Historical Encyclopedia*. Santa Barbara: ABC CLIO, 2009.

Swanger, Joanna. *Rebel Lands of Cuba: The Campesino Struggles of Oriente and Escambray, 1934–1974*. Lanham: Lexington Books, 2015.

Sweet, James H. *Domingos Álvares, African Healing, and the Intellectual History of the Atlantic World*. Chapel Hill: University of North Carolina Press, 2013.

Sweet, James H. "Manumission in Rio de Janeiro, 1749–54: An African Perspective." *Slavery & Abolition* 24, no. 1 (2003): 54–70.

Takagi, Midori. *Rearing Wolves to Our Own Destruction: Slavery in Richmond, Virginia, 1782–1865*. Charlottesville: University Press of Virginia, 1999.

Tannenbaum, Frank. *Slave and Citizen, The Negro in the Americas*. New York: A. A. Knopf, 1946.

Taylor, Nikki M. *Driven Towards Madness: The Fugitive Slave Margaret Garner and Tragedy on the Ohio*. Athens: Ohio University Press, 2016.

Thornton, John K. *Africa and Africans in the Making of the Atlantic World, 1400–1800*. New York: Cambridge University Press, 1998.

Thornton, John K. *A Cultural History of the Atlantic World, 1250–1820*. New York: Cambridge University Press, 2012.

Thornton, John K. "The Slave Trade in Eighteenth Century Angola: Effects on Demographic Structures." In *Revue canadienne des études africaines/Canadian Journal of African Studies* 14, no. 3 (1981): 417–427.

Tillet, Salamishah. *Sites of Slavery: Citizenship and Racial Democracy in the Post-Civil Rights Imagination*. Durham, NC: Duke University Press, 2012.

Tin, Louis-George. *Esclavage et réparations: comment faire face aux crimes de l'histoire*. Paris: Stock, 2013.

Torpey, John. "Legalism and Its Discontents: The Case of Reparations for Black Americans." In *The Limits of the Law*, edited by Austin Sarat, Lawrence Douglas, Martha Merrill Umphrey, 75–108. Stanford: Stanford University Press, 2005.

Torpey, John. *Making Whole What Has Been Smashed: On Reparations Politics*. Cambridge, MA: Harvard University Press, 2006.

Tutino, John. *From Insurrection to Revolution in Mexico: Social Bases of Agrarian Violence, 1750–1940*. Princeton: Princeton University Press, 1986.

Twinam, Ann. *Purchasing Whiteness: Pardos, Mulattos, and the Quest for Social Mobility in the Spanish Indies*. Stanford: Stanford University Press, 2015.

Ulentin, Anne. "Garantir leur avenir: Les gens de couleur libres de Saint-Domingue et l'indemnité de l'indépendance de 1825." *Bulletin de la Société d'Histoire de la Guadeloupe*, no. 173 (2016): 63–82.

Velázquez, María Elisa and Gabriela Iturralde Nieto. *Afrodescendientes en México: Una historia de silencio y discriminación*. Mexico: Consejo Nacional para Prevenir la Discriminación and Instituto Nacional de Antropología e Hisoria, 2012.

Verger, Pierre. *Flux et reflux de la traite des nègres entre le Golfe de Bénin et Bahia de Todos os Santos, du XVIIe au XIXe siècle*. Paris: Mouton, 1968.

Verger, Pierre. *Fluxo e Refluxo do tráfico de escravos entre o Golfo do Benin e a Bahia de Todos os Santos*. Salvador: Corrupio, 1987.

Vincent, Theodore G. "The Contributions of Mexico's First Black Indian President, Vicente Guerrero." *The Journal of Negro History* 86, no. 2 (2001): 148–159.

Vincent, Theodore G. *The Legacy of Vicente Guerrero: Mexico's First Black Indian President*. Gainesville: University Press of Florida, 2001.

Walker, Tamara J. "'He Outfitted His Family in Notable Decency': Slavery, Honour and Dress in Eighteenth-Century Lima, Peru." *Slavery & Abolition* 30, no. 3 (2009): 383–402.

Walvin, James. *Atlas of Slavery*. Harlow: Pearson, Longman, 2006.

Warren, Charles. *History of the Harvard Law School and of Early Legal Conditions in America*. New York: Lewis Publishing Company, 1908. vol. 1.

Webster, C. K. *The Congress of Vienna, 1814–1815*. London: Oxford University Press, 1918.

Welch, Clifford Andrew. "Vargas and the Reorganization of Rural Life in Brazil (1930–1945)." *Revista brasileira de história* 36, no. 71 (2016): 1–25.

Whitfield, Harvey Amani. *The Problem of Slavery in Early Vermont, 1777–1810: Essays and Primary Sources*. Barre: Vermont Historical Society, 2014.

Whitman, T. Stephen. *The Price of Freedom: Slavery and Manumission in Baltimore and Early National Maryland*. Lexington: University Press of Kentucky, 1997.

Williams, Eric. *Capitalism and Slavery*. Chapel Hill: University of North Carolina Press, 1941.

Williams, Rhonda Y. *Concrete Demands: The Search for Black Power in the 20th Century*. New York: Routledge, 2015.

Wise, Terence and Richard Scollins. *The Knights of Christ: Religious/Military Orders of Knighthood 1118–1565*. London: Osprey, 1984.

Wood, Peter H. *Black Majority: Negroes in Colonial South Carolina from 1670 Through the Stono Rebellion*. New York: Knopf, 1974.

Wrigley, C. C. "Historicism in Africa: Slavery and State Formation." *African Affairs* 70, no. 279 (1971): 113–124.

Digital repositories and other media

Amazonia. http://amazonia.org.br/

African Origins: Portal to Africans Liberated from Transatlantic Slave Vessels. Emory University. http://www.african-origins.org/.

BBC News, http://www.bbc.com/news

Brown-Tougaloo Cooperation Exchange. http://cds.library.brown.edu/projects/FreedomNow/.

Caribbean Community (CARICOM). http://archive.caricom.org/.

Columbia Center for New Media Teaching and Learning and the Center for Contemporary Black History. Columbia University. http://ccnmtl.columbia.edu/projects/mmt/mxp/speeches/index.html.

Comissão Pró-Índio de São Paulo: http://www.cpisp.org.br/terras/

Discursos e intervenciones del Comandante en Jefe Fidel Castro Ruz, Presidente del Consejo de Estado de la República de Cuba. http://www.cuba.cu/gobierno/discursos/.

Griffith, D. W. *The Birth of a Nation*, 1915.

Huffington Post. http://www.huffingtonpost.com/

Institut National de l'Audiovisuel, Jalons Version Découverte. http://fresques.ina.fr/jalons/accueil.

Instituto Nacional de Estadística y Censos. Ecuador. http://www.ecuadorencifras.
  gob.ec.
Legacies of British Slave-Ownership. https://www.ucl.ac.uk/lbs.
McQueen, Steve. *12 Years a Slave*, 2013.
National Coalition of Blacks for Reparations in America. http://www.ncobraonline.
  org.
Planalto, Presidência da República do Brasil. http://www2.planalto.gov.br.
Political Database of the Americas. http://pdba.georgetown.edu/.
Rhode Island Department of State, Virtual Exhibits. http://sos.ri.gov/
  virtualarchives.
Royall House & Slave Quarters, Medford, MA. http://www.royallhouse.org.
Salon. http://www.salon.com.
Senado Federal do Brasil, Atividade Legislativa. http://www25.senado.leg.br/web/
  atividade/legislacao.
"Speech of Maya Angelou and guest speakers at Million Man March on
  Washington." October 16, 1995. https://www.youtube.com/
  watch?v=SeLfvkaobos.
The Avalon Project: Documents in Law, History, and Diplomacy. Yale Law School.
  Yale University. http://avalon.law.yale.edu.
The Conference on Jewish Material Claims Against Germany. http://www.
  claimscon.org/.
The Holy See. http://www.vatican.va/.
The Huffington Post. http://www.huffingtonpost.com.
The Movement for Black Lives, *A Vision for Black Lives: Policy Demands for
  Black Power, Freedom & Justice.* https://policy.m4bl.org/reparations.
Trans-Atlantic Slave Trade Database: Voyages, Emory University. http://www.
  slavevoyages.org.
US Constitution, Cornell University Law School, Legal Information Institute,
  Cornell University. https://www.law.cornell.edu/constitution.
United Nations Documents: Gathering a Body of Global Agreements. http://www.
  un-documents.net/.
United States Congress. https://www.congress.gov/.

INDEX